BACKPACKER
and HIKER'S
HANDBOOK

WILLIAM KEMSLEY JR.

STACKPOLE
BOOKS

0 11557 03462 2

Dedicated to Florence and Albert Kemsley, my grandparents,
who homesteaded far beyond the "end of the road" in the Canadian northwest,
and particularly to my dad, William Kemsley,
who spent his early years growing up on the homestead.
They instilled in me the lure of the wilds through family homestead stories.
And Dad, by taking me frequently into the woods, passed on to me
his own special love of the woods.

Copyright © 2008 by William Kemsley Jr.

Published by
STACKPOLE BOOKS
5067 Ritter Road
Mechanicsburg, PA 17055
www.stackpolebooks.com

Printed in China

First edition

10 9 8 7 6 5 4 3 2 1

Photographs by the author except where otherwise noted
Illustrations by Kate Kemsley except where otherwise noted
Cover design by Caroline Stover
Cover photograph courtesy of the National Outdoor Leadership School

Library of Congress Cataloging-in-Publication Data
Kemsley, William.
  Backpacker and hiker's handbook / William Kemsley,
Jr.—1st ed.
      p. cm.
  Includes bibliographical references and index.
  ISBN-13: 978-0-8117-3462-2
  ISBN-10: 0-8117-3462-5
  1. Backpacking—Handbooks, manuals, etc. 2. Hiking—Handbooks, manuals, etc. I. Title.

GV199.6.K44 2008
796.51—dc22

                                                                    2007021147

Contents

Foreword

One day in 1974, I met the founding publisher and editor of *Backpacker* magazine, Bill Kemsley, in his midtown Manhattan office. I had an outline for an article in my pocket and some color transparencies in a briefcase. I had founded the Florida Trail Association a few years earlier and thought the newly formed *Backpacker* magazine should run an article about us. Bill gave me a chance to tell him why. All these years later, Bill and I are still hiking and still writing about it . . . and we're still good friends.

A lot of trail miles have passed under our boots. For the past decade, Bill has hiked the Four Corners area, particularly the Grand Canyon, in part because it's close to home for him and in part because it's his special place. But he also recently hiked in the French, Swiss, and Italian Alps.

By contrast, I am as comfortable hiking a trail in ankle-deep water as I am on the trails of the Rocky Mountains. But I have strayed far enough away to hike on the South Island of New Zealand, in Nepal, northern Pakistan, Patagonia, and the French Alps.

When Bill had the magazine, one of the sections I enjoyed most was "Elders of the Tribe." And now Bill himself is an elder of the tribe. I can think of no one the title fits more appropriately. After World War II, when durable, lightweight fabrics and sturdy lightweight aluminum became available to the likes of Skip Yowell, who started Jan-Sport, and Dick Kelty, who started Kelty Packs, Bill conceived of a magazine for the huge numbers of people who were then taking to the backcountry for days at a time and carrying everything they needed on their backs.

The editor of the leading hiking magazine had to have a broad knowledge of the subject, and a deep one too. And he had to have a vision of where hiking ought to go. Bill had all of these, one reason why *Backpacker* prospered when the fallout began and other, similar magazines disappeared.

I had the good fortune to join Bill on many outings and benefit from his companionship. We traced John Burroughs's climb through the Catskills to the headwaters of the Roundout. We joined Gudy Gaskill, the founder of the Colorado Trail, on a hike through deep snow down into the Grand Canyon for five days. We took our children across the Presidential Range in the White Mountains of New Hampshire, and we took inner-city kids into the Selway-Bitterroot Wilderness of Montana on a Big City Mountaineers high-adventure trip. In these and many other places, I had the opportunity to share campfires and conversation, trails and aching backs, personal difficulties and business successes, environmental issues and trail policies with a man who thought deeply and clearly.

I can't imagine anyone who could write more authoritatively on the subject. If you have ever walked a trail and intend to walk another, I encourage you to peruse the pages of the book now in your hands.

JIM KERN
Founder, Florida Trail Association
Cofounder, American Hiking Society
Founder, Big City Mountaineers

Acknowledgments

A number of people have given me generous amounts of their time and talents to get things right for this book. Still, if it isn't right, the responsibility rests squarely with me.

Near the top of the list is my wife, Joy, who encouraged me to undertake this project and who buoyed me up during the long, dreary days when I would rather have been hiking. And my friend Harry Franks, who persisted in trying to get me to understand things that are simple for him but somewhat dense for me. Likewise, my friends at the Enchanted Forest Cross Country Ski Area—John Miller, Geoff Goins, Dave and Linda Mieras—in our chats about my book in between ski runs, when we might have talked of more important things. Friends, too, like Alison Guynes and Jock Fleming, who inadvertently gave me tidbits that I slipped into the pages of this book. And there is Joy Dillingham, who gave inspiration as well as the title to the book. There is my daughter Kate, son William, and my brother Brian, who heard more than they needed to hear when they asked so politely about the book's progress. And then there is someone I got to know through an Internet introduction, the survival expert Greg Davenport. Greg and I have never met face-to-face, but we need to, and I hope it will be on a week's trek somewhere in the Idaho or Montana mountains. He has been an invaluable help on some highly critical life-or-death issues.

The folks who helped me when I asked many of the same questions over and over, checking and fiddling with details, included those hikers who have known me almost a lifetime in our founding *Backpacker* magazine and the American Hiking Society: Laura Waterman, Jim Kern, Paul Pritchard, Chuck Sloan, and Kenn Petsch. And those also who were so key to the development of AHS: Susan "Butch" Henley, Destry Jarvis, Louise Marshall, Reese Lukei, Dave Lillard, Bob Leggett, and Bill Schneider. Butch especially had to endure repeated requests for details and never faltered in her enthusiastic support, going through voluminous files to extract as precise a fact as possible. She never tired, never faltered, was as steadfast as she has been in her long-distance hiking.

The second tier, of course, is "second" only because of coming on the scene later, though these folks were nonetheless industrious and committed to helping me get the facts right. They include Eric Seaborg, Shirley Hearn, Mary Margaret Sloan, Marceline Guerrein, Joe Shute, Celina Montorfano, Jane Thompson, and Pete Olsen, who conveys current information in his Internet newsletter for the American Hiking Society. And most recently, a great supporter of the project, AHS president Greg Miller.

Then there were my Big City Mountaineers resources—Mark Godley, Jonathan Dorn, Skip Yowell, Bill Stoehr, and Mary Kay Stoehr. Gudy Gaskill, of the Colorado Mountain Club and founder of the Colorado Trail, as well as Bruce Ward and Steve Fausel of the Continental Divide Trail Alliance were all very helpful, as were Sherry Fletcher and Baxter Brown of the Campo Espinoso Wildlife Refuge. And from the Boy Scouts of America, I received special assistance from Dave Bates at the national office, Mark Anderson of Philmont Scout Ranch, Rob Langsdorf at the High Adventure Team, and Thyme Osborne. Kendall McGlynn and Sean Matthews at Wildlife Conservation Society provided extensive material on bears and other wildlife. Molly McCahan at the Sierra Club, Kate Borgelt at Outward Bound, Nate Hintze at National Outdoor Leadership School, Laura Hurley of the Appalachian Mountain Club, and Cindy Carpenter of the Tenth Mountain Hut Division Association were unstinting in providing information. So was David White at the Catskill 3500 Club. Tom and Barbara Springer of the New Mexico Rails-to-Trails Association were a great help, especially because of their intimate relationship with the Lincoln National Forest rangers. And authors Jo Deurbrouck, Kerry Smith, Ashleigh Morris, Bridgitte Mars, and Natalie Baca helped in their quiet ways.

Those experts I called upon in the women's field began with a man, Mike Buchheit, the director of Grand Canyon Field Institute, which hosts a considerable number of all-women backpacking trips each year. Mike put me in touch with Melanie Miles and Marjorie "Slim" Woodruff, who both graciously answered e-mail after e-mail and allowed me to attend their orientation classes for backpacker groups heading out on the trails. And they, in turn, put me in touch with veteran GCFI hikers Janet King and Paula Blankenship. Mike also introduced me to Denise Traver, who founded the GCFI all-women program and still leads trips for GCFI as well as Call of the Wild—which brings up another name, Carole Latimer, who helped me in many ways, including sharing a superb recipe and some very useful trail tips. Other women who helped include those I've already mentioned, as well as Betty Leavengood, who is an inspiration just to chat with; my sister-in-law, Kit Kemsley; and in their own way, Heidi Seller and Judith Niemi, author of *Women in the Outdoors*. Then there is Jack Pennington, who swiftly responded to all my requests.

The rangers and land managers who did yeomen's work for me include my friend Steve Bridgehouse at Natural Bridges National Monument, who not only helped with his own good counsel, but also directed me to dozens of other land management employees who shared their expertise. Some of the most helpful were at Grand Canyon. Mike Anderson straightened me out on many points of history; Mike Quinn waltzed me through the GCNP archives; Dr. Tom Myers, official Grand Canyon physician, coached me on risks and accidents to hikers in deserts and canyons. Along with his writing partner, Mike Ghiglieri, he coauthored the excellent book from which I quote extensively, *Over the Edge: Death in Grand Canyon*.

Those who helped me from the National Park Service were Stephen Frye at Glacier; Tom Vandenberg at Wrangle-St. Elias; Terry DeBruyn, the Alaska National Park regional wildlife biologist; Gary Somers at Shenandoah; Lindy Russell at Western Arctic National Parklands; Debra Schweizer at Yosemite; David Elkowitz at Big Bend; Kyle Patterson of Rocky Mountain National Park; William Stiver at Great Smoky; Jennifer Shaw at Lake Clark-Katmai National Park and Preserve; Richard Martin, superintendent at Sequoia-Kings Canyon; Tim Manns at North Cascades; and Superintendent Suzanne Lewis and Stacy Vallie at Yellowstone.

Forest Service people who assisted include Cindy Schacher, who dug up valuable information about Moose Creek Ranger Station in the Selway-Bitterroot Wilderness; Brian Long at Lincoln National Forest; Kent Wimmer Forest Service liaison with the Florida Trail Association; and John Neely at Steens Mountain, Oregon.

Industry people helped enormously, including Dennis Madsen, Randy Hurlow, and Mitch Herbert at REI; Laurie Gitman, Janet Wyper, and Marlene Hensley at L.L.Bean; Mark Van Saun at EMS; Jack Gilbert of Mountain Hardwear; Kathy Cabrera at Eureka Tent; Paul Gagner at Gregory; and Kirsten Johnson and Pride Johnson at Counter Assault Bear Spray Company. There were also those connected tangentially to the field, like Ursula Beck with her Taos Institute of Art; Mary Jane Butters and her MaryJanesFarm; and Dick Spas, who helped in countless other ways as well.

Others helped me understand the scope of the outdoors market today and its recent changes: Tom Doyle, Dan Kasen, and Larry Weindruch of the National Sporting Goods Association; Terrance Hunter at Market Research; Chris Frado at Cross Country Ski Areas Association; and Kent Ebersole at *Backpacker* magazine.

I have met on numerous trails many folks whose names I either have forgotten or never asked. Some whom I've been in touch with since are Gary Kruse and his buddy Bob Fukamoto from Colorado; Hal Braun from Montana; and Mac McGlann and his son, Rob McGlann, who hiked with me down the North Kaibab Trail into the depths of Grand Canyon on a fall day recently.

To all of you and to those whom I have forgotten to mention, I am sincerely grateful.

Introduction

Why another backpacking handbook? Even more, why would a guy like me write a handbook *about* backpacking when he could *be* backpacking? After all, I'm living in the midst of the best hiking in the world—the mountains of northern New Mexico, with 13,000-foot peaks to climb just minutes away from my door, craggy canyons, deserts, and spruce, piñon, and ponderosa forests.

The answers are simple—three, really.

First, it seemed no handbook adequately dealt with the changing trends in backpacking. So my book goes into the most notable of them, such as the following:

- A new hiking hazard has surfaced: hyponatremia. Up to recently, most cases were dangerously mistreated because they were misdiagnosed. I tell what to do to protect yourself from hyponatremia, and prevention isn't what power-drink advertisers claim. See chapters 16, 29, and 30.
- There's been a boom in innovative backpacking gear, especially clothing—some of which makes sense, a lot of which doesn't. I cover this in chapters 2 and 10.
- The most startling trend is in the increasing number of wild animal attacks on hikers. Cougars are taking their toll, and so are predaceous black bears. Notice I said *black* bears, not grizzlies. I also used the innocuous-sounding word *predaceous*. But don't be fooled by its innocent sound. *Predaceous* means bears stalking hikers, to attack and make lunch of them. There aren't enough of these attacks to keep us out of the woods yet. But the shocker is that with certainty, we can expect more of both black bear and cougar attacks in future. I cover bears in chapter 18 and cougars in chapter 19. I tell how and where the attacks are occurring and what you can do to reduce the risk.
- We've seen a steady increase in the number of women backpackers and a more recent boom in all-women backpacker groups. Being a man, I recognize I am no authority on women hikers, so I enlisted outstanding women backpackers, guides, and outfitters to aid me in writing chapter 22.
- With baby boomers reaching retirement years, we might have expected increasing numbers of older backpackers. But a growing number hoisting packs today are a lot older even than boomers. Chapter 23 explores who we are and why.

My second reason for writing this book is that I see a great failure of hikers to accept the reality of many hazards of the trail. And I do not mean just beginners. I believe these risks are highly underplayed in other handbooks, as well as by rangers in various parks and forests. I treat the risks more seriously throughout my book, putting

The author on the trail to the summit of New Mexico's highest peak, 13,000-foot Mount Wheeler.

them into realistic perspective. Some say I go too far. Well, Mom always said, "An ounce of prevention is worth a pound of cure."

A good example of what I mean is a risk that virtually all hikers believe they know how to handle, yet kills more of us than all other causes of trail deaths taken together. Still, it is a risk quite easily avoided. This sneaky killer—hypothermia—afflicts the body when it gets so cold its inner core temperature can no longer sustain life. Hypothermia is killing increasing numbers of hikers today simply because there are more hikers—not because the risk has become more severe.

The good news is that you can completely eliminate this risk on all your hikes. It is not complicated. But it means following advice, which most of us hate to do. In chapter 16, I tell how to avoid hypothermia and what to do if you find someone suffering from it. Too, I confess my own bout with this sneaky culprit—even after decades of extensive backpacking experience!

Then, probably the biggest fear hikers *ought* to have is not being sufficiently afraid of the *real* risks of the backcountry—what many rangers call "the 911 syndrome." More and more people that go into the backcountry are complete novices depending upon cell phones or GPS units, figuring, sort of TV-like, that if they get into trouble they can just dial 911 and help will be on its way. This seems to be part of the extreme-sports mentality that now regards the backcountry as some sort of large outdoors playground. I need say very little about this—suicidal is, after all, well, *suicidal!*—but I do cover trail risks seriously and in some depth throughout.

Finally, I've yet to find a handbook on hiking and backpacking that introduces readers to the love of trails as I have experienced it. A telling photo in our family album is one of me at age eight with a long, sad face because it was time for us to return home from our backcountry vacation.

Everything today—including introducing people to the lure of the land—is done with an impatient passion for the *instantaneous.* This is antithetical to the type of backcountry experience I thrive upon and am promoting in this book.

The Real Threat of Death in the Wilderness

"In essence, we are surviving great-great-grandchildren of the wilderness. Our five senses were fine-tuned by its demands. To see its vastness, hear its thunder, smell its springtimes, and to feel the bite of its winds, the heat of its sun, and the chill of its rains brings us back to our childhood, to our very roots.

"Most of us know, however, that the wilderness in turn cares not a whit for us. It reciprocates neither our fascination nor our love for it. If we fail to respect its dangers, we realize, not only might those dangers hurt us, they may kill us—or an innocent child who is depending on us.

". . . The people who die traumatically in [the wilderness] . . . die mainly—almost universally—due to their own, or their guide's, poor judgement. It is impossible for the rest of us to protect them fully from these personal failings. We can only hope to do our best to inform people of the real dangers the . . . wilderness poses and always will pose.

"Forewarned, it is then up to the personal responsibility of each of us to avoid killing ourselves—and thereby also avoid tacitly accusing the wilderness of being our murderer."

From *Over the Edge: Death in Grand Canyon,* by Michael P. Ghiglieri and Thomas M. Myers. 366–67.

How many men have I met at social gatherings who talk about their climbs of Acacongua, Kilimanjaro, or some peak in the Peruvian Andes, who never set foot in the woods before this trip or ever do so again?

This sort of instant indoctrination is like someone becoming a surgeon simply by leaping from undergraduate classroom to operating room, scalpel in hand—not exactly the surgeon to whom you want to entrust your life. And let's face it, expedition outfitters take anyone along who has a fat enough wallet. Recall the commercial trekkers' disaster on Mount Everest!

Maybe this quick-acquaintance thing is good for the wilderness, as well as for business, but I seriously doubt it. Anyway, this book is not about any quick success in getting acquainted with the backcountry.

That steady, firm-footed affinity I've had for the woods and crags is not obtainable quickly. I want this book to appeal to the few readers who already have—or are eager to develop—an intimate, enduring friendship with the outdoors. I want it to appeal to those who would like to feel as comfortable camped beneath pines on a cool evening in fall as they would in their comfy bed, and happier still eating dinner from camp pots in desert sands among ocotillo, cholla, and saguaro as at their dining-room tables back home.

Oh, I have hundreds of friends who are as at ease among forest creatures as I am. And I've spent many nights with various friends out there. I hope to take you with us down the trails as we talk—deciding where to go, figuring out the right time of year to go there, planning what to take on the trips, chatting about how to find our way even when we get lost, talking, too, about clothes and equipment, cooking and eating, choosing our companions and taking our families into the backcountry.

Once you become so addicted to the serenity of the woodland camp, you'll have a proprietary interest in preserving it, seeing even a rustic structure in it as an intrusion.

As I ruminated over all these things in the writing of this book, I've seen that it rather summarizes my long lifetime spent in the backwoods—from my earliest recollections of waking in the morning, camped on the shore of a Michigan lake, to the smell of a campfire with bacon frying. My sister June is waking up too. Dad is out fishing while Mom prepares breakfast in an iron skillet. The writing also brought memories of early days camping with my Boy Scout troop and taking my first solo overnight hike at age twelve to earn a merit badge. It took me back through my rock-climbing and mountaineering years, on through life into the Southwest canyons and deserts, and the mountainous terrain of Scotland, England, Wales, France, Switzerland, Italy—and virtually every major mountain range in the United States.

These ventures have never been the competitive kind, which rather takes the pleasure out of it for me. Even in rock climbing, where I eventually climbed at what we termed a "respectable" standard, what I appreciated was the feel of the conglomerate rock in the warm spring sun or the beauty of red, orange, and yellow leaves spread like a blanket across the Hudson Valley below, eschewing any need to ever push my limits beyond what was fun for me.

Come share some of this with me. If just a few of you enjoy it and get hooked enough to tread some of these paths more than somewhat, it would give me the kind of kick I get when one of my daughters, Kate, calls to say, "Dad, could we take a few days' hike in Colorado this July?" Or when another daughter, Diane, asks if I'd like to join her and husband Chuck with their boys, Andrew and Jeffrey, for a hike down into Grand Canyon.

It's something about the solace, the peace, the return to the harmony of the natural world from which we all emerge that has no equal anyplace else. A favorite poet of mine, Robert Service, has caught a sense of this lure of the wild, and I've sprinkled some of my favorite verses throughout the book.

I was fortunate enough to have a career that justified my spending something like a hundred nights a year camped out on trails somewhere or other. It also gave me cause to associate with other like-minded trail hounds.

For this book, I've taken advantage of my long list of trail acquaintances. Many of them know me strictly from our hikes. Others know me more professionally—that is, from an organizational and office point of view, when I got more involved in trail concerns. These friends span trail clubs such as my beloved Catskill 3500 Club, the Adirondack Mountain Club and the Appalachian Mountain Club, organizations like Explorers' Club, Wilderness Society, National Wildlife Federation, and Sierra Club, as well as federal

The author checking map directions atop peak in Snowdonia National Park, Wales, United Kingdom.

Dave Sumner and me camped atop Continental Divide in San Juan Mountains of southern Colorado.

bureaucracies—the National Park Service, USDA Forest Service, and Bureau of Land Management.

I've gathered a good deal of their wisdom into the pages of this book. It occurred to me as we were putting it all together that since we enjoy our campfire conversations so much, it might be fun to put some of my friends' really personal trail tidbits into the book as well. So I asked each to share some choice item he or she just wouldn't go out on the trail without. The first ones I asked mostly mentioned particular packs or tents to which they had become so attached they have applied numerous jury-rigged repairs. So to avoid monotony, I made a proviso and asked the rest, "What would you take along—*other than the tents-boots-packs-compass sort of thing?*" That's when the chatter became fun. I interspersed their comments throughout the book. To me, this may be the most interesting part of it. You get a shot at either—the main body of the text or the trail tidbits—or both.

See you along the trail. Meanwhile, why not sit down, open the book at any page, and let's talk.

Section One
PREPARATIONS

The author atop cliff overlooking a fjord in Gros Morne National Park, Newfoundland, Canada.

They have cradled you in custom, they have primed you with their preaching;
*   They have soaked you in convention through and through.*
They have put you in a showcase; you're a credit to their teaching—
*   But can't you hear the Wild?—it's calling you.*
Let us probe the silent places, let us seek what luck betide us;
*   Let us journey to a lonely land I know.*
There's a whisper on the night-wind, there's a star agleam to guide us,
*   And the Wild is calling, calling . . . let us go.*

*   —from "Call of the Wild," Robert Service*

1
Getting Started

Some 165 million Americans say they walk for recreation. If you are one of them, then it is merely a matter of getting perhaps a bit more adventurous, taking to woodland trails and stretching the distances you cover in a day. So just skip the next section and go along to the following one.

If you are just getting started walking for pleasure, then I'd take it easy. Start taking short walks on local streets near home. Or if you can, go out on some nearby country roads. Just about anyone, in any shape, can get into hiking and backpacking. It may take some getting into shape, but that too can be enjoyable.

Be honest. If you've never walked more than the few steps between a taxi and a restaurant, don't leap right into heavy-immersion backpacking in Patagonia or the Everest Base Camp. Not a wise way to go!

BEGIN WITH EASY RECREATIONAL WALKING

My view is to start out with the idea that you want to enjoy this. So begin with afternoon strolls. No matter how busy your schedule, you can almost always find an hour or two on a weekend for a walk.

Don't dismiss the idea of walking on country roads if you haven't tried it. It is the most popular type of walking for millions of Brits on Saturday afternoons in their beloved Lake District, and it has been for generations. Millions of Europeans in every country on the Continent take walks on their backroads. Get into the romance of John Denver's old tune "Country Roads."

Another option for easy walking is the beautiful new trails that have been made from old railroad tracks. The Rails-to-Trails organizations have been busy turning 1,225 abandoned railroad tracks into thousands of miles of trails for hiking, running, and biking. Check their website, www.railstrails.org, for trails near you.

Walking country roads, converted railroads, or trails in parks—the idea of walking for pleasure now attracts more than half the population of the United States.

Wherever you live, whatever the weather conditions or terrain, there are good places to walk for pleasure. Unless you enjoy Sunday afternoon strolls, why in the world would you want to take the leap into backpacking?

STEPPING UP FROM RECREATIONAL WALKING
TO MORE STRENUOUS DAY HIKING

I'm talking here about moving up from strolls to serious hiking. I don't think I have to tell you the difference. You are fully capable of knowing which is which.

Now you are carrying water, food, and a few other things and mostly heading out on more woodland trails, though this is not essential.

You likely already have all you need to get started day hiking—sneakers, a pair of jeans, a shirt, and a light jacket or sweater. And it would be nice if you had a daypack to carry a lunch and sweater. A book-bag-type knapsack is just fine.

Let's talk frankly about ways of stretching from easy Sunday walks to exploring woodland trails to full-day hiking and on into backpacking. This is the way most of us who continue backpacking for a lifetime have become addicted—a little at a time, loving each incremental aspect of the sport.

There are many ways to get started in serious day hiking. The best is to

I'd never go out on a trail on even a clear, sunny day without my raingear.

—John Miller, operator of Enchanted Forest Cross-Country Ski Area, after seventy-seven climbs up New Mexico's highest peak, 13,610-foot Mount Wheeler, including several winter ascents

have a hiking member of your family or a friend take you along on a hike. Another way is to find a hiking club to go with on a beginners' hike.

Don't be embarrassed about signing up for a beginners' hike. It is always best to take things one step at a time. With hiking clubs, you will find that there are sometimes stalwart hikers who just love to get out there and race down the trail. It is the macho thing to do and gives them extra pleasure to be out front. That is discouraging to newcomers.

Frankly, after a lifetime of hiking, I am not eager to go along with most of these groups. My style is a lot more laid-back. And I am writing this book for people who,

---

Practice Good Trail Etiquette

- Step to one side when encountering horse riders, to the inside of the trail if you're on a steep hillside or canyon. Stay still and refrain from making sudden moves or noise that might frighten horses.
- Keep to trails. Cutting switchbacks causes trail erosion.
- Bury human waste at least six inches deep and at least 200 paces from all water sources—streams, lakes, ponds, springs. Pack out used toilet paper in zipper-lock bags.
- Pack out all garbage and trash.
- Wash 200 paces from all water sources—streams, lakes, ponds, springs.
- Erase all signs of campfires, including rock rings. Better still, use a stove instead of a campfire.

like me, hope to find the backcountry a peaceful, beautiful, and joyful place to recharge their emotional and spiritual energies. So join the recently ex-sedentary group. You will be with people whose company you will enjoy.

Most cities and towns have more than one hiking club. Call your local newspaper for names and contacts. Another source of information could be a sporting-goods store—one that sells backpacking and hiking equipment, of course. Or your librarian may help.

Probably the quickest source of information, though, may be the Internet, where the American Hiking Society lists some 150 independent hiking organizations. Visit www.americanhiking.org and click on "Find a hiking club near you." Another possibility is the Sierra Club or Audubon Society, both of which have numerous local chapters offering various types of hiking groups.

HOW TO GET STARTED ON YOUR OWN

I've given you the easy ways first. Of course, you also can get started on your own. A major question you may want to put to yourself is, Are you the kind of person who likes to have someone else tell you about new things, or do you get a certain joy in finding out about them yourself?

If you don't have a club, friend, or family member to start off with and are eager to get going, don't wait. Find an easy trail somewhere close by, and take on two or three miles for your first jaunt.

Build on that the next time you go out. Keep on doing these hikes as long as you enjoy them. I used to find that an afternoon's hike with a baguette of Italian bread, a handful of Greek olives, a piece of imported provolone cheese, and a bottle of cool water was about as close as I could get to heaven in the woodlands. I had been a Boy Scout and spent many afternoons with my family taking walks in the woods as I grew up, but I took my first *real* hike as an adult living in San Francisco after my tour of duty in the navy. It was in a park adjacent to Berkeley, and I had no idea where the path led. My friend and I hiked along it for a couple hours before returning by the same route to the car.

The one luxury I always take with me when I camp is a book. Some of the most relaxing times of my life are reading next to a tranquil lake or on an Appalachian Mountain peak.

—*Doug Shafer, former ranger, Camp Deerwood*

One thing that stands out about that hike after many years was the mysterious carousel music we heard sifting through the trees as we walked. Eventually we saw that the music was not a fantasy. Far below, through the trees, there indeed was a real carousel. It was circling slowly with children giggling and joshing with each other from its horses. We thought this a fairy-tale sort of thing to find in the woods, where we naively thought civilization would leave off at the edge of the wilderness.

Those were exciting days of discovery. I very likely took to trails more often than most other people, for it led, after a time, into backpacking, because I wanted to stay out in the woodlands while the sun was sinking beyond the treetops, and I also wanted to experience its rising through the early-morning mists.

My passion for the woods actually dates back to the enchantment my father gave them when my sister and I were kids. When we were out on one of what Dad called walks in the woods, he'd spice up our curiosity by saying things like "I wonder what is over this next hill?" or "What do you think is around that bend in the trail up ahead?" I believe Dad was genuinely curious about these things. He had a way of honing our curiosity about so many things in life, always raising such seriously inquiring thoughts. So, yes, you too can sharpen your curiosity by discovering, on your own, the fascinating things in store for you out there in the backcountry. I guarantee you one thing: You will never lack for the thrill it can offer.

> **When I'm hiking, I fall into the ancient sleep pattern of "first sleep" from soon after sundown until about midnight or so. Then often I wake up and write. I have scrawled meaningless blather and the best ideas I've had in months in these circumstances. So pen and paper are always in my pack.**
>
> *—Christine Woodside, editor of Appalachian Mountain Club's magazine,* **Appalachia,** *and Appalachian Trail end-to-ender*

WHERE TO GO DAY HIKING

There are hiking guides for almost every section of woodlands anywhere in America, especially around cities. Call the outdoors editor of your local newspaper. Check with your librarian. Go to amazon.com. You're bound to find something.

You might also check out the Internet for trails in your area. Again, probably the best source of information is the American Hiking Society's website which lists some 30,000 trails in the United States. *Backpacker* magazine also has a trail finder, as do some other well-known websites and publishers. Many of these online trail finders are powered by trails.com, which has partnered with nearly every guidebook publisher in North America to publish trail descriptions and maps from the guidebooks themselves.

2

What To Wear

Were you to see me on the trail, you might want to pass by and listen to more fashiona-bly attired hikers about clothing. So, forewarned, forearmed. You might say I am more "utility oriented" or, for a more sophisticated term, more "clothing Bauhaus" than many, as I go for what works best for me and stick with it regardless of whatever new comes along.

I've hiked with people who have many different styles of clothing on their treks. One memorable guy was a cardiologist from San Diego who was with a dozen of us on an eighteen-day trek in Grand Canyon. And I swear this to be true: Every morning Peter put on a different clean shirt. We could never figure out how he carried all of them as well as food for eighteen days and large quantities of water.

Having said that, there are a number of basics that apply no matter what the style of your clothing. So stick with me as long as you can. Dr. Peter got through almost three weeks with me without even flinching.

Day hiking does not require anything much other than clothes you already have in your closet. Not until you intentionally begin taking your hikes in inclement weather do you have to worry about special clothing. Then you need raingear and boots. The most basic item of clothing you need for backpacking is boots, so let's discuss them first.

BOOTS

The most important consideration in selecting a hiking boot is fit. If the boot fits, buy it. All other considerations are unimportant if your boots don't fit properly.

Most good sporting-goods shops stock several brands of boots because manufactur-ers use different lasts to make them, and each brand of boot therefore fits feet differently. A knowledgeable sales person can tell you which brand will more likely be appropriate for your feet—whether it has, for example, a wide or narrow heel, a high or low arch, and other particulars to fit your feet. It is you, however, who is the final judge. You know how the boot feels on your feet. Don't let anyone try to tell you differently.

How to Tell if the Boot Fits

Forget about your shoe size. When hiking with a pack, your feet stretch and expand to about a half size larger than normal. It is said that the foot actually lengthens and widens a half inch every time you step down on it with a fully loaded pack on your back. Likewise, manufacturers' boot sizes often differ from street shoe sizes. Finally, wearing heavier socks along with an extra pair also increases the boot size you need.

Though most hiking stores have a variety of socks for customers to put on when trying on boots, it is far better for you to take along your own socks that you will be wearing on the trail. It's best to wear two pairs—a thin pair next to your foot and a thick outer pair—even in the heat of summer. The thin sock reduces friction between foot and boot and lowers the risk of blisters.

Have the sales clerk measure your foot size with both pairs of socks on and while you are standing with all your weight on the foot being measured. Nothing has changed since Horace Kephart gave directions on how to size a backpacking boot in his classic *Camping and Woodcraft* back in 1917: "Put on thick socks, put up a weight equal to the load you are to carry, slip a tape measure under the sole, then throw your whole weight on that foot, and have someone do the measuring."

Today's Brannock foot scale seems to accomplish the same pack-compensated measuring of your foot even while you are seated. Trust it. But again, you are the sole judge as to whether the boot fits when it's on your foot.

How to Test the Fit of the Boot

When you try on a boot, kick your heel all the way into the back of the boot and lace it up as tight as you can. Then squat into a couple of deep knee bends to see if the heel slips up and down. If it slips more than about an eighth inch, try on another pair.

To test the correct width at the ball of the foot, have someone hold your foot firmly on the floor while you try to rotate it. You should not be able to feel any movement when you do this. The key is that the boot should fit so that there is enough toe-wiggle room, but no leeway for rotation of the ball of the foot, which will cause blisters.

Now try to kick your toes to the front of the boot. Being sure that the boot is tightly laced, kick the toe of the boot against the floor. Walking down an incline, such as the

fitting stool, can also test for toe fit. Your toes should not touch the front of the boot when trying these tests. Try on several different sizes and brands of boots, regardless of price or looks. It is imperative that the boots fit properly. My wife recently bought a new pair of boots that she chose partly for their good looks and partly because of their attractive price. She was enormously disappointed after one hike in them. Fortunately, the store she bought them from, REI, was customer-friendly enough to exchange them for another brand that fit her better, though they cost a good deal more, and she is so pleased now that she hates to take them off, even when not hiking.

A good way to try on boots is to put one of a pair on one foot and a different-size boot on the other foot. Compare the

Since blisters and foot injuries can cause a bad trip, I take good care of my feet, washing them and keeping them clean, on the trail. I always carry extra pairs of good-quality socks.

—Linus Meyer, BLM rangeland management specialist

Seven Steps to Good Foot Care

1. Avoid any pressure on the bone or soft tissues of feet that can give you undue pain and at worst develop blisters.
2. Be sure socks fit properly without wrinkles or lumps.
3. Wear clean socks to avoid chafing, bacteria growth, and potential blistering.
4. Keep socks dry to prevent hot spots and blisters.
5. Take at least one or two extra pair of socks, even on day hikes.
6. Carry moleskin, a lightly padded adhesive sold in foot-care sections of drugstores, and duct tape to apply to hot spots to prevent them from forming blisters.
7. Give your feet special attention. On longer rest stops, take off your boots to air your feet.

---

feel of the two. Take off the one that is less friendly to your foot, and put on another boot from a different size or model, comparing the feel of these two. Take off the one that feels less comfortable, and so on, until you find the boot model and size that feels best. Then put on both boots from the same pair, and walk around the store for a while to see how they feel.

Try to shop for boots at the end of the day, when your feet are the most swollen. After a ten-mile slog with a heavy pack, they'll swell even more than that.

Boot Weight

Back in the 1960s and 1970s, when boots were more popular in classrooms than on the trails, the heavier, the better. Today most manufacturers have gone for lightness in weight. Good thing, too. The significance of this is old hat. Again, let's hear what Horace Kephart had to say back in his 1917 advice: "The importance of going light shod when one has to do much tramping is not appreciated by the novice. In ten miles there are 21,120 average paces. At one extra pound per pace the boots make you lift over ten tons more footgear."

If two model boots fit equally well, choose the lighter one. Kephart even advocated canvas sneakers for this reason. And Grandma Gatewood hiked the 2,000-mile Appalachian Trail three times in her sneakers. Today, though, we tend to be more tender-footed than either Kephart or Grandma Gatewood. So at least a thicker-soled boot will be more comfortable, especially on rocky trails.

Stiffness of Boot Soles

You want a sole that is thick enough that your princess-and-the-pea tender feet do not feel every pebble you walk over, yet flexible enough to bend under pressure of your hands. Stiff soles are for mountaineering, so as to affix crampons. They may look macho but will be hell on the feet after a few miles of trail.

Waterproofing

With the latest materials such as Gore-Tex, many boots are water repellent, if not outright waterproof. There are pros and cons about waterproofing. In summer, you don't want waterproof boots. They make your feet sweat, because waterproofing also means they are airtight, and thus your feet become more susceptible to blistering. For summer hiking, you needn't care about wet feet. You can comfortably dry them in camp at night, as well as the boots. And cold feet are generally not a problem in summertime. This is one reason why you take along an extra pair of wool socks in your pack. Regardless, it is a good idea to try to avoid walking in deep water with your boots.

If you'll be hiking in snowfields at higher altitudes, of course, the waterproofing is more critical, as it is also in spring and fall snow. If this is your concern, talk to the salesclerk about it and be advised accordingly.

Besides buying boots that are already waterproofed, also buy some waterproofing agent, such as a silicone spray. Trial and error will guide you to the best results on the boots you buy.

Breaking In Boots

Before you treat the boots with a waterproofing agent, be sure they fit to your comfort. Wear them around the house, in the office, wherever you can do so without soiling the soles. This enables you to see if they indeed are the right fit for you. Once you have decided that they are going to do the trick, then you can start the break-in process in earnest.

In the old days, the foot soldier broke in his boots by standing in water until they were thoroughly soaked, then walking until they were dry. This enabled the leather to conform to the contours of the foot in all its subtleties and avoided many of the blisters.

An easier and just as effective way to break in leather boots is to run the hottest tap water you can into the inside of each boot, let it stand only a moment or so, and pour it out. Then put on the boots and walk them dry. Not a bad idea to do on a Sunday-afternoon hike.

Although I am sounding the warning, there will still be people who read this and wait to buy their boots just before leaving on a weeklong backpacking trip, putting on their boots at the trailhead for the first time. If you happen to be one of them, I feel sorry for you. Yet neither would I miss a weeklong hike if all I had was a new pair of un-broken-in boots! So make the best of it. And enjoy it the best you can.

SOCKS

First and foremost, do not hike in cotton socks. They absorb moisture, are slow to dry, and increase the risk of blistering the feet.

My choice is thick wool socks that are knit for me by a special wool merchant woman in a tiny town in Texas. (I just had to get that in, for I have been in love with her socks for more than ten years now.) I sometimes wear a pair of thin silk socks underneath them to reduce irritation to my feet.

There are other options that also are enormously gratifying to the feet. I've bought socks when hiking in Switzerland that had cushioned bottoms and elastic that let them conform to my ankles and feet. Then at a backpacking equipment trade show, I was given a pair of Thorlos. They were very much like those Swiss socks. I've worn the Thorlos on my daily hikes for several months now and love them. They are very comfortable—actually, I have to confess, more comfortable in my hiking boots than my homemade wool socks, though I will stick to them for reasons I mentioned earlier.

Thorlo makes its socks in three "levels of protection." These are three levels of thickness, which really provides a nice choice. Now it wouldn't be nice not to mention another important sock maker or two. Wigwam and Smartwool specialize in wool socks, which I have already indicated have a sweet spot in my heart. REI carries its own fine brand of merino wool socks.

The key things are that the socks, whether wool or synthetic, be thick enough to provide cushioning and have the capability of drying quickly once you take them off at the end of the day.

The trick I usually use for drying my socks in camp is to leave them on at night when I crawl into my sleeping bag, provided the temperature is not too hot. In the morning, the socks are toasty dry. And my feet were warm all through the night. This is particularly good in late-fall and early-spring hiking.

CLOTHING FOR BACKPACKING: LAYERING

Now let's talk about clothing. Clothes from your closet are sufficient for your first hikes. But be sensible. Wear outdoors clothes, not fashionable attire. Jeans or shorts and a denim shirt, wool sweater, and light jacket will do the trick for most summer hiking. As you become better acquainted with the trails, you will learn more about your needs.

Once you decide to go backpacking, there are a variety of other things to consider. In addition to the comfort of daytime trail hiking, you will need to keep warm in the cool of evening and early morning, as well as deal with the warmer midday temperatures. There is a lot to choose from in the way of fabrics and cuts of clothing.

I confess my preferences from the beginning so that you know from whence I come. Make your adjustments accordingly. My inclinations are toward natural-fiber clothing and away from synthetics. Not that I don't have some perfectly wonderful synthetic clothing. But my first choice is natural fibers whenever possible. With that in mind, let's talk layering. My ensemble gives me layering capabilities that will take me into temperatures down into the thirties comfortably. And it still keeps my pack weight to reasonable levels, about the same as my synthetic-fabric friends' pack weights.

The Undergarments

In the heat of summer, for most hiking I simply wear my Hanes underclothes. But for extra warmth as temperatures cool in fall and in spring hiking, and even in the mountains in summer, I like silk long johns. They are so comfortable. And on cooler nights, delightful to put on in the evening in camp and to wear inside my sleeping bag.

There are a variety of synthetic fabrics, which a lot of my friends prefer, that seem to serve as well. But the idea here—whether natural fiber or synthetics—is to have a very lightweight pair of long johns, top and bottoms, for cooler evenings.

Also, should you run into a cold snap on your hike, you can put this layer on and be very comfortable hiking with it as your base layer of clothing.

The Second Level

There are big arguments, very sound ones, against wearing blue jeans and denim shirts. They say that when cotton gets wet from rain or body moisture, the fabric loses its capacity to keep you warm; in fact, it tends to suck the body warmth away. True. But it is still my choice.

My best, most sensible hiking friends go for shirts and pants made of synthetic fabrics. They are right, of course. My choice requires me to be far more sensitive to keeping the cotton denim dry, which I've learned to do over the years. You'd best follow my friends' example, not mine. I am confessing it here so that if I meet you on the trail and you notice what I am wearing, you will not call me a hypocrite. So, a light pair of pants and shirt for this second layer.

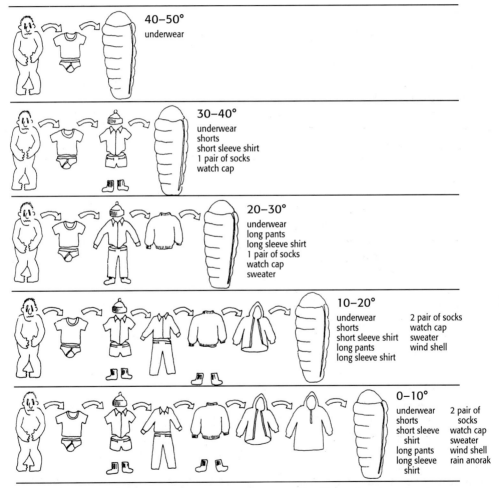

40–50°
underwear

30–40°
underwear
shorts
short sleeve shirt
1 pair of socks
watch cap

20–30°
underwear
long pants
long sleeve shirt
1 pair of socks
watch cap
sweater

10–20°
underwear
shorts
short sleeve shirt
long pants
long sleeve shirt

2 pair of socks
watch cap
sweater
wind shell

0–10°
underwear
shorts
short sleeve shirt
long pants
long sleeve shirt

2 pair of socks
watch cap
sweater
wind shell
rain anorak

Think thin layers of clothing rather than heavy garments. This illustration shows how layers can keep you warm even when you're sleeping outdoors in cooler temperatures.

FROM THE WINTER 1974 ISSUE OF *BACKPACKER* MAGAZINE

I always take sufficient clothes for the worst possible weather, even on an afternoon hike in the summer.

—*Geoff Goins, outdoors enthusiast and owner of Night Sky Adventures, a company providing private tours of the universe in northern New Mexico*

The Warmer Outer Layer

Here again, I differ from most of my more sensible hiking friends. They have mostly gone to thicker polyester pile or fleece clothing, which is soft and lightweight. I wear a light angora wool sweater. It isn't much heavier than the fleece or pile pullovers. But oh, I love the feel of the soft wool. Likewise, it is as good at keeping me warm should it pick up moisture.

In cooler weather, I substitute an L.L.Bean chamois shirt for my denim one. For even cooler weather, I switch to a Woolrich wool shirt in lieu of the sweater. The advantage of shirt over sweater is its flexibility of being buttoned up or down. Of course, the wool shirt does add some weight to the pack.

The Outer Shell

I use my rain parka to serve dual purposes, as a windbreaker as well as for rain. There are many good breathable fabrics that raingear is made of today, the most famous of which is Gore-Tex. Mine is made of an REI ripstop nylon laminate. It keeps me dry while at the same time allowing my perspiration to be wicked out. Whatever you choose for your outer shell, you will still need a rain parka or poncho.

I also have rain pants, which serve as wind pants as well. I can pull them on over my jeans or wear them instead of jeans, depending upon the weather. Then, sometimes I do carry both wind pants and rain pants. Should my jeans get wet, I can take them off and wear the wind pants, which are nylon and very lightweight.

3

Getting in Shape for Backpacking

Today, with the Internet, numerous spas, and health nuts, there is no shortage of experts on how to get into physical shape. I am not one of them. But what I can share with you is my personal experience over the years with my own physical condition for hiking and backpacking.

My first bit of advice for anyone who wants to get physically fit for backpacking is simply this: Get into hiking first.

I am not a spa person, but if you work out at a club, do StairMaster climbing or incline your treadmill steeper and steeper. I had a friend who got into shape for a serious climb up 22,834-foot Mount Aconcagua in South America by climbing stairs for all the floors of the Empire State Building once a week until he was ready for the trip. Not a bad idea.

You too can condition yourself for backpacking by doing as much walking as you can, even during busy city days. Try parking a bit of a distance from the office, store, restaurant, or mall each time. Add a few steps to every stop you make. Climb stairs instead of taking the escalator or elevator whenever possible.

There is nothing like the workouts you do on your feet for conditioning yourself for the trail. Whether you are a new backpacker or are taking your pack down from the hook for the first time in the spring after a winter of indolence, you will suffer the same difficulties the first day out on the trail. Your load will be unwieldy and uncomfortable, not to say exhausting. For years, I suffered this perennial problem. Eagerly anticipating the first hike of the year, I would invariably bite off more miles and carry more pack weight than I should. And I suffered agonizingly for it.

For a number of years, I tried different approaches to this out-of-shape phenomenon. None of them were very successful. Then, one year I discovered what I called the "four-day syndrome."

On the first day of my first backpack of the year, I would suffer all the pains of being out of shape. I'd fall asleep the first night early and exhausted. The second day was worse, because then I had to start out hiking with sore and aching muscles. I would suffer the entire day. And at the end of that day, I hardly cared whether I even ate dinner before going to sleep. The third day, though, was somewhat miraculous. While the legs and feet still would be sore, I had far more strength than on either of the first two days. That would be encouraging and spur me on with the hike. Then there was the glorious transformation of the fourth day. Almost always on this day of the hike, while my muscles were still a bit sore, I would start the day off with an enormous

The author trekking Colorado's Snowmass Wilderness.

burst of energy. I was a superhiker! From that day on, the hike was sheer joy. As were the rest of my hikes that summer.

In those days, I went out on at least a weekend backpack once a month to be sure I would not lose any of the strength I was building up from that first hike onward.

Once I discovered this four-day syndrome, I made two resolutions. I determined to take at least a four-day hike early in the year. And a weekend hike once a month all summer and as long into the fall as weather permitted. Then I skied as often as I could afford and snow conditions permitted.

Despite these resolves, I always had the same resistance to taking my first backpack of the season. I used to wonder if anyone else had these thoughts. As I would get huffing along on my first hike of the season, slogging up the first mile of the uphill trudge, identical thoughts would fill my mind year after year.

"Why the hell am I doing this? I could be back home watching a good movie. This isn't even fun. It is all pain. This is the last—the very last—backpacking I'll ever do. I'm going home after this hike and hang up this pack for good, so help me."

Those were not merely whimsical thoughts. I was always dead serious. Until . . .

If you are an experienced backpacker, you already know that once you have reached your first good viewpoint or your second-breath rest stop, taken off your pack, and sat awhile, you have changed your mind and wondered why you waited so long to get back on the trail. And after

My "luxury item" is a pair of binoculars my wife gave me one Christmas. They're small, yet have a good optics and allow me to see birds and other animals, as well as what's on the other side of a valley. I hike to get closer to nature, and these let me get much closer.

—Pete Olsen, director of membership, American Hiking Society

Four Ways to Shape Up For Backpacking

So here is my prescription for keeping in shape for backpacking.

1. Walk and take stairs as a regular part of your daily activities whenever you can avoid escalators or elevators. Park some distance away, and walk to office, shops, restaurants, and malls.
2. Go day hiking as often as you can, year-round. Try to get in at least one good, strenuous day hike a month. Get into either snowshoeing or cross-country skiing or both.
3. Get in a good jaunt at least once a month during the season, or substitute your monthly day hike.
4. Plan your first big backpack of the season to be at least four days long. Plan to cover modest distances each day for that first trip of the season. Depending upon the terrain, I go for no more than four to five miles a day for the first two days. Keep in mind that days are still short and nights long at that time of year, limiting the number of daylight hours available for hiking.

the fourth day, I would be transformed again into superhiker. I would sheepishly repent for my first day's thoughts and resolve to take my next backpacking trip as soon as possible.

I did get into workouts at a club. And that would get me into somewhat better shape for hiking the following season. But for me, club workouts are the most boring thing I can imagine doing. Furthermore, I have found that my ordinary club workout just didn't cut it for the first day I shouldered my fifty-pound pack in the season. (This was in the days before I decided to go light and pare down the weight.)

A simple thought then occurred to me one year, so simple I wondered why it had never occurred to me before. Why not continue hiking through the year—fall, winter, spring—and be ready for the trail when summer came around? I could at least hike all winter, even if I didn't backpack.

So I did.

Next, I got into mountaineering. That required making camp in freezing weather on glaciers, even in the middle of summer. So of course, the thought occurred: Why not get into winter backpacking? How much different could it be from high camps in mountaineering?

That was the answer I needed. I resolved to backpack at least once a month all year round. I found I really enjoyed cold-weather backpacking. I bought snowshoes and a good winter tent. And kept on backpacking into January, then into February and March. And finally it was time for the first spring backpacking trip of the season in April. That did it. Ever since then, I have not suffered the spring agonies of past seasons being out of shape for the trail. For more thoughts on extending your hiking and backpacking season into the cooler months of the year, see chapters 31 and 32.

These days, I still go backpacking in the wintertime. But I also love cross-country skiing. And I go about two or three times a week. I am fortunate to live in an area where the skiing is terrific most of the winter and to have a special place that I love to go.

4

Buying Your Outfit

Perhaps the most daunting thing about buying backpacking equipment is the excessive options available in any good sporting-goods store today.

For this chapter, I spent a few days at the mammoth Outdoor Retailers Trade Show. When you consider that *Backpacker* magazine has reviewed 367 packs, 371 sleeping bags, and 263 tents—in all, 1,567 products checked by fifty-one testers in just one Gear Guide issue—it is a bit overwhelming. The magazine *Hooked on Gear* lists almost as many items.

Now the good thing about this is that there is substantially little difference among the items in each category. Blindfolded, you could just about throw a dart at *Backpacker*'s list and come away fairly well served, so far as quality and design are concerned. The better equipment on the market today is largely a result of the magazine's evaluations. When *Backpacker* lauds one manufacturer's product for certain features, other manufacturers are quick to follow suit.

But there is a hitch.

You do need to take into consideration your own particular needs that have little to do with quality, some to do with design, but most to do with you. So I will talk mostly about how to assess those needs and give some down-to-earth (ahem!) clues about going about your shopping.

Don't become the proverbial Grand Canyon rescuee, whom the rangers chortle about having come to the trailhead way overequipped and terribly underexperienced. Your rescue—if approved by the rangers—will cost you several thousand dollars more. Hence, if you have a fat wallet, do not fear. You'll make some mistakes in your initial purchases that money can easily correct when you find out what your true needs are.

If, on the other hand, you have a bit more caution, even if you do have a deep pocket, you may want to examine some of your essential needs versus the nice-to-have ones, and find a balance along the way.

It would be impossible to make any kind of competent survey of equipment that wouldn't be out-of-date before this book even made it through the editorial process. So I am going to take a more practical approach. I'll give some general guidelines of what to look for in equipment. I'll mention the products I use. They're obviously a reflection of my bias toward my style of camping, of course.

The worst that will happen if you go with my choices is that some items will not be as comfortable for your own style of backpacking. As you discover from trail experience what your particular tastes are, you'll fine-tune the outfit, tweaking it here and there with a new and different sort of pack or a different sleeping bag, pad, stove, or tent.

But then, many people will passionately disagree with my choices. If you are one of them, you won't go wrong by ignoring my preferences and going your own way. You'll more than likely still end up with great gear that works for you and is safe.

My bargain-basement REI backpack after ten years has more duct tape and stitches in it than it's worth. I use a lot of hand-me-down equipment.

—Mike Buchheit, director,
Grand Canyon Field Institute

STARTING INEXPENSIVELY

Most backpackers I see on the trails today seem to have something in the range of $2,000 worth of clothing and equipment. There is a lot to be said for the fine, innovative comfort gained from these latest fabrics, designs, and materials. I've certainly had the opportunity to own the best and the latest of these over the years. Reflecting on my early days on the trail and how little I could afford then, I checked out what it would cost a newbie to get started reasonably well-outfitted today. I was shocked at how inexpensively this could be done.

I get along with equipment and clothes that would cost you about $250 if you were to buy them all new. And for the trip I planned as I wrote this chapter, I even could have done it for considerably less.

CHEAP STARTER BACKPACKING OUTFIT

For the completely abstemious, this Wal-Mart outfit is far better and more complete than the old army surplus one I had when I began my overnight treks.

Tent	$ 19.88
Sleeping bag	18.98
Sleeping pad	6.47
Propane stove	19.96
Fuel cartridge	4.46
Mess kit	5.44
Cutlery	.96
Flashlight with batteries	2.97
Rain jacket and pants	29.93
Total cost	$109.05

Add to this a $74.93 internal-frame pack from rei-outlet.com and you have an outfit for less than $200. Or add my favorite pack of all time, the external-frame Kelty for $109 and you have a complete outfit for $218.05.

Now you may want to upgrade some of the gear as you get more experienced. But then, remember that I went on one of my longest backpacking trips on which there were three physicians and two lawyers, and we all had the hokiest, cheapo equipment you can imagine. So don't let the dollars keep you from getting out in the backcountry overnighting.

EQUIPMENT NEEDED FOR AN OVERNIGHT BACKPACKING TRIP

Here is a list of basic equipment that will put you on the trail overnight in most parts of the United States during the warmer months. As your needs become more refined, you can replace them with better-quality items as they become more critical to you.

pack	cookpot	first-aid kit
tent	bowl	compass
sleeping bag	cup	flashlight
sleeping pad	spoon	rain parka or poncho
stove with fuel	pocketknife	water bottle

There is no sense in going into the backcountry if you are going to be embarrassed about the gear you are carrying. Tell the truth, I once took a wilderness trek with a group of eleven other trail-hardened hikers who had the most embarrassing collection of *el cheapo* hiking gear you could ever imagine. Yet each of these men was capable of undertaking this severely difficult trek entirely on his own. It was as if they couldn't afford any better, but the group included two lawyers, three physicians, a former Denver Broncos linebacker, and the ranger who ran the mountaineering program at Grand Teton National Park. A half dozen of these fellows got together to climb Mount Denali in Alaska for their next adventure.

The moral is to love the backcountry more than you love your image of yourself with your hiking gear. Nor do you have to go to Grand Canyon to enjoy yourself. I do now because I've moved out to a place a day's drive from all Grand Canyon trailheads. And it is my favorite place to hike in the whole United States.

But I grew up in Michigan, where I could hike backroads to county campgrounds. Or I could find farmers who would let me camp on their untilled acres. There were state parks too, with no entry fees. And in New York, where I lived in the city for most of my adult life, I never exhausted the hiking possibilities within a couple hours' bus ride of the city.

Outdoors is outdoors. Trails are trails. And if you come to love them as much as I do, you'll find ways to tweak your equipment here and there as you find a few extra bucks now and then, or know someone who asks what to give you for your birthday. If you've got the yen for it as I have, then nothing will keep you off the trails—especially inexpensive equipment.

BOOTS

I talked in more detail about boots in chapter 2. This is more of a summary for those of you who are further along in your hiking life.

Boots are the most important gear you need, but there is not much to say about buying a pair. You carry into the store the single most important criterion for buying a pair of boots—your own judgment. Do the boots fit your feet comfortably? You are the only one who can answer that question truthfully after trying them on and walking around with them under some test conditions the store will be pleased to provide. First be sure to put on thick enough socks to simulate what you will be wearing on the trail. It is best if you bring your own socks with you to the store, though most stores will have socks that you can use in trying on boots.

Lace up the boots tightly. Kick your toe to the floor to see if your toe touches the front of the boot. If it does, you need a bigger size. The store should have an inclined surface for you to walk up and back down. How do the boots feel when taking this walk? Don't be bashful. Be sure the boot is right for your feet. Try on several pairs to see the difference in how they fit on your feet. A good way to do this is to put a boot from one pair on one foot and a boot from a different pair on the other foot. This gives you a direct comparison of two pairs without having to guess what one pair was like while trying on the next pair.

The market today has a broad offering of lightweight boots. You do not—in fact, *ought not*—buy heavy mountaineering boots for backpacking. They may look terrific but are way too much overkill for the trail. They add weight to what you have to carry along on the trail and provide little to no extra value. Some salesclerks will hype their "extra ankle support." That is sheer nonsense. You get no more ankle support from a mountaineering boot than you do from an ankle-high walking boot.

Just this past year, I had to replace a pair of boots I'd worn for years. They were great boots, but my feet had grown larger for some reason. And on this particular trip, we were carrying very heavy loads, causing my feet to spread out more than usual. Well, my toes pounded against the toes of the boots ever so slightly, but enough that when I returned home, the big toe on one foot was black and blue. Ergo, I needed larger-size boots. So that is another consideration. When carrying a heavy load for any distance, especially in hot weather, your feet are going to grow about a half size bigger on that trip. Good thing to account for this before you decide upon a new pair of boots.

BACKPACKS

The first and most important consideration in choosing a pack is the comfort factor. Only you know whether carrying a load in it is going to make your back sore.

Second, it has to be big enough to carry all your supplies and gear. Common sense ought to rule here in that you ought to buy the pack that serves most of your hiking needs—which obviously will be weekend trips, rather than the two-week dream trip in your "someday plans." For weekend backpacking, you will most likely do fine with a pack in the range of 2,500 to 4,000 cubic inches in capacity. That is a large range. The smaller end assumes you carry your sleeping bag strapped outside the pack.

There are basically three types of packs. Well, just one moment—there is also a hybrid frame that bridges two categories. The multitude of offerings are simply variations on these themes.

External-Frame Packs

Today this is an almost dying species. Yet I believe it is the best, most comfortable, and safest of the three types. Incidentally, virtually all of the people I backpack

> I am sure to test all equipment before I take it on a hike. Most important, when I get a new pack, I make sure it fits comfortably before I go out on the trail.
>
> —*Linus Meyer, BLM rangeland management specialist*

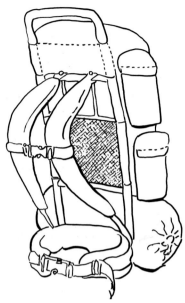

External frame packs have the advantages of carrying the load high, safe, and comfortable.

Internal frame packs are most useful in cross-country skiing, winter backpacking, and mountaineering, as they carry loads lower and snugger to the back.

with, as well as all the group backpacking tour guides I know, prefer external-frame packs.

The external-frame pack is more often than not lighter weight than internal-frame packs. It carries your load higher, which is more comfortable, and you can walk upright, which is best for backpacking, especially hauling long distances. The frame holds the pack away from your back, allowing more ventilation in between, keeping your back cooler. And the external-frame pack is easier to pack, because you can prop it up and its hold-open bar will hold the main compartment open while you load the pack. And most important, the external-frame pack is the safest when negotiating precipitous places, walking narrow ledges with steep drops, crossing swift streams—anyplace where you might take a tumble.

The Appalachian Mountain Club hut men and women, who haul humongous loads up to mountain huts almost daily, use external-frame packs that do not have hip belts and carry the weight of the load up high. If they should stumble or fall, they toss the pack up and over the head, away from themselves. That way, they can get out of the pack harness far enough away from the load that it does not come down on them.

I am clearly prejudiced, as must be obvious by now, toward the external-frame pack. I have used a Kelty external-frame pack ever since I first discovered it some years ago. I've also used the JanSport external-frame pack with equal success. Two old standbys!

Internal-Frame Packs

On the other hand, you may choose to make the trade-offs inherent in using an internal-frame pack because of its particular conveniences.

Most packs sold today have internal frames. The advantage of these packs is that they have many extra features that ordinarily do not come on external-frame packs. One type has a removable top compartment that can serve as a fanny daypack. Most have a number of side pockets designed for various functions. Many have an internal water bladder that snugs up against the back and has a plastic tube extending within easy reach of the mouth for drinking while walking.

And because the internal-frame pack was originally designed for wilderness skiing and mountaineering, it usually has fittings for carrying an ice ax, crampons, skis, and climbing rope.

Flexible-Frame Packs

The flexible-frame pack is the "hybrid" I spoke about. It was designed by Skip Yowell of JanSport back in the days when Dick Kelty's external-frame pack was taking over the market. This pack's frame is an aluminum tubing, usually external to the pack, that flexes a bit when hiking. It has most of the advantages of the external frame and provides some additional comfort in its flexing with the body's stride.

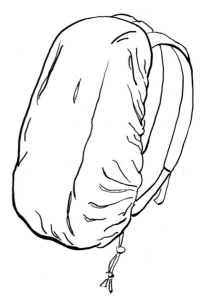

Rain covers are available to fit all types of packs.

Frameless Packs

Frameless packs are the latest trend in lightweight backpacking gear. Dispensing with the pack frame reduces the weight of the pack considerably. No doubt for certain racing backpacking trips, this is the ideal. The big name in this type of pack is GoLite, which is doing a fourteen-day backpacking hike along the Continental Divide Trail without resupplying to demonstrate the value of its ultralightweight gear.

Though this advantage is wonderful for some people, these packs just aren't my cup of tea. In my view, the disadvantages of the frameless pack far outweigh the advantage of its weightlessness. These frameless packs do not have the sturdiness of frame packs, nor do they have hold-open bars like external-frame packs.

Yet I must say, on one of my recent treks in Grand Canyon, I encountered a man obviously in his eighties who was outfitted entirely in ultralightweight gear and was covering some enviable hiking distances in enviable times.

You may not know which type of pack is best for your particular hiking style until after you have tried them out on the trail, an excellent reason for renting rather than buying your first outfit. Salesclerks at outfitting stores, especially at the large chains like REI and EMS, are very knowledgeable about gear. They can be a great help to you in winnowing down your choices.

SLEEPING BAGS

There are a few decisions you have to make that will influence the type of bag you buy. First is the bag's shape. You have basically three types of sleeping bags from which to choose: mummy, square-cut, and semimummy or barrel-shape.

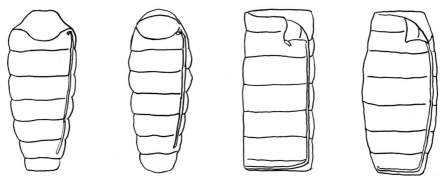

Most common sleeping bag shapes are the mummy, semi-mummy, square cut, and barrel bags.

The Mummy Bag

The most common shape for backpackers is the mummy bag. Because the mummy shape hugs the body, it can better retain body heat. Also, for the same amount of loft, the mummy bag is lighter weight.

The Square-Cut Bag

This is the type you used to take camping when you were a kid. It has several advantages over the other shapes. It is roomier and has ample girth for the restless sleeper. It usually zips open on three sides, allowing it to serve double duty as a blanket at home when not being used for backpacking. And it usually costs far less than the other shapes.

Don't be put off by its association with kids' summer camp or slumber parties. There is a square-cut sleeping bag among *Backpacker* magazine's top recommended sleeping bags. It is snappy looking, very lightweight, and made by one of the top brands in backpacking sleeping bags, Marmot Mountain Works, and its price is right. Check out Marmot Trestles 35. See for yourself.

Semimummy and Barrel-Shape Bags

These bags are a compromise, having advantages of both mummy and square-cut bags.

Warmth Ratings and Fill

The next consideration in buying a sleeping bag is its warmth rating. Many people buying their first bags go for one that is rated far too warm for the uses to which they actually put the bag. If you are starting out in summer backpacking at places that are below 10,000 feet in elevation, buy a bag that is not rated below thirty-two degrees. You can always wear extra clothes to enable you to sleep at lower temperatures. But you can't take the down out of the bag on warmer nights. Besides, inside a tent, the temperature will be about ten degrees warmer than the outside temperatures.

I have two sleeping bags—one summer weight and the other for winter. I also have a sleeping-bag liner that serves as extra warmth for either bag and can be used as well for a sleeping bag itself in hot weather when I need not much more than a sheet around my body.

In summer, I use a lightweight REI down bag. It is slimmer, cutting down the weight to a little over a pound. The winter bag is heavier, even though it is down-filled. It is a Marmot Mountain zero-degree bag weighing about four pounds.

My summer-weight bag is perfect for Grand Canyon spring and fall, where weight is a major concern because of the need to carry large amounts of water. And in summer, my sleeping-bag liner is plenty warm enough.

Flexible Temperature Range Sleep System

I noticed at a recent Outdoors Retailers Trade Show that my old friend Jack Gilbert had come out with a line of sleeping gear that follows the same principles for all-weather camping that I have been using all these years.

The firm Jack founded, Mountain Hardwear Company, calls it a Sleeping System, suggesting that you own both a three-season sleeping bag rated to five degrees and an upgrade rated down to forty degrees. Slip the upgrade into the three-season bag and *voilá*, a winter bag that will take you down well below zero.

Then the other day, a good friend told me about a lesser-known outfit in Grand Junction, Colorado, called Wiggy's. It seems they coined the term Flexible Temperature Range Sleep System (FTRSS) for the U.S. military and claim to have been the first to introduce the sleeping system. In fact, they registered the patented system under a national stock number assigned by the U.S. Navy, NSN 88465-01-395-4084.

Jerry Wigutow, Wiggy's *patrón*, says he has been at this business for thirty-two years, a dozen of them field-testing his system. He has an impressive list of credentials, developing sleeping gear for the military, including the Alaska National Guard and the U.S. Navy survival gear for its ships and aircraft. And he asserts that his "FTRSS is the most widely purchased sleeping system by all the U.S. Armed Forces."

Hand it to him, for he not only guarantees that his sleeping gear will do what he claims, but also gives a lifetime guarantee that if anything does not hold up or perform, you can return it and he will either repair it satisfactorily or replace it. This goes for the temperature ratings, the loft, weight, durability, and such. And the price is right—it's some of the lowest-priced gear on the market.

Why I Bought a Wiggy's Sleeping Bag

by Dick Spas

I checked with my favorite retail outfitter for a sleeping bag that was made in America, for I have a strong loyalty to American-made products. It didn't have any. I checked with several other retailers, the last of which laughed, saying, "Lots of luck. But not here. All of the sleeping bags we carry are manufactured 'abroad,' which mainly means made in China." So I did a search on the Internet and came up with Wiggy's, whose products are made here in the United States. I bought one and have been greatly impressed that it is even better than any I owned before this. It lives up every bit to Jerry Wigutow's claims.

Wiggy's has patented what it calls its Lamilite insulation system for manufacturing its sleeping bags and winter attire, which now brings me to the type of insulation filling in sleeping bags you will want to consider when buying a bag.

Down Versus Synthetic Fill

Both down and synthetic fills will keep you just as warm. There are two major differences in the fills: Down is lighter weight and compresses into smaller space, whereas synthetics stay warm when wet and are less expensive. And then, there is also Wiggy's hybrid known as Lamilite, which is a combination of insulation fills and a manufacturing process designed for it. This fill is also lightweight, fluffy, and impervious to failing when damp. I personally have not tried Wiggy's Lamilite system, so can't vouch for it. But I do think it is worth a shot. Take a look at his website, www.wiggys.com.

Let the salesclerks give you their stories on the virtues of each. It makes for interesting listening.

Choosing the Type of Sleeping Bag

For weekend backpacking in moderate to hot temperatures, just about any sleeping bag will do fine. Answer these three questions to make the right choice for you:

1. What is the honest-to-goodness lowest temperature you are likely to be sleeping out in? Unless you intend to camp at high altitude much of the time, you will find summer-rated bags suit all your needs. Best to get a bag that is rated about ten degrees warmer than the lowest temperature you expect to encounter. There are other easy ways for you to increase your sleeping warmth by ten to fifteen degrees.
2. Do you want down or synthetic? Don't be turned off by the word *synthetic*. Many excellent bags are filled with synthetics. And synthetics have a warmth factor that down-filled bags do not have. When down gets wet, it loses its capability to keep you warm. Not so with synthetics. Also, synthetics are less expensive.
3. Do you toss and turn in your sleep? If so, roominess is a factor. You will especially want extra inches at the shoulders. You may want to consider either a semimummy or square-cut bag instead of the mummy bag. Another advantage here is the lower cost. Square-cut bags are the type you took camping when you were a kid. I include one in my budget outfit list; see the sidebar titled "Start Backpacking with a Complete Outfit for Under $250."

Care of Your Sleeping Bag

Whether your bag is filled with down or fibers, there are certain ways of caring for it that will give you maximum comfort and increase its life.

Use on the Trail

For the trail, in order to keep your bag dry and avoid accumulating trail dust, line your stuff sack with a trash bag. Then stuff the sleeping bag into the stuff sack feetfirst, stuffing it as tight as you can.

Three Ways to Increase the Warmth of Your Sleep

1. Your tent will raise the temperature about five to ten degrees above the outside temperature. Close down most of the tent openings without cutting off good ventilation.
2. Put on more clothes, especially in layers.
3. Put on an extra pair of socks and a wool cap. Your feet and head are the two parts of the body that, if exposed, cool down the whole body fastest.

Once you have set up camp on the trail, take out your sleeping bag and lay it out loosely inside your tent. Be sure to zipper tight all tent openings to keep bugs out of your bag. Laying out the bag, especially a down-filled one, an hour or more before bedtime will allow it to loft optimally before you retire.

In the morning, turn the bag inside out and lay it out in the fresh air while you eat breakfast. This airs out the body's moisture and odors from the night's sleep. Wait until after breakfast to stuff the bag for the trail. If you are staying in the camp more than one night, leave the sleeping bag spread out loosely inside the tent.

Proper Storage

After each trip, I turn my bag inside out, unzip it, and lay it out to air for at least twenty-four hours before storing it.

When you store the bag at home, place it inside out in a stuff bag large enough to allow it to fluff out to its maximum loft while not in use. Some people prefer to hang the bag by tabs on the foot from a clothes hanger inside the closet. This stores it just as well. Just do not store the bag stuffed in its stuff sack.

Cleaning

Follow the manufacturer's instructions on tags on your bag telling you how to care and clean your bag.

I seldom clean mine. Each cleaning diminishes some of the lofting capability of the filling. So I choose to live with the bag's natural state, uncleaned, as long as possible.

When it does need cleaning, I wash it in a bathtub, allowing it to soak in mild detergent for a few hours. Then I gently rinse it out two or three times to get all the soap out of it. I take care in lifting the bag while it is soaking wet for fear of having the water-logged filler breaking through the baffles inside the bag.

Once the bag is rinsed, I lay it outdoors on a porous surface, such as a lounge chair with the cushion removed, to let most of the rinse water drain out of the bag. After an hour or so, while it is still wet, I put the bag into the tumble dryer set at a very low temperature. I put an old sneaker with the bag in the dryer to help loft up the bag's filler while it is drying. The tumbling makes an awful sound with the sneaker in there, but it does the trick nicely.

Though dry cleaners claim to do a safe job of cleaning bags, I am leery of any other procedure than washing my own bag. After all, I don't wash the bag more than about once a year.

SLEEPING PADS

There are many very comfortable sleeping mattresses available. You know your sleeping comfort and can choose accordingly. I prefer my old EMS bare foam pad for its light weight. But then I sleep well on firm surfaces, sleeping at home on a hard futon with thin pad. You may want a more comfortable pad than I use. This is one item where you will have an easy time determining which to buy.

An interesting pad that is now offered by a few companies converts the sleeping pad into a camp chair for use around camp. The one I saw was made by Mountain Hardwear.

TENTS

If you think choosing pack, boots, and sleeping bag is complicated, tents will be your undoing. In buying your first tent, I would definitely stay away from anything but a simple design. The sturdiest design for a few hundred years, almost universally around the world, has been the A-frame tent. But once Skip Yowell at JanSport developed the dome tent back in the 1960s, manufacturers have been tweaking the design so that it provides much of the sturdiness of the A-frame but is usually a bit more commodious.

The most common tent material is breathable nylon, which is not waterproof, though it may be water repellent. The fabric is breathable, so it does not trap your body vapor as condensation inside the tent, wetting your sleeping bag and clothes.

A tent should come with a waterproof fly, either separate or attached to its roof. The fly is meant to cover the top of the tent in such a way that it keeps rain out and also keeps it from dripping from the fly onto the tent wall fabric. If the fly is attached to the tent, be sure that it is amply cut so as to cover all the main tent's surface fabric by several inches all around.

Price is absolutely no guarantee of good tent design. I actually saw an expensive tent made by a leading manufacturer at the trade show that had a fly that did not adequately cover its doorway. Furthermore, the fly's zipper opened at an outward-sloping angle above the doorway so that there was no way of getting into the tent during a rainstorm without bringing in substantial moisture with you.

Here are some things you will want to pay attention to when you buy a tent:

- All windows and doors should have adequate insect-net covering.
- Windows and vents should provide adequate cross ventilation.
- Be sure the tent is waterproof. The main body of the tent should be made of breathable material, while the fly should be waterproof, not merely water repellent.
- Seams should come sealed. Most tents do come this way today. Not a bad idea, though, to get a tube of seam sealer to be sure. Regardless of the maker's presealing of the seams, I like to seal my tent seams before my first use as an extra precaution.
- Some tents come with a footprint or floor saver, which is a tarp shaped to the bottom of the tent that is placed beneath it for added floor protection from damage from rocks. It also provides another layer of protection against water that runs beneath the tent in rainy weather. I cut mine out of sheet plastic, as well as another for the inside of the tent. I hate getting wet unless I am swimming.

Tenting Safety

For your safety in the backcountry, heed the following precautions on tent use. Some mistakes can be life-threatening.

Be sure to vent your tent when you go to sleep. Leave an opening in one of the vents for fresh air to come in. Resist the temptation to want to batten down all the openings on cooler evenings. If you do, and your tent wall fabric is not porous enough, you may be in danger of suffocating from lack of oxygen.

Do not cook inside your tent. The most important reason is that fumes from a stove contain deadly carbon monoxide. Second, stoves can flare up unexpectedly and catch tent fabric or clothing on fire. Third, it is difficult to maneuver around a stove in such a small space, and hence quite possible to tip it over.

Do not leave your tent set up in direct sunshine, especially at higher altitudes, as this allows ultraviolet rays to damage the tent fabric. Best to take down the tent as soon as you can after use in the morning. Although ultraviolet rays do not immediately cause damage, I have seen a friend's tent, which had been used extensively in the mountains, ripped to pieces in heavy winds midway on one of our backpacking trips.

Beyond this, you are on your own. Tents come today in a huge variety of shapes and designs, with myriad additional features. I am wary of some of them, for good reason.

Over the years, I have had two bad experiences with what were represented as "the ultimate" in tent design. In each case, the tent blew apart on me in weather that was more severe than the designers had anticipated. Sometimes, I suppose, calculations in an office will tell an engineer one thing, but the weather may say something quite different. So my suggestion is to beware of tents that don't come with full money-back guarantees.

This is where both magazine field evaluations of products and knowledgeable sales personnel in large retail shops will serve you well.

I own two tents today. I have a Eureka Timberline two-person tent that is roomy enough for winter camping as well as for trips with my wife. She is more comfortable with our gear inside the tent on days when we are pinned down in inclement weather. The nice thing about this tent is that I am able to add a commodious vestibule as well as a gear loft, which we suspend from the inside tent top for extra gear storage at night. Altogether, including stakes, it weighs just under eight pounds. It is a sturdy A-frame tent that has been a standard of the Boy Scouts for more than thirty years.

The Timberline is simple, inexpensive, and probably the most popular tent for backcountry use. It has been used widely by the Forest Service, Bureau of Land Management, and commercial camps for decades. At this writing, it can be found on the Internet for less than $150, including vestibule and gear loft, and I believe it is better than some tents costing upward of $600.

I recently spent three weeks camping in my Timberline at trailheads while exploring wilderness areas on day hikes. I can hardly say enough about this tent. The more I use it, the more I discover little things I simply took for granted, such as a reinforced tab at the zippered corner of the door opening where wear is most likely to occur, a raised lip of fabric covering the place where the zippers meet at the corner. It is designed so that the vestibule and the fly naturally overlap at their edges to keep out rain and snow.

The entrance zippers are placed beneath an overhanging eave and are flapped to keep out rain or snow when you enter. Entering, in fact, is easy because of the tent's maximum opening entranceway. The vestibule fastens onto the front quickly and is designed to minimize wear on the parts of the fabric that get the most use. It has a vent that can be drawn closed. The vestibule's zipper entrance is placed well back on its most vertical point and tucked close to and beneath the fly's eave so as to minimize the amount of moisture that gets in when you enter or exit the tent during rain or snow. The vestibule provides ample storage space, with rain flaps along the bottom edges to keep it dry during inclement weather.

What I like most about the Timberline, though, are the many quite simple but ingenious design features. Its shock-loaded poles make erecting the tent easy and speedy. It is freestanding, needing no pegs except to anchor it in heavy weather. The edges of the tent have clips that fasten to the poles to maximize its interior space.

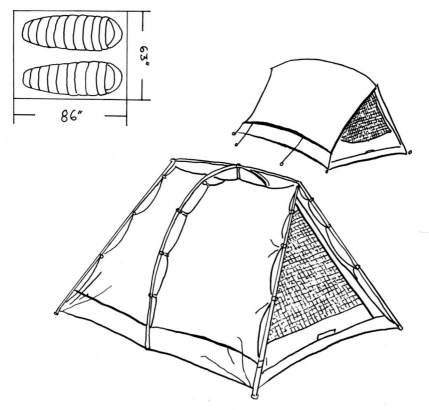

The Eureka Timberline tent has been a standard for thirty years. It has many fine, well-designed details for withstanding severe weather.

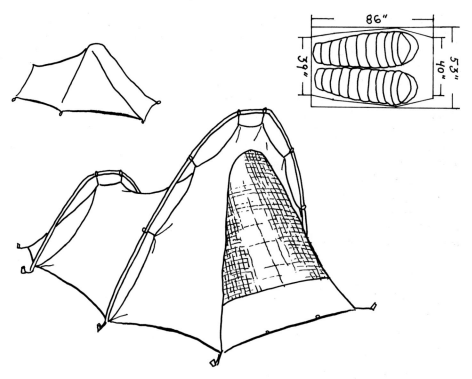

The Sierra Designs Flashlight tent is a prototype that has been imitated by most other manufacturers because the design is perfect for solo backpacking.

The company has obviously listened to its customers' suggestions and incorporated them into little design features that continue to improve this very sturdy, useful product, which explains why more than two million of these tents have been sold over the years.

And please note that I do not have any vested interest in the company or tent. My sole purpose for telling about it is to provide readers an added value to my book.

When I go alone, I take my Sierra Designs Flashlight tent, which is much lighter weight, coming in at a little under four pounds with stakes and two ground cloths, one for outside and one for inside the tent.

Camp can be protected from weather with a tarp slung among trees. Jim Kern and I camp in a Catskill mountain retreat.

Tarps can be strung over a sequestered spot among trees, as here with Forest Service officials Bill Worf, author of the 1964 Wilderness Act, and Bill Holman, former supervisor of the Selway-Bitterroot Wilderness Area.

I am taking it on a week's backpack soon, because at the altitudes I will be hiking and at this time of year, I expect a fair number of bugs. And they usually are more abundant in the evening as I am trying to get to sleep.

This tent has been so successful for Sierra Designs that it is being imitated by many other tent manufacturers today.

Oftentimes when I am going out in better weather, I will merely bring along a tarp, which I stretch over my hiking staff for rain protection. It weighs ounces rather than pounds and is my typical three-season camping preference in Grand Canyon, where weight is so critical because of the amount of water you must carry.

Many lightweight tents offered today are variations of my simple tarp and are touted as the "ultimate lightweight tent of the future."

How Two Can Backpack for a Weekend in Grand Canyon for $149

Why not take your first trek into Grand Canyon for $149 for two people? Start by first of all obtaining your backcountry camping permit and your camping permit at Mather Campground on the South Rim well in advance of your hike. Allow three months, if possible. Then pick up your rental equipment at Peace Surplus in Flagstaff, Arizona, en route to the canyon. It would be advisable to make these arrangements in advance as well. All of this can be done over the Internet. Following is the breakdown of approximate costs, including three-day equipment rental and permits for two nights, but not food or transportation to and from Flagstaff and Grand Canyon. The prices may have changed since my last visit, but they are likely still a bargain.

Two-person backpacking tent	$ 21
Two external-frame backpacks	30
Two summer-weight sleeping bags	18
Two sleeping pads	6
Backpacking stove	9
Entrance fee	20
Campground on rim	15
Backcountry permits	30
Total cost	$149

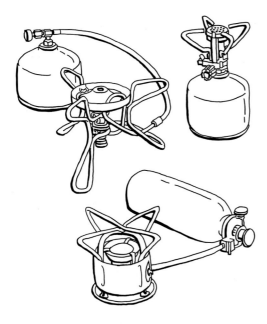

There are many stoves to choose among. Considerations are weight, fuel, and use. The top two in this illustration are fueled by canisters of butane, propane, or a mixture of the two. They have lots of advantages for short trips during warmer weather. Disadvantages are that when the canister runs low cooking time is painfully prolonged, you must carry out the empty canister, and sometimes you have to change canisters in the middle of meal preparation.

The bottom illustration is my MSR, which I've used since Larry Pemberthy invented it back in the 1970s. It has never failed me and because it's intensely hot, it melts snow quickly. Its disadvantages are that it needs priming, is more dangerous, can spill easily, and is difficult to turn down to a simmer. But since it's served me without fail for so many years, I'd be hard pressed to give it up.

STOVES

My choice has been the Mountain Safety Research (MSR) stove since it was first invented by Larry Pemberthy way back in "the olden days." Its advantages are still its compactness, light weight, fast and hot flame, and durability. It is difficult to operate, though, until you get the hang of it. In fact, even some old trail hands I sometimes backpack with aren't very handy with the MSR. Today's version is much easier to use than older models. Some MSR models will burn virtually any type of fuel. This is really important if you plan to backpack in underdeveloped parts of the world where camp-stove fuel is not available.

Some of the other stoves on the market today are far easier to operate than the MSR, and just as compact. Many of the other stove makers are mimicking the MSR design. And with most of these, you can reduce the flame to a more comfortable simmer, if you need that function. Few, though, are as quick to heat up to blowtorch capacity for melting snow and boiling water in winter temperatures.

Unless you find that the screen on your stove does all that you want of it, I recommend an inexpensive aluminum windscreen as additional help in cooking in those open spaces that we often find ourselves in while on the trail.

Other types of gear, such as water purifiers, compasses, and first-aid items, are discussed in the appropriate chapters throughout this book.

Start Backpacking with a Complete Outfit for Under $250

Here is an outfit I priced out at an outstanding sporting-goods store, Peace Surplus, in Flagstaff, Arizona. They assure me that should you call an order for these items that do not appear on their website, they will ship them to anywhere in the United States with shipping charges additional to the price of the merchandise.

Kelty pack	$ 99.00
Eureka Solitaire tent	79.00
North Peak sleeping bag	29.95
Texsport pack light foam mattress	8.99
Texsport rain suit	27.99
Total	$244.97

Note that this outfit does not include stove or cooking gear, nor boots and clothing. But all of these can be supplied from what you have at home, except for the stove. And I am highly recommending that you take along a couple of seven-ounce cans of Sterno with a metal cup to heat your water. You will probably need to create a windshield to keep your Sterno can from blowing out. A large supermarket paper bag will do just fine. Cut it down to about six to eight inches high. Open it up, place stones in each corner, set the Sterno inside, and place your cup of water on top of it to heat the water.

Wear your sturdiest sneakers and wool socks, blue jeans, and a shirt. Take along a sweater for the cooler evenings. And enjoy yourself.

BORROW OR RENT BEFORE BUYING

Let me advise you not to buy any backpacking gear until you have made a few overnight hikes with borrowed or rented gear. The beauty of getting started backpacking today is that there are many places where you can rent very good packs, tents, and sleeping bags. The advantage here is that you get to try them out on the trail. This lets you know a number of things about gear that you only theorized about before, or at best took a salesclerk's advice.

The one item you may well want to put some money into before this, though, is your boots. And this is not a difficult decision to make at all.

5

Planning Your Trip

Planning a backpacking trip is much like planning a mountaineering expedition, taking almost as much time as the trip itself. Obviously, going for a weekend backpack on trails a few hours' drive from home needs less planning than a weeklong trek on trails a plane ride away.

This chapter will deal with the latter. You can scale back a bit to adjust for the near-to-home weekender, though much of the planning is the same, except on a smaller scale.

PLAN FOR THE WEATHER

As you plan a backpacking trip, you'll want to know what kind of weather to expect for that time of year in that location. Guidebooks as well as land managers are very helpful about this. But it is just as important for you to get your own long-range weather forecasts from the Internet before setting off to your destination, especially if you are traveling some distance.

You want to be sure to carry sufficient warm clothing for the cool evenings— whatever they might be for that area. Likewise adequate raingear.

HOW MANY MILES SHOULD YOU PLAN TO HIKE PER DAY?

This is where even highly experienced backpackers make big mistakes. I call it the "living-room syndrome," for it occurs on my living-room floor when I pore over topographic maps figuring out all I want to do on my next hike. All hiking trails look easier on the topos than they turn out to be when I get there. I anticipate, too, that I will be in far greater hiking form than I usually am. It's a habit I don't seem to be able to break.

One way to compensate for this syndrome is to plan to hike in and out on the same trail rather than trying a loop hike, as is so tempting on a map. This way, you have a lot more control. You know how long it takes you to get in to a place. Ergo, you know pretty much how long it will take you to get back out. The trick is to stop hiking in so as to give yourself sufficient time to hike back out.

After you have gained some experience backpacking, you will be better able to estimate hiking times that are closer to those used in guidebooks. You may be a faster or slower backpacker. That is not a problem, for you can adjust guidebook times to the pace most comfortable for you.

The hiking time estimates in the *AMC White Mountain Guide* have always seemed comfortable to me, as are those in the *Guide to Adirondack Trails,* although in recent years I have slowed down a bit. Both seem to calculate roughly two miles in an hour,

Here I am camped solo in a Pennsylvania wildlife refuge along the Appalachian Trail.

adding an additional half hour for each 1,000 feet of elevation gain. I have found some guidebooks, though—particularly the guides to Colorado's Fourteeners—to be a bit of a stretch. That may be due somewhat to the altitude, both in the Rockies as well as in my boots.

Some places like Zermatt, Switzerland, which is my other favorite place to hike, have trail signs up at every juncture giving time and distance to each of the points along the route ahead. These are hiker-friendly times, perhaps influenced by the Swiss Tourist Office.

If you check your actual walking times against the guidebook times, you can calculate the difference in time it takes you to cover those same distances. I've gotten familiar enough with my own hiking pace that I can calculate just about how far I have backpacked simply by checking the time it took me to get there.

My calculation today is customarily made by figuring it takes me about an hour to cover two miles of fairly level trail with a pack. Then I add an hour for each 1,000 feet of ascent. Descending is usually faster, though long, steep descents can slow me down. Those are clearly not record-book times.

They do enable me, however, to estimate the time it will take me to cover the distances. When I hike out of Grand Canyon on the Bright Angel Trail from Phantom Ranch, which is about ten miles and a climb of about 5,000 feet, I figure it will take me five hours for the distance of ten miles, plus an hour for each 1,000 feet of ascent—an additional five hours—for a total of ten hours. I usually make it out in a bit less time

The Three-Two-One Rule for Calculating Hiking Times and Distances

Here is a method some hikers use to reduce the guesswork in estimating hiking times. On a smooth-surfaced country road without a pack, you can probably cover about three miles an hour. Take a backcountry trail through the woods and it will take you longer to cover the same distance. Figure two miles in an hour. Pick up a backpack and it will take you even longer. Estimate that it will take roughly an hour to cover one mile on a backcountry trail. Get it? Three-two-one!

Time yourself on a smooth-surfaced country road and use that to calculate the other times. For example, if you discover that you comfortably cover only two and a half miles an hour on a road, divide that by three and multiply it by two to estimate the time it will take you on a trail, and it will be one-third of the road time to backpack that distance on a trail ($2.5 \div 3 = 0.83 \times 2 = 1.67$). Thus if it takes you an hour to cover two and a half miles on country road, you should be able to hike one and two-thirds miles on a trail, or to backpack three-quarters of a mile on a trail in an hour.

than that, though there are times it takes somewhat longer. A lot depends, of course, on how often and how long I stop to rest or take photos.

That is not a trail on which you can feel comfortable taking your time, inasmuch as there are a huge number of gung-ho day hikers and trail runners. My intention in writing this book is not to produce speed champions. Pleasure is my sole objective in hiking—merely to get in tune with the backcountry. The more I am out there, the more deeply immersed in nature I become.

If I could write a script for your experience, I'd have you enjoying the backcountry as much as I do. If you come to say that there is nothing you would enjoy more than a backpacking trip in to your favorite spot, I'd be a happy camper.

PLAN SOME REST DAYS EVEN FOR YOUR SHORTER TRIPS

Inevitably, Murphy plays a role in most of my hikes; things that can go wrong often do. Not that they are terribly big and disruptive things that go wrong. But, for instance, it rains on a day I didn't expect rain, or I lose a piece of gear and have to spend some precious time looking for it. Or it takes a lot longer finding a campsite than expected. Or one of us gets a crick in the knee that slows us all down. There are hundreds of unexpected difficulties that you and I are not even able to imagine that are going to creep into one or another of your overnight hikes. Expect it, live with it, don't fight it.

This is one good reason for building in an extra day here and there on your backpacking trips for rest and taking day hikes. This is a particularly important aspect of family backpacking with children. They love to have a day in camp when they don't have to hustle down a trail. It leaves all sorts of time for exploring various parts of the backcountry you never would have imagined were there.

My nephew Kenn and I do a great deal of backpacking together. We always set aside the second day of our treks for rest. Sometimes he goes off exploring while I loll about camp. Sometimes I do the exploring while he lolls. And other times we both explore together—or both loll. What a cherished time this is for us!

We have a special place in Grand Canyon that takes us only about five hours to pack in to, where we love to spend our second day meandering about the slopes of the Hermit Shale. We have found a lot of interesting things down there in our meandering. For example, we found some very old, peeling paint marks on the ceiling of an overhang in a remote part of the canyon. Some painter obviously wiped his or her brush upon the rock surface while painting a scene from the canyon. More than likely, we speculated, it was for the Santa Fe Railroad Company, which paid many artists to paint beautiful scenes of the park to promote tourism back in the 1920s and 1930s.

When I later mentioned our discovery to Grand Canyon Park Archivist Mike

When I find something I like, I stick with it. My Kelty Redwing is very comfortable. My REI Down-Time sleeping bag, Eureka Timberline tent, and Svea stove have been with me a long time.

—*Kit Kemsley, author of* **Places of Power,** *NPS, USFS, BLM fire control dispatcher.*

Trip-Planning Schedule

Three Months Ahead
- ☐ Decide who is going.
- ☐ Get permits and regulations.
- ☐ Buy or order guidebooks and maps.
- ☐ Break in new boots.

Two Months Ahead
- ☐ Plan route, water sources, hiking times, and emergency escape routes.
- ☐ Make up gear list. See that everyone has one.
- ☐ Check out gear to be sure it is in good working condition.
- ☐ Plan a menu for each meal and make up food list.

Two Weeks Ahead
- ☐ Buy and repackage food.
- ☐ Confer with hiking partners on gear and departure plans.

One Week Ahead
- ☐ Gather together all gear and check against list.
- ☐ Gather together all food and check against list.
- ☐ Check advance weather forecasts.
- ☐ Check with rangers on trail conditions.
- ☐ Give a copy of your itinerary to a friend or relative.

Day Before Departure
- ☐ Pack all gear, checking against the list again.
- ☐ Pack food and get all items ready for departure.
- ☐ Check that all other hiking partners have done the same.
- ☐ Take care of any last-minute items not thought of beforehand.

Day of Departure
- ☐ Check gear against list for any items not accounted for.
- ☐ Load gear and be sure all others have checked their lists.
- ☐ Depart.
- ☐ Enjoy!

Quinn, he knew about it and speculated more romantically that these peeling paint spots may have been left by Tomas Moran back in the 1890s, when he painted the most famous painting of the Grand Canyon, which hangs in the National Museum in Washington.

In Death Valley on a rest day on one of our family hikes, my daughter Kate found the most perfect arrowhead I've ever seen. Once while exploring the rim of the Black Canyon of the Gunnison, we found a perfect set of deer antlers. On a hike in the Wind River Wilderness in Wyoming, a fisherman pointed out that he had his pick of the kind of trout he wanted to catch, for there were different species in each of the ponds in that area—speckled in one pond, rainbow in another, brown in still another, with cutthroat in yet another pond. Who'd have noticed, if we had just bombed on through there?

Those rest days may be the reason you go in there in the first place.

IMPORTANCE OF USING A CHECKLIST

In the sidebar "The Essentials," you'll find a checklist of items I consider to be essential for any overnight backpacking trip. In the sidebar that follows, "Nice to Have Along," you'll find another list of things that might be useful on some of your hikes. I would bet there aren't two other backpackers who would wholly agree with my breakdown of the two lists. Nevertheless, most would agree that nothing should be taken off the "Essentials" list. Add to this list whatever you feel you can't leave home without.

Make copies of both lists, and tuck them into your backpack when you store it. Next time you plan a backpacking jaunt, use the lists, checking off items as you prepare for the hike. The "Nice to Have Along" list will tip you off to things that you didn't take along on your last hike that you might like to have along on the next one.

I've pared my "Essentials" list down substantially from a three-day July 4 weekend when I sweated along a Pennsylvania section of the Appalachian Trail under my fifty-two-pound pack full of "lightweight" gear.

The Essentials

- ☐ pack rain cover
- ☐ tent
- ☐ tent rain fly
- ☐ poles
- ☐ stakes
- ☐ ground cloth
- ☐ sleeping bag
- ☐ stuff sack for sleeping bag
- ☐ plastic bag to line stuff sack
- ☐ sleeping pad
- ☐ water bottles
- ☐ water filter
- ☐ rain parka
- ☐ cook stove
- ☐ stove windshield
- ☐ extra fuel
- ☐ funnel or pouring spout
- ☐ cook pots
- ☐ plate or bowl
- ☐ cup
- ☐ spoon
- ☐ fork
- ☐ pocketknife
- ☐ matches
- ☐ can opener
- ☐ flashlight
- ☐ extra batteries

- ☐ extra flashlight bulb
- ☐ compass
- ☐ maps
- ☐ trail guidebook or copies of relevant pages
- ☐ first-aid kit
- ☐ repair kit
- ☐ sunscreen
- ☐ insect repellent
- ☐ extra nylon cord
- ☐ plastic trash bags
- ☐ zipper-lock bags
- ☐ boots
- ☐ two pairs long pants
- ☐ two shirts
- ☐ two pairs socks
- ☐ underwear
- ☐ sweater
- ☐ silk long john top
- ☐ silk long john bottoms
- ☐ jacket or windbreaker
- ☐ wide-brimmed hat
- ☐ gloves
- ☐ warm wool hat
- ☐ toilet tissue
- ☐ toothbrush

Nice to Have Along

- ☐ hiking staff or trekking poles
- ☐ rain pants
- ☐ gaiters
- ☐ shorts
- ☐ toothpaste
- ☐ comb
- ☐ biodegradable soap
- ☐ plastic trowel
- ☐ pen and notebook
- ☐ sunglasses
- ☐ binoculars
- ☐ camera
- ☐ film
- ☐ thermometer
- ☐ altimeter
- ☐ field guides
- ☐ swimsuit
- ☐ towel
- ☐ washcloth
- ☐ camp shoes
- ☐ paperback novel for a rainy day in camp

I had started out with visions of all the things I wanted to do on that hike. I carried my heavy Nikon F-2 camera with a couple of long lenses, five field guides—birds, wildflowers, trees, mushrooms, and ferns and lichens—as well as a variety of comfort items, such as camp mocs, camp chair, and mats. Then, too, I took along far more cooking pots and utensils than I would ever use. That trip wised me up and led me to trim my pack weight down for all my hikes since.

After a number of trips, you may find that you gather together your backpacking gear without feeling you need to use checklists. I've done that, gotten lazy over the years and overconfident. But when I still use my checklists, I avoid the kinds of mistakes I have made in my overconfident period.

Once I forgot to bring tent poles! We were sleeping out under the stars and did not discover that until the middle of the night, when it began to rain and I started to put up the tent. My wife reminds me of this often—*very* often—for she did not sleep well that night, cramped up among all the gear in the back of the station wagon.

Another time, at a remote spot on the North Rim of Grand Canyon just west of the park boundary, we started to fix dinner when I discovered I had forgotten to bring along the plunger for the pump on my MSR stove. Hence, there was no way of firing up the stove to cook dinner. It was late, so I was prepared to go without dinner. But my wife insisted we build a fire to cook it.

On a recent hike in to Colorado's San Luis peak, I forgot to bring fork and spoon. I had my Swiss Army knife. Not difficult to make do. I also failed to bring along my backpacking binoculars. Again, not critical, but it would have been nice to have a closer peek at that particularly large owl I saw hovering on a branch of a ponderosa pine over the trail ahead of me.

> I make sure that in my backpack or day-pack is a small plastic trash bag, Ziploc bag, paperclip, rubber band, and shoe-string—all items that have multiple uses and almost no weight and take very little space.
>
> —*Reese Lukei, VP legislative affairs for American Discovery Trail Society*

HOW TO PACK YOUR GEAR
Preparing Your Gear for Your Pack

First, repackage all food items into more portable and less bulky containers. Do not even consider carrying glass jars. They're far too heavy, and what's worse, they can break in your pack, causing you endless grief. Cans also are heavy. If you can safely empty cans into plastic containers, do so. Zipper-lock plastic bags are terrific for food items. But realize that plastic bags do not keep food protected from animals and birds. You need an overall container that is varmint-proof for this.

I'd never go without my bandanna. It serves so many purposes. I wear it wrapped around my head, use it as a sweat band, towel, to clean my glasses, and as a hot pad when handling cook pots. You won't believe this, but I have used it to lower eggs into a pot of scalding water to boil them. I'd also hate to go on a hike without my camera.

—Kate Kemsley, faux finisher and mural artist, the hikingest of the author's offspring

Likewise, pack your clothes in plastic bags. I hate to get my gear wet on the trail. It is not only uncomfortable, but unsafe as well. Individually wrap each item of clothing separately in its own zipper-lock bag. If the item is not easily distinguishable from other items when folded up, write what it is on a note card and slip the card into the bag so that the note faces out. This enables you to identify each item of clothing quickly. Family hiking can be made a whole lot easier if each item is labeled, such as Katie's socks, Will's T-Shirt, Andrew's shorts, Dad's long johns.

Line your stuff sack with a plastic trash bag before stuffing your sleeping bag, to give it extra protection against rainy weather. Then double-protect everything. Place a large, heavy-duty plastic trash bag into each compartment of the pack before loading anything into it. Finally, since I am a little paranoid about rain, I have a waterproof pack cover to put over the whole pack at night at camp and during downpours. I just hate getting wet!

Carry tent stakes in separate bags that keep them from puncturing the tent or any of your other gear.

Loading the Pack

1. Load heavier items at the top of the pack, lighter ones on the bottom. Your sleeping bag ought to be at the bottom of your pack, clothing next, with food near the top along with tent and stove fuel.
2. Load weight of items evenly from side to side so that your pack will not pull you to one side or the other as you hike.
3. Adequately cover all sharp edges and corners so that they will not puncture or tear other items in your pack.
4. Separate food from fuel and stove so as not to contaminate food with the scent or taste of fuel.
5. Keep all items you'll need on the trail in handy locations: water, map, and compass in side pockets; windbreaker and lunch easily handy near the top of the pack.

> I don't take a wristwatch. It gets in the way. And I can look at the time too often. I take a pocketwatch and bury it in my pack.
>
> —*Jim Kern, founder, Florida Trail, Big City Mountaineers, and cofounder of American Hiking Society*

Check Your Pack Weight

Before you take off for the trailhead, pack and weigh your gear.

Using your checklist to be sure you have everything you plan to take, load your pack with all your gear, food, and water. In desert country, figure on a gallon of water for a day's hiking. Check the weight of your fully loaded pack on a scale. The best way to do this is to get on the scales without your pack, then with it. Subtract your body weight from your weight with the fully loaded pack, ergo your pack weight. As a rule of thumb for the maximum pack load, calculate one-fourth of a woman's body weight and no more than one-third of a man's body weight. These are maximums for slim-bodied people. Figure less for overweight people.

I almost always find that my pack weight at this point is far heavier than I intend to carry on the trail. So now is a time of paring back. Examine every item you have in your pack to see if it is worth the extra weight. You will be surprised at how a few ounces here and a few ounces there add up.

USEFUL KNOTS FOR BACKPACKING

There are a few knots that are useful to the backpacker and easy to learn. They have a multitude of uses in the backcountry, and the more practiced you are with them, the safer and more secure your use of ropes will become.

Keeping Your Tent Dry Inside

I hate waking up in the middle of the night with a wet sleeping bag. It has happened in the best designed and constructed tents. For protection, I cut two tarps for my tent out of plastic.

Lay out the tent on the living-room floor on top of a sheet of clear plastic. Trace a line all around the tent with a marker. Cut one tarp a half inch wider all around for the inside of the tent. Then label it "inside" with unerasable marker. Cut a second tarp from the plastic about a half inch smaller than the tracing all around the tent and label it "outside."

You want the outside tarp to be a bit smaller than the tent so that water does not come down the side of the tent and gather in puddles beneath it. You want the inside tarp larger so that it forms sort of a boat inside the tent and keeps your sleeping bag dry in the event that any moisture does get into the tent.

I leave the tarps in place when I roll up the tent with poles and pegs to store inside the carrying bag.

There are tents now for which you can buy footprints or floor savers that serve the outside tarp function. I still prefer to have both inside and outside tarps.

The most common use of these knots is to secure your tent tie lines so that they will be both secure in stormy weather and easily adjustable when required. Though many tents come with tie lines that are already fitted with an adjusting device, these can break, get fouled, or be lost, rendering the tie lines inoperative.

It's a good idea to learn to tie these five knots before taking your first serious overnight excursion into the backcountry. Learn what they look like when properly tied. Learn to tie them by memory, without hesitation. They will serve many useful needs in the backcountry, as well as provide that extra margin of safety that can mean your or your companion's life.

Overhand Knot

The overhand knot is the simplest of all knots and is the point of departure for many of the more elaborate knots, which is the reason for demonstrating it here.

Rolling Hitch

Use the rolling hitch to firm up your tie line. Run the loose end of your line around a stake, then tie the loose end to the standing end of the line with a rolling hitch. After firming it up, run the knot up the standing end until the line is taut. It can be slid by hand to either lengthen or shorten the rope, but left alone, it stays put.

Square Knot

The square knot is useful for many purposes, such as tying up bundles and attaching items to your pack. But do not use it to tie two ropes together. In *The Ashley Book Knots,* the world's foremost expert on knots, Clifford Ashley, states that using this knot to tie two ropes together "is probably responsible for more deaths and injuries than have been caused by the *failure of all other knots combined.*"

The basic overhand knot.

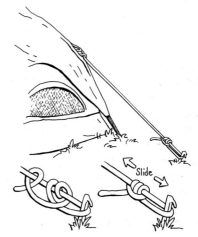

The rolling hitch can be used for adjusting the tautness of tent ropes.

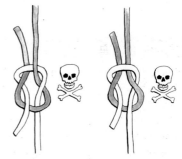

The square knot is one of the most versatile knots, but it also can be the most dangerous. Nautical knot expert Clifford W. Ashley claims that more lives have been lost from improper use of square knots than all other knots combined. Never use the square knot to tie two lengths of rope to each other, as the knot can easily come untied.

The improper way of tying the square knot is known as the granny knot. This is extremely dangerous!

There is no "almost right" way of tying this knot. Study it, and be sure you have crossed the ends the right way and not the incorrect way. You should be able to tie this knot without hesitation before using it for lashing anything.

The water knot is the most reliable way of fastening the ends of two lengths of rope.

Water Knot

The water knot is easy to learn and an excellent way of fastening the ends of two ropes together; it will not fail. It is also called an Englishman's knot, a fisherman's knot, and a true lover's knot. You simply tie an overhand knot at the end of each of the ropes to be fastened together, but tie each of them around the end of the other rope. And be sure that the ends of the overhand knot are facing away from its own rope.

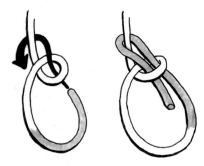

The bowline knot is the sturdiest means of forming a loop in the end of a rope. It is the basic knot in mountaineering.

Bowline Knot

Ashley says: "Properly tied in ordinary rope, there is little or no danger of a Bowline Knot's capsizing before the breaking point of the rope itself is reached. It is so good a knot that the sailor seldom uses any other loop knot aboard ship." Use it wherever you want to tie a firm loop in the end of a rope to hitch over a post. It has long been used by mountaineers to tie their waist loops onto the ends of climbing ropes. And it can be used to fasten tent tie lines onto stakes or onto the tent itself.

Section Two
TRAIL SAVVY

The summer—no sweeter was ever;
  The sun shiny woods all athrill,
The grayling aleap in the river,
  The bighorn asleep on the hill.
The strong life that never knows harness;
  The wilds where the caribou call;
The freshness, the freedom, the far-ness—
  O God! how I'm stuck on it all.

  —from "Spell of the Yukon,"
    by Robert Service

6

On the Trail

Start slowly with day hikes. After you have taken several day hikes, you will find out what pace is good for you. Once you have day-hiked sufficiently to want to extend your hiking to overnighting, this chapter will help you on your ventures.

PACK WEIGHT

There is a distinct difference between the pack weight you *can* carry and the weight you *want* to carry. All sorts of formulas are offered by authors of various of books. Obviously, there is a certain amount of gear and food you will need to carry. Then there are items it would be nice to have. Start with what you have to carry, including food and water, and weigh your full pack. Ideally, your pack will weigh no more than one-fourth your body weight, assuming you are of average weight for your height. I weigh 150 pounds and find that a pack of 35 pounds is about as much as I care to carry. The essentials in summer weigh somewhere around 25 pounds for a two-night, three-day backpack, allowing for no more than 10 pounds of "nice to have along" items. I am usually quite comfortable with that weight. And sometimes I have to pare that weight down further when I will be hiking in desert areas where I have to carry greater quantities of water.

SETTING YOUR HIKING PACE

Whatever your comfortable pace has been on day hikes, it will slow down considerably when you are carrying a pack. Most guidebooks assume you can hike with a pack at about two miles per hour on level ground and add a half hour more for every 1,000 feet of elevation. This is *average* and will have to be adjusted for your pace, based upon what you have discovered from your day hikes. I've found I'm comfortable enough with two miles per hour on the level; in fact, I do a bit better than that. But uphill, I need to add more like three-quarters of an hour for every 1,000 feet of elevation, depending upon the steepness of the trail.

Ideally, you will hike at a pace slow enough that you can enjoy the outdoors. Even more important, the pace of your group should be throttled down to the pace of your slowest hiker. If you are the leader of the group, it is best if you hike last and allow your slowest hiker to lead.

A number of walking books recommend how you should put your foot upon the ground. I think that is damned foolishness. You will find out quickly that your feet can very well decide for themselves how they want to hit the dirt each time you swing them forward. Let them find their own comfort level, and just watch for hot spots on the foot, which ought to be taken care of immediately once you notice them. Apply moleskin, a lightly padded adhesive sold in the foot-care section of drugstores, to the whole area that is being irritated so as not to develop a blister. An excellent substitute for moleskin that works even better for preventing hot spots from turning into blisters is ordinary duct tape. Carry a supply wrapped around your hiking staff. When needed, simply cut off a portion and spread it over the hot spot, smoothing out all wrinkles.

UPHILL HIKING
The tendency is to want to stop more often when hiking uphill, for you are expending a good deal more energy than on the level ground. It is said that a fifteen-degree slope (however you want to measure that!) takes about four times the amount of energy to climb than the same distance consumes on level ground. Better to shorten your stride and go slower, and stop less often. It takes far less energy to keep going at a slower pace than it does to go faster and take frequent rest stops. Go for the feeling of these things rather than actually measuring them.

Try the rest step on steeper grades. After planting your foot and beginning to step up, lock your knee into a straight-leg position and hold it like that while you swing the other leg forward. Literally feel yourself rest for a micromoment before pushing off into the next step. If this does not come easily for you, forget it and find your own way of economizing on the uphill slog. I use this infrequently, if at all, though at one time I did find it useful.

DOWNHILL HIKING
At first this is a relief from a long uphill climb. If downhill hiking continues for long, though, it becomes more wearisome than uphill hiking. They say that uphill is hard on the lungs and downhill is tough on the knees. I'd agree, especially at higher altitudes.

There is a way of walking downhill that is easiest on the legs. As you take a step down, keep the knee flexed a bit to allow it to cushion the jarring, sort of like skiing. Another trick that I have devised for my long downhill slogs is to turn somewhat sideways to the right for a few paces, then turn to the left, then straight downhill again, alternating the direction I face from right to left every few paces. Obviously you need to find your own comfort in doing this. But I find this eases the stress on the knees.

HIKING WITH AND WITHOUT TRAIL MARKERS
Most trails in heavily wooded areas, particularly in the East, have been marked with distinctive trail blazes—emblems or, more often, colored rectangles painted on a visible surface such as tree trunk, rock face, or fence post. When some of these trails rise above the tree line or cross barren rock sections, they may be marked by rock cairns or blazes painted on the rock surfaces. It is important to know which marker designates the trail you are going to hike. Where this trail crosses other

I always carry ibuprofen to take before going to bed at night to ease aches and pains.

—*Sherry Fletcher, school superintendent, Truth or Consequences, New Mexico*

trails, they will have their own distinctive trail blazes so that you don't get confused about which way to go at these junctures.

If the trails become at all confusing to you, do not move ahead until you can see two trail markers—one ahead of you and one behind you. This is easiest to do when there are two or more in your hiking party, so that one of you can stay by the marker you can see while another goes ahead to locate the next marker.

Please be considerate of the next hikers and do not put up rock cairns or paint markers of your own. This will merely add more confusion to the trail situation.

Many backcountry trails, in both the West and East, are often not marked, though many of the trails may be fairly well worn into the terrain and fairly easy to follow. This makes route finding a bit more difficult, and you can become confused as to which direction to take at certain junctures. In this type of terrain, you should be more proficient at map reading and have along trail guidebooks, good topographic maps, and a compass to avoid getting lost.

There may be times when you are hiking above tree line where you will have to hike off-trail, going cross-country where you can see no trail markers. First of all, a warning: This can be quite dangerous if you have not had a considerable amount of experience in route finding on your hikes. So avoid this type of hiking until you feel very confident. Realize that should you turn an ankle, lose your way, or have something else unforeseen happen, such as a sudden whiteout, there will be no one out looking for you. Some deaths at higher elevations have been due to the inability of even highly experienced hikers to find their way during sudden whiteouts from a thick, foggy cloud or sudden snowstorm.

This is wilderness, regardless of whether it is marked as such on the map. That is what wilderness is all about—the raw elements with no cell phone.

I always have my Zeiss 10X40 binoculars around my neck. An important part of the adventure of being in the backcountry is being watchful for the birds and animals. You never know what you're going to see around the next turn in the trail.

—*Timothy Manns, chief interpreter, North Cascades National Park Service*

REST STOPS

Ideally, you will take your first rest stop after twenty minutes to a half hour to adjust your clothing and pack straps, check your bootlaces, and take care of calls of nature.

Keep a light windbreaker on top of your pack within easy access, and slip into it on your rest stops. The body cools down rapidly, especially if you are perspiring or there is the slightest breeze.

The average pace mentioned in guidebooks also includes rest stops. And the so-called average hike assumes a two- to five-minute rest every half hour or so, depending upon your hiking pace and the kind of terrain you are covering. Be flexible. It really is unwise to set a pace

Sunscreen Warning

It is best to apply sunscreen before starting your hike in the morning. This is particularly important in the mountains, deserts, and in snowy conditions, all of which intensify the power of the sun to burn the skin. The higher the elevation, the more intense the sun's rays. Use a sunblock on cheeks and nose, even with a wide-brimmed hat. Longtime mountain and desert backpackers are known to become victims of skin cancer at early ages. It's a severe type of cancer and not worth the risk.

that is going to be uncomfortable for anyone in your group. You should be out there to enjoy the experience, not to prove anything.

Rest stops ought to be determined more by the landscape and trail than the clock. Many times on a hike, you will come to places that are far better to take a rest than others—a view, a nice set of rocks or logs to sit on, a lovely shaded spot after you have been hiking through the sun for a while. Let these natural settings govern your stops as much as possible.

If hikers in your group need rests more often than a few minutes every half hour or so, perhaps your pace is too fast.

Taking off your pack and putting it back on at a rest stop consumes a substantial amount of energy, so it is best to have packs-off rest stops less often and for longer periods of time. I'm talking five minutes versus two minutes for your shorter stops. Too long a period of time saps your energy more than you realize and makes it difficult to get up and get going again.

A better way is to take short packs-on breaks, usually at places where there are rocks or logs on which you can rest the load of your pack while you lean against them or even sit for a moment.

While hiking uphill, the tendency will be to take more shorter rest stops in order to catch your breath, particularly at higher altitudes.

Use your rest stops for minor trail chores. Check your feet for hot spots or blisters. Read your map. Adjust your bootlaces. Get out your snacks. Drink some water.

HOISTING THE PACK

A lot of unnecessary energy can be expended in putting on and taking off the pack. So, simple as it may sound, the art of hoisting the pack and taking it off is a useful exercise. There are a couple of basic ways of putting on the pack.

The one way most useful for beginners is to first set the pack upright on the ground. Sit down in front of it, slip your arms through the straps, then roll out sideways onto your knees and stand up. Reverse the process in taking it off.

Once you've gotten more used to backpacking, you will probably use one of the various ways of grabbing the pack by the top, hoisting it to your knee, slipping one arm through a strap, then swinging the pack around on your back so that the other strap hangs free from your body and you are able to slip your other arm into it.

The external-frame pack provides a cardinal advantage for this method, as it offers the top crossbar as a convenient handle for grasping and hoisting the pack to your knee.

Warning: Far too many newcomers, at the end of a day's backpacking, toss their packs off and let them crash to the ground. Bad, very bad, practice! It not only crushes anything breakable in the pack, but damages the pack itself as well.

DETERMINING THE DISTANCE FOR THE DAY'S HIKE

Yes, if you've already been backpacking several times and you are on a long-distance hike, you will probably want to cover somewhere between fifteen and twenty-five miles a day. But for your first few hikes—actually, for most of your hikes—you may want to cover far less distance and enjoy your afternoons in camp.

I like to spend no more than four to six hours hiking and the rest of the day puttering around camp, perhaps even taking short walks. Thus the distance covered for this sort of hike is about four to ten miles a day, depending upon the terrain. This summer my daughter Kate and I will be hiking around Mont Blanc in the Alps. It's a two-week trek and we plan to hike only four to eight miles a day. How often will we have the opportunity to sink into such grandeur! For first hikes, I would definitely recommend the shorter of these distances, somewhere between four and five miles a day, with some elevation gain.

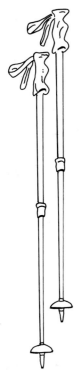

Hiking poles can be adjusted for height and are quite popular, especially in Europe.

HIKING POLES

There is a widespread use of trekking poles for backpacking. I'm told they are very useful and reduce the possibility of falling. I am sure that is all correctly observed. My choice, though, is quite different. And I am not necessarily recommending it.

I have a number of different hiking staffs that I have acquired over the years; mostly they were gifts from friends. Some of them were quite nicely crafted by the gift giver. One that has become sort of a favorite was crafted out of the stalk of a century plant. What is particularly nice about this staff is its lightness and incredible sturdiness. I use it especially in Grand Canyon—which, as you may have noticed, is one of my all-time favorite places to backpack.

Mostly, though, I use a shorter walking stick I picked up in Switzerland a number of years ago, which is of the old-style type that European hikers use, tacking on emblems from the various places they have hiked. Mine too has a long line of these nailed to one side. So as they say, it is sort of "salty."

Hiking staffs are most important for keeping your balance, especially for stream crossings. They are also said to scare away snakes by their continual rhythmic pounding upon the earth as you hike along.

Wear a Broad-Brimmed Hat

It has always seemed to me the wisest thing to wear a wide-brimmed hat wherever I hike. There are many reasons, not the least of which is that it prevents severe sun-burned noses, neck, and ears at higher elevations or when hiking in direct sunlight on snow or deserts. The wide brim should encircle the hat, keeping the sun off the tops of the ears and neck as well. Attach a stampede strap to the hat before leaving on the trail, with a slide that can shorten the strap to hold it up under your chin in windy conditions, which you are almost certain to run into at some point on every hike. Should you need relief from wearing the hat, say on overcast days, then fasten the stampede strap to the top of your pack, allowing the hat to hang down behind. A carabiner-type clip serves well for this.

I have never found this to be true. In fact, the one rattlesnake that I scared up enough to shake his rattle at me was unperturbed by my walking stick.

Another use to which I put my hiking staff is to prop up my tarp when I use it for my shelter instead of a tent.

RAINY WEATHER

As soon as you feel the first raindrops, put on your raingear and see that everyone else in the party does the same. The quickest way to get hypothermia is in wet weather, regardless of the temperature. Hypothermia is a particular concern in temperatures in the forties to fifties. Rain brings a quick drop in temperature with it.

There are a number of precautions you should have taken before you left on the trip to keep things dry in case of rainy weather. If you have done these things, you are prepared to weather it out. These were described in chapter 5. If you didn't do them, take the time to do so when the first raindrop falls.

You should be carrying in your pack a number of zipper-lock plastic bags in a variety of sizes, as well as a number of extra trash bags. Now is the time you need them.

First and foremost, do you have your sleeping-bag stuff sack lined inside with a plastic trash bag? Second, are all of your spare clothes in zipper-lock bags or trash bags? If not, do these things at the first sign of rain.

Third, store anything else in plastic bags that might be harmed by getting wet, such as camera, matches, and toilet tissue.

Fourth, see that your map is folded with the section you are traveling on the outside, and stuff it inside a zipper-lock plastic bag so that it does not get wet.

If your feet are getting sopping wet, stop often to wring out your socks to avoid having blisters develop in the softening skin.

A simple item I always carry along that makes for easier life on the trail is a small, fourteen-inch square piece of closed-cell foam. It's great for sitting on wet or cold ground, or just extra sitting comfort anywhere.

—*Bob Leggett, cofounder, Blue Ridge Center for Environmental Stewardship*

What can be a simple stream crossing at most times can become a risky business when swollen by spring snow runoff. This crossing of the Wassataquoik Stream going into the Northwest Basin up Mount Katahdin in Maine became a technical, roped crossing with snowmelt runoff from the Klondike in early spring.

CROSSING STREAMS

Few backcountry trails cross streams on bridges. Often you will have to cross on rocks or logs. It is critical that you watch your footing. Don't take unnecessary chances. Here are some pointers:

- Stream crossings are the biggest cause of hiker deaths after hypothermia.
- Even large rocks in streams can be slick as ice. Test everything before you step on it. This goes for the smallest streams as well as for bigger ones.
- Cross at wider spots where the water runs slowest.
- Use your walking stick for support.
- *Be sure to unfasten your waist belt and sternum straps before starting to cross a stream.* Falling with them still fastened can be dangerous, as your pack will push and hold your head facedown underwater.
- Do not try to cross a stream barefoot unless it has an absolutely smooth sandy bottom. If you are able to cross the stream in warm weather by wading into it, then do so with your boots on. Take off your socks first. Then empty the water out of your boots on the other side and put your dry socks back on. Do this *only* in warm weather, when your boots have a chance to dry out without making your feet fearfully cold.
- If the stream is too fast, don't try crossing it. If the water is more than knee-deep, it's too fast, and you need a more advanced technique to cross it. There is always another day—provided you are still alive to enjoy it. Never be embarrassed about turning back in the backcountry. It is a sign of wisdom, not of cowardice.

7

Where and How to Set Up Camp

You will be doing three types of camping that are very different: trailhead camping as well as two kinds of backcountry camping. But before you start any type of camping, there are a number of precautions to take.

PRETRIP TENT TESTING

When you plan your first overnight hike with a new tent, give it a test run before you go. It is never a good idea to take a tent on the trail without having set it up at home and running it through a few rudimentary tests. It would be like taking off on a small-aircraft flight without the routine checkout, and almost as dangerous.

Set up the tent to be sure you know what tricks there are in setting it up and taking it down. Find out how your tent performs in real-life situations. Here is where familiarity breeds success.

First of all, spread out your sleeping pad and bag inside the tent, and bring in your pack to see if the tent really is roomy enough for you and whoever else will be camping with you. I use one tent when I go alone and another for when my wife goes with me, because she wants lots of extra room.

See if there are any adjustments you ought to make before you are out on the trail. You can easily fix anything you like while materials and tools you need are still at hand.

Make sure that all poles are there and fit together as they are supposed to. Are all clips and tent stakes there? Are they appropriate to the terrain where you will be setting up your tent? For instance, will it have to be pitched to stand up free on a flat rock surface with only tie-downs to large rocks and no stakes? Wire pegs are good for most woodland terrain in summer, rather than the thick pegs used for snow camping.

Do all the poles, clips, and zippers work the way they are supposed to? Do you have a ground cloth to layer beneath the tent? Would you like an extra ground cloth inside the tent? It helps protect the tent floor from punctures from tiny pebbles beneath the floor when stepped on from inside the tent.

Most important of all, find out if the tent is waterproof enough. You don't want to discover on the trail that your tent leaks through its seams in a downpour. So after your routine checking, take the garden hose to it. Do this first with the fly on, then without the fly, to be sure that all the seams will protect you from getting wet in even a heavy storm. Be aware, though, that the tent wall fabric without the fly is not supposed to be waterproof. So you are just being fussy at this stage, extra-checking the seams of the tent itself, not the fly. I want my seams sealed and usually end up doing this myself.

Give Your Tent a Trial Run

Take an overnight near home, a short distance from your car. Try a state or county park near home for your first night out on the trail, especially in a new tent. Or try it out in the backyard. If you have children, they'll love the idea.

Some hikes have a tendency to be more rainy than others, and I hate to get wet. So I go through these extra precautions.

TRAILHEAD CAMPING

You will often set up housekeeping at the trailhead the night before your backpacking trip, usually close to your car. There are many options to this camp. Some people camp inside their cars or trailers. Many set up their tents much like the camp they will be using out on the trail, but with camp tables, chairs, and other conveniences too cumbersome for the trail.

The trailhead camp is another good practice area. Unless you arrive at the trailhead by public transportation, the advantages are that you still have access to all the items in your car that you will be leaving behind once you set foot on the trail.

BACKCOUNTRY CAMPING

The other type of camping is backcountry camping. Since you won't have easy access or safe retreat to your car once in the backcountry, it's much more important to make sure your shelter is properly prepared and ready to go.

There are basically two types of backcountry trail camping: camping at designated campgrounds and choosing your own campsite at large someplace along the trail. The difference most often occurs in national parks, which more often want you camped in designated campgrounds. National forests quite often will give you more latitude.

The two types of camping require different sorts of techniques and considerations.

I won't go on a backpacking trip without my inflatable washtub. It's a quick and easy way to wash dishes or take care of personal hygiene. I use it to bathe on backcountry trips. I just inflate the tub and bathe in the middle of my tent in privacy. And it weighs less than eight ounces. I think I would consider carrying eight ounces less food just to be able to carry my washtub. One like mine can be seen on the Campmor website, www.campmor.com.

—Shirley Hearn, manager,
Volunteer Vacations Program,
American Hiking Society

Designated Campgrounds

Some of the places you backpack, particularly in national parks, will require you to pitch camp only in designated campgrounds. It is useful for you to arrive early enough to have a choice of sites at which to set up your camp. Though all sites are comfortable, you'll find some more suitable to your tastes.

There are regulations about how you must set up camp in designated campgrounds. Be sure you understand them and can comply with them *before* you start off on the trail. For example, almost

Tenting and sleeping under the stars on the Tonto Plateau in Grand Canyon.

all forbid campfires, requiring you to use a camp stove for cooking. All forbid tying anything to trees or shrubs, such as a cord to hang clothes to dry.

Many have regulations about where to cook as well as where and how to store your food. These are very strictly enforced in places like Yosemite and Sequoia-Kings Canyon National Parks, because bears can be a problem. Other parks, such as Grand Canyon and most in Alaska, provide animal-proof containers at each campsite in which to store your food as well as your garbage for similar reasons. In Alaska it is bears; in Grand Canyon it is more squirrels, skunks, and mice.

The regulations are in place for serious reasons, mostly for your own safety. You can even be fined for not complying, if not harmed by an animal.

When you are given a camping permit, you are asked to sign a small-print statement that indicates you are aware of the regulations and agree to comply with them. Best you read them before starting off on the trail.

Some parks, like Yosemite, require you to watch a video on camping and hiking safely in bear country before you are granted a permit. It has become a serious issue ever since a National Park Service study discovered that although 92 percent of backpackers claimed they knew how to hike and camp safely in bear country and did so, a field check of them discovered that only 3 percent actually did conduct themselves as they claimed they did.

Prepping Your Tent for the Trail

There are a few things you can do to prep your tent that will prove invaluable once out on the trail.
- Seal the seams. Most tents today already come with a good measure of seam sealing. But don't find out in a storm that it would have been better to reinforce the sealer before leaving for the trail.
- Lubricate the zippers with WD-40, soap, or a commercially prepared zipper wax.
- Apply light lubricant to tent pole connections.

Hiker deaths from bear attacks have increased substantially in the past fifteen to twenty years and are still on the increase. And though you may not be bothered by a bear if you do not deal with your food properly in your campsite, your leavings could well attract a bear that molests the next party that camps there.

Choosing a Place to Camp at Large

Other times—and this may be more the rule after you have become more experienced—you'll be camping in the wild, or "at large," as national parks call it.

Camping at large brings other skills into play. You need to look for a variety of conditions all at the same time. Follow these guidelines for best results.

Make Camp Early

It is far better to have a safe, comfortable campsite than it is to make a military march to a predesignated mark on your topo. So while you have plenty of light to find a suitable place to camp, take advantage of it.

Choosing a Tent Site

Obviously, a level spot is the most important aspect of the campsite, though not always attainable. If you have to tent on an incline, then pitch your tent so that your head will be on the uphill slope. It is an excellent practice to test the tent spot first by spreading out a groundsheet and lying down on it. Imagine what it will be like at 2 A.M.

Pick high ground. When choosing a camp spot in a meadow, it is tempting to select a depression in the ground because of the comfort it promises. The problem is that it has usually been formed by an animal wallow, which collects a puddle of rainwater that doesn't evaporate or run off very quickly after a storm. You need the opposite—a place high enough that rain will run down and away from it, leaving your tent dry.

I once took a group of teens into the High Uinta Wilderness Area in Utah for a five-day backpack. We got hit by a sudden summer storm our first night out. Two groups of youths had ignored the leader's instructions and set their tents in one of these meadow basins. Rain filled their tents, drenching their sleeping bags and clothing, so much so that we had to cancel two days of hiking in order to dry out their gear before setting off on the trail again.

Check the campsite for insects too. Ideally, your site will be on a bit of a rise where a breeze will waft away mosquitoes.

In cooler weather, a rise is also the warmer spot, since warm air rises during the night from the lowlands below.

NONTENT CAMPING

There are many of us who camp with a tarp. Or we sleep under the stars. I recently hiked rim-to-rim in Grand Canyon,

I have an old three-season, brand-no-longer-known sleeping bag that won't quit. My Walrus two-man tent is easy to put up, with a high ceiling and good ventilation.

—*Mike Buchheit, director,*
Grand Canyon Field Institute

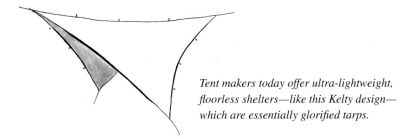

Tent makers today offer ultra-lightweight, floorless shelters—like this Kelty design—which are essentially glorified tarps.

sleeping under the stars each night. I did carry a tarp, though, just in case. Weight was my primary consideration, inasmuch as the heaviest thing in my pack on Grand Canyon treks is water. A gallon of water adds eight pounds of deadweight to the pack, the equivalent of my tent and sleeping bag together.

Few backpackers I know are willing to sleep under the stars. For one, there are the critters. A young man found a rattlesnake in the campground in which I camped the last night of my cross-canyon hike.

A disadvantage when using a tarp as a ground cloth and sleeping under the stars is that it is damnably uncomfortable to try to double it as a cover for yourself in the middle of the night if it starts raining.

There is another obvious way of camping with a tarp that provides protection from inclement weather. String it up as a makeshift tent shelter by running a cord between two trees, draping the tarp over the cord and staking out its corners. Simple solution, but not always so easy to do.

On my rim-to-rim Grand Canyon hike, I met two women, Gwen and Dinah from San Francisco, who were also camping out under the stars. I was impressed with the breadth of what I believed to be their backpacking experience. After chatting with them a bit, however, I discovered they were only on their first backpacking trip. In planning their vacation for the Grand Canyon, they had set their vacation and flight dates several months in advance. They tried repeatedly to get reservations for bunks at Phantom Ranch without any luck. So out of desperation, at the last minute, they were able to obtain a camping permit for Bright Angel Campground, which is next to Phantom Ranch. They didn't have a tent, and neither wanted to buy one for a one-night stand. So instead, they did what nature called them to do—slept on a ground cloth out under the stars.

Danger! Places to Avoid Tenting

There are some places where you never tent. Open ridges and mountaintops attract lightning and are very dangerous. Climb a few Colorado 14,000-footers and notice the memorial markers for hikers killed by lightning on the ridges.

Also avoid camping in narrow slot canyons or dry washes in the deserts. They are tempting spots to camp, because their sandy, smooth surfaces are very inviting. But each year, campers die in flash floods in such terrain. These floods come suddenly, without warning, and carry away everything in their paths.

How to Camp near Lakes and Streams

- Set up camp at least 200 feet from the shore of lakes and streams. That is about a hundred normal hiking steps from the edge of the water.
- Wash yourself the same distance from the water's edge, without soap if possible—even if using biodegradable soap. Though biodegradable soap was developed for use in the backcountry, the term means different things to different manufacturers. And biodegradable at best means that it takes three weeks to break down into the soil. So never use it in lakes, streams, or ponds. And if you do use it, dump the soapy water far away from streams, ponds, or lakes, and well away from other campers. Dump it in cleared soil, preferably in a sun-warmed area to help break it down.
- Wash dishes and utensils equally far from water's edge, again without soap. A good way to clean pots is the old woodsman's way, using handfuls of gritty dirt or sand. When clean, they can then be rinsed in the lake or stream, for only the earth needs rinsing. Some will disagree with me about not using soap on dishes and utensils. If you are one of them, then do the washing 200 feet beyond your camp. It leaves a far cleaner camp for the next party.
- Dump no trash or vegetable garbage into lakes or streams, including fish scales or guts.
- Bathe in streams or lakes, but absolutely do not use soap, not even biodegradable soap. This is the rule whatever public lands you are on.

THE BEST WAY TO USE GROUND CLOTHS

You will frequently see tents in campgrounds, set up with ground cloths beneath them. Good idea. But they are often badly set up. Too often campers allow the ground cloth to protrude from around the edges of the tent. The problem here is that it allows water running down the sides of the tent to collect onto the ground cloth, which then runs underneath the tent, the exact opposite of what you want to have happen.

Preferably, the ground cloth beneath the tent floor should be tucked in on all sides so that it can't possibly collect water beneath the tent. I prefer to use two ground cloths—one underneath the tent and another inside, covering the entire tent floor and up the sides a bit all around.

The advantage of the two-ground-cloth system is that it gives added protection to the tent-floor fabric, which is the part of your tent that will get the most wear over time. And in reading the rest of this book, you will understand my fervor about keeping dry. The inside ground cloth gives added protection from any moisture that accumulates on the inside walls of the tent from running down and under the sleeping bag or clothes. In a downpour, a certain amount of moisture accumulates on the inside walls of the tent, if from nothing other than your own breathing. In freezing weather, this moisture accumulates more obviously as frost on the inner walls.

WATER FOR YOUR CAMP

Besides drinking water, you need water for washing, cooking, and cleaning your cooking utensils. The simplest way of getting water is to camp near a source—a lake, stream, or faucet. Most federal, state, and county campgrounds have faucets of potable water. In the backcountry, these are rare, though there are many spots near streams or lakes.

Public backcountry areas have rules about water. And if there aren't rules, there is a consideration with which all backpackers ought to be both familiar and willing to comply. Generally, camp at least 100 paces from the shores of lakes, ponds, streams, and springs. Carry water at least as far from the water source to wash yourself and your camp utensils. Dump the wash water even farther away from the water sources, and well away from the trail.

SETTING UP CAMP KITCHEN

Set up a separate area for cooking and eating, well away from your sleeping area. If you are in bear country in particular, cook and eat at least 100 paces from your tent where you sleep. If not in bear country, your food remains will attract other varmints, which can become annoying during the night. In the Northeast, it's usually raccoons and squirrels. Some places attract skunks and porcupines.

More often than not, if there is an option, I avoid developed campgrounds in the backcountry, because there are usually remains of food from previous campers, which attract wildlife—porcupines and raccoons in the Northeast, bears, gray jays, and ravens in the West.

Nonetheless, for safety as well as comfort, cook and eat as neatly as you can, well away from your sleeping area. Avoid dropping scraps or grease anywhere. Keep food in well-protected, covered containers at all times. A common sight in Grand Canyon, for example, is a wild scattering of food bits and shredded plastics in a campground where ravens have had a feast of an unsuspecting camper's food supply. Plastic bags are no protection from birds or varmints or bears. You need a varmint- and bear-proof container to store your food in.

At developed backcountry campsites such as those provided in Grand Canyon, the Park Service provides large, animal-proof boxes to store food and garbage.

Cook in a Safe and Protected Area

It is always best to use your cooking stove well away from the camp traffic area, and preferably protected by trees or rocks so as not to be easily knocked over by you or others in your party. I learned this the hard way.

Mornings can be chilly, even in mid summer.

> **My Crazy Creek camp chair and the cigars, and reading and writing material are things without which any multiday jaunt into the backcountry is almost not worth taking.**
>
> —*M. John Fayhee, former editor*
> *of* Mountain Gazette

One night in the Cascade Mountains of Washington, I was cooking dinner after a long day's climb up Mount Saint Helens. We were famished, our mouths watering from the aroma of the fine feast in the frying pan. Without realizing it, I'd set up the cooking area directly in the line of camp traffic. And it was I, no one else, who went to the tent for something warmer to put on; when I returned, I accidentally knocked over the cook stove with the evening's meal. My buddies were not charitable, and I understood their consternation!

HOW TO LEAVE A CAMPSITE

Before leaving camp, give it a thorough policing. Not only is this the correct way to camp, but it assures that you do not leave any of your personal items behind. On heavily used campsites, there is always a temptation to overlook trash that you know full well you did not create. Well, it isn't your duty, for sure. But wouldn't it have been nice if the previous campers had picked up after their predecessors? What does it hurt to pick up a little extra trash—despite the fact that you didn't cause it?

The way to identify an experienced camper today is by their no-trace camping. The words mean exactly what they say—leave no trace that you once camped there. The secret is to become exceptionally sensitive to what impact your camp will have on the ground and foliage in, around, and under your camp.

A ranger I camped with in the Kanab National Forest in Utah insisted we camp on flat rock and not on the earth or grasses. His reasoning was that our camp would leave no trace of its having been pitched on the rock.

A large group of no-trace campers hang hammocks and lay down thick sheets of metal foil on which they build small campfires, both practices being most sensitive to the delicate environment of the backwoods campsite.

One wild area even requires that you carry out your own feces. As I write it, there is a gross distaste about the idea in my mind. Yet I do understand, for this is through a very narrow slickrock canyon that takes a few days to traverse and is so popular that it soon turns into a sewer if this rule is not followed. Ergo, if you want the experience, then go by the rules.

The Camp Latrine

When you set up camp where there is no outhouse, find a place that you will use for a latrine that has fairly easy access but is a good distance from the campsite. Make sure all campers in your party know where it is and how to properly use it.

For solid human waste, dig a hole a good six inches deep. Carry out all toilet paper, which you can store in zipper-lock bags, and cover the hole after use. Do not burn toilet paper or bury it.

Camp Housekeeping

Keeping things tidy in camp is a great way of keeping the camp clean and not losing things when you leave. The old shipboard principle of "a place for everything and everything in its place" saves the camper many unpleasant experiences.

One way to be sure you do not lose your Swiss Army knife or your altimeter is to keep them in the same pocket of your pack or vest at all times when you are not using them. And having the rest of your gear always in the same place in your pack saves countless hours of sorting and searching at rest stops on the trail as well as in camp.

HOW TO KEEP FROM LOSING ITEMS ON THE TRAIL

A terrific habit is to put anything that you are not using, even for a moment or two, on or near your pack. You aren't going to leave without your pack. So this habit is a sure way to see all of your loose gear before you pick up your pack to move on.

What a pain it is to get down the trail a few miles and find out, as I did on a hike in a slickrock canyon one March day, that I had left my 28-millimeter lens on a log at a rest stop while I changed to my 85-millimeter lens to shoot some people photos. Fortunately, a couple arrived at our lunch stop and asked if any of us had inadvertently left a lens back along the trail.

THE ROMANCE OF THE CAMPFIRE

Nothing is more evocative of the backwoods than visions of smoke curling heavenward from the warm glow of a campfire near a stream in the forest. Yet nothing is more restricted in the backwoods today than campfires.

Virtually every national park limits their use to fireplaces in campgrounds. This is true as well in most other public parks—federal, state, and county. Some permit no fires at all, except to cook on camp stoves. Where fires are permitted, there are regulations.

So let's talk about the need for fires at all. *Backpacker*'s first editor, Laura Waterman, in an early *Backpacker* article, argued that there is no need for fires in the backwoods at all. She and her husband, Guy, wrote in their book *Backwoods Ethics* (Stonewall Press, 1979), which set the stage for the new no-trace camping:

> First of all, reliance on fire-building in the backwoods has become a highly questionable policy in light of the new environmental concerns. If we could be sure that everyone going into the backcountry would disperse to a different spot every night, knew how to construct a small fire and then leave no trace when they were through, maybe fires would be OK. But the dead wood supply has long been used up at most commonly visited campsites and the devastation wrought by irresponsible hatchet-wielders is an ugly sore.
>
> As long ago as 1893, the Appalachian Mountain Club was urging a halt to the cutting of firewood in the fragile area of the Presidential Range. . . . Also, many inexperienced fire-builders don't appreciate the risks of underground fires that smolder for days under the duff and may spring to conflagration long after the fire-builder has left, thinking he has put out all his embers. . . .

When having a campfire, be sure to restore the site exactly as you found it.

And a subtle and sensitive argument against fires concerns their effect on the relationship between the camper and the night. Fires have a hypnotic effect—that's part of their attraction. They draw your eyes and you sit gazing into the flickering flame and glowing embers. Meanwhile, you lose contact with the woods around you, the stars above you, the wildlife (which gives your fire a wide berth), and the silence and sounds of nocturnal nature. The campfire is its own uniquely satisfying world—but tends to isolate you from the larger natural world around you.

As to building fires for emergencies, the Watermans said the only time this is justified is to create an emergency rescue signal if you are lost in a remote corner of the wilderness. Citing the famous Jack London story *To Build a Fire,* Laura noted that the man died, while the dog lived.

Although Laura and Guy's view is no doubt a bit uncomfortable for those who love their hot dogs and s'mores, it does make sense. And perhaps we just may be willing in time to give up the romance of campfires for a better, more environmentally pure camping experience.

Where fires are permitted outside of developed campgrounds and not restricted, as in some national forests and Bureau of Land Management (BLM) lands, there are proper and safe ways to build fires. Mostly, they should be built small, using twigs not much larger around than your thumb, never left unattended, and put dead out before leaving camp. All signs of campfires should be erased, including rock rings. Only dead wood gathered from the ground should be burned.

When planning your trip, check the Internet to see what the regulations are for the time you will be visiting. Though some places usually permit campfires, they may be restricted or forbidden at certain times because of fire danger.

8

Purifying and Carrying Water

Water is always a serious consideration on the trail. There are three factors to think about: its level of purity, how much to carry, and how much to drink.

WHERE TO FIND WATER ON THE TRAIL

There are obvious sources of water in the mountains and forests—streams, ponds, lakes.

In the Northeast and the higher mountains, it is rare not to cross numerous streams and springs. Sometimes you'll hear the water running but not see it, for it will be beneath the rocks of the talus. These springs of water emerging from beneath the tundra are the quintessence of pure water, the "nectar of the gods," about as sweet as water can be.

As I write this, a memory rises in mind of a hike I took with Jim Kern in the Catskills. We had been bushwhacking all day and were high on the side of a forested mountain, where we decided to spend the night. I went around a corner of the mountain 100 feet or so from our site to take care of a call of nature, when to my surprise I heard a gurgling of water, went a bit farther, and found a gift of God, the mountain giving us our private drinking fountain.

Though we had brought along ample canteens of water, Jim and I indulged this freshwater gift that evening. How delicious! The Catskills have the finest-tasting water of any I have ever drunk in the backcountry. And there was a time when I would have bet I could tell the difference between it and water from any other place, including the Adirondacks farther up in New York.

You will want to purify any water you use from these backcountry sources. The best means of purifying the water is by boiling it. The next best is to filter it with a commercially available backpacking filter, available at all good backpacking outfitting stores. Try it out before going on your hike to be sure you know how it works and how to use it.

Finding water in desert hiking, as well as in drier mountains such as those in Nevada and Arizona, is quite a different story, however. First and foremost, do not rely upon the maps for water sources. Springs may run infrequently or become dry altogether. If possible, check first with local rangers about the reliability of the springs indicated on the maps where you will be hiking. In desert country, where you see green trees, there is water somewhere. But don't spend too much time looking for it, if it isn't obviously flowing in a spring or seeping from a rock wall.

What is it about water that attracts children to play in it, no matter the weather?

Be concerned about water. It is the most important ingredient of your hike so far as safety and comfort are concerned. Be sure you have enough and know how you are going to replenish your supply en route.

There are a variety of situations you can get yourself into where water is at a premium and you may well have difficulty with that. Most important, do not panic. It will only make things worse. And usually your situation is not as bad as it first appears. Calmly think things through. Likely you will find that the solution is right around the next corner, so to speak.

Of course, if your car is only a few hours away, you can stretch the water you have left and it will get you through.

There was one hike I took with three other men. We had miscalculated the length of daylight for one part of our hike down into the Grand Canyon. We knew the trail would require an overnight before we got to the bottom, so we took sufficient water for that night and some extra. What surprised us, though, was that—its being February—the sun dropped a lot earlier than we anticipated. In fact, we hadn't even considered that in our plans, for this was an eighteen-day backpack trip with many extraordinary details. Sunrise and sunset were near the bottom of our list somewhere.

So this miscalculation required bivouacking out on the trail an extra night, even though we were within sight of our next water source, a beautiful clear stream that flowed in from a side canyon. It meant rationing what little water we had left to half-cup proportions where we ordinarily would have needed a pint or so each, including for our meals.

Well, one of our group went almost crazy with fear of not getting enough to drink, even though in the morning, it took us less than a couple of hours to get to the stream. When we got down there, our companion plopped down in the middle of that stream, scooped up liters of water, and drank and drank. He astounded all of us by drinking something like six liters of water before he got up out of the stream.

Now that is an extreme case. But the psychology of hikers is probably as important as getting the water itself. In the desert, there are sometimes potholes that collect rainwater. And if all else fails in desert country, carefully carve a barrel cactus in two and squeeze the juice from its innards. I have never tried this and would have to be mighty thirsty before I did. But I've seen enough old westerns to know this survival trick.

Survival manuals give techniques that usually are not much help where you are most likely to need water most—in the desert. Don't count on collecting evening dew or condensation from foliage in a desert. You will be lucky to find trees with leaves of any size, never mind dew. These techniques probably work in forests of the Northwest or Northeast, but not likely in the Anza-Borrego Desert or the Superstition Mountains.

HOW MUCH WATER TO CARRY

Ideally, you should carry at least two quarts of water per person for each day you are hiking, on the assumption that you will find water on the trail for your evening camp. If you are hiking in the desert, you should carry substantially more than this. For desert hiking, it is strongly suggested that you carry a gallon of water per day, presuming you will camp by water at night. You should drink often to avoid dehydration. The caveat is to drink often, *before* you are thirsty, and not wait until you are. But eat, too. Eat a snack as often as you drink. Best to eat salty foods to replenish the salt you are losing in your perspiration. This is also serious business, and lots of drinking without the salt replenishment can cause hyponatremia.

The drawback of carrying all that water, of course, is the weight. A gallon of water weighs eight pounds.

You have many choices of containers in which to carry your water. Many hikers today carry packs with bladders built into them. I've not used them, though I have used something similar. On a particularly long desert hike, we carried World War II army two-and-a-half-liter bladders. The advantage of these was that when not in use, they could be rolled into compact bundles taking up less room in the pack. We filled them at points where water was available, then carried them a day's trek ahead of us and cached them in the place where we would have to camp dry another day before moving on to the next water source. We then returned to our first camp to pick up our packs.

Though they had the advantage of portability and worked for the caches—and there are those who claim they distribute the weight of the water better than carrying the same amount of water in large water containers—they were cumbersome to use in camp. Unlike water bottles, they could not be set down without closing up the tops tightly after each use, which was bothersome during meal preparations. They were also less convenient to use for pouring and drinking from.

Today's bladder systems have tubes that you strap around the shoulder so that you can drink while walking. A nice convenience, I am sure. But you can tell I am prejudiced, for I can't see how they overcome the cumbersomeness of use in camp. A water bottle can be handed around, brought to the cooking area for easy access, and so forth, whereas the bladder is far more cumbersome and limited in these ways. Furthermore, I have long ago learned that carrying many water containers is far safer in desert country than carrying one large one.

I know of a couple guys who each carried a one-gallon container of water on a hike down the Tanner Trail in Grand Canyon. This trail is twelve miles from rim to river. And while down there, one chap's water container developed a severe leak, leaving them with only the one container to carry enough water to get out the next day. That is a tough trail to hike in one day, especially in the heat of summer, when these fellows were doing it. They ran out of water before they were halfway out. They suffered severely the rest of the hike and almost became rescue victims. Ever since I heard this story, I make doubly certain to carry my water in the desert in several half-liter bottles—just to be safe.

There are a host of beautiful "designer" water bottles available that are very popular. I'm still using emptied plastic soda bottles. My best are the thick-walled twenty-four-ounce Propel bottles.

Do as I say, Not as I Do!

Refreshing drink from spring emerging from rocky slope of Culebra Peak, Colorado's southernmost 14,000-footer

I have rarely purified water in the back-country and have never had giardiasis or any other problem from the water we drink or used for cooking.

Hence, a warning. Should you hear some of us boasting about stout stomachs, resistant to backcountry water critters, consider this: There is a line of medical thinking that giardiasis is like turista. Gringos who go south of the border usually have a bout with it, though local Mexicans rarely suffer similarly. This thinking presumes that Mexicans have a bacterial immunity system that counteracts Montezuma's revenge, whereas gringos lost this immunity long ago.

The same may be true for longtime users of the backcountry, who somehow have built up an immunity to this nasty little critter, *Giardia.* I've known so many others who privately confess to drinking even the muddy water of the Colorado River without purifying it.

I recommend you always purify your backcountry water before you drink it!

Unless you are a longtime outdoorsman or woman and know your system provides this immunity, then don't take a chance.

PURIFYING YOUR WATER

Water is always a concern in backpacking—whether there is too little, as in deserts, or too much and it needs purifying. We've heard from the most reliable studies that 10,000 samples were taken from streams all over the United States, including Alaska, and every one of them contained *Giardia lamblia,* an infectious little amoebic critter that causes so much stomach and intestinal difficulties among backpackers that it has earned the sobriquet "backpacker disease."

So water purification is a serious matter for backpackers.

Giardiasis is but one affliction that you can get from backcountry water. And you won't ruin your trip if you do get a case of giardiasis, for you won't show any symptoms until you return home from your trek. It takes one to two weeks to manifest, in the form of diarrhea, cramps, bloating, and nausea. One fellow said he dropped from 165 to 115 pounds within a week of first symptoms!

Water purification is not a simple discussion. I once tried to get sanitation engineers from three cities to provide information for an article for *Backpacker* magazine on water purification. To a man, they refused to talk. I was mystified. Apparently, none wanted to stick his neck out on this testy topic.

I had to gather other scientists to research the article for *Backpacker*. This was some years ago. Since then, there have been an army of "experts" who have studied and written articles and books on backcountry water, and another army of companies selling products to purify it.

This is not surprising, inasmuch as backpackers as a group tend to be highly educated. Naturally, they'd put a good dollop of scientific reasoning and research into a subject like this. As one author told me, "My interest was sharpened when acquiring giardiasis after drinking from a partly frozen stream on the Long Valley trail to Mount San Jacinto, yet human habitation was sparse and snow covered the ground."

Those who know me know that my patience with ccs, ppms, HCIOs, and pH 7s is as limited as water in a burning desert. So for my sake, if not for yours, I'll keep it real simple.

For ease of use, the filter seems to me to take the prize. For safety, boiling is the only solution. The other systems work to varying degrees, depending upon whose book you read and the degree of need your system has for purity from all protozoans, bacteria, viruses and cysts. You have to be the judge here, for only you know your own stomach's tolerance.

Let me say a little more about each of these techniques, confessing that I am an entire innocent in this area. My innocence, though, could be good inasmuch as I approach the subject with few preformed views.

Filters

Were I starting out to find a filter, I would go to some major backpacking outfitting store like REI, find out who their most knowledgeable salesperson is, and ask for advice about which filter I should buy. Then I would buy it.

The reason I say this is simple. All the manufacturers have enormous claims for their filters and write them in highly convincing language. Why shouldn't they, since they each believe their own product to be the best on the market?

But it would be foolish of me to think I could evaluate the comparative differences among the various brands of filters from merely reading their hype. Besides which, since I have already been down this water treatment road some years ago and understand there are many hidden complications, I would want someone who had some experiential knowledge of what has worked well for others in the field. The knowledgeable salesperson is no doubt a good source of this information.

Not enough for you? If you want to read the literature on the subject and make the best choice as a result, then there is a whole different way of going about it. I'd start with a 1996 article in *Backpacker* by Mark Jenkins. Then take a look at David O. Cooney's book *Purification of Wilderness Waters*. If that is not enough, I'd check *Backpacker* magazine's

> **I don't carry a water filter. I take Portable Aqua, now in Part 1 and Part 2. Part 2 takes away the iodine taste.**
>
> —*Jim Kern, founder, Florida Trail, Big City Mountaineers, and cofounder, American Hiking Society*

Five Ways to Purify Water in the Backcountry: An Overview

The following information is from an article by J.E. Ongert, called "Backcountry Water Treatment to Prevent Giardiasis":

1. *Use a filter.* Kills *Giardia* if it has a four-micron filter or smaller. Most filters do not meet all of the EPA water purification standards. If the purifier meets *all* EPA standards, it will "remove, kill, or inactivate all types of disease-causing micro-organisms from the water." Filters clog and need cleaning and special considerations, which require you to talk with the salesclerk and study the product's literature. Filters that do best take considerable time to pump the water through. They leave water clean and tasteless. And most filters for backpacking do not filter out viruses and bacteria.

2. *Purify with halazone.* Kills viruses and bacteria, but won't kill *Giardia* or cryptosporidium. Loses its effectiveness in colder water and when some desert minerals are in water. Leaves a taste of chorine in water.

3. *Use chlorine for same.* Kills viruses and bacteria, but won't kill *Giardia* or cryptosporidium. Loses its effectiveness in colder water and when some desert minerals are in water. Treated water has chlorine taste.

4. *Or iodine.* Kills viruses and *Giardia,* but not cryptosporidium. Works only in warmer waters and is rather slow in purifying the water. Treated water has distinct iodine taste.

5. *Boil the water.* Boiling the water is safest of all. Kills all disease-causing microbes. For safety, boil for a full minute at altitudes below 24,000 feet. Boiled water must be aerated, poured back and forth from one container to another, to overcome "flat" taste.

"Gear Guides." And if you are obsessed enough with important details, then go to the FDA website and check out its *Bad Bug Book.* Search for *Giardia,* cryptosporidium, *E. coli,* and hepatitis A. If backcountry water doesn't get you sick, this sure will.

More than likely the reason I could not persuade sanitation engineers to talk to me about purifying water is that municipal water systems do not, as a rule, purify for *Giardia* or cryptosporidium, both of which elude chlorination. In defense of city water systems, however, there is little need for them to purify for these critters, since they get into water supplies mainly from animal or human feces. Thus the risk of them getting into your tap water is fairly low. Not so in the backcountry, though, where all streams are polluted at one point or another by some animal or another that carries the germs. Cities spread *Giardia* and cryptosporidium mainly through public swimming pools. Get it? *Yuck!*

Ultraviolet Purification

There is one product I found out about at the Outdoor Retailers Trade Show that may have some potential and some advantages. It purportedly kills all germ types in water via ultraviolet light. It is said to be quick and easy to use and leave no aftertaste. But it is very pricey, nearly four times the cost of the average filter.

This purifier is about twice the size of a fat Waterman fountain pen. To use it, dip its tip into about a pint of water. Turn on the switch, and in seconds it kills all bacteria, viruses, and cysts, leaving the water pristine tasty. The drawbacks are price, as I said, and the special care for a quartz tip, batteries, and electronic circuit, all of which can be a bit temperamental. Still, you may want to take a look.

Halazone or Chlorine

Halazone (chlorine) was the standby water purification technique used by the U.S. Army during World War II and by backpackers for many years thereafter. It is still used by many. The shelf life of the tabs, though, is limited. And they do not eliminate *Giardia* or cryptosporidium, even though most municipal water systems use chlorine to disinfect their water supplies. A cheap and quick alternative is liquid—*not* powdered—chlorine bleach, which can be used conveniently if nothing else is available. Carry a couple spoonfuls in a small plastic container, and use a couple drops per quart of water.

The argument is sometimes made that since halazone is basically chlorine, which is the purifying agent used by most municipalities to treat their water, it would be good enough for backcountry use. I repeat that the primary source of *Giardia* and cryptosporidium is animal feces, which is much more likely to get into backcountry streams and springs and less likely to get into your tap water at home.

Iodine

Iodine is cheap and easily used. While it does protect against *Giardia,* it doesn't kill cryptosporidium cysts. Furthermore, it creates a godawful taste. I've been told that putting chunks of orange peel into the iodized water diminishes that awful taste. You might want to try this at home before taking it out on the trail. My palate wrenches so badly at the taste of iodine, I can't even stand it when the water is brewed into strong, black coffee.

Boiling: The Safest Method of Purifying

Boiling is the only entirely safe way of treating water. Filters are the next safest way to go, and the easiest. So a few words about boiling.

Water Purification Bottom Line

Some useful facts: Virtually no municipal water purification system is able to filter out *Giardia lamblia* and cryptosporidium. And according to the FDA website's *Bad Bug Book,* an estimated 80 percent of us have had one or both of these diseases at one point or another during the course of our lives. They are responsible for "25 percent of gastrointestinal disease and may be present asymptomatically." Still, either of these will cramp your life, if not your gut, for a miserable period of time. And could lead to other complications. It's hardly worth the risk. Then there's this: After public swimming pools, the backcountry is the place where you are most likely to pick up a case of either. So common sense says, when in the backcountry, purify your water either with a filter or by boiling.

Boiling is the safest way to purify water.

It is a simple procedure, but it takes some time. All that is necessary is to bring the water to a boil. It doesn't have to boil for any length of time, just come to a boil. This will kill all bacteria and cysts, no matter the elevation of your campsite, for the purification takes place at 135 degrees F. Water boils at that temperature or higher up to an altitude of 24,000 feet. So you are safe unless you happen to be taking on Everest.

There are several disadvantages of boiling: It takes time to boil enough water for a day's backpacking needs; it takes time to cool down once boiled, and the water tastes flat once boiled. Boiling also uses up much of your fuel in the process, although I'm not sure that isn't offset by the weight of the filter carried on the average three- to four-day backpack.

A cure for the flat taste is to pour the water back and forth between containers a few times to aerate it. Not so bad tasting after this.

And one way of getting the boiling down to a science is to boil up your water after dinner in the evening, just after you have made your last cup of hot chocolate. Pour it into your water containers and let it cool during the night. In the morning, pour it back and forth between your water containers to aerate it.

9
Eating and Cooking on the Trail

There are three things to consider about eating on the trail. First and most obvious, you need to carry everything with you that you will be eating. Second, weight and portability are key considerations—particularly for longer trips. When you get to the trailhead, you have already passed the last grocery store. Finally, on backpacking trips, you will more likely want cooked meals.

EATING ON DAY HIKES

Obviously, like picnics, you may bring along just about anything you like for a day hike, so long as you can carry it in your pack or pockets. Many people like sandwiches, which will keep as well in a pack as they do in your picnic basket.

Some people are concerned about replacing the energy consumed on a strenuous day hike. If you are one of them, take along some high-carb foods. A handful of gorp, dried fruit, a PowerBar, or a bottle of power drink could be useful.

I particularly like fresh fruit on day hikes—an apple, orange, or banana—after my bread and cheese hit the spot. I particularly like an orange at a rest stop along the trail. Please carry out the apple cores and banana or orange peels. Though they are biodegradable, they will be an eyesore to other hikers for weeks.

Most of us do not cook meals on day hikes, though in colder weather, this is sometimes a real treat. Instant soup on a winter hike makes a terrific midday meal. It simply requires the complexity of bringing along a stove to heat the water for the mix. But when I treat myself to such, I have always been grateful for the extra effort.

EATING ON BACKPACKING TRIPS

The overnight part of a hike is what adds so many more things to plan and do on the trail. You now have two more meals to eat each day. Weight of the foods becomes more important than their freshness. I often do carry fruit, for instance, on a backpacking trip, but usually only enough for lunch the first day, so that I do not have to carry that extra weight more than part of the first day's hiking.

Nor is it wise to carry canned foods or any in jars. The cans and jars add extra weight that you also have to carry back out. Besides, glass jars can be broken in your pack, which creates a mess I don't want to mess with.

Do consider high-energy foods, for you are going to be putting out far more energy than on day hikes, and for a more sustained period. So carry high-carb foods as part of your food kit, such as dried fruits, granola, candies, PowerBars, and power drinks.

Kenn Petsch cooks dinner on our rest day in Horn Creek.

There are two ways to go for backpacking foods: the freeze-dried prepackaged meals and the put-it-together-yourself route. I've given several recipes for foods you can prepare at home to take along on the trail; see the recipes later in this chapter. Imagination can help you think of others of your favorites that can be prepared and packaged prior to your hike from natural food stores or gourmet shops.

There is actually a third route, which is something of a modification of the put-it-together-yourself theme. Today's supermarkets offer a wide variety of prepackaged meals that are cheapo competition for the freeze-dried fare. This is the option I am most likely to take for its lower costs as well as because it makes it so much easier to put together meals for a trip.

Freeze-Dried Menus

The offerings here are luxuriously gourmet. And provide many advantages. They are already packaged, including all ingredients you will need for a meal. They are easy to use. You simply heat up water, open the foil package—which opens out to a container—and pour in your hot water. Wait the few minutes it takes for the meal to reconstitute. Then eat and enjoy. No pots or even dishes to clean up afterward, only a fork or spoon. Tuck the empty container in your trash bag, and *voilà*, lie back and watch the sun set. The variety of meals offered is lavish these days. I highly recommend that you try at least one or two of them at home before you decide on the foods for your future trips.

But . . . there is always a "but," right? But there are some drawbacks. These meals are pricey. Still, one way of looking at it is that they are not as pricey as if you were eating them in a restaurant with as great a view as you will have when you eat them.

The other drawback is more easily overcome. Freeze-dried packages lie about how many portions are contained therein. If you simply adjust the figures by a multiple of

Petzold's Bedtime Snack

A little trick that Paul Petzold has instructed NOLS wilderness students to use on their trips is worth considering here. He has them bring along a pocketful of hard candies that they can pop into their mouths and suck on just after they crawl into their sleeping bags at night, so they can draw upon the quick energy as they drop off to sleep. The quick energy fix warms the body in the sleeping bag as a bonus for the day's efforts.

two, you will do fine with freeze-dried menus. Having said that, I have to admit I am only passing along rumors from other backpackers. Since I eat rather light anyway, I find the package claims of portion sizes of freeze-dried meals to be adequate.

Put-It-Together-Yourself Grocery Store Backpacking Menus

As I confessed earlier, I am of the "third way" school of backpacking meals. At least when I backpack by myself, I opt for the supermarket prepackaged food items, being sure that they contain all the ingredients needed to prepare them. I must warn, though, that the Hamburger Helper type prepackaged meals do need hamburger to help them. So don't make my mistake of finding this out on a hike into the Snowmass-Maroon Bells Wilderness, looking forward to a fine outdoors dinner and discovering, of course, that I was supposed to bring along hamburger. The package meant what it said: It was a "helper" only. I learned to read labels before loading my food selections into the supermarket cart.

Two Extremes of Trail Cooking

There is the gourmet trailside cookery on the one hand. And on the other is the severely abstemious, monklike fare of Sierra Club founder John Muir, as well as the Grandma Gatewood version. Muir carried a tiny amount of food in his overcoat pockets, usually crusts of sun-dried bread, grain meal, sugar, and tea.

Grandma Gatewood end-to-ended the Appalachian Trail a few times, beginning in her sixty-fifth year, carrying no more to eat than a pocketful of uncooked oatmeal. She generally mooched her meals from hikers camped at lean-tos along the trail. Characteristically, she would arrive in camp with her belongings in a bag slung over her shoulder, chat with other campers for a spell, then childishly inquire, "My, what is that you're cooking? It smells so good."

This would lead campers to offer her a portion of their meal, since she would confess she had not brought anything to eat except a handful of uncooked oatmeal.

Now, on the other hand, I cannot count the number of hiking companions I have had who were trailside gourmet cooks. There was a time when Jim Kern, Gudy Gaskill, and I backpacked through an eighteen-inch snowstorm down to the bottom of Grand Canyon for a few days, and Gudy surprised us all at our last night's camp by baking a Dutch-oven peach cobbler with whipped cream for dessert.

How about Danish salami with fried bannock and strawberry jam?

BUYING YOUR FOOD

This section will sound exceedingly elementary. But please pay attention. Because it is so simple, this is where I tend to make many mistakes.

Planning is key to eating well on the trail. For shorter, two- to three-day hikes, planning the food is paramount to a good time. Make a list of the meals you will be having: today's lunch and dinner; tomorrow's breakfast, lunch, and dinner; and so on, for each day's meals. Then fill in the blanks.

What will you have for each meal? It is useful to do this on paper, especially while you are buying. I have found over and over again that I overlook items when I'm buying food for a trip—things like bread or crackers to go with the cheese for lunches, milk for my coffee, and such.

When you see the list on paper and review it, missing items tend to pop to mind because of their absence. And do read the instructions on the packages, to be sure you can actually prepare the foods on a one-burner backpacking stove.

Weight is a key consideration, of course. Some hikers could not care less about weight and go out carrying way beyond what I like to tote, but they are assured of a much more abundant variety of foods for meals. I will confess, though, that on many of my backpacking trips, I will indulge myself with my favorite trail food: a couple of hot dogs and a can of pork and beans. I'm a sucker for this dish on the trail. But never at home. And I carry the extra weight of the canned beans for only the first day.

The longer the trip, the more planning goes into the menus and the more weight conscious I become. One fifteen-day trip with a dozen other friends found the bigger guys complaining fiercely about the sparseness of the diet, which had been intentionally limited because of weight considerations.

In addition to the freeze-dried and prepackaged meals, you can buy bulk at a health food store and package your own. And that is not to mention preparing some of your own recipes for trail foods in advance of your hike. The more experienced a backpacker you become, the more you will want to include some of your favorite trail recipes.

Whichever route you take on your food-shopping stint, read the labels carefully. You need to know approximate cooking times and whether all ingredients are included in the packages. To wit, my experience with Hamburger Helper, which does not include the hamburger.

TRAIL FOODS SIMPLIFIED—MY IDIOSYNCRATIC BENT

The past several years, when it is up to me, camp cuisine leans heavily toward the utilitarian. As long as the food is nourishing and meals are simple to prepare, it is fine with me. I'm out to immerse myself in the backcountry. Food is secondary, a mere necessity.

Having said that, I've truly enjoyed the fine fare I've been served by friends on many different hikes. There was Gudy Gaskill's Dutch-oven peach cobbler, of course. Then there were the fish and mushroom appetizers that Jim's friend Shirley served us on the banks of the Suwanee River in Florida. And the numerous delectable vegetarian dishes that Guy and Laura Waterman served up on our hikes in Maine, Newfoundland, and the White Mountains of New Hampshire.

Packing Food for Longer Trips

When packing food for even groups of two or three for a trip of more than a weekend, prepack each meal for each day of the trip, and label them accordingly: DAY ONE BREAKFAST, DAY ONE LUNCH, DAY ONE DINNER, on through the entire trip's meals, including some for an extra day in case of an emergency.

This may seem like such a bother. But on a longer trip, it is such an incredibly important aspect of the packing. The time saved and the difficulties avoided in trying to figure out meal portions once on the trail are worth every bit of the extra effort. It also gives you far better control over the weight on your back.

For longer hikes and larger groups, package each meal beforehand and label as Lunch Day 1, Dinner Day 1, Breakfast Day 2, and so on. It makes life so much easier on the trail.

Still, when I am alone, meals are spartan. I boil a pot of water, from which I ladle enough into my cup to prepare instant soup, a little more for an instant entrée in my bowl, and finally the remaining hot water for my hot chocolate. And I want to tell you, with today's supermarket offerings, I am never less than content with my evening meal.

My breakfasts are much the same. I boil enough water for my whole meal, which amounts to about three cups of water. First I ladle out enough boiling water to prepare my instant oatmeal. Though I never eat instant oatmeal at home, on the trail it's not bad. While I wait for the cereal to bulk up in the hot water, I add a couple heaping tablespoons of coffee grounds to the remaining water, bring it to a boil again for one full minute, turn off the stove, and flick a few drops of cold water to help the grounds settle. I then pour a cup of coffee with instant creamer and drink my coffee while eating my cereal.

It is a simple, delicate orchestration, but once completed, I have a fine relaxed breakfast in the dawning daylight. I get nostalgic as I write about it, even though it is but a couple weeks since my last morning meal on the trail!

I am left with a cup, bowl, and one pot to clean up before packing up for the day's hike. I usually clean them by merely wiping with a paper towel. The soiled towels go into my plastic garbage bag. No problem.

GOING COOKLESS

In summer when hot food is not necessary, it is occasionally a pleasure to leave cookware and stove behind. Going cookless, I have no need for fuel, pots, lids, handles, or even soap to wash them after eating. What a joy it is at times to simply be there in the backcountry, lie back, chomp on a handful of granola, drink a cup of cool water, and enjoy the sun slipping down beyond distant peaks.

Trail Utensils

What you need is probably going to be less than what you'll take on your first backpacking trip. No problem. Better to have taken too much than not enough. Still, here is a checklist of items you will want to take:

- ☐ Cup. Tin preferable. I use an enameled metal cup, which I prefer to plastic, since it does not carry the taste from one meal to the next. And it can be used in an emergency as a small pot to warm something up directly on the stove.
- ☐ Bowl. Again, I prefer an enameled metal bowl, for same reason as for the cup.
- ☐ Fork.
- ☐ Knife.
- ☐ Pot. Bring two pots for two or more people, preferably nesting ones.
- ☐ Pot lifter.
- ☐ Can opener. Probably on your Swiss Army knife.
- ☐ Lightweight backpacking stove.
- ☐ Biodegradable soap.

The only thing I miss when I go cookless is my morning coffee. But I have sometimes solved that by bringing along a can of Sterno upon which I heat the coffee water in my metal cup.

SELECTING THE RIGHT BACKPACKING STOVE

The limitations of cooking on lightweight backpacking stoves is that they have only one burner, and unless you are a party of four to six, you usually lug along only one stove. This means planning meals and cooking each course while you are eating another.

I've used three different types of stoves over my backpacking career. The first was the old standby of mountaineers, the Svea-123. It is still a neat, compact, and reliable little machine. This is the stove that author Colin Fletcher carried on his two-month backpacking trek through Grand Canyon. In *The Man Who Walked through Time,* he describes a memorable backcountry scene of his first night on the trail on the floor of Hualapai Canyon in which his Svea figures prominently in great detail. This description characterizes the essence of the Svea cult that was so widespread at that time. The sound of that stove, which is one of its qualities that inspire devotion, conjures up all sorts of images of "the whole, clean, open, primitive freedom" of the trails, as Fletcher so pointedly puts it.

The SVEA-123, the old standby of mountaineers.

My next stove was one of those first used on an Everest expedition, a little Bluet that used LPG cartridges. It worked fine, was a bit lighter weight than the Svea, and was a lot easier to use. This stove had a short life with me, though, for my patience would run out when the cartridge ran low of fuel and it took forever to boil water.

My next stove was one of the first MSR stoves that Larry Pemberthy ever made. And all I have done over the years since is replace some of the parts.

Your taste in foods and style of cooking are the key factors in determining what stove is best for you. There are many good ones on the market, in a range of prices. No doubt you will be a great judge of which serves your own needs best after you have done a patient bit of shopping and questioning salespeople.

Protecting the Stove's Flame from the Wind

The biggest difficulty of lightweight backpacking stoves is protecting the flame from the winds. Yes, of course, you can shelter the stove behind rocks or beside a large tree. It's a good idea, but it sometimes does not do the trick. Winds have whimsical minds of their own and seem to choose to change directions and gusts whenever they like. Then, too, sometimes rocks or trees are not available anywhere near your campsite.

Why have I not mentioned that most of these stoves come with some sort of wind-protective shield? Well, I've never found the shields supplied with the stoves to be particularly effective for the winds I have encountered at my campsites. There is one exception—the MSR's foil shield. It has best suited my backcountry camping needs for many, many years.

Should you choose a different brand stove, you can still fashion a similar shield from heavy kitchen foil. I have not tried this but have been told by others that it works well. Then, too, other stoves do not have the limitation of the MSR, which is its burner's inability to reduce the flame down enough for simmering. That has never been a problem for me, but it is to many other backpackers. The other side of the short-coming of the MSR is its blowtorch capa-bility of burning very hot. This is ideal for winter camping, when you may have to melt snow for water.

You know your likes and tolerances. Buy a stove that best fits those needs.

Windshields are essential for your stove. This is the typical one used with MSR stoves—it's actually a sketch of my own MSR windshield. Don't leave home without it. FROM MOUNTAINEERING: FREEDOM OF THE HILLS. COPYRIGHT © 2005 MOUNTAINEERS BOOKS.

Cooking in Inclement Weather

Rainy or windy weather cooking can be tricky. One way is to rig up the tarp you use for a ground cloth beneath your tent as a shelter to protect stove and hikers while you cook and eat. You need to be imaginative in how you rig it up, depending upon trees, rocks, terrain, and direction of the weather for best protection. Not always easy. But don't cook in your tent, especially if you are in bear country!

The tendency today is for lightweight. And a good selection of stoves keep the weight to a minimum. For reliability and durability, however, you may want to consider some of the heavier stoves. My friends Laura and Guy Waterman carried a heavy Optimus for years because it fired up so reliably in the winter, when they did most of their backpacking.

COFFEE OBSESSION ON THE TRAIL

Though a number of my hiking friends take along more elaborate fare on our backpacking treks, I go far simpler. There is an exception: I'm something of a coffee nut.

I recall one notable backpacking jaunt I was on with a favorite hiking companion. This was maybe the first hike on which he prepared all the food for the trip. I've always appreciated leaving this chore to others. Well, our first morning on the trail was almost our last one together. After the oatmeal was cooked and he had pulled out the fresh cream for it, I asked where the coffee was.

"Coffee?" he said. "No, I didn't bring any coffee."

"!!!!!" Dead silence out of deference to my friend.

Ever since then, even if someone else is preparing the food for the trip, I bring my own coffee. And let my confession become even juicier. Yes, I bring fresh-ground coffee, which I boil up in a pot, grounds and all. I let it settle a minute or two, then drink it very hot.

But even more telling—I bring along coffee that I have roasted myself. Yes, I'm about as nutsy about coffees as some of my friends are about wines.

If you want to join my fun, check out www.sweetmarias.com. They'll send you their free newsletter, which

I always take my battered pot, which was a gift of an old friend, Peter, who first used it out West in the 1970s, and my Peak One stove. I have had this outfit in use from the time I was through-hiking the Appalachian Trail as a slightly overwrought twenty-eight-year-old. The outfit was so forgiving of my blunders that I nicknamed it "the cousin." The pot is compact, holds a neat four cups of liquid, has a nice pour spout and nifty lid, and the stove fits inside it for compact carrying.

—*Christine Woodside, editor of AMC's magazine,* Appalachia, *and an AT end-to-ender* is worth a few pounds of coffee in itself. Here's Tim on a recent shipment of Timor organic coffee beans: "This is quintessential crowd-pleasing coffee, what I used to think of in the coffeehouse business as 'good house coffee,' because everyone will enjoy it. It has an initial hint of its Indonesian roots, just a touch of pleasant woody-forest flavor (it's a good flavor, trust me!), nestled in a low-acid cup profile with a thick heavy mouth feel. As it cools, hints of cocoa and vanilla emerge in the background." And he goes on and on. Love it. And raw coffee beans cost less than half the price of Starbucks roasted beans! So for fun with your morning coffee, www.sweetmarias.com.

I carry my own concoction of oatmeal, which I can eat at any time of day. I dry mix roughly in these proportions: one cup rolled oats, half cup blueberry granola, quarter cup each of raisins and walnuts. When hungry, I boil up enough water to cover the mixture, and let it sit covered for about five minutes. Then if I have a banana, I slice it up on top and gorge myself. But when I don't take this mixture, I can be just as satisfied with a cold can of corned beef and some bread or crackers.

—Dick Spas, commercial photographer and photography teacher

TRAIL RECIPES

GORP BREAKFAST BARS

These high-energy gorp bars are a bit messy in really hot weather but guaranteed to get you along that last mile of the day.

2 12-oz. pkgs. semisweet chocolate chips	½ cup shredded coconut
2 8-oz. pkgs. butterscotch bits	½ cup chopped cashews
½ cup honey	½ cup uncooked oatmeal
½ cup chopped dates	½ cup muesli
½ cup yellow raisins	½ cup wheat germ
½ cup chopped dried apricots	

Melt chips in double boiler. Add honey. Pour over remaining ingredients in large bowl. Mix well. Pour mixture onto greased cookie sheet to cool. Cut or break into hand-size chunks. Wrap in plastic foil. Store in refrigerator.

MOUNT RAINIER LOGAN BREAD

I first ate this bread on a mountaineering summer in the Cascade Mountains of Washington State. I bought it from REI when it was closeted on the second floor of a downtown building in Seattle.

Laura Waterman, the first editor of *Backpacker* magazine, reconstructed the recipe for me. I love it with strawberry preserves and some Danish salami. Great trail lunch to eat at home as well.

It can be stored for long periods of time at room temperature, and longer still when frozen. What isn't used on one hike can entice you to the next one. The recipe makes two loaves.

2 cups rye flour	½ cup chopped dried peaches, apricots,
1 cup whole wheat flour	dates
¾ cup wheat germ	2 tbsp. peanut oil
¼ cup brown sugar	½ cup honey
½ cup powdered milk	½ cup molasses
½ cup chopped walnuts or pecans	¼ cup sorghum (or maple) syrup
½ cup raisins	6 eggs

Mix flours, wheat germ, sugar, milk, nuts, raisins, and dried fruit with a wooden spoon in a large bowl. In separate bowl, beat peanut oil, honey, molasses, syrup, and eggs. Then mix into dry ingredients. It should be the consistency of and heavier than bread dough. Press into oiled 1-inch-deep flat pans.

Bake at 275 degrees, or the lowest temperature setting on your oven, for two hours or until done. It burns easily, so it is important to keep the temperature low and watch as it bakes. The bread should appear like fruitcake when done.

Store in portions in foil or plastic wrap in refrigerator or freezer.

CURRIED MUSHROOM TOP RAMEN

This makes a hearty meal for a cool night on the trail. It is easy to put together, satisfying, and inexpensive. Serves four.

    1 oz. dried sliced mushrooms
    3 tbsp. dried curry powder
    1 pkg. any flavor Top Ramen noodles

Place mushrooms in cup of cold water to soak for twenty minutes. Pour mushroom water in large pot. Add water to make up 4½ cups. Bring to boil. Add curry powder and Top Ramen noodles. Add mushrooms. Boil for three minutes. Add soup mix from Top Ramen package. Stir, serve. Have a good supply of cool drinking water handy, as it is quite spicy.

GREEN MOUNTAIN STEW

My friends Laura and Guy Waterman, authors of *Backwoods Ethics,* treated me to this one on some especially memorable hikes. There are two I recall in particular: one across Mount Katahdin's massif in Maine, and the other along the shores of Westmoreland Pond in Newfoundland.

    ¾ cup bulghur
    ¾ cup dehydrated peas
    5-oz. can Vienna sausages

Add 3 cups of water to the bulghur and peas. Bring to a boil and cook ten to fifteen minutes, or until all water is absorbed. Add sausages five minutes before end of cooking. Stir. Serve with plenty of butter and salt.

The Watermans served soup first and cocoa afterward. Especially good for winter camping. Now that I think about it, they also served it for dinner on a snowshoe trip we made in January to a lean-to in the White Mountains of New Hampshire. Outstanding. But I think that night they served hot Jell-O instead of the cocoa.

Romance of a Midnight Campfire Meal

Not so long ago I did most of my cooking over campfires. There is one meal that stands out in memory for its special romance. It was an early-October weekend.

I hiked after dark to the top of a mountain in New York's Catskills. There was a beautiful full moon that night, and the weather was still a bit balmy. I made camp, built a fire, put some small potatoes beneath the coals and an ear of corn on the edge of the fire, laid a grill atop, and set a T-bone steak sizzling midst the flames, sending up its mouthwatering aroma.

It was well past midnight before dinner was ready to eat. I can just about savor that meal still, so many years later, as well as the warmth of that camp.

Today fires are no longer permitted on that mountaintop. But oh, what a delicious memory!

CATARACT GULCH THAI CURRY SOUP

No doubt freeze-dried foods will beat the pants off this gourmet meal by several ounces. But this meal will beat the pants off the taste of any freeze-dried packaged meal. Daughter Kate concocted this for us on a recent hike to the Continental Divide in the San Juan Mountains of Colorado. It is really easy to make. All items are off the shelf of a natural food store.

4.9-oz. pkg. Thai Kitchen brand curry rice noodle soup	5.5-oz. can Thai Kitchen coconut milk
5-oz. can chunk chicken, drained	1 stalk fresh celery, chopped
	1 small fresh carrot, chopped

Follow directions on the package, boiling noodles three minutes in enough water to cover them. Pour off water. Rinse noodles in cold water, drain, and set aside. Separately, mix together 1½ cups water, coconut milk, celery, carrot, and chicken. Bring to boil, then simmer until vegetables are tender. Add noodles. Stir and serve.

It is so deliciously sweet and mildly piquant that you won't need dessert.

GRAND CANYON JAVA

This is an energy-packed food for strenuous hiking. I got it from Scott Thybony, author of *The Official Hiking Guide to the Grand Canyon.* Scott goes exceedingly light, not even carrying a stove and fuel. He uses a tin cup and heat tabs to bring a dessert like this one to warmth.

1 oz. powdered milk
1 oz. sugar
1 oz. margarine

Mix dry ingredients. Melt margarine in tin cup. Stir in dry ingredients. If you want the java to be true to its name, then add a teaspoon of instant coffee. Bring to desired warmth. Drink for dessert to pump up energy for next day's hike.

Obviously, this is not a dish for the fat-sensitive, nor diabetics.

MOUNTAIN BARS

Make-at-home recipe you can store for long periods and take on trips as needed. This recipe originally came to me from Judy and Gary Bunce.

2 cups crushed vanilla wafers	1 cup seedless yellow raisins
1½ cups finely chopped nuts	2 tbsp. light corn syrup
(your choice; I particularly like pecans)	6–8 tsp. honey
½ cup finely chopped dates	½ tsp. vanilla or maple syrup
1 cup finely chopped dried apricots	2 cups powdered sugar

Combine all ingredients except the sugar in deep bowl. Knead. Press. Add enough water to bind. Shape into 2-by-5-inch logs. Roll in powdered sugar, wrap in plastic, and store in refrigerator.

Be sure to save some for the trail.

FAST COLD-WEATHER ENERGY

This is a quick fix for cold winter nights. Particularly good for bedtime. And so simple.

2-oz. pkg. Jell-O (do not substitute other gelatin desserts, which don't have the great taste)

Simply stir package of Jell-O into 3 cups of boiling water, and sip it as hot as you can. Drink before dinner or just before bedtime. I found that it gives me a quick and short-lived high—better than a martini. And it supplies much of the energy that is used on winter ski or snowshoe trips.

Diabetics beware!

10
Going Light

How light can your gear get? There are certainly a wide variety of options for shedding pack pounds today. Equipment makers are using the latest stretch, double-weave, abrasive-resistant fabrics and pliable, anatomically contoured polystyrenes to lighten your load.

One outfit specializes today solely in lightweight gear and clothing. And there is a new magazine, *BackpackingLight,* that debuted recently on the Internet and has been called by the *L.A. Times* "home to the most fanatic pound shedders on the planet."

I obtained a GoLite catalog at the manufacturer's booth in a recent trade show. The catalog carried twenty-four packs, none of which exceeded two and three-quarter pounds; a line of eight sleeping bags, the heaviest of which was two and three-quarter pounds; and ten tents and tarps that weighed less than four pounds each with poles and pegs.

How to make a comparison? No doubt a GoLite outfit similar to my basic outfit—pack, tent, and sleeping bag, with same carrying capacity, cold-weather rating, and rain cover—weighs only about five pounds, fifteen ounces. My outfit, on the other hand, weighs two and a half times this, at twelve pounds, six ounces, which is a substantial difference.

The GoLite outfit also compares favorably to similar products from other manufacturers. I made a quick check in the REI catalog and found that the GoLite outfit beat the lightest-weight comparable REI outfit of tent, pack, and sleeping bag for similar trail conditions by two pounds, thirteen ounces.

In going this light, though, either with GoLite or REI gear, I would give up comforts of my outfit that I'm not yet ready to sacrifice. When I do need to trim back weight, as in primitive desert areas where it is essential to carry as much as two gallons of water per day, I have my ways, as they say, and I will go into them at the end of this chapter.

The lightest-weight packs either have no interior frame or are made of body-contoured plastic, whereas my pack's external frame is made of aluminum struts that have a variety of uses, especially on longer treks.

The lightest-weight sleeping bags achieve their lightness by giving up a longer, sturdier zipper and more room around head, neck, and shoulders. I need a bag with a sixty-inch girth at the shoulders and plenty of headroom in the hood. I also need a full-length two-way zipper to allow better ventilation for feet and legs on warmer nights. The longer two-way zipper makes for a far more versatile sleeping bag.

The lighter-weight tents, especially the ones sold by GoLite, are made of a single-wall waterproof fabric. The top of GoLite's line was recently named by a *Backpacker* magazine equipment evaluator as "the best three-season shelter. Tent of the future."

Note the difference between the words *tent* and *shelter.* My tent has two walls—a breathable nylon interior wall covered by a waterproof fly—with a layer of several inches between them. I prefer this construction for various reasons. It reduces condensation on the inside of the tent from the body's evaporating vapors. This is particularly important at higher altitudes, where nighttime temperatures frequently drop to freezing, even in midsummer, turning the condensation into frost, which falls on and dampens sleeping bag and clothing. Also, the layer of air trapped between the tent wall and fly provides additional warmth on cooler nights. So a three-season shelter may well refer only to three seasons at lower elevations, mainly in the South. And *shelter* means more tarp than tent.

Then there is the inexpensive route. For truly irreverent, though highly useful and entertaining text on lightweight hiking, check out the Guru of Lightweight's 504-page book, *Beyond Backpacking: Ray Jardine's Guide to Lightweight Hiking.* You'll find a quite cantankerous, though often charming author who knows what he's talking about, for he's used these techniques hiking end-to-end on the Pacific Crest Trail as well as on dozens of other long-distance hikes. In fact, the guy works at a job less than four months in any one year, he is hiking so much. You will earn back the price of the book if you just follow a couple of his cost-cutting suggestions about gear. Jardine says he gave many of his design ideas to the GoLite company, since he realized that making lightweight products to sell would require him to be off the trail much more of the time.

Crusty ranger Roger Chase checks Guy and Laura Waterman's pack at his stone-age "weigh-in station" at Russell Pond in the center of Maine's Baxter State Park. His sign says: "Weigh In Station. Packs Only. Don't Fool with the Scales. They Are Set by a Certified Fisherman," Scale uses stones for weights.

Some of his advice is highly dubious, though, such as his views on *Giardia* and storing food in bear country. But when trading off comfort for lighter weight, Jardine is a master at the trade-offs. And a lot of the weight chucked is in the items he doesn't take along.

A small, lightweight 128-page book is Don Ladigin's *Lighten Up!* Ladigin teaches the ultralightweight packing class at University of Oregon. His book is lightheartedly illustrated by NOLS instructor Mike Clelland, whose specialty is *Mad* magazine humorous-style illustrations. But the meat of the book is serious.

If you are hell-bent on ultralight, you may be perfectly willing to make these trade-offs. I recently bumped into a man in his eighties breezing up a steep trail. He seemed highly pleased with his ultralight outfit, which altogether probably weighed less than a third the weight of mine.

Today's lightweight trend is nostalgic, for it's a generational version of the perennial call back to nature and its impulse to go light, which has occurred with regular frequency in subsequent generations over the past 150 years or so among those of us who get the primeval yearning to return to the woods.

Backpackers want lighter gear. New materials come along, enabling lighter gear to be made. Then enough lightweight gear lumped together just turns into heavier loads. This then is followed a decade or so later with still newer materials used to lighten the gear yet more, followed again by this too becoming a heavy load. And this then is followed by still another cycle of more new materials enabling still lighter gear, followed again by its turning burdensome on our backs. And so the cycle goes. On and on . . .

Once more today, backpackers want to lighten gear. Dutifully, equipment makers take turns in the cycle, designing still lighter equipment.

THE HISTORY OF GOING LIGHT

Late in the nineteenth century, John Muir formed the Sierra Club because he saw on his 1,000-mile hikes the beauty of the Sierra backcountry and how America was desecrating its natural wonderlands. Muir stayed in the mountains weeks at a time, going about as light as one can go, carrying his entire outdoors kit in his pockets. This kit was, simply enough, his food supply—a few crusts of bread and a handful of tea leaves.

A decade or so later, on the East Coast, the Adirondack guide Nessmuk (George W. Sears), in *Woodcraft and Camping,* admonished backcountry campers that "the temptations to buy this or that bit of indispensable camp-kit has been too strong, and we have gone to the woods handicapped with a load fit for a pack mule. This is not how to do it. Go light. The lighter the better."

I confess to becoming one of Nessmuk's twentieth-century versions of the hikes "handicapped with a load fit for a pack mule," puffing up a Pennsylvania mountain on a section of the Appalachian Trail one blistering July 4 weekend. Fifty-two pounds of lightweight gear for a three-day trek!

Nessmuk also boasted, "My own load, including canoe, extra clothing, blanket-bag, two days' rations, pocket ax, rod and knapsack never exceeded 26 pounds; and I went prepared to camp out every night."

I got the hint, got some lighter-weight gear, but mostly I left a lot of "this or that bits of indispensable camp-kit" at home. Still, I did not trim back enough to match Nessmuk's twenty-six pounds, less his ten-and-a-half-pound canoe, ergo, a fifteen-and-a-half-pound pack load including two days' food.

Another generation after Nessmuk's boast, there was another wave of back-to-nature, go-light hiking. At that time, Joe Knowles went out into the Maine woods, having cast off about as much extra baggage as a human can shed. Barefoot, dressed only in undershorts, he hiked off to survive two months in the barren woodlands. To prove he wasn't faking, he repeated this feat the following year in the state of Washington under closer observation.

> **I always have a good paperback in my pack, one that I don't want to keep so I can tear off the pages when I have read them and toss them into my campfire.**
>
> —*Betty Leavengood, author of* **Grand Canyon Women** *and* **Tucson Hiking Guide**

About a decade later, we had a back-to-nature movement that fascinated industrialists like Thomas Edison, Harvey Firestone, and Henry Ford, who chummed around in the Catskill Mountains with "the other John," John Burroughs. This generation begot a rash of national parks from the bully hand of President Theodore Roosevelt. When Teddy Roosevelt wasn't shaking his big stick at foreign powers, he was flexing his muscles with executive decrees to create a hog's feast of national monuments, as they were then called. Part of Teddy's inspiration for national parks came from his backpacking with John Muir, asking him to go "just the two of us" for a few days into the Yosemite backcountry.

Another generation later, land lovers Aldo Leopold, Howard Zahniser, and Bob Marshall went light on their fifty-mile day hikes. At that time, the young David Brower put out a Sierra Club book entitled *Going Light.* He said it was "written by backpackers" to convince folks that "one gains a great deal by getting just as far from exhaust fumes and ringing telephones as his feet will let him . . . for the backpacker enjoys a certain degree of independence from trails because the equipment is with him and he can camp almost any place." Brower, and other Sierra Club leaders like Ansel Adams, were hying people off to backcountry camps to observe nature's magnificence, which they would lose if these lands were not protected.

Shortly after *Going Light* was printed in 1951, gear designers like Richard Kelty used new materials to substitute lighter-weight packs for the old Trapper Nelsons and Adirondack pack baskets. At about this time, in 1953, a British party climbed Mount Everest. Mountaineers everywhere clamored for lighter-weight sleeping bags, tents, and camp stoves.

The backpacking movement burgeoned, and newer and newer materials were available to make increasingly lighter-weight gear. Nonetheless, the desire to carry along more "this or that bits of indispensable camp-kit" paralleled this go-light cycle.

World War II veterans returned to the woods, at first trying to go light with army-surplus gear before discovering the Kelty pack, Larry Pemberthy's MSR stove, and the Eddie Bauer down-filled mountaineering sleeping bags. They joined the enthusiastic outdoors lovers who led the charge to turn roadless lands into designated wilderness areas. Along with Rachel Carson and her *Silent Spring* as well as a generation of back-to-nature boomers, they ushered in a host of environmental acts to preserve the earth for posterity, beginning with the 1964 Wilderness Act.

HIKING LIKE THE ORIGINAL GO-LIGHT TRAVELERS

It was in this milieu that Albert Saijo made a Zen-like advocacy for going light in his classic little book called *The Backpacker,* as well as his articles in *Backpacker* magazine. A lot of what Saijo said in the early 1970s rings as puissantly today as it did back then, and his little book is still being reprinted.

So I have to ask: Isn't what keeps us from truly going light that impulse described so well by old Nessmuk—our own temptation to carry just a few ounces more of seductive bits of technologically perfect gear?

How about just a ten-ounce folding camp chair? Or a neat little thirteen-ounce pair of binoculars that shoot digital photos? Hey, you can leave the film cans behind. Or the UV tan tracker to avoid sunburn, only one ounce? Maybe even a 1.2-ounce pedometer that also reads your pulse and helps prevent overexertion? You know what I mean. We all have our favorite little backpacking widgets we love to take along. One of mine, to which I don't usually confess, is a tiny whisk broom to sweep out my tent. Tearing off the tags on the tea bags just does not make up for the accumulation of these extra ounces!

I believe that Albert Saijo had it right back in 1972. Saijo's thought-provoking writing was exceedingly popular at the time, and his words left a deep impression on me, albeit I have never yet risen to his standards.

Going Where Ancient Indians Once Trod

Saijo wrote from his high camp on a California mountain plateau. Insects coming out at dusk roused thoughts of their ancient lineage, older than the conifers and grasses, older even than the granite rock upon which he sat.

Thoughts of ancient times brought up visions of Indians who likely camped at the same spot. This raised questions of how they moved to the high meadows in summer when the valley got too warm, and back down to their winter home in the warmer valley when the mountains got too cold. Saijo reasoned they were the original go-light travelers, taking with them only what they needed, getting by with whatever was there before them, living in harmony with plants, animals, and the land.

As dusk grew dimmer, Saijo found a level spot on which to lie down, stretched out his ground cloth, and rolled out his sleeping pad with his sleeping bag atop. While crawling into the bag, he envisioned how Indians would camp at the same spot and need so little from nature—only enough to eat, drink, and keep warm.

He didn't build a fire. Didn't have a stove, nor pots, pans, or utensils. He simply ate a handful of pemmican.

He reminisced on how he had gotten started going lighter, the many hikes he had taken when he came back with uneaten food, having carried it the entire trip. When planning trips in those days, he had always thought his pack would lighten up as he ate the meals over the days. But it never turned out that way.

Making this observation after several hikes, he began to trim back. He thought, "The only way to break this cycle is to begin thinking in terms of an ultra-light wilderness style. . . . And ultra-light comes to mean not only cutting back on the load, but also treading light on the wilderness, thus helping to preserve it."

He became ecologically concerned that increasing numbers of backpackers would repeat the depredations of the land done by sheep, cattle, and loggers before us.

Saijo argued that in America, because of our abundance, we had come to believe we must eat more food than is necessary or good for us. We believe that unless we eat three meals a day, every day, we'll be undernourished. We are obsessed by "dietary deficiencies" and whether there is enough of this or that mineral or vitamin per day in the food we eat.

So we eat on schedule, eating not so much because we're hungry, but because it's time and we must eat the right foods. Eating has become compulsive behavior. By taking that food attitude into wilderness, we're bound to take along far more than we need to eat.

Saijo said he "leaned toward the not enough, rather than more than enough." He chose natural foods, many of which he prepared in advance, especially his pemmican, Indian buccan, and mixtures of seeds, nuts, and dried fruits.

"The notion that we must cook outback is really an encumbering one," he said. "Must we carry a kitchen everyplace we go? Why should we want to eat in the wild as we do at home?"

He pointed out that our kitchen and food are the heaviest items in our packs. And they are the ones that keep us from melding more completely into the harmonies of the outdoors.

Saijo's gear on his treks consisted of a sleeping bag, lightweight sleeping pad, over-the-pack poncho, space blanket, and five-by-seven-foot waterproof nylon tarp, which he used either as a ground cloth or in combination with the poncho to pitch as a tent in rainy weather. He also carried as versatile and spare an ensemble of clothes as possible.

He summed up in caustic language what he thought of people like me who lug too much gear and food on the trail: "The overload psychology of too much food and gear and the heavy, home-outdoors style of camp ultimately rest on the early American urbanite pioneer's idea of wilderness as a foe to be fought and subdued—a domain of unfriendly forces to be penetrated at great risk to life and limb. Following this psychology, we often try to provision ourselves absolutely fail-safe."

John Muir was exemplar of the wilderness style Saijo embraced. Muir carried two blankets, bread and tea, a notebook, and a few small items in his trouser pockets. If he decided at times to go any lighter, he dispensed with the blankets.

HOW I LIGHTENED MY LOAD

All right, so Saijo did have his influence on me. How did I lighten my load? Fair question. I have to confess, I seesaw back and forth, for a while becoming abstemious about what I put in my pack, and at other times going out with a pack-mule syndrome. One thing persuades me to go light more than anything else: water! When I have to carry a lot of it, I tend to reduce my pack weight as much as possible.

Let me tell you what I took on a recent hike. First a little background about the hike. There were good reasons why I made this hike with as little weight as I could while still being safe. I hiked a section of trail that I had never done before. It goes into a part of Grand Canyon that has intrigued me for a number of years.

The problem with this trail, as with many of the primitive trails, is that there is a full day's hike of about eleven miles between water sources, the most magnificent section of the three-day hike. I wanted to camp waterless one night at a particularly beautiful spot I'd been to before. Which meant, of course, I'd have to carry a lot of extra water on one day, adding about eight pounds of deadweight to my pack in addition to the rest of my backpacking gear.

The quickest way of lightening your pack is to eliminate much of what you don't really need for a hike. A lightweight tarp trims a minimum of three pounds from your pack alone, and it's easy to pitch and will keep you dry. But the trade-off is that it won't screen out bugs or create the warmth of a tent. William Kemsley Jr. camped in a primitive area of Grand Canyon.

It never sounds like much extra weight back home as I plan the trip. But I've had my share of lugging heavy loads of water and thus was not easily lulled into pretrail complacency.

I picked the perfect time of year for this hike, when the days are long but not exceedingly hot. I expected the weather to be reasonably warm and the days long—sunup at about 5:30 A.M. and sunset about 7:30 P.M., with a good half hour of twilight at each end of the day.

First I decided on my clothes. I'd wear a nylon shirt and pants and carry a light-weight set of silk long johns, top and bottoms. Should I get wet perchance, I could set up camp and slip out of the wet clothes and into the long johns and my sleeping bag if necessary.

At this time of year, the temperatures at the campsites below the rim rarely tip below fifty degrees. So I carried a lightweight sleeping-bag liner, cutting another pound and a half from my three-season bag weight. But I wanted to be prepared for an emergency that could surprise me by dropping ten to fifteen degrees below that. Thus the silk long johns, for silk is a good insulator and extremely light weight.

I decided not to take my four-and-a-half-pound tent. Instead, I carried a lightweight tarp. I can rig it up as a shelter quickly using my walking stick as a pole. Substituting the tarp with a ground sheet cut another three pounds of weight from my pack.

Following Saijo's lead, I left behind my stove, fuel, and cook kit. This saved me another pound or so of pack weight. I kept my food weight down to just two pounds altogether for the entire three-day trek. The only real weight was in my lunches, which were cheese and crackers. Breakfasts and dinners were granolas and dry fruits and nuts. Then I also had some favorite trail snacks—dried sugared ginger chunks and shelled pecans. But I carried only two meals for two of the three days: lunch and dinner on day one; breakfast, lunch, and dinner on day two; breakfast and lunch on day three.

These were relatively easy choices to make. What was more difficult was trying to sort out the widgets to carry. Ordinarily I carry about five pounds of them, including flashlight, altimeter, toilet tissue, rain cover for my pack, lightweight camera and film, notepad and pencil, first-aid kit, snakebite kit, extra fittings for pack repairs, moleskin.

I wrestled with this decision for some days before the hike. I changed my mind again and again. Finally I eliminated the camera and film, pack rain cover, notepad and pencil, snakebite kit, altimeter, and repair kit, getting the weight to the minimum.

My Kelty pack weighs four and a half pounds. So I opted instead to carry my day-pack, an Austrian Bergsport Kohla, which though considerably smaller is also considerably lighter. I can carry everything I need in it, strapping my sleeping pad on the outside. My sleeping pad is plain, bare three-quarter-inch foam. I've had it for years, and it weighs eight ounces.

With this exercise in lightening up, I reduced my pack, without water, to thirteen and a half pounds total, including three days' food and my walking stick. I carried six twenty-four-ounce empty Propel water bottles, for a total capacity of a gallon and a pint of water.

This amount of water would get me though just over twenty-four hours. Here is how I justified this in Grand Canyon. At this time of year, the heat is not intense. I started out the day from a water source where I drank until I could drink no more before leaving. I knew that I would be at a water source sometime midafternoon the following day, so I had water for the day of hiking, including lunch and dinner the first day and breakfast the next, and would wait to eat lunch until I hit the water source.

Here are the items in my three-day Grand Canyon outfit:

- Bergsport Kohla daypack
- sleeping-bag liner
- foam sleeping pad
- eight-by-ten-foot tarp
- three-by-six-foot space blanket
- cup
- aluminum spoon
- Swiss Army knife with seven blades
- six empty twenty-four-ounce soft-drink bottles
- eight aluminum wire tent pegs
- rain parka
- rain pants
- silk long john top and bottoms
- silk balaclava
- ski glove liners
- fifty feet nylon eighth-inch parachute cord
- AAA Maglite flashlight
- extra batteries
- matches
- toilet paper
- compass
- map
- small container of sunblock
- walking stick
- plastic trash bags and zipper-lock bags
- first-aid kit

While you can see from this list that Saijo, Muir, and Knowles are a bit too austere for me, I nonetheless did come close to Saijo's standards.

Section Three
USING THE TRAILS

The woods where the weird shadows slant;
The stillness, the moonlight, the mystery,
I've bade 'em good bye—but I can't.

—from "Spell of the Yukon," by Robert Service

Dave Sumner photographing wildflowers in Weminuche Wilderness in southern Colorado's San Juan Mountains.

11

Finding Your Way

For many reasons, it is wise to get accustomed to day hiking before you attempt backpacking. First of all, the risk of getting lost is greatly reduced in day hiking, for you are never more than a few hours from the trailhead, whereas on a backpacking trek, you can be days from the nearest access point.

Second, instead of trying to learn several backpacking skills simultaneously, when day hiking you can focus entirely upon learning the most essential outdoors skills—how to follow trails and how to read map and compass. Basic route finding is easier on day hikes, because trails are more heavily trodden and thus easier to follow. On the other hand, trails in more remote areas where fewer people hike become appreciably more difficult, and the deeper you go into the wilds, trails actually disappear altogether in some places.

You don't want to end up like the old Adirondack guide Nessmuk on a trail he took across Michigan in the late nineteenth century. He found the trail easily, but as he wrote in *Woodcraft and Camping:* "It was filled with leaves, dim, and not easy to follow. It ended as nearly all trails do: it branched off to right and left, grew dimmer and slimmer, degenerated to a deer path, petered out to a squirrel track, ran up a tree, and ended in a knot hole."

So, a caution: Learn basic map reading and how to use a compass. Before departing on even a short hike, define an emergency heading that takes you to the nearest well-traveled road, no matter where you might be on the trail. It is the best insurance against spending a miserable night in the woods or heading in the wrong direction if you get lost.

Another caution: Stick to well-marked trails. Most trails are marked with distinct trail markers, usually maintained by volunteers who, by keeping trails highly usable, prevent many hikers from getting lost.

Finally, while you are learning your route-finding skills, always hike with other experienced hikers who know how to use map and compass. Never hike alone. Some places, even on well-marked trails, are not all that easy to follow. At switchbacks, for example, hikers sometimes miss the turn and wander off the trail in the wrong direction. Should you happen to follow their missteps, which happens a lot more easily than you might suspect, finding your way back to the trail can be tricky.

In the event you do lose the trail like this, immediately stop and keep calm. This is a key reason for hiking with someone. Stay where you are and have the other person retrace your footsteps back toward the switchback to find the trail. Be sure that both of you are always within eyesight of each other.

If your companion does not find clear signs of the trail, have him or her come back to you and perhaps try another likely direction to look for it. Stay calm. And do not make off blindly through the woods looking for the trail, believing you know where it might be situated. You could be wrong and get even farther away from where you want to be. No matter what, do not go forward on your hike without knowing that you are back on the trail again.

> **I've been caught a couple of times in survival situations. And I tell you, the most comforting thing I had along was a whistle.**
>
> —*Dave Bates, National Boy Scout Association camping and conservation director*

Should you be alone for some odd reason and find yourself in this situation, stop, stay calm, and slowly retrace your footsteps back to the switchback. Frequently look behind you at the terrain to be sure you can go back there if need be. Also mark the path you are taking back with easy telltale signs, such as leaning a dead branch against a tree or bush every few feet. Do not panic, but do *not* continue your hike until you are certain you are on the trail you intend to be hiking.

Nessmuk was able to find his way by the "feel of the woods," but far too many search-and-rescue missions are due to beginners who have taken a hike without having basic navigational skills or a guidebook that details intersections and which way to go next.

There are a number of organizations that offer training in map and compass. Some outdoor sporting-goods stores, local hiking and mountaineering clubs, and local search-and-rescue organizations usually provide good training.

After you have made a number of day hikes, you'll begin getting your feel of the woods, which will become an enormous asset to your hiking. There is no better teacher than actual hiking experience.

When I was a youngster, our family frequently took afternoon walks in the woods. They were always short and undramatic walks on unmarked paths or simply through the woods where there were no paths. These walks, early in life, gave me my feel for the woods and a sense of the logical direction a path might take around the next bend or over the next knoll. This sense of the woods is difficult to describe to anyone who does not have it. But you will begin developing your own sense of the woods as you spend more time on day hikes.

You'll know when you are ready to add backpacking to your hiking agenda. Backpacking simply adds yeast to the day-hiking dough for me. It enables me to stay out longer and provides a quiet, more lasting afterglow. There is only one pleasure in life that's equal to it, that also does not dim with the years, and that is opera. Just as a CD of Maria Callas singing *Vissi d'arte* hypes me for my next opera, topos get me psyched to such a pitch I can barely wait for my next Departure Day.

USING GUIDEBOOKS, MAPS, AND COMPASS

As soon as you can, start using guidebooks, maps, and compass. They will give you a much better feel for finding your way. The advantage of guidebooks is that they spell out in useful detail how to get to a trailhead, what the trail terrain is like, and hiking

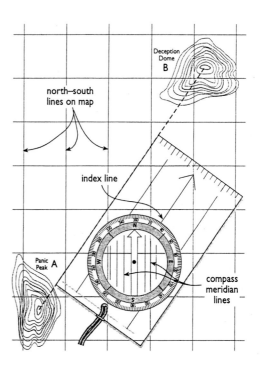

To take a bearing, line up your compass needle to north, then align it with vertical meridian lines on your compass housing with the north-south lines on your map. Keeping the needle pointed north, take your bearing along the index line of your compass as shown in the illustration. FROM *MOUNTAINEERING: FREEDOM OF THE HILLS*. COPYRIGHT © 2005 MOUNTAINEERS BOOKS.

distances from one point to another. This information is not so easily obtained from topographic maps. But the joy of topographic map reading is their way of unraveling the mystery of the terrain. I simply love to use a topo map to figure out how to get in to a particular spot, plot the route, and then actually try hiking it.

An excellent reason to get topographic maps of areas you are hiking in, even if you do have a guidebook, is to get the feel of the topo and greater detail of the terrain. And should you get lost off the trail, you will have considerable difficulty getting back to the trail with only a guidebook and no map.

Mapping my trips enables me to take a hike three times. The first is when I sit down with topo to figure out where I want to hike. This gets the juices flowing, building my anticipation for the hike. The second time, of course, is the real thing, when I head out to hoof it along the trail. This part is always a lot better than I even imagined. The third time is when I've returned home and am putting away my gear. Invariably, I am going over the topo maps once more, seeing where I went and laying plans for my next hike. As often as I've hiked, as many trails as I have traversed, I'm always amazed at what a joy I get from these jaunts—all three of them.

I can tell you how to read a topographic map. A great book to get is Cliff Jacobson's *Basic Essentials: Map and Compass.* In the end, the map and your feet will be the most effective teachers. The best way to learn is through actual field training from a school, mountaineering club, or local search-and-rescue organization.

The best topographic maps are U.S. Geological Survey (USGS) maps. They come in quads for various areas. An index to topographic maps of each state is available from the USGS regional offices at various places throughout the United States. Check with your outfitting shop, your local librarian, or online at www.usgs.gov.

Then, in this computer age, there are a variety of other sources of topo maps as well. You can purchase any number of manufacturers' digital products, CD-ROMs that not only contain all of an area's scanned USGS topos, but sometimes also include additional information to help in route finding. Two useful products are the National Geographic Maps' TOPO and Maptech's Terrain Navigator. There are also websites, such as trails.com, topozone.com, and terraserver.com, that provide much the same topographic material, or at least downloads of a local trail's topo quad.

These CDs and websites are obviously more convenient to use than having to make trips back and forth to the map store. A word of warning, though: At least one company offers what it advertises as "topo maps" that are anything but. They are a hokey version that comes nowhere near the accuracy and detail of USGS topographic maps. Be sure to read the fine print and see samples before you buy.

USGS maps come in two different scales: 15-minute quads on a scale of 1:62,500 and 7.5-minute maps on a scale of 1:24,000. The scale is indicated on the map's legend. The most useful for hikers are the 7.5-minute maps at the scale of 1:24,000. This scale gives details in one mile to two and an eighth inches, with contour lines for every forty feet of change in elevation. But you are mostly going to be able to obtain maps only on the scale of 1:62,500, which is a scale of one mile to an inch, with contours of eighty-foot intervals. Though this is the general rule, there are a few variations. Some of the more recently surveyed maps have contour lines every twenty feet, with forty-foot intervals in mountainous terrain.

More than likely, the trail you plan to take will be on the map. As you learn to follow the trail and read the map, you will become more and more familiar with map reading from actual field practice.

Now let me interject a couple of other cautions. USGS maps are often out-of-date. Most were surveyed some twenty years or so ago. Hence they may not have newer trails on them, or newer routes of old trails. Sometimes they show trails that have been abandoned long ago.

An even more serious caution about out-of-date USGS maps: They likely have incorrect compass declinations on them. For example, I have a USGS map for Rocky Mountain National Park that I used for years. It is based on a survey made in 1957. The declination is 15 degrees east. Since magnetic north and declination change daily, the most recent USGS declination on the quad is 10.455 degrees east. This may not sound like much of a difference while reading this book, but it could make the difference of

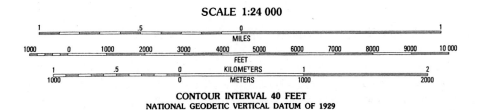

Each map has a scale on it to indicate how the map's measurements correspond to actual miles or feet. Simply use a ruler to calculate how many miles are indicated from one point to another on the map.

Understanding and Compensating for Declination

When using a map and compass, you need to compensate for declination. Basically, declination is the difference between true north and magnetic north. The Geographic North Pole, the point where the earth's axis of rotation intercepts the earth's surface, is some 900 miles north of the magnetic North Pole. A compass always points to the magnetic North Pole.

If you draw a line from any particular geographic location to both poles, magnetic and true north, the angle between the two lines is the declination for that location.

If you draw a line from the true geographic North Pole through the magnetic North Pole and continue it on south, a compass reading anywhere along that line south of the magnetic pole will point directly at the true geographic North Pole. The two poles and the hiker holding the compass are all on the same line. So declination anywhere on that line is zero degrees.

This is the agonic line. In the United States in 2004, that line ran roughly along the Mississippi River from Duluth on the north to New Orleans on the south. But the agonic line shifts: Just a few years earlier, it ran from Grand Rapids, Michigan, down through St. Petersburg, Florida.

If you are west of the agonic line, your compass will point east of the true geographic North Pole. This is called east declination. If you are east of the agonic line, your compass will point west of the true geographic North Pole. This is called west declination.

All this requires you to keep several factors in mind. Are you east or west of the agonic line? If the former, you have west declination. If the latter, you have east

continues on next page

Declination for magnetic north can be found in the lower corner of U.S. Geological Survey maps. True north is indicated by the vertical line, usually with a star at the top. Magnetic north at the South Rim of Grand Canyon is indicated in the illustration as 13 degrees east in 1988. Note, though, that the declination changed by .55 degrees to 12.45 degrees east in 2007. Magnetic north is constantly changing. Because declination is constantly changing, many mapmakers no longer indicate it on their maps. Be sure you know what the declination is for the area you are heading into, and get it corrected on Topozone (www.Topozone.com) before your departure.

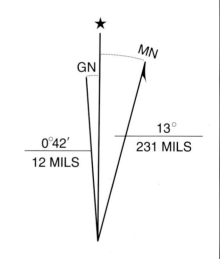

UTM Grid and 1988 magnetic north declination at center of map diagram is approximate

Understanding and Compensating for Declination *continued*

declination. If you have east declination, you subtract the declination from your map direction, but you add the declination to your compass reading. If you have west declination, you add the declination to your map direction, but you subtract the declination from your compass reading.

I find this far too complicated to be able to recall in difficult emotional situations when I might need it the most. It is much easier to follow the simple pretrip procedure that Harry Franks calls his KISS declination system for regridding topo maps.

First of all, set your compass for magnetic north and leave it on that setting permanently. Then regrid your USGS topo maps. Begin by laying a yardstick along the magnetic north direction shown on the lower corner of USGS maps. Rule a magnetic north line across the entire map, then draw several lines on the map parallel to this one.

Harry regrids his own maps at home for each area he plans to hike. Then, when he is on trails on those quads, he simply lays the compass on the map with the needle pointing along the lines he has ruled on the quad. This makes it simple and requires no thinking in tight situations where it is critical to get accurate compass bearings.

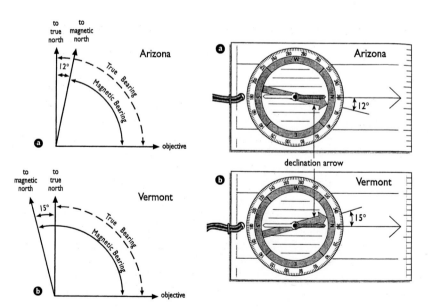

The differences in magnetic declinations can throw you way off course unless you adjust for them. At the left are recent declinations for Arizona and Vermont. The illustration on the right shows how to adjust your compass for those declinations. It should be obvious how much 27 degrees of difference would make if you had your compass set for Vermont and used it to find directions in Arizona without making the adjustment.

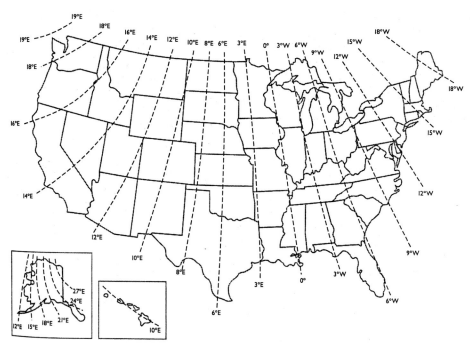

Magnetic declination changes from day to day. This illustration shows the lines of declination for the United States in 2005. Check declination for the area you plan to hike at www.Topozone.com. It's free and they offer great maps that you can download at a competitive price.
FROM *MOUNTAINEERING: FREEDOM OF THE HILLS.* COPYRIGHT © 2005 MOUNTAINEERS BOOKS.

life or death if you were trying to find your way out of the Rocky Mountains in a whiteout!

A real danger in desert country is that indications of springs are often inaccurate. So although they are highly useful, topos need to be augmented by other, more up-to-date information on the trails you are taking.

One of the difficulties in using CDs and Internet sources is that the USGS maps that they are licensed to use in their databases are not always the most recent editions. Topozone.com is one site that updates its declinations daily. Other map sources may do likewise, but it will serve you well to ask before you buy.

A quick way to be sure your topo declination is correct for the time of your trip is to check out the declination at topozone.com or www.ngdc.noaa.gov/seg/geomag/icons/us_d_contour.jpg, and adjust your maps accordingly if necessary. Topozone.com also offers some amazing map features, such as a portion of any group of USGS quads in laminated plastic.

Local land management agencies will have more up-to-date maps, though they are often not as easy to read. In conjunction with USGS topo maps, they will enable you to readily find your way. And trail guidebooks are very useful in providing more up-to-date information, but it's a good idea to check the publication date to see how current the information is.

For many popular hiking areas, the National Geographic Society produces assemblages of about eight USGS topographical maps on one map sheet. These come in a more useful format, with trails more clearly marked, as well as other features such as campgrounds, trailheads, road gates, cross-country ski areas, ranger stations, even avalanche danger areas. They are printed on waterproof and more durable paper stock. See www.nationalgeographic.com/trails.

COMPASS READING

I cannot in this short space give you a comprehensive course in compass reading. There are good books on this, as well as courses in orienteering given by local hiking clubs and outfitting shops. Take advantage of them.

Nonetheless, let me touch upon a few basics. First, all USGS maps have a magnetic north correction on them, usually in the bottom left-hand corner (see illustration). Find it, and adjust your compass accordingly. Or use Harry Frank's KISS method and regrid your topos. It can make a critical difference in finding your way—or *not* finding your way at all.

For example, using 2005 compass settings, if your compass is set for New York's Adirondacks, it would be 14.845 degrees west of true north. If you did not change your compass setting and took the New York setting out to Colorado to backpack in the Rocky Mountains, where magnetic north would be 10.455 degrees east of true north, you would be off course by 25-plus degrees. In other words, the compass setting that you had for the Adirondacks when you got to the Rockies would take you off course roughly one and two-thirds miles for every mile you hiked, which would put you almost seventeen miles away from where you want to be in ten miles!

Second, your compass is probably going to be of greater use when you are lost in dense woods and are least able to use it for triangulating your position, since you are unable to see key distant landmarks commonly used for route finding in open country.

In dense woods, you want to be able to know you are heading in the right direction and keep a steady course in that direction. Hence, following your compass bearing can be a way of finding your way out of the woods. A problem when being lost in dense woods is that hikers tend to walk around in circles and really get disoriented. So following a steady compass course is critical. Note that this can occur on short hikes as well as longer ones.

A compass can also aid you in locating various landmarks when you are in the open where you can see them.

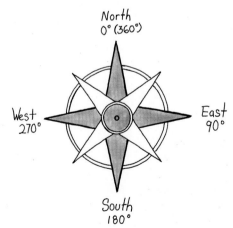

Each map has a directional indication, such as a rosette, that shows how to orient the map. North is always true north, and you must adjust your compass declination to magnetic north to aid in route finding.

Important Considerations When Using a Compass

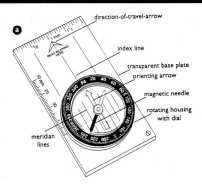

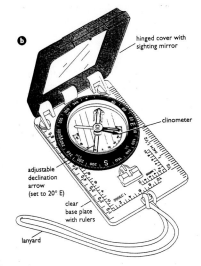

A good compass offers essential features for route finding and useful optional features. FROM MOUN- TAINEERING: FREEDOM OF THE HILLS. COPYRIGHT © 2005 MOUNTAINEERS BOOKS.

1. Be able to tell which direction is north from your compass. The red end of the needle points north; the other end points south. Line up the lines on the housing of the compass with the north end of the needle, and you have the basic orientation of the compass.

2. Take your map reading, adjusting it for the declination. Your compass needle actually points to magnetic north, while your map is plotted around true north. This indication of true north and magnetic north is found in the legend on the bottom left-hand corner of USGS maps. (See the illustration.) Adjust for the declination of your map by simply turning the compass housing around the same number of degrees in the direction of magnetic north indicated on your USGS topo map. A highly recommended alternative is the Harry Frank KISS method, a simpler and safer way of adjusting for declination.

3. Before you leave home for your hike, be sure you understand number 1 above and make one of the adjustments indicated in number 2. Do not wait until you are on the trail to figure these things out.

4. On the trail, orient your map on the ground so that its top is headed toward true north on your compass reading. Get a feel for the land. Does it make sense to you as you see it laid out before you along the compass directions indicated?

USING AN ALTIMETER

When I want to quickly locate my position on the trail, using an altimeter is far faster than finding it with a compass.

I carry an altimeter all the time in addition to my compass. At the trailhead, I set it to the elevation on my topographic map. Then on the trail, when I want to know where I am, I simply take a new altitude reading and use the contours on the map to see where that elevation intersects the trail. This gives me a reasonably quick check of my position. For a more accurate reading, however, I confirm it with my compass. The altimeter's readings can change with a change in the weather, which leads me to the other reason I carry my altimeter—for weather alerts.

An altimeter is simply a barometer calibrated for altitude. I always check the altitude of my camp in the evening before I go to sleep. If I discover in the morning that the altimeter reading is higher than it was when I went to sleep, it is telling me the barometric pressure dropped during the night. This is cause for concern. It means a storm is likely coming in.

Altimeters indicate elevation by the barometric air pressure. The higher we go, the lower the air pressure and the higher the elevation registered on the altimeter. So a rise in altitude when I have not budged from camp means the barometric pressure dropped, ergo an imminent storm.

If you are going to use an altimeter, be sure to reset it at the trailhead just before you start your hike. Likewise, check your altitude every morning, and reset the altimeter if necessary before leaving camp. Otherwise you could have inaccurate readings, both for positioning yourself on the trail and for weather forecasting.

USING THE GLOBAL POSITIONING SYSTEM

The Global Positioning System (GPS) has become a valuable trail tool. *But be warned: The GPS should not be used in lieu of adequate understanding of map and compass. It is not a substitute!* This could be very dangerous. Consider: What happens if you drop and break your GPS? Accidents happen. What if your batteries die? Do you want your life to depend upon a pair of AA batteries? What if you have miscalculated your original position and feed in incorrect information? Errors also happen.

A GPS can be used as an excellent safety measure for finding your way back to the trailhead in an emergency. The trick is to log in your position at the trailhead and retain it in the GPS until you return to the trailhead. Should you have problems and need to find your way back out, you then follow the beeline back to your starting point.

Caution: There are many errors that the use of the GPS cannot resolve. Your GPS can be thrown off by cold, moisture, terrain, batteries, or human errors. If you haven't adjusted between the data and the map, this leads to errors in the coordinates and your subsequent headings. Be sure that if you use a GPS, you also know how to find your

Harry Frank is director of the Ski Patrol at Enchanted Forest in the Carson National Forest of New Mexico. Though he is emeritus professor of psychology and associate professor of earth and resource science at the University of Michigan, he continues to teach winter survival skills to instructors for the Mountain Travel and Rescue program of the National Ski Patrol.

> One thing I won't go into the back-country without, whether it be for work or for play, is a compass. It is an indispensable tool for tracking radio-collared animals, finding that elusive piece of paradise in mountains, or finding my way back to my truck after getting helplessly lost in the process of doing these activities.
>
> —*Sean Matthews, project director, Wilderness Preservation Society*

way by map and compass as a reliable backup and have them along for this purpose.

No doubt, the GPS is an enormously useful tool for search and rescue. But it can also be a problem if relied upon too heavily.

A GPS is all but useless when the tree canopy is too dense overhead, such as in eastern hardwood forests. Satellite signals are inaccessible in dense forest covering. In canyons, the walls are usually too high to permit reception. And cold weather can cause batteries to dim or die altogether.

I have used a GPS when sailing offshore. It was far handier than the use of a sextant, though we always carried one aboard and knew how to use it. When I go into the backcountry, though, I avoid as much as possible all electronic gear. I do not carry a GPS or cell phone, and I'd prefer not to hike with anyone who carries either. Or at least I hope my hiking companions don't tell me they have them along, if they do, and are discreet enough to keep them out of my view.

Once when I was the editor of *Backpacker* magazine, I was taken on a backpacking trip by the head of trails for the Forest Service, Bill Holman, and Bill Worf, one of the key authors of the 1964 Wilderness Act. They wanted to show me some difficult problems in managing wilderness lands.

Holman's superiors made a stipulation for this trip—that a backcountry ranger accompany us with a radio to keep in touch with home office daily in case anything went wrong. Though the radioman kept the equipment out of sight and did his reporting well out of our range of hearing, I have to tell you that just knowing he had the radio with him took a good bit of the joy out of that trek for me.

I go back to nature with my pack and as little gear as I can get by with and still be as safe as common sense allows. A GPS, cell phone, radio, and all other connections with the outside world are just not appropriate for my hikes, even though one of my daughters keeps insisting that I take a cell phone with me—"just in case, Dad!" I love Maggie dearly for the thought. But truly, were I to carry one, I might just as well be in downtown Albuquerque as in the heart of Grand Canyon.

If you want to carry a GPS or cell phone, so be it. You'll just have to get instructions on how to use them from someone else. Some of the best instructions can be obtained from outfitters.

12

How to Deal with the Weather

I am going to describe weather here in the broad brushstrokes with which it has been shown to me. I have never found it necessary to know a lot of detail about weather forecasting other than to be able to identify a few fairly consistent patterns throughout the various types of terrain I've hiked over the years. Elsewhere I cover special conditions in mountains (chapter 28), deserts (chapter 29), and canyons (chapter 30). And weather conditions for winter hiking are discussed in chapter 32.

Of course, we would like to have great weather on our hikes. But it doesn't always work out that way. So how is it possible to assure ourselves of these conditions when we have to plan our hikes so far in advance? For one thing, we can plan to take our hikes at the more propitious times of year for the area.

CHECK THE AREA'S WEATHER HISTORY

The history of an area's weather is a big help. Today there is ample literature available for about any hiking and backpacking area you care to hike. Most trail guidebooks give historic weather conditions for these areas during various times of year. This is a good place to begin.

If you're headed for a national park, the Park Service website (www.nps.org) has historic weather data as well as weather forecasts. The Forest Service (www.fs.fed.us) has similar sets of weather data for the national forests, and the BLM (www.blm.gov) does for some of its lands as well.

I've often looked for a warm place to backpack in early spring after a particularly long, cold winter. It was difficult to find such a good place, until I discovered Organ Pipe National Monument in Arizona and Big Bend National Park in Texas. Both are prime spots to hike in February and March. And since it is not easy to get to either by plane, their backcountry areas are not nearly as heavily trafficked as so many other hiking spots.

Lest I lull you with too much romance, let me warn that both these spots are stark Southwest deserts and have all of the risks of desert hiking, albeit during early spring without the intense heat of summer.

Wherever you may be headed, as you get closer to departure date, check the long-range weather forecasts regularly. The website I find most useful is weather.com, which will give you a ten-day forecast for just about any area you like.

As I write, I have just canceled a week's backpacking trip because the ten-day forecast indicated rain or thunderstorms for every day but one. I don't mind if it rains on a hike, but I see no sense in starting out on one when the forecast is so grim.

Being prepared for the weather enables you to enjoy various moods of the wilds.

CARRY APPROPRIATE GEAR FOR THE WORST WEATHER CONDITIONS

Now what I have to say concerns both day-hiking and backpacking, though on multi-day hikes you are more at the mercy of the weather over a longer period of time. Still, the greatest number of hiker deaths occur from hypothermia. This strikes worst in fairly mild weather. And it can occur just as easily on a day hike as on a backpacking jaunt. So do not presume that because you are out for just a three-hour hike, it is perfectly safe to jog along in skimpy attire or that you are safe from the weather even if the sky is not threatening and the temperatures are in the forties or low fifties—though obviously you won't need a full pack with tent and sleeping bag on such short hikes. I'll send up the warning signals assuming a backpacking trip; use common sense for which applies on your particular hike. But do remember that it is far better to be safe than sorry—and alive than dead.

Even when we do schedule our hikes to coincide with the best possible weather forecasts, Mother Nature may still choose to ignore our plans. There is not much you can do about hot weather, other than strip down as much as possible. But for cold weather, you can carry extra clothes. And for wet, you can carry raingear to protect you and the things in your pack. Carry extra trash bags and various size zipper-lock plastic bags in which to store your clothes and other items you don't want to get wet.

I store my sleeping bag in a plastic bag inside my stuff sack—for those just-in-case times. Likewise, I put each item of clothing in a separate zipper-lock plastic bag and put the small bags inside a large plastic trash bag in each compartment of my pack. It may sound like overkill, but I have done so much of my backpacking in the Northeast and Northwest that I know what to expect of the weather.

I carry an umbrella summer and winter, and use it.

—Laura Waterman, first editor of **Backpacker** *magazine, author of* **Backcountry Ethics** *and many more*

The weather does not have to be severe to take you down. Hypothermia is the number-one killer of hikers. It occurs most frequently in temperatures in the forties and fifties, especially when it is rainy. Better to be safe than sorry with regard to extra clothing.

Keep yourself and your hiking companions dry as you hike in cooler weather, especially if it is wet. This means stripping off some clothes if you are perspiring enough to dampen your shirt. It means adding a layer if it is getting chilly, especially at rest stops. And it means donning raingear at the first few drops of drizzle.

I always carry a pair of thin glove liners, for I hate having cold hands. The liners keep my hands comfortable when it's even just a bit chilly. My headband-earwarmer serves the same purpose for my ears, even if I have a hat. And I'm never without a bandanna; it has so many uses on the trail.

—*Celina Montorfano, vice president, American Hiking Society*

Another thing: Do not get exhausted hiking in cooler weather. The exhaustion can add to the possibilities of hypothermia, for it depletes energy more rapidly when you have to replenish both the energy consumed in hiking and that needed to keep the body warm.

WEATHER FORECASTING

You can pick up a few signs from the sky that will warn you of inclement weather coming in your direction. Forewarned is forearmed.

As I said in the beginning, I have never seen much need for more detailed comprehension of weather forecasting. The few vital tidbits I have picked up from various sources have been quite enough to get me out of the toughest weather conditions. There is the old standby, "Red sky in the morning, sailors take warning. Red sky at night, sailor's delight." It still seems reliable in my experience. And the most predictable indicator to me are mare's tail clouds. They indicate a storm within thirty-six to forty-eight hours.

Though the sky is beautiful and the weather fair, this classic mare's tail cloud formation is a harbinger of precipitation to come anywhere from thirty-six to forty-eight hours after it's seen. It is the best weather forecaster of inclement weather that I know about, and it has been for millennia, as indicated in the seaman's rhyme: "Mare's tails and mackerel scales/Make tall ships take down their sails."
GORDON RICHARDSON,
WWW.CAPETOWNSKIES.COM

Quick Checklist of Telltale Weather Signs

- High, white, filmy cirrus clouds indicate a storm coming in twenty-four hours or so.
- Mare's tails are highly predictable of a storm within thirty-six to forty-eight hours.
- A ring around the moon is created by thin cirrus clouds, ergo a storm is likely coming.
- Thickening clouds, lowering and approaching, indicate a storm is on its way shortly.
- Thickening wave clouds in the mountains and snow plumes on ridges indicate high winds at mountaintops and perhaps increased moisture, with a possible storm. Take heed!
- Clouds lifting and thinning indicate a storm passing.
- Snow pellets and wind shift may indicate a storm moving away.
- Altimeter falling (rising altitude) indicates an approaching storm.
- Altimeter rising (lowering altitude) indicates a storm departing.

Typical of the predictability of this cloud formation was a recent observation I made. On November 27 at about 11 A.M., I noticed mare's tails building up overhead. During the night of November 28, between midnight and 5 A.M.—thirty-seven to forty-two hours later—it began to snow, lightly at first, then heavier during the afternoon, until eight inches had accumulated before it stopped snowing at 3 P.M. on November 29, fifty-two hours after I'd spotted the mare's tails. Right on schedule. Works at any place in the United States that I've tried it, particularly in the Rockies, where it is not so easy to forecast the weather. Nice clue, for it gives you a good amount of time to either get back out or hunker down to wait out the storm.

Mare's tails are not always in the classic form. Sometimes they only roughly approximate the classic. They are cirrus clouds, which are clusters of ice crystals high in the sky at about 20,000 feet. In the form of mare's tails such as these, they forecast inclement weather within thirty-six to forty-eight hours.

Mackerel scale cloud formations are cirrus clouds high in the stratosphere, also indicating pre-cipitation within a day and a half to two days. Be prepared. As sailors warn: Mackerel clouds in sky, expect more wet than dry.

I also depend a lot upon my altimeter for clues. If I notice, for example, that the altimeter reading puts me at a higher elevation in the morning than it read the night before, but I haven't moved the camp, then I know that the barometric pressure has dropped and I should expect a change of weather to the misery side shortly.

Sometimes you will be confronted by an approaching front, which can be quite dramatic. This is indicated by a long row of clouds appearing on one side of a straight line with clear sky on the other side of it. It means a sudden deterioration of the weather is likely imminent.

Some people don't seem to mind the weather as much as I do. But I would just as soon not be wet or cold. And frankly, that fits with common sense. An ounce of prevention is worth a pound of cure when it comes to inclement weather in the backcountry.

I've kept it very simple. If you want more extensive knowledge of the weather signs, there are many good books on this. One short, simple primer is Michael Hodgson's *Basic Essentials: Weather Forecasting.*

13

Health, Safety, and First Aid for the Trail

I will only touch upon these topics in this short chapter. Some of the more complicated first-aid concerns are covered in other chapters; see the sidebar "Helpful Cross-References." But I will point out some red flags here about how things could be difficult on the trail.

The best thing you can do for first aid on the trail is follow the old Boy Scout motto, "Be prepared." Though it may seem extreme, it is an excellent idea to take a Red Cross first-aid course. It teaches skills that are useful not just for hiking, but for the home as well.

Carry a first-aid kit even on short hikes. Know what's in it as well as how to use its contents. If you buy a commercial kit, check to be sure it has instructions on how to use its contents.

The most common conditions that need treatment on the trails are blisters, scratches, cuts, burns, sunburn, fatigue, sprains, and frostbite in colder weather or at higher elevations. And this chapter doesn't discuss how to deal with any of them. This chapter mostly explains the kinds of first-aid problems that can come up on the trail and where you can go for medical advice on how to deal with them.

PRETRIP PHYSICAL EXAMINATION

If you are not actively engaged in some aerobic sport and do not get regular medical examinations, it is wise and good common sense to get a physical checkup before you undertake physical, stress-related activity. You can do it. But easy does it. Start gradually, dare I say—one step at a time.

MEDICATIONS

If you are currently taking medications, take along a sufficient supply for the duration of the trip and then some. Add a few extra days' supply in case an unexpected emergency prevents your getting back home when you expected.

A physician friend, Allison Guynes, told me recently about a backpacking trip he and his wife, Cathy, took in Wyoming's Wind River Mountains with a couple other doctors a few years ago. The trip almost cost one of the doctors his life because of such an oversight.

The doctor was a diabetic. But he may have been more concerned about expending the extra energy used in backpacking and being sure to replenish that energy than he was about his diabetes. So he was eating more energy-producing foods than usual,

First-Aid Kit Contents

The most important thing to have in the first-aid kit is a set of instructions about how to use its various contents. If you buy a ready-made first-aid kit, inspect its contents to be sure it has instructions for use of all items in it. Your kit should contain the following:

- antiseptic towelettes
- antibiotic ointment
- Band-Aids
- burn ointment
- gauze compresses
- gauze roll
- butterfly closures for cuts
- adhesive tape, 1- and 2-inch
- salt tablets to prevent heat exhaustion and hyponatremia (dissolve in water before ingesting)
- scissors
- sunscreen

- tweezers
- insect repellent
- triangular bandage
- elastic bandage
- pain relievers (aspirin, ibuprofen, or acetaminophen)
- rubbing alcohol (small amount in plastic container)
- safety pins
- moleskin
- snakebite kit
- coins or phone card for pay-phone calls

For longer trips, your physician may provide the following items:

- prescription antibiotic
- prescription painkiller

which are high in carbohydrates, and the exact opposite of what a diabetic ordinarily can safely consume.

Likewise, he had not taken sufficient insulin to counteract the hyperacidic effect of the excess glucose he was ingesting. He went into a diabetic coma, and his companions had to get a helicopter rescue for him. Luckily they were still within range of some rangers who could radio out for help.

Be sure you and all members of your trek have sufficient supplies of medications to take care of your health on the trip, plus enough for a few extra days' emergency!

HIKING SAFETY DURING HUNTING SEASON

Check hunting season dates for the area in which you will be hiking, especially deer season. If there is hunting at all, protect yourself from being mistaken for a deer by wearing a blaze orange vest and hat. These are available at local hunting outfitting shops. Too many people are shot after being mistaken for a buck in the woods.

Helpful Cross-References

See the following chapters for treatment of various first-aid concerns:

- Hypothermia, chapter 16.
- Heatstroke, chapter 16.
- Altitude sickness, chapter 28.

- Snakebite, chapter 17.
- Hyponatremia, chapter 16.

Forest Service officials Bill Worf and Bill Holman at a mountain pond near Moose Creek Station in the Selway-Bitterroot Wilderness Area explain difficulties of managing wilderness lands.

Hunting seasons vary from state to state and depending upon the type of game. The best way to find out the seasons for any type of hunting in the area you plan to hike is to phone the Fish and Game Department of the state it is in. These offices pretty much set the seasons and issue the licenses.

NEVER HIKE ALONE

This advice will sound hypocritical in a book with a chapter entitled "Going Alone," which extols the joys of solo backpacking. Nonetheless, it is given in every list of advice prepared for beginners. It is sound advice. Yet there is hardly a highly experienced hiker who doesn't seek the joys of solitude of the backcountry by occasionally hiking solo.

Stick to the rule of hiking in groups until you just must go by yourself.

If you do hike alone, you take far greater risks than when hiking in a group. Should you get hurt while with a partner or in a group, even in a minor way, you will have someone to assist you or go for help. If you are in a group of three or more, you have someone to stay with you while another goes for help.

A cross-country skiing friend of mine, Madeleine Herrmann, had just such an occurrence on a day hike near her home in New Mexico recently. She was a highly experienced hiker, having hiked, skied, and biked all her life, and having been a triathlon champion in her younger days.

Madeleine misstepped and broke an ankle. Fortunately, she was with a friend who hiked out to get help to carry her out on a litter. So although I hike alone frequently, I realize the far greater risks I take when I do. In the chapter "Going Alone," I explain some of the extra precautions that need to be taken to lower these risks. But note that they *do not* eliminate the risk.

14

Insect and Plant Nuisances

One of the first things you must learn to contend with on the trails is the nuisance plants and insects that make backcountry life at times unpleasant at best, if not outright hellish.

BEES, HORNETS, AND WASPS

Ordinarily, bees, hornets, and wasps are not more of a nuisance in the backcountry than they are in your backyard. For most of us, their sting is but a nuisance. For some people, however, and you most likely know if this applies to you, it is a serious condition that requires immediate treatment. Laura Waterman, the first editor of *Backpacker* magazine, had a serum vial hung around her neck wherever she went because of her dangerous allergy to their sting. And she had to use the serum several times that I recall.

While hiking, be alert for hornet and wasp nests in hollow trees and nests hanging from branches. Also beware of turning over logs, not just because of snakes, but hornets and wasps as well. Their nests can be beneath rock ledges and along mud or dirt banks of streams.

Bees are more likely to be found by flowers. They are attracted to bright colors and sweet odors. Good reason to wear drab clothes and avoid fruity-smelling soaps, shampoos, lotions, and fragrances.

Should you encounter a swarm of bees or wasps, try to stay calm and avoid running or other swift movements, which simply attracts them all the more. If you are attacked, the best defense is to duck underwater if possible, dive into your tent or car if nearby, or cover your head and face the best you can with shirt, sweater, or whatever is at hand.

If stung, scrape the stinger out, rather than trying to squeeze it out, which will spread the venom. Apply cold water if you can to ease the pain. Otherwise, tough it out. Should you experience extensive swelling, nausea, shortness of breath, or a rapid pulse, you may be experiencing an allergic reaction and should seek medical help as soon as possible.

MOSQUITOES, BLACKFLIES, CHIGGERS, AND NO-SEE-UMS

Depending upon the area and the season of the year you plan to hike, you may have to deal with mosquitoes, blackflies, chiggers, or no-see-ums.

At their worst, they can turn your hike into hell.

The best way to deal with the worst is to stay off the trails during their hatch season. I long ago discovered that the worst mosquito hatch in my favorite hiking area in the

Safer, Natural Insect Repellents

One advocate of the natural oils that can keep bugs at bay is Bridgitte Mars, the author of a new book on the raw vegetarian lifestyle called *Rawsome!* In an article titled "Bug Off! Natural Insect Repellents," she says: "Bug banishing essential oils include bay, bergamot, camphor, cardamom, cedarwood, cinnamon, clove, eucalyptus, geranium, lavender, lemon, lemon grass, orange, patchouli, pennyroyal, peppermint, rosemary, sage, tea tree and vetivert. . . . Pregnant women should use essential oils cautiously, and avoid the use of pennyroyal."

Some of those sound rather appetizing, don't they? The method she suggests is to apply the oils to your pulse points every hour or so. Bridgitte is also one of the advocates of garlic: "take three or four garlic capsules a day to make you an unappetizing target for blood-sucking bugs." Another repellent she suggests ingesting is vitamin B1, which "creates a smell that many bugs don't like."

Then there are those things she suggests we not ingest. "Avoid consuming sugar, alcohol, tropical fruits and juices—they'll make you more appealing targets."

Bridgitte can be contacted at bridgitte@indra.com.

Adirondack Mountains was the third week of May. So I planned my hikes before or after that time. Blackflies in the Catskills are at their worst in late July and early August, a good time for me to hike elsewhere. In Wyoming's Wind River Mountains, I suffered a robust hatch of mosquitoes in late June.

So when planning your trip, find out as best you can about what the worst insect seasons are for the area. This is usually not difficult. Check with park or forest rangers, or even local businesspeople near the area.

Regardless of when you go hiking, though, by all means take along bug dope. The most effective brands contain DEET. Look for it on the labels of the bug dope you buy. There are those who claim the harmful effects of DEET are not worth its repellency. And they advocate repellents such as citronella.

As we know, mosquitoes can carry some dread diseases—typhoid and West Nile, for example—which you want to protect against.

Something else worth mentioning about insect repellents: Various brands seem to have different effectiveness for different people. It is good idea to take along a few different kinds on family hikes. One of my daughters, Kate, seems to attract blackflies like sugar attracts ants. Another of my daughters seems to attract mosquitoes. I must have something odious in my blood that mostly frightens away these pesky critters.

Speaking of odious odors, I have been told that garlic works even better than bug dope. They say that if you chew a couple of garlic tablets a day for a while before leaving on a hike, it helps reduce the attraction of bugs to you. It's certainly worth a try, if your garlic doesn't drive away your friends as well.

There are some precautions that you can also take besides bug dope that can make your trip more enjoyably bug-free.

Wear long-sleeved shirts and long, loose-fitting pants. Tuck your cuffs into the tops of your socks. The pesky insects come out in fuller strength at dusk, so your tent may be the last resort to be free of them. Be sure you keep the tent well zipped when not using it, and unzip it only long enough to quickly get inside. In bug season, it is not a bad idea to spray some insect repellent on the tent fly and window mesh when you set up the tent.

TICKS

These critters don't sting. They just burrow in. And they are far more dangerous than the biters. They can carry Rocky Mountain spotted fever and Lyme disease.

Ticks are picked up by walking through brush or grasses, where they attach to your clothes. Best way to protect yourself from ticks is to wear long-sleeved shirts and long pants, tucked into the tops of your socks. Spray insect repellent on your clothes as well. There is also a tick repellent that can be sprayed on clothes. But caution: Do not spray it on bare skin—your own or others'.

Check your body as often as you can, especially hairy parts, which is where ticks like to burrow in. When you find one, grasp it with tweezers near its mouth and pull it gently out, being careful not to leave its head burrowed beneath your skin. Applying a dab of either bug dope or your stove fuel to the tick before trying to extract it will help free its grip on your skin.

Lyme disease has been contracted in virtually every part of the United States. Rocky Mountain spotted fever, though, despite its name, is most common in the East. The symptoms of these tick-borne diseases show up from two days to a month after contact. Symptoms of Lyme disease are usually a red rash or flulike symptoms—achy muscles, fatigue, nausea, and fever. Rocky Mountain spotted fever symptoms can also include a fever accompanied by a rash on hands and feet that spreads upward.

If anything at all suspicious appears after a hike in the woods, it is always best to have it checked out by your doctor.

One time while camped on a section of the Appalachian Trail in Pennsylvania, I apparently set up my tent in the midst of some sort of insect that produced a burning rash all over my legs and torso, with weeping blisters similar to poison ivy. But even my doctor could not identify its source. He gave me a salve and a pill and told me to get lots of rest. And the rash did eventually clear up.

SPIDERS

The two most common poisonous spiders you may encounter in the backcountry are the black widow and the brown recluse.

The female black widow is the one that bites and has a shiny black, spherical body with a red hourglass mark on the belly. The bite looks like a small pinprick. It can develop into severe pain and cramps within two to three hours. If bitten, take a painkiller if you have one, and sit it out as quietly as possible.

Treatment after You've Been Bitten by an Insect

A company that claims to be "the leading producer of insect repellent and insect bite products" is Tender Corporation in Littleton, New Hampshire. It produces Bens, Natrapel, and Family Medic. Its website is www.tendercorp.com, where it offers a good bit of detailed information on insect bites and treatment. It has more than you will ever want to know about West Nile virus, for example. Worth a visit.

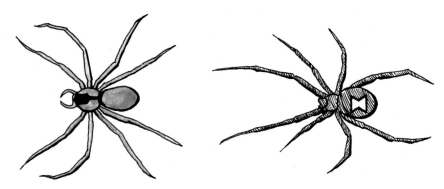

The two venomous spiders you may find in the backcountry are the brown recluse and the black widow. The brown recluse ranges in size from ¼ to ¾ of an inch and is generally about a fourth the size of a black widow. It is brown and can be distinguished by the violin shape on its body.

The female black widow is shiny black with a red hourglass on its belly. Its legs stretch out from 1 1/16 to 1½ inches. The male is smaller and less distinct, but harmless. For more details in identifying all venomous spiders in your area go to www.termite.com, where you can request a free spider identification chart, which also includes information on spider bite first aid.

The brown recluse has a small brown body with a violin-shaped mark on the belly. Its bites are painless. Symptoms do not occur for hours, possibly not until days later. Ulcerated skin and fevers are the telltale symptoms. This is a more serious bite that can have serious consequences if not treated by a doctor within a day or so of noticing the symptoms.

The spiders are most likely to be found in outhouses or when gathering wood on the trail. Don't poke your fingers in nooks or crannies. And above all, shake out your boots before putting them on. Keep the tent tightly zipped. And shake out your sleeping bag before crawling into it.

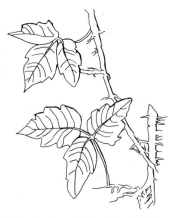

Poison ivy has distinct three-leaf clusters.

POISON IVY, OAK, AND SUMAC: "LEAVES OF THREE, LET IT BE"

Learn to identify the three-leaved plants before starting backpacking. You'll have a high likelihood of running into poison ivy or poison oak unless you are hiking in Alaska, Hawaii, or Nevada. California has no poison ivy but lots of poison oak. All other states have plenty of both.

Poison sumac is found only in the swampier areas of the East and is not so likely to be contacted while hiking on trails, for it is a high, bushlike tree with its leaves higher from the ground.

All three contain urushiol, which is a potent allergen, a tiny drop of which can cause a rash on most people. You get exposed to the allergen by touching leaves, stems, or roots. It cannot be blown about in the air.

Should you burn poison ivy in a fire, however, the smoke can carry its urushiol juices, which will attack your skin very severely. Beware of vines growing on firewood that you put into a fire. The vines very likely could be poison ivy. It's difficult to tell without its leaves attached. If in doubt, don't burn the vines. Pull them off with gloved hands. Better still, don't burn the wood.

Poison ivy, oak, and sumac can also be carried on your clothes if you brush against the vines along the trails. Be especially careful of spreading poison ivy to yourself and others after a hike in poison ivy country. If in doubt, clean your clothes the best you can. Wash the washables in a washer, and sponge down with soapy water those garments that can't be tossed in the washer, such as raingear and boots.

The moment you believe you have contacted one of these plants, wash your hands, arms, and other parts of the body that may have been in contact with the plant, using strong soap and water. There is another school of thought among some physicians that washing with soap and water may spread the urushiol oil. This view is propounded by William Epstein, professor of dermatology at University of California, on the website http://pediatrics.about.com/. He advocates washing exposed skin first with rubbing

Poison oak has small oaklike leaves, often reddish in color.

Poison sumac has distinct red berry clusters and is most often found in swampy areas.

How Outdoors Professionals Deal with Poison Ivy, Oak, and Sumac

People who work regularly in the outdoors have long known how to protect themselves from poison ivy, oak, and sumac, as well as how to treat their rashes or insect bites should they get nailed.

They pretty much all know about a small Oregon company, TechLab, which accidentally got into what it calls "the itch niche" a few decades back. TechLab has a particularly good product to use for washing away toxic oils once you have come in contact with any of the poison plants—ivy, oak, or sumac.

The company markets its products primarily for outdoors workers who come into contact with these plants most often—foresters, surveyors, firefighters, utility and telephone line workers. But today its main product, Tecnu, is sold in major drugstore chains. The company has an interesting history and line of products useful for plant-caused irritations as well as insect bites. Visit www.techlabinc.com.

Your Best Defense against Pesky Insects, Spiders, and Poison Plants

- Find out which bugs are likely to be out in the seasons you plan to hike in an area.
- Don't place your hands or feet underneath logs, rocks, bushes, or even your tent without having a careful look.
- Wear a long-sleeved shirt and long pants, snug at wrists and ankles. Wear heavy socks and a wide-brimmed hat.
- Avoid scented soaps, shampoos, cosmetics, lotions, and hair sprays.
- Avoid wearing shiny jewelry and buckles.
- Cover exposed areas of your body with insect repellent. Reapply often, especially when perspiring. DEET is the most reliable repellent, *but do not use on children.* Citronella is an acceptable, natural alternative repellent.
- Apply insect repellent to clothing, pack, and tent.
- Use tent with sewn-in floor and mosquito netting on doors and windows. And keep openings zippered tight at all times.
- Keep camp free of garbage and debris, and especially strong-scented foods.
- Don't walk about camp in your bare feet.

alcohol, then with clear water, then washing with soap and water. This may not be possible on the trail unless you carry rubbing alcohol with you, and I've hiked with folks who carry a small plastic container of it that they use to wipe down their feet after a hot day's hike. But there is a caution with this method. Unless you know for sure that you will not be anywhere near poison ivy thereafter, you may be more sensitive to contact with it. The alcohol leaves the skin yet more sensitive to catching poison ivy.

For decades, woodsmen and foresters have washed with soap and water. And most Boy Scouts still do. David Fairbanks, medical director of the Goshen Scout Reservation, advocates the old standby, washing affected areas with soap and water within fifteen minutes of contact. Take your pick.

But there are also other choices. Several products on the market today claim to be more effective than soap in removing the toxic oils once you have had contact with the poison plant. I have had personal experience with Tecnu, the one that has been around the longest.

Tecnu is a particularly effective product for washing both body and clothes after exposure. Tecnu is sold in major drugstores and is so effective that I keep a bottle in our home all the time. Its makers say it removes poison oils that cause rash and itching, stops irritants from spreading, and decontaminates clothing and tools.

Should you get a poison ivy or oak rash, do not scratch it. You may cause infection. Washing with cold salt water and cool salt water baths will provide relief from the itching. There are over-the-counter cortisone creams that are also palliatives. Your druggist can likely give you other suggestions for treating the rash. In less than two weeks, though, it will usually have run its natural course and leave you healed, unless you happen to be one of those supersensitive types who get more severe reactions.

15

Getting the Most from Your Trail Photography

A few simple photography tricks of the trail can turn snapshots into photographic triumphs for even a rank amateur with a throwaway supermarket camera. I've taught outdoor photography to people who've paid thousands of dollars for a week's photographic field trip. All the basics taught on these trips are yours for a quick perusal of this one chapter.

There are two parts to this chapter: one for the basics of hiking photography, and another for those who want to further refine their trail photography. First some preliminaries.

FUNDAMENTAL PRINCIPLES

The fundamental principles sound so simple, easy, and so, so obvious—it is easy to overlook them. But these few tricks of the trail are what made the difference to me when it came to buying a story for use in *Backpacker* magazine. They require a bit of pretrip planning. But not a lot.

Digital versus Conventional Film Cameras

There are some great advantages to using digital cameras. You get to see immediate results, you can take pictures in a wider variety of light conditions without changing film, and you need not carry a lot of film canisters.

Disadvantages: the extra effort it takes to sort through your eventual photographic take and begin selecting the ones you want to print to show your family and friends.

I'm partial to film for the tangible results of holding all the prints in hand when I sort through the take after the hike.

What Type of Film to Take

Unless you have good reason to do otherwise, take ISO 200 film for the outdoors. The film boxes of all brands are plainly marked for this.

Five Hints that Can Turn Snapshots into Prize Winners

Whatever I have to say about the five basics, though, will apply no matter what type of film you use or even if your camera is digital. These five hints were even found by a CBS television journalist to be useful on one of my field trips.

Bill Holman, Selway-Bitterroot, Idaho.

1. Take Two to Three Times More Film Than You Ordinarily Take on a Hike

Film is cheap compared with the cost of your backpacking trip, no matter how inexpensively you go. Don't stint. Take three times as much film as you planned to take. I'll tell you why in a moment.

When we see a great photograph by Ansel Adams, Galen Rowell, Phil Hyde, or other fine outdoors photographers, we wonder how in the world they managed to capture such magnificent beauty. And in a classroom analysis, it's likely to revolve around their greater sense of esthetics.

I used to think this way, too, until I ran a story about Ansel Adams in an early issue of *Backpacker.* His representative gave us a wide assortment of photos to select from

Shooting photos with my Nikkormat in Grand Canyon.

to accompany our article. They were mostly on 35-millimeter contact sheets, where the photos on a full roll of film are printed on an 8-by-10 sheet of photographic paper.

What was immediately evident was the huge number of shots on each contact sheet that were mediocre at best and poor at worst, with one great photo amongst them. I came to a very pedestrian conclusion—that Adams routinely took thirty-six photos to get one good one.

It was simple, too simple, really. It deflated the esthetic sensitivity theory considerably. Not that great photographers don't have a great eye for a photo. They do. But like a concert violinist practicing the same tune over and over again, so, too, the fine photographer must shoot pictures over and over again to get one good photo.

So why shouldn't we do the same? You can improve your chances of getting good photos of your next backpacking trip by taking more shots than you have in the past. Just keep in mind Ansel Adams shot photos at a thirty-six–to–one ratio.

2. Take a Lot of Your Photos at the Best Times of Day

You won't always have the opportunity to take advantage of the light at the best time of day to photograph. However, often the best camp photos are available at those times—morning and late afternoon giving the best light. I am sure there are those professionals who can explain why this is so. Colors and hues seem to be more vivid at these times.

And since we're usually cooking, eating, breaking camp, or setting it up at those times, we've generally got our minds too occupied with these activities to take time for photographs. If you can break away to get some shots, these are likely to be the most memorable of your trip.

Yes, you will no doubt irritate your fellow hikers by taking photos during these times. So warn them in advance, and don't do it every day of the trip. Discretion, as you know, is the better part of . . .

3. Getting People in Your Scenes Guarantees Interesting Photos

Have you ever returned from a hike with dozens of photos of beautiful scenes to see your own mother yawn after seeing just four or five of them? Well, you know what I mean.

One way to get Mother to take a look at the sixth scenic shot and eagerly ask to see the next is to use a simple trick of the trail.

Dave Sumner, Rocky Mountain National Park, Colorado.

Dave Sumner, Maroon Bell Wilderness, Colorado.

Put people in every one of even the best scenery photos on your trip. And most especially, get yourself in as many of these shots as possible. It takes more effort than just pointing and shooting. But it's well worth it. Try it and see for yourself.

There is a bit of finesse required for this type of photography, to be sure. But not as much as you may expect. To reduce irritating your hiking companion, give advance notice of what you want to do. But at the site, try a little courtesy.

Say to the person, "You know, this is such an impressive view of the scene out there. But even better with you in it. Mind if I take one with you standing there?" Now, take your time. Get a good angle. Take three or four shots from slightly different points of view. Then it isn't difficult to ask your hiking partner, "Would you take one of me in that same spot? It's such a great shot that I'd love to remember myself right there in the scene."

Include people in your photos. They give perspective to the size and distance of objects. Do you see the string of hikers atop the mountain ridge?

Opposite: *People in your photos also make scenes more interesting. Compare these landscape photos to the same scenes with people in the photos.*

You can even do this with total strangers if you should meet one at some of these scenic spots along the trail. On a recent hike along a busy corridor trail in Grand Canyon, someone asked me to take her photo at this breathtakingly grand scene. I did, of course. And while I was taking it, the next hikers had to wait a moment for me to shoot. They then asked if I would mind doing the same for them, which I obliged. Pretty soon I'd taken photos of almost a dozen groups of hikers. We all had a good laugh about it.

The worst that has ever happened to me is that the stranger was too shy to want his picture taken and couldn't figure out how to use my camera. And, oh yes, I've often gotten photos back from the finisher with my feet cut off at the ankles, or more often, the framing of the shot was just not what I had in mind when I asked someone to snap the shutter. But still, they were more interesting than just plain scenery photos.

4. Silhouette Your People against a Contrasting Background
This seems only too obvious when you're at a viewpoint that overlooks a vast mountain horizon. Yet it is often missed because we fail to simply change the angle slightly. Get the photographic angle that silhouettes the person against the sky, for example, so that the figure in your photo stands out in contrast against it.

There are a variety of ways to do this. Depending on the situation, you can get the person in the bright sunshine silhouetted against a dark shadow on the wall of a canyon or against a dark forest background. Check the angle for the best way to get the figure to stand out against the background.

One sure way of getting the person to stand out from the background is with the color of the clothing. I got into the habit of wearing a bright red shirt so that, with my red pack, I stood out against the contrasting dark green forests when I did most of my hiking in the woodlands of the Northeast.

I learned this trick from a Vermont photographer whose photos often appeared on calendars. He carried a red shirt and a bright red felt hat in the trunk of his car with his

Take Extra Batteries for Digital Cameras

For film cameras, it is advisable to carry lots of extra film. With digital, it is more important to carry extra batteries. The ones that come with the camera last only about a couple of hours and are expensive. Furthermore, they are seldom found on the racks of drugstores on the road. Best to plan ahead.

And, of course, take along extra memory cards. Not easy to find when you are ten miles from the trailhead!

Not only is it difficult to find the batteries at photo retail shops, but price may be a consideration for you. Best to go online well in advance of your trip and be sure you have what you want.

Most batteries have to be bought direct from camera manufacturers' sites, such as www.canoncompanystore.com or www.nikonmall.com. You may get good price results from www.amazon.com. Then there are third-party generic suppliers as well, such as www.delkin.com, that sell batteries for most camera brands at lower prices.

Silhouetting figures against a contrasting background gives very dramatic photos.

photographic gear, so that he could outfit an impromptu model he would persuade to pose for him in a scenic shot of a snowy Vermont village, for instance. A little pretrip planning of your clothing can prove useful in your photographs.

5. Take the Same Photo Several Times Using Different Exposures

Professional photographers usually "bracket" their shots, taking three to five shots of the same scene to be sure they have a variety of color densities of their finished photos from which to choose. It is surprising what a difference these bracketed exposures can make.

This is not as easy as it sounds. Many autoexposure cameras have an override feature that enables you to manually adjust the exposure, by changing either the shutter speed or the lens aperture opening. If so, you are in business. If in doubt, check the operating manual that came with your camera.

If you can, and it is a particularly impressive picture you want to take, then take three to five photos of the scene. Take the first one with the "correct" exposure your meter tells you to use. Then move either the shutter speed or the aperture opening one stop to underexpose the photo, and snap the shutter at this exposure. Do the same photo again, but change the exposure in the opposite direction, overexposing one stop. Do the same, but now two stops under and two stops overexposing.

You will be surprised at the quality of your photos you have to choose from when you get your take back from the photo finisher.

Bracketing is not as important with digital cameras, as they have wider exposure latitudes.

Getting Better Wildflower Shots

Get low, and try to silhouette the flowers against the sky with the sun coming over your shoulder onto the face of the flowers. When you see your photos after your trip, you'll feel it was well worth the grubby elbows and shirtfront to get them.

Try to set your flowers or other feature of your photo off in color contrast to the surrounding background. JIM BARKER

HOW TO REFINE YOUR TRAIL PHOTOGRAPHY

Decide before your trip what type of photos you intend to take. Will they be mostly camp and scenic shots? Or do you want to focus on wildflowers? How interested are you in taking photos of wildlife?

Not that you can't take several types of photos on the same trip. But since it takes time to get decent photos, it really is rare to get many types on the same trip. The main reason for deciding in advance is to determine the kind of lenses you will carry.

What Lenses Should You Take?

There have been times when I've packed a 200-millimeter lens to photograph wildlife. Other times I've taken a 55-millimeter for close-ups of flowers. For people shots in camp I prefer a 70- to 85-millimeter lens. It enables me to get close-ups of people without getting in their faces. For trails in forests or tight canyons, its better to have a wider-angle lens, like a 28- to 35-millimeter.

I eventually ended up carrying a cumbersome zoom lens, 35- to 70-millimeter, which provides ideal capabilities for 90 percent of the shooting I like to do. The drawback, of course, is the weight and bulk of the camera and lens. Nonetheless, it is so versatile without having to change lenses that I even take it on my solo hikes.

Positioning a figure in sunlight, with a color of clothing that contrasts against the background, makes the scene more visually appealing.

There are other times I've gone out strictly to shoot alpine wildflowers. It's one of my favorite types of trail photography. I've spent hundreds of hours on hikes with my friend Dave Sumner, after setting up a camp in the Fravert Basin high in a meadow on a shoulder of Colorado's South Maroon Peak, crawling around on my belly with my 55-millimeter lens, photographing alpine wildflowers—paintbrush, columbine, alpine sunflower, and elephant head in fullest bloom.

Getting the Right Exposure

My good friend Jim Kern does it all by simply visually estimating the exposure for each shot. He has been shooting outdoors photographs professionally for several decades for *National Geographic, Audubon* magazine, and the like. His eye is no doubt far more accurate than his light meter. Jim uses Kodak-32 slide film almost exclusively. He knows its characteristics so well that he rarely ever misses.

This is not to knock light meters. They do have their immense value, especially for those of us who are not as experienced as Jim. It is useful, however, to know the limitations of the light meter and how it works.

Try this. On a bright, sunny day, point your camera—I am presuming you have a through-the-lens light meter—at the sky,

I would never be on the trail without my 35-millimeter Leica camera with Fuji film.

—*Steve Bridgehouse, backcountry ranger, Natural Bridges National Monument, southeast Utah*

Jim Kern takes a nature shot on a December hike in Grand Canyon.

and note the reading of what f-stop it is suggesting at what shutter speed. Then point the camera at the darkest part of the scene you are about to photograph and see what readings it gives you for this. Notice the difference?

The difference is because the film requires a lower light exposure for the bright area and a greater light exposure for the darker area. Your light meter tries to mediate the difference, taking an average of the brightest part and the darkest portions of the scene you are pointing the camera at. And the average exposure is not exactly what you may want in a particular photograph.

The early morning at the bottom of Grand Canyon, for example, before the sun comes up over the canyon rim, is a magnificent time of day for photographs. But you really do have to adjust for this average. If you expose for the brightest part of the scene—say, the light striking the top of the canyon walls above you—the rest of the canyon will fall into pitch dark shadow. It is a pleasing photographic effect. But if you expose for the shadows, the top of the canyon walls in the sunlight will wash out as if in angelic paradise.

Because the light meter gives you average readings, professionals bracket their shots, using different exposures for the same scene.

Take several shots of any scene that is particularly interesting to you, not just from various angles, but from entirely different perspectives as well. These two photos were taken from outside and inside the ruins of Ben Beamer's cabin at the confluence of the Little Colorado and Colorado Rivers at the bottom of Grand Canyon.

Get Yourself in Your Photos

Take a couple or more self-timer shots to avoid getting shots of your back with the sole of your boot in the air. Know what I mean?

Adjusting for Neutral Gray

Now, there is another average that your light meter is assuming as well. Its standard optimum exposure is based upon a color called neutral gray. This is a standard color value. If you want to get technical, you can find a colored piece of cardboard called a neutral gray card. Point your light meter at the card, and it will give you the optimum exposure readings for that particular light condition.

To save the time and extra nuisance of carrying a neutral gray card, pros know that the palm of the hand will do the trick just as well. They hold up one hand with the palm facing the light meter. This gives them the same value as the neutral gray card. So using the neutral gray palm of your hand, you can get an accurate optimum exposure reading for the scene you are going to shoot.

Here's the way to do it: Decide what it is you want to stand out in your photo of a scene. If it's in the shade, then hold your hand open in the shade with the palm toward your camera, focus your light meter upon it, and take the reading. To optimize the average of a scene that has both sunlight and shadow, take two readings, one with your hand in the sunlight, and the other with it in the shadow. Now decide whether you want to average your exposure toward the sunniest or the most shadowy parts of the scene. Again, this is a perfect reason why it is wise to bracket your shots. If you have these extreme exposure readings, try taking a shot with the highest exposure readings as well as one with the lowest readings. Then take another somewhere in between the extremes. And see what kinds of photos you get.

Keep a Notebook of Your Shots

If you want to refine your photography, take along a small pocket notebook. Number your rolls of film. Head a page of your notebook with the number of the roll as well as its type and ISO rating. Then list the f-stop and shutter speed of each shot you take on that roll.

This will give you a log of how you obtained the quality of the better photographs that come back from the finisher.

Can You Use Tripods on the Trail?

Hikers may carry any kind of tripod on the trail, even a cumbersome, heavy tripod for a large-format view camera. Dave Sumner and I spent several days one January at a camp in

Landscape photographs can often be enhanced by including figures that give the scene a sense of perspective.

William Kemsley Jr., San Juan Mountains, Colorado.

Colorado's Mosquito Mountains. We'd skied in with clothing, gear, and food for five days at below-zero weather. Dave was on a professional photography trip.

Dave carried not only a Hasselblad and a Nikon with extra lenses, but also a 4x5 Linhof field camera with film holders, extra lenses, and all the accessories. Don't ask how he managed all that weight. I can only confess that I didn't carry any extra weight except a few candy bars.

The point is that Dave also had a heavy-duty tripod upon which he could mount his field camera. That is extreme, of course, but I've seen many backpackers carrying rather sturdy tripods strapped to the outside of their packs.

My preference is to go light, with one of those little backpacking tripods you can get at a sporting-goods store like REI for about $10 to $25. The reason I carry one is for self-timer photos of myself. For a longer hike with the family, it's nice to have shots of yourself in the family group.

Section Four
RISKS ON THE TRAIL

It's the cussedest land that I know;
From the big, dizzy mountains that screen it
  To the deep, deathlike valleys below.
Some say God was tired when he made it,
  Some say it's fine land to shun;
Maybe; but there's some as would trade it
  For no land on earth—and I'm one.

—from "Spell of the Yukon," by Robert Service

As the weather moved in, these hikers dropped off the ridge of Mount Katahdin in Maine to a safer position from possible lightning strikes.

16

Dangers from the Weather

Most newcomers fear snakes and bears, yet weather presents far greater dangers—from dehydration, heatstroke, hypothermia, hyponatremia, and lightning—than all other hiking risks. More hikers die from hypothermia alone than all other causes combined. Yet hypothermia is the one risk over which hikers have most control.

DANGERS FROM COLD WEATHER
There are two main types of cold-weather risks: freezing and hypothermia.

Frostbite and Freezing
Frostbite is more easily detected in its initial stages, because the biting cold penetrates the skin's sensibility, becoming noticeably painful. It attacks exposed parts of the body—ears, nose, cheeks, chin, fingers, toes. It is actually the freezing of the outer layers of the skin from exposure to cold temperatures and chilling winds. But the external factors are not the only things contributing to frostbite. A lot depends upon the physical condition of the body. You are far more susceptible to frostbite when exhausted and when in need of heat-producing foods.

For hikers, the most likely situation that will put you at risk of frostbite is when there is a sudden inclement change in the weather, such as a sudden sleet and snowstorm at higher altitudes in summer when you are not prepared for it. Prevention of frostbite is simple common sense: Cover the exposed parts of your body with warmer clothing. The cure is more demanding.

Symptoms
Frostbite can progress from its milder forms to an irreversible injury, which in its extreme form can mean amputation as its only remedy. Frostbite progresses from a biting cold feeling to numbness of the affected area, which then loses all feeling. As the chill continues, the affected area may begin to actually feel warm. This is an alarming symptom suggesting that the frostbite has penetrated to deeper, more dangerous levels.

Treatment
Treatment depends upon how far the frostbite has progressed. If it is early-stage frostbite, the afflicted area should be warmed as quickly and gently as possible. Frostbitten cheeks, nose, or ears can be cupped by warm hands and covered against further exposure. Frostbitten fingertips can be warmed by tucking them under your own bare

armpits. Toes can be warmed against another person's warm belly, then dressed in dry wool socks. Do not rub frostbitten areas; this may cause tissue damage.

At first the treatment will cause unpleasant tingling in the affected part, which may show purplish or mottled color as blood circulation is restored. The affected area may swell or even blister. Do not break the blister or tamper with the skin.

Though not a direct treatment for frostbite, it is also a good idea to drink warm fluids—tea, warm water, whatever is available. But avoid all alcoholic beverages.

Treatment of more severe frostbite—when tissue has already frozen—is a far more serious matter. Trying to rewarm frozen tissue on the trail is a dangerous thing and may cause complications later. It is far better to leave the frozen part alone until the victim can be moved to a place where rapid rewarming can be accomplished and medical attention obtained.

Hypothermia: The Sneaky Cold Killer

One October morning in dry, moderate fall weather, an eight-year-old boy went for a walk in the woods with his dog. He was wearing a cotton shirt, blue jeans, light jacket, and tennis shoes. His mother became concerned when he did not come home for lunch.

That afternoon, the weather deteriorated into a cold rain. And when he was still not home by 4 in the afternoon, his mother called for help to go looking for him. The search went on until dark, then with flashlights through the night in the rainy forest. At almost dawn, the searchers found the boy and his dog huddled together in a hollow by a tree stump. The dog was still alive, but the boy was dead. The newspapers said he died of exposure.

That word, *exposure,* is a vague term referring to a combination of conditions that lead to death—exhaustion, inadequate nourishment, dehydration, panic, fear, and hypothermia. It was the last of these that caused the boy's death. His body temperature had cooled to the extent that its normal metabolism broke down; his body lost more heat than it could replenish.

Basically, the human body is a highly efficient regulator of its own temperature. The foods we eat are digested and assimilated by the cells in the tissues throughout the body to produce both heat and energy. Carbohydrates such as sugar and starches produce heat and energy quickest. Proteins such as eggs, meat, and cheese do the same but produce heat and energy at a much slower rate. Fats produce twice as much heat and energy for the equivalent amount of weight as proteins and carbohydrates.

Muscular activity is another source of heat and energy. Exercise utilizes the foods stored in the body, turning them quickly into heat and energy. Bursts of quick activity can produce as much as ten times the heat and energy than sitting at rest.

The body produces heat by shivering, which is an involuntary rhythmic contraction of the muscles. It is an important lifesaving mechanism that kicks in whenever the body's temperature drops to a certain level of risk. Then there are outside sources of heat for the body—the sun, fire, and the warming effect of drinking hot liquids.

The body's core temperature is maintained at roughly ninety-nine degrees at all times. This varies somewhat among individuals but is consistent within each individual. The homeostasis function of the body metabolizes just the right amount of your

I never leave home without my L.L. Bean combination whistle-compass-waterproof match-box. This convenient little item provides three essentials in a compact, lightweight container, especially good for short trips in familiar terrain.

—Harry Frank, ski patrol director, Enchanted Forest, Carson National Forest, New Mexico

food intake to maintain your baseline temperature. The rest of the body's food intake is stored as fat until it is needed for conversion to maintain the bodily core temperature.

When the body begins to chill down, there is a constriction of the blood vessels in the outer extremities to keep the core temperature at its ninety-nine-degree base. When this gets out of balance, as in damp, cold weather, the temperatures of hands, feet, and head may drop to the sixties or even the fifties, as the body's way of preventing its internal core temperature from losing its warmth of ninety-nine degrees.

The body's heat is lost through the breath, perspiration, and radiation. This heat loss is exaggerated when the weather turns cold, wet, or windy and we don't do something to preserve the body's warmth, such as getting into a warm shelter, putting on warmer clothes, or in some other way protecting the body from losing this greater amount of heat.

Temperatures do not have to be freezing for the body's core to lose dangerous amounts of heat. More often than not, this occurs in fairly mild conditions. Temperatures that caused the boy's death described earlier never dropped below forty-five degrees.

Hypothermia occurs any time the body loses more heat than it is able to replenish. Heat loss occurs from strenuous backpacking, and the loss intensifies in lower temperatures and dampness for any period of time. It creeps up on a person quite deceptively. And the danger point can approach quite insidiously, without the hiker even realizing it.

Symptoms

Hypothermia is a very sneaky condition that brings the body's core temperature down to dangerously low levels. It happens in cool but not particularly cold temperatures, when you least expect it.

The symptoms of hypothermia proceed in a very orderly manner. Prevention comes through the knowledge of and sensitivity to its symptoms. This will enable you to do something to prevent further risk.

The first clue is that you begin shivering to such a degree that you cannot perform simple tasks such as striking a match, buttoning your clothes, or working a zipper.

As the body's core temperature drops a bit more, you shiver more vigorously and in waves. You feel lethargy, tiredness, and irritability. You begin to have difficulty speaking. Your coordination deteriorates. Your pace slows and you begin stumbling and fumbling, even falling. You may have difficulty carrying on the thread of a conversation.

An Almost Deadly Mistake

Hypothermia can sneak up on highly experienced hikers at unusual times. It happened to me on a fairly warm day in Grand Canyon. Had I not been hiking with friends who were able to help me, I hate to imagine a more embarrassing way for the founder of *Backpacker* magazine to die!

We were hiking to our camping destination for the night. It had been raining mildly most of the day. At midday it got so hot that I stopped to take off most of my clothes from underneath my raingear. It was good thinking, for I did not want them to get wet from my perspiration.

By the time we reached our destination, the temperatures had fallen, and I hadn't realized that my body was cooling down while I was hiking. In fact, I thought it was just comfortable.

But . . . we stopped at our campsite, and as I began pitching my tent I started to shiver. I could not find the tabs of my zippers, as my fingers were increasingly numb. I fumbled with the tent poles. Nothing seemed to be working right.

I did not even think of getting out more clothes to put on. Nor did I dig out my gloves. Dexterity of my fingers was simply gone, like stubs of wood dangling from my hands. This all occurred in less than fifteen minutes. The cold by then was cutting deeper. And the minutes seemed exceedingly long.

What was worse, I began to not care. After my friends had their tents up, they noticed I was still struggling halfheartedly with mine. One came over to help and in seconds had it up. He was then savvy enough to realize what was happening to me. Not wanting to embarrass me, he unstuffed my sleeping bag and laid it out for me. I managed to get out of my raingear and climb into it. Then the shaking became even more uncontrollable. I couldn't get warm.

Minutes later, my friends had their stove fired up and brought me a cup of hot Jell-O to drink. Then a cup of heavily sweetened hot tea. These went down with difficulty. But soon I could begin to feel the warmth inside me, though my body was still shaking. It took well over an hour for my body to feel comfortable. All this simply because I had been too foolish to pay attention to my body temperature as the afternoon cooled.

The temperatures that day were well above fifty degrees. It was raining, as I said. I had tired more than I realized from our eleven-mile backpack. Combine all of those, and we had this sick puppy suffering from hypothermia.

What was the lesson? I should have noticed the temperatures cooling in the afternoon and my body tiring, then put on warm clothes beneath my raingear sometime in midafternoon.

Don't dismiss this as a minor brush with fate just because I can chuckle about it now. My friends likely saved my life!

By this stage you should have tried to find help and a way to begin to warm up the body. If not and the condition progresses, your body temperature still dropping, you will exhibit irrational thinking with impaired judgment. When the symptoms get to the stage where you are shivering uncontrollably, lack coordination of fingers and limbs, and become unable to think properly, you are headed toward the last stages, which are collapse, coma, and death.

If the body's core temperature drops further, your muscles become rigid and you go into a zombielike stupor. The final stage is when you lose consciousness and die.

There are times when these stages progress quite rapidly. Someone who falls into cold water can drop to a dangerous level of hypothermia in a minute and a half and be dead in three minutes. Hikers have been known to progress from the onset of hypothermia to unconsciousness in less than thirty minutes.

Treatment
It is essential that any indications of hypothermia be treated quickly and aggressively. Three things are essential:
1. Prevent further loss of the body's heat. The first and most vital thing is to get the victim out of the wet and cold into some kind of shelter, however primitive, out of the wind, rain, and cold. If clothes are wet, get them off and dress the victim in dry clothes.
2. Warm the body from the outside. Place the victim in a prewarmed sleeping bag. If the chilling is deep, then get other companions to lie next to the victim, being sure that there is ample insulation both beneath and above the sleeping bag.
3. Have the victim drink hot fluids as much as possible—soups, tea, hot water. Get the victim to eat high-carbohydrate foods such as candies, dried fruits, or any other foods with a high content of sugars or starches.

Preventing Hypothermia
For starters, let's keep in mind that it is easier to keep warm than it is to warm up once you get cold. So being sensitive to your body's warmth is key to keeping safe on the trail.
- Be prepared to put on or take off clothes as temperatures change. It may seem bothersome, but consider the consequences of not taking the trouble to do so.
- Do not let your clothes get wet from perspiration or rain.
- Slip on a sweater or jacket whenever you stop for a rest.
- Snack often on the trail, particularly with high-carb candies, PowerBars, or gorp.
- Drink more often than you think you need to.
- Wear a warm hat. Put on gloves when temperatures drop.
- Wear clothes that will keep you warm when wet—wool or polyester, not cotton.

DANGERS FROM THE HEAT
There are four types of problems that can arise when hiking in hot weather: muscle cramps, heat exhaustion, hyponatremia, and heatstroke. Most of these can be avoided by cooling the body, eating salty foods, and drinking greater amounts of water.

The body's mechanics are such that we give off two to three quarts of water a day. Half evaporates through pores and breath; the other half is lost through urine. In drier desert hiking, this increases fourfold; the body giving off eight to twelve quarts a day. If this isn't replaced, it causes the blood to thicken abnormally. And hence the problems.

But while the body is giving off this excess moisture, it is also giving off excessive quantities of needed body salts. Drinking plenty of water is the quickest, easiest

Preventing Heat Exhaustion, Heatstroke, and Hyponatremia

The way to avoid all of these heat disorders is simply to stay as cool as possible while hiking, drink at least a half to one quart of water every hour, and eat salty foods as often as you drink.

1. It is best to carry your bottle in your hand and drink frequent small quantities, at least a half to one quart per hour. This is an excellent place to use bladder drinking systems.
2. Eat as often as you drink. Nibbles of a salty snack are essential to avoid both heat exhaustion and hyponatremia.
3. Take frequent rests in the shade if at all possible.
4. Avoid hiking at midday between the hours of 10 A.M. and 4:00 P.M. when temperatures are in the high nineties or above.
5. When you pass streams or ponds, wet your body down. Wet your clothes so that you can walk wet to cool your body.
6. Avoid caffeine and alcohol. They increase your kidneys' loss of fluids.
7. Should you notice any signs of heat exhaustion or heatstroke, stop immediately to rest and drink some more. Pour cool water over the body to bring down temperatures. If possible, immerse the body, especially the head and neck, in a stream or pond.

measure to prevent heat exhaustion and heatstroke. But the salts must also be replaced to avoid hyponatremia. Replace them by eating every time you drink, preferably some salty snacks.

Dr. Tom Myers, the park physician at Grand Canyon from 1990 to 2000, recently instructed leaders of group trips on how to protect their clients against hyponatremia. Contrary to advertised claims, he told them not to rely upon power drinks alone for the source of salt to prevent hyponatremia. He advised that the best preventive is simply to eat salty foods and avoid drinking too much water. When it is suspected that a person has been stricken by mild to moderate hyponatremia as a result of inadequate salt intake and relative overdrinking of water, Myers advises to take in salt from salty foods, restrict further fluid intake, and avoid any use of the power drinks at this point.

I opt for Myers's view and say that the way to avoid hyponatremia is to consume salty snacks at every rest stop in desert and canyon hiking and not depend upon consuming power drinks alone. After all, it was in Grand Canyon that hikers were first diagnosed as suffering from hyponatremia. Previously these symptoms may have been misdiagnosed as dehydration and possibly treated the opposite from how they should have been treated.

Heat Exhaustion

Perspiration and moisture dispersion through breathing and bodily evaporation is the body's way of cooling itself down.

When the body is unable to dispose of sufficient amounts of heat, it develops heat exhaustion. This occurs in hotter temperatures, especially when you are working up a strong sweat, and even more so if it is very humid. Heat exhaustion can even develop slowly over several days of hiking in intense heat.

Symptoms

Dehydration from intense sweating can cause heat exhaustion. It can occur suddenly or develop slowly over a period of several days. Hiking in hot weather causes the body to lose one to two quarts of moisture an hour through perspiration, urination and evaporation. Heat exhaustion symptoms are extra tiredness, weakness, and malaise. You begin to feel awful and sweat even when you have stopped to rest. You develop a pale face, nausea, cool and moist skin, headache, and cramps.

Treatment

Immediately have the victim do whatever possible to cool the body's temperature down, such as the following:
1. Get into the shade and rest there.
2. Drink lots of water.
3. Eat quick-energy foods.
4. Pour water over the head and neck; wet the clothes if possible.

Heatstroke

Heatstroke is far more serious than heat exhaustion and comes on a lot faster. This life-threatening emergency results from the body's heat-regulating mechanism getting overwhelmed by too much bodily exertion and too much external heat. It is aggravated by lack of sufficient water consumption. This condition is highly dangerous and must be treated at once.

Symptoms

First signs are that breathing becomes difficult and you begin to feel tired. You experience shortness of breath, and muscles feel as though they are weakened and on fire. If it develops further, you may experience muscle cramps, dizziness, diarrhea, and nausea, and your vision may become blurred. As your condition worsens, you could stop sweating and your skin gets dry. A sure sign of serious heatstroke is the deterioration of mental functions—confusion, delirium, ataxia. You could even lose consciousness. The victim may exhibit a flushed face, dry skin, weak and rapid pulse, high body temperature, poor judgment and an inability to cope, and even unconsciousness in advanced states.

Treatment

It is essential that the victim get medical help and be cooled as quickly as possible.
1. Send someone for help while you cool the victim down.
2. Get the victim into a cool, shaded spot.
3. Pour water on the victim's head and torso continuously.
4. Fan to create evaporation to help cooling.
5. It is essential to get the victim evacuated to a medical facility as quickly as possible.

Hyponatremia

In recent decades, we've been warned about taking in too much sodium in our diets. This came about mainly because until then, most foods were heavily salted, and a link between sodium and high blood pressure was discovered. Suddenly the words "sodium-free" and "low-sodium" began to appear on food packages everywhere.

To some degree, this sodium-free diet was useful inasmuch as many diseases are aggravated by excessive intake of salts. And because of their health, many Americans have to watch the amount of sodium in their diets.

The sodium-free food fad has negative consequences, however. Some amount of sodium is required for normal body functions, for the sodium in the body is dissipated through perspiration and urination. The reduction of the body's sodium has not been particularly noticed in normal, everyday activity, since the body has a remarkable homeostasis mechanism that adjusts to retain needed minerals under normal conditions.

Press the body to greater limits, though, and the homeostasis mechanism is overridden. Extra exertion in particularly hot weather conditions can readily disturb the normal sodium-water balance of the body. The result can be an attack of hyponatremia. This is a serious, life-threatening disorder. If not caught and corrected in time, hyponatremia can lead to death.

One commercial group backpacking leader, Marjorie Woodruff, told me that of all the backpackers she has taken on hikes, the single most serious health threat she has dealt with was three cases of hyponatremia.

Until recently, this was not recognized as a separate disorder in the backcountry. The first few cases diagnosed as such were reported in 1994 in the journal *Wilderness and Environmental Medicine* (www.wemjournal.org.) A thorough report on salt and the athlete can be viewed free at www.rice.edu/~jenky/sports/salt.html.

I have purposely avoided using the word *electrolyte*. It is not clear to me what people mean by that word and whether it includes sodium, which is dissipated in perspiration and urine and must be replaced by food or drink. According to Webster's Collegiate Dictionary, an electrolyte is "any substance which when dissolved in suitable liquid dissociates into ions and thus renders the liquid electrically conducting." Salt contains both sodium and chlorides but is a good source of sodium.

The www.rice.edu website mentioned above says that one loses about two to three grams of sodium per hour of strenuous athletic exercise and gives a comparative list of products, their salt content, and the amount you need to ingest to replace this amount of sodium. It takes about one to one and a half gallons of Gatorade, for example, to replace this amount of sodium, but it takes only forty to sixty baked Rold Gold hard sourdough pretzels to do the same!

Symptoms

This physical disorder resembles the early symptoms of heat exhaustion. It is caused by low sodium in the blood as a result of drinking too much water without also eating salty foods. Its symptoms ought to be compared with those for heat exhaustion to distinguish them from one another. They include nausea, vomiting, an altered mental state, and frequent urination.

Warning! Sports Drinks Alone Will Not Prevent Hyponatremia

Dr. Tom Myers, Grand Canyon National Park physician, 1990–2000

I have seen plenty of people who believed a bladder bag filled with power drink was an answer to all electrolytes needed in desert hiking. In fact, I believe strongly that sports drinks and their related ads, which became the vogue in the late 1980s and early 1990s, have been a great contributor to the hyponatremia problem in Grand Canyon.

It was essentially an undocumented problem in the 1980s, but I saw hundreds of cases through the 1990s, and nearly 40 percent of heat-related illness in Grand Canyon are now from hyponatremia.

Tom Myers, MD, Grand Canyon National Park physician since 1990 and coauthor with Mike Ghiglieri of Over the Edge: Death in Grand Canyon. ELIAS BUTLER

The problem is that for best taste the maximum tolerable levels of salt in sports drinks is only about <20 mEq/liter of sodium. (For example, in Gatorade there is only 18.7 mEq/liter of sodium.) In sweat, one loses 20 to 60 mEq/liter of sodium in a day of hiking. In urine, the losses are even higher, 75 to 116 mEq/liter. Combined, the losses can be substantial. This is especially true for unacclimated people, who lose up to ten times the sodium in sweat as someone who is acclimated to the heat.

It is true that caloric and carbohydrate needs are highly elevated during extreme exertion in heat. The carbohydrates in sports drinks come in the form of simple sugars. The problem with pushing the carbohydrate (i.e., sugar) level in a sports drink is that it can cause an osmotic diarrhea in the gut and accelerate electrolyte loss. That's why hyperconcentrating power drinks can be a mistake. These companies have designed drinks that push the limit of carbohydrates and electrolytes but are still palatable and not harmful. Because of their good taste, there is increased voluntary consumption of power drinks over plain water. This makes them a good option to help prevent dehydration, but even when mixed correctly, sports drinks alone remain inadequate to replace the body's electrolyte losses.

In short, sports drinks alone are inadequate. I've seen it. Trust me; I'm a doctor!

Treatment

Treatment of hyponatremia is similar to that for heat exhaustion.
1. Have the victim rest in a cool place.
2. Give the victim salty foods.
3. If the victim's mental condition deteriorates, seek medical help.

LIGHTNING CAN STRIKE MORE THAN ONCE

More people are killed each year in the United States by lightning than by snakes, spiders, bears, and mountain lions. And there is no absolutely safe way to avoid the danger. But a little knowledge and a bit of common sense can reduce the risks immeasurably.

Some of the more dangerous places during any sort of electrical storm are on exposed ridges and mountaintops and near edges of canyons. These are treated more fully in chapters 28 and 30.

First of all, it is very useful to assess the potential danger when you hear thunder, then see the lightning flash. A simple thirty-second rule works well. Count the number of seconds between hearing the thunderclap and seeing the lightning flash. More than thirty seconds means the storm is still far enough away to enable you to take precautions. If you want to be technical, divide the number of seconds you count by five, and that will give you the number of miles the storm is from you, inasmuch as every five seconds equals a mile.

There are a number of precautions you can take that will greatly reduce the risk of being struck by lightning. Most importantly, stay away from areas where you are the tallest object, for you will serve as a lightning rod, conducting lightning down through you to the ground.

Find shelter if you can. But beware of overhanging ledges or shallow caves. There was a mountaineering casualty in the Bugaboo Mountains when some climbers took refuge in a cave on Bugaboo Spire. Lightning struck and killed two of them. They were no doubt near the mouth of the cave, for it was shallow.

These precautions may seem excessive. Keeping it simpler, you are trying to avoid metal objects, being wet, or being the tallest thing on the landscape.

Should you feel your hair standing on end or your skin prickles, an electric charge is building up near you—an indication that lightning may strike you soon. Keep calm, but do get into the best possible situation that can offer some protection. See the list below.

Lightning Precautions

1. First, avoid hiking in a thunderstorm as much as possible. When you are already on the trail and a storm comes up, take the other precautions listed here.
2. Avoid handling metal objects. It's a good idea to put your pack down and get well away from it. Take your sleeping pad or sleeping bag with you to sit on as a cushion to give you a little protection and insulation from the ground.

Jim McVey hunkering down during an afternoon storm in Schofield Basin of the Colorado Rockies.

3. Do not get into your tent. And get away from any metal gear you have with you.
4. Get well away from water—streams, ponds, lakes.
5. Take shelter. If buildings are nearby, get into one. If you can find a cave that is deep, then get into it. But caution: Caves are dangerous unless you can get deep inside.
6. Seek lower ground. Find an arroyo, ditch, ravine, or such where you can get down below the higher terrain around you.
7. Find a cluster of small trees to hunker down in. Be sure they are surrounded by larger trees. It is the height that attracts the lightning bolts.
8. Stay away from tall trees. Do not take refuge beneath a tall tree. It attracts lightning. Also avoid tall rocky outcroppings.
9. Avoid wide-open spaces such as a mountain meadow where you would be the tallest object.
10. Stay off ridges and away from the edge of a cliff.
11. If caught in the open with no place to hide, crouch on the balls of your feet and cup your hands over your ears. Do not put your hands on the ground.

How to Treat Someone Struck by Lightning

Do not be afraid to help victims who have been struck by lightning. It is perfectly safe to touch them. Even if they seem to be dead, first aid can save their lives. Victims of lightning strikes can appear dead but be resuscitated by CPR. They have often been "brought back to life" by the quick action of someone giving CPR. Get treatment for other injuries, such as burns, as soon as possible.

17
Snakes

When I teach classes in backpacking, most people who've never hiked say their greatest fear is snakes. Yet snakes are actually among the lowest risks of the backcountry.

In their book, *Over the Edge: Death in Grand Canyon,* authors Michael P. Ghiglieri and Thomas M. Myers could find no evidence of a single death from a snakebite among the 550 deaths they counted in the 150 years of recorded history of the canyon. Most snakes you see while backpacking in the United States are harmless. And those that are poisonous are more frightened of you than you are of them. They behave accordingly, slithering away from you as fast as they can.

Snakes bite about 8,000 people a year in the United States. Of these, fewer than 15 die from the bite. These typically are very young children, the elderly, or people who are sick. About a third of the bites are "dry" bites, in that they do not break the skin of the victim. Most of the bites occur to zookeepers, research workers, or other people near home who carelessly move stones, boards, or other objects without taking proper precautions. Some are bitten while molesting, teasing, or trying to kill or catch snakes.

Poisonous snakes are shy and will try to slip away when they hear you coming. Should you come upon a snake suddenly, though, it will likely be a rattlesnake and warn you with its spine-chilling rattle, a sound you will never forget.

While in the backcountry, it is difficult to see a snake basking in the shade under a bush or in its branches. So the first precaution to avoid problems with snakes is to keep your eyes open, being aware of what is around you in all directions.

TYPES OF POISONOUS SNAKES

There are two basic types of poisonous snakes: those with hemotoxic venom and those with neurotoxic venom. The hemotoxic venom travels through the bite victim's blood, whereas the neurotoxic venom travels more quickly through the nerves. As a general rule, all poisonous snakes in the United States have hemotoxic venom except the coral snake, which is neurotoxic.

The most dangerous snakes of the world, such as the cobra and black mamba, have neurotoxic venom. On a list of the deadliest snakes, the coral snake ranks eighth deadliest in the world. Yet deadly is different from dangerous. Many of the deadliest snakes, such as the coral snake, rarely strike anyone, even though their toxins are more deadly than those of snakes that strike more frequently. So although the coral snake is the *deadliest* in the United States, the timber rattlesnake is more *dangerous,* attacking and hence killing more people than the coral snake.

How to Avoid Snakebite

- Wear appropriate footwear such as boots, chaps, or high-top hiking shoes. Baggy pants are also a help. With most snakes, if they have to go through boots or pants when they strike, they do not penetrate the skin.
- Step on logs or rocks rather than over them, in case a snake is resting beneath them.
- Don't put your hands into ledges, holes, or other places you can't see into.
- Walk well away from brush alongside the trail, and keep an eye alert for snakes that may be resting in their shadows or branches.
- Don't turn over rocks or logs with bare hands. Use a tool or branch.
- Don't hike in snake country by yourself.
- Watch where you are walking.
- Learn what dangerous snakes are in the area where you will be hiking. Get a book with good pictures of the snakes in that locale.
- Don't molest, catch, or kill a venomous snake.
- Don't walk around after dark without a flashlight. Snakes are nocturnal, especially in the summer. They are less so in spring and fall, and usually hibernate in winter.
- Don't gather firewood after dark.
- Shake out sleeping bag, boots, and clothes before using.

One day a few years ago, I was with a group of American Hiking Society members in the Forest Service office of Ranger John Neeling in Utah. The group was being prepped for a trail maintenance project several miles in the interior of the Kanab Creek Wilderness Area.

The subject of rattlesnakes came up, and John said, "There is one unique species in the area where you will be working, the Mojave rattlesnake. It is particularly dangerous because unlike other rattlesnakes, the Mojave is neurotoxic as well as hemotoxic." He told us how to identify the Mojave and avoid contact with it.

I thought to myself at the time, "Amazing for a forest ranger to be so misinformed." Before writing this chapter, though, I talked to Bob Meyers, director of the American International Rattlesnake Museum in Albuquerque, New Mexico. He told me that John was on the money: Mojave rattlesnakes are indeed neurotoxic as well as hemotoxic. In fact, Bob believes that a few other rattlesnake species are also neurotoxic, most notably the eastern timber rattlesnake.

Furthermore, on lists of the deadliest snakes in the world, the Mojave rattlesnake ranks right up there with the black mamba as eleventh deadliest, higher even than the king cobra. So mentally, at least, I owe John Neeling an apology.

POISONOUS SNAKES OF THE UNITED STATES

There are four species of poisonous snakes in America: coral snakes, water moccasins (aka cottonmouths), copperheads, and rattlesnakes.

Coral Snake

Little need for hikers to worry about the coral snake, which is the deadliest of all North American poisonous snakes, for they are extremely reclusive. There is almost zero likelihood of you ever seeing one on the trail, never mind being bitten by one.

The coral snake's natural habitat is in Florida and the extreme Southeast, mostly in coastal regions. They don't look particularly fearsome, and bites occur most often to people who handle them without realizing how venomous their bites can be. The coral snake can be encountered in any type of environment, usually in early morning, at night, or in the evening.

The bites of all coral snakes are highly dangerous. One subspecies that lives only in a narrow region of southern Arizona is the deadliest of all. There is just no antivenin for this particular species.

Water Moccasins

Water moccasins, as the name implies, are found in swamps and along streams and ponds, mainly in the Southeast. They are slow-moving and more aggressive. They will ordinarily stand their ground rather than run from you. Their defensive posture is to cock themselves into a striking position with their mouths wide open, showing their fearsome fangs. The interior of their mouths are white, giving them the alternative name of cottonmouths. Though their bite is highly toxic and very painful, it is usually not lethal.

Copperheads

Copperheads are fairly widespread in forests, mostly in rocky outcroppings in the eastern United States. They have no way of warning you. But they need to be highly antagonized before they will attack. And fear not, their bite is only mildly toxic, and deaths from copperheads are almost unknown. Far more deaths result from bee stings.

Rattlesnakes

Rattlesnakes are the most common poisonous snakes in America, with some sixty varieties spread across the states. Half the number of rattlesnake species are found in the southwestern deserts. Rattlesnakes generally warn you if they feel threatened. And their rattle is spine-tingling enough to cause you to jump well out of their way. Since snakes are cold-blooded creatures, they are usually out in the cool of evening—a good reason not to hike in rattlesnake country after dark. It is wise to move only with flashlight and caution if you have to go about at night.

For more information on poisonous snakes of the world, see Dr. Manbir Singh's website, www.manbir-online.com.

And if you are ever in Albuquerque and looking for something interesting to do, check out the American International Rattlesnake Museum at 202 San Felipe Northwest. The museum has the largest collection of different species of live rattlesnakes in the world. It hosts a greater number of species than the Bronx Zoo, Philadelphia Zoo, National Zoo, Denver Zoo, San Francisco Zoo, and San Diego Zoo all combined! Director Bob Meyers also has lots of solid information on his website, www.rattlesnakes.com.

HOW TO TREAT SNAKEBITE

The object of first-aid treatment is to keep the venom from spreading. If you are not out in the backcountry, then get the victim to a doctor or hospital as quickly as possible.

When in the backcountry, the first thing to do is to be sure that the wound has venom in it. Simply examine it to see whether there are puncture holes from a snake's

How to Identify a Snakebite

All poisonous snakes except the coral snake have two large fangs. If the victim is bitten and the snake escapes before identification can be made, the following signs should be noted:

- Two, sometimes just one, puncture holes in the skin made by the fangs.
- Pain follows five to ten minutes after the bite, and swelling begins as well as discoloration around the bitten area. The symptoms progress up the victim's limb. Should the fangs enter a vein or artery, the swelling and discoloration may not appear.
- Coral snake bites are different from all other poisonous North American snake bites in that these snakes bite by chewing with smaller teeth, for they have no fangs. The bite is not usually painful, and little to no swelling appears until an hour or more after the bite. But when the symptoms do appear, they progress rapidly—nausea, drowsiness, marked salivation, and difficulty in breathing. Paralysis can also develop quickly.

fangs, indicating that the snake actually injected poisonous venom. Within five to ten minutes, swelling and a fiery pain usually occur around the bitten area. There may also be tingling and numbness. Treat the victim as follows:

1. Do not panic.
2. Keep victim as calm and as still as possible. Moving about causes the venom to spread more rapidly.
3. Keep the bitten area lower than the heart.
4. You can administer acetaminophen or ibuprofen to reduce the discomfort and pain, but do not give the victim alcohol or aspirin. Both increase the danger of the bite.
5. Wash the wound with soap and water.
6. Get medical help as quickly as possible.
7. If medical help is not available within half an hour, wrap around a wide bandage two to four inches above the bite to slow the spread of the venom. Do not cut off circulation. Tighten it only enough that you can still slip a finger under it.
8. Then use a suction device to extract as much venom as possible from the wound. The best suction device is the Sawyer Extractor. It is small, compact, and has powerful extracting capabilities. In the event you don't have an extractor, then (now get a grip on yourself!) you may suck out the venom by mouth. Spit it out, of course, as you draw out the venom.
9. Do not cut the bitten area according to the now obsolete cut-and-suck method. It often causes infections.

First aid is just that—emergency treatment. It is most important to get medical help as soon as possible. But move the victim slowly, with lots of rest stops, to keep the blood from circulating the venom through the body.

A final word, though. If no treatment at all is obtained, the likelihood of fatality is almost nil, unless the victim is a very young child or someone who is elderly or already very ill and debilitated.

18
New Bear Attacks: Take Them Seriously

Those new to the backcountry often have excessive, unfounded fears of grizzly bears. Bear expert Stephen Herrero tells of a woman who wanted to be close to nature and retired to the backcountry in northern British Columbia, Canada. But after two years, she "still hadn't gone for a hike because she was so afraid of bears." A friend suggested she call Herrero.

"I tried to assure her," he said, "that if she took time to learn about bears she could enjoy nature as she'd hoped. . . . I said bear attacks are rare. . . .

"I wrote my book, *Bear Attacks: Their Causes and Avoidance,* for people like her."

Many park rangers in bear country also try to allay unfounded fears of bears, often citing comparative figures to illustrate their point, such as that while only 29 people were killed by bears in the 1990s, some 250 people were killed by dogs from 1977 to 1998.

It is also pointed out to hikers that twenty-one times more people are killed by lightning in a year than are killed by bears. More than twice as many die of bee, hornet, or wasp stings, and twice as many of spider bites. But for hikers, it is more important to note that while 3 people were killed by bears in an average year in the 1990s, some 600 died of hypothermia in a single year. Thus the odds are 200 to 1 of a hiker dying of hypothermia compared with a bear attack.

All of these facts are true, of course, and have done a great deal to assure hikers and backpackers of the relatively lower danger they face from bear attacks. But I wonder if they haven't also instilled a false sense of confidence in the hiker.

A study of visitors in Yosemite by William B. Cella and Jeffrey A. Keay tried to determine the way people respond to warnings about handling food safely in bear country. In his book, Herrero reported that "a study carried out in Yosemite National Park found that 92 percent of the backcountry users stated that they stored their food properly, whereas only 3 percent actually did so."

OVERCONFIDENCE CAN BE DEADLY TO BOTH HIKERS AND BEARS

There is one piece of critical information that I think is missing in the educational material on bear safety. None of the material I have put my hands on gives the incidence of attacks and injuries that occur when hikers are following all the safety measures. This seems an egregious oversight, one that engenders an overconfidence that many hikers have about the real risks of bear attacks. And overconfidence breeds higher risks. With the extreme-sports mentality that prevails among so many today, there is something macho about swaggering out in front of danger.

The numbers of incidents are low, but they have been increasing. And with the increase, more bears are killed, increasing the endangerment of the species and the antibear mood of the public. Herrero studied all he could find on bear incidents covering an eighty-year period from 1900 to 1980. He found only seventy deaths from bear attacks during that period, which amounts to a little less than one death per year. Yet he also found there were twenty-nine deaths from bear attacks in the decade of the 1990s. That is more than a 300 percent increase. Though the numbers are still small, and a lot lower than those for deaths by hypothermia and lightning, there is a lot more at risk here than hikers' lives, though that of course is the chief concern.

I have given far more emphasis to the dangers that bears pose to the hiker largely because it is lacking elsewhere in the literature. I have checked other hiking guides and find little to no mention of the reality of the risk. If you willingly go out into bear country with the risk in mind, it ought to be a full-face reality risk.

THE NEW KILLER BEARS

A steadily rising number of people are killed each year by bears in the United States and Canada. And those doing the killing are black bears, not grizzlies. More than half of the victims are in the backcountry—hiking, camping, fishing, hunting, skiing, running, researching, working.

If that is alarming to you, it was meant to be. It was alarming for me to discover this deadly trend. And I write this book the way I would want to read it.

The bottom line is that if you are going to hike in bear country—especially black bear country, and that is just about any place in the United States or Canada—you'd best follow bear safety guidelines, carry bear pepper spray deterrent, and know how to use it.

The reasons follow.

By Hiking Safely, the Life You Save May Be a Bear's

When I first began to write this chapter, I got together with bear expert Bill Schneider to seek his guidance. Bill was my bear expert when I began publishing *Backpacker* magazine. Back then, he set me straight about a lot of bear concerns and wrote a number of articles for the magazine.

The first thing he told me this time around was that things had changed in the past few years regarding bears, and more important, there were new ways to cope with bear attacks.

No, the numbers are not large. Neither are the number of deaths from heart attacks in the backcountry. But who would be so foolish not to do everything possible to take the risks seriously?

Need I say, bears are an emotionally charged issue? On one hand, there are the "bear people" who will do all they can to protect them. They see facts from their point of view. On the other hand, there are those who feel there are bears enough already. And they see facts to support their views.

Contrary to many of the arguments on either side, there are precious few Americans or Canadians who would actually want to remove bears from national parks. That's even true of those who have been mauled by bears. As Steve Herrero reports in his authoritative book, among people who have been injured by bears, less than 15 percent would have them removed from the parks.

Some of the same facts become interpreted completely differently by both sides. Then each side has highly convincing bear "experts" who give scholarly backing to their point of view.

Right from the get-go, each side differs dramatically in how it thinks I should present the dangers of hiking in bear country. The one side would like me to minimize the dangers so as to avoid feeding any unrealistic fear of bears you may have. The other side would like me to dwell upon the grislier side of bear maulings to be sure you really do understand.

My challenge is to present a balance between the two. Quite frankly, I believe both sides tread in dangerous waters, thus making my attempt at balance all the more important.

When people are given the impression that the risks of bear attack are minimal, they tend to become careless about following the guidelines. That brings on bodily harm to some that could be avoided.

This business of ignoring the rules because they are regarded as trivial can be seen everywhere. The signs at trailheads along the rim of Grand Canyon, for example, warn hikers not to attempt to hike to the river and back in one day, but the trails swarm with hikers who ignore this guideline, causing hundreds of needless helicopter rescues every summer, not to mention the deaths. Drivers ignore speed limits, and in our town drivers merely slow down but drive right on through stop signs. The same is true of myriad rules or guidelines in the parks and national forests, including bear safety rules about storing food in camp.

On the other hand, hikers should not be so frightened of bears that they avoid hiking in bear country altogether.

All my life, I believed the risk from black bears was minimal, because I had heard it repeated over and over again by the experts I admired. They were right, of course. But the more I studied the material to put together this chapter, the more seriously I now consider black bear dangers. I, incidentally, also take just as seriously the risk of having a heart attack in the backcountry. And I take all the necessary precautions for both types of risks.

I care less about proving a point in this chapter than I do about saving lives. It so happens that saving a hiker's life from a bear attack is as good as saving the life of a bear—for whenever a human is hurt or killed by a bear, the bear is almost always hunted down and shot.

In moving through the morass of bear material, I leaned on Bill Schneider's thirty years or so of bear expertise. He has written some seventeen books and dozens of magazine articles about bears and taught numerous classes on the subject. I believe him to be a rather balanced sort with regard to bear emotions.

I checked most facts against data from Stephen Herrero, whose scientific authority in the field is acknowledged by those on both sides of the emotional divide.

I also gleaned as much information as I could from superintendents of national parks with significant bear populations. While both Schneider and Herrero would largely agree with my facts, there are some they would likely question. For I also

Bear Encounter Warning!

by Pride Johnson, Counter Assault Bear Spray Company

I train U.S. government land agency employees for the U.S. Geological Survey, U.S. Forest Service, and National Park Service how to deal with bear encounters. Most of these employees are scientists in forestry, geology, water quality, and such, but they are not bear experts.

In bear encounters, I recommend that they take a proactive approach and assume the worst-case scenario, meaning they assume that the bear will charge. When the bear is within thirty to fifty feet, I recommend they start spraying in half-second to two-second bursts of bear pepper spray deterrent.

And for the common person, I DO NOT recommend trying to distinguish among and respond to the various behaviors. Things may change rapidly for both the bear and the intruder. Therefore, I recommend a proactive approach by being prepared with bear pepper spray deterrent in an actual charge. Assume the worst-case scenario—that the bear will charge.

gathered data from such disparate views as the Maine Guides Association and *High Country News.* And I've taken extra effort to provide my sources for all of the data.

How They Tell You to Protect Yourself From Bears

I found out more about bears than I really wanted to know. The chief thing was that safety from bears certainly isn't all it is cracked up to be. Though there is much you can do to avoid being attacked, once you are attacked by a bear there is precious little you can do to protect yourself from a severe mauling or death.

More often than not, whenever journalists report bear attack stories, they fit them into some sort of statistical context. It may be a very sketchy context, in words such as "this is the first attack since 1970" or "bear attacks are very rare."

Bear experts are continually cautioning us not to be concerned, since "even national parks with viable grizzly bear populations average fewer than one fatality per year," and there are "8 times more deaths due to spiders than from bear attacks," and "190 more people are killed by lightning than die of bear attacks."

I take exception to these numbers. Here's why.

Rangers and bear experts assured Glacier Park visitors that "there has never been anyone killed by grizzlies in the park's history." They said, "Leave them alone and they won't bother you." They said this until the park was fifty-seven years old. And they told the truth.

Then, in a single summer, several backcountry users were injured in various bear attacks, including the brutal slaughter of two nineteen-year-old female college students in the early-morning hours of the same night, though the women were camped in separate campgrounds some twenty trail miles apart.

Each national park keeps its own statistics of bear incidents, and rangers are encouraging, assuring us that few backpackers ever fall victim to bear attacks. They said that in the Great Smoky Mountains National Park right up to the year 2000. The park management even cut the number of bear incidents in half. But then a black bear unaccountably attacked and killed a hiker. Bear expert Schneider's comment: "Wherever there are bears and hikers in the same spot, it is an eventuality that somebody will be killed. Nobody has been killed by a black bear in Yosemite, but this will happen sooner or later. We have to accept that as part of the deal while doing all we can to prevent it."

What is not in the statistics, nor in those assurances, is that of the nine to ten black bear attacks reported in newspapers each year from 2000 to 2003, two or more resulted in deaths. (See "Black Bears in the News" at www.maineguides.org. Newspaper clippings in their files record twenty-three bear attacks on twenty-seven people, with six deaths.) Nor do they tell that more than half of the bear attacks occur to hikers, backcountry campers, or hunters—which narrows down the 150 million park visitors more than somewhat.

Also, what is not in the National Park Service (NPS) literature is that most of the new deadly bear attacks were not caused by careless campers and reckless hikers. They were unprovoked bear attacks on people who seem to have been following all the guidelines for bear-resistant hiking and camping. In fact, most fatal attacks are attributed to "predaceous" black bears. According to Bill Schneider, "Some of the worst incidents have been caused by black bears, which appear to be slightly more likely to develop predatory habits than grizzly bears." This makes the statistics more alarming. And the assurances less comforting.

Still . . .

PROTECTING YOURSELF IN BEAR COUNTRY

Though statistics say that there is far more likelihood I will be involved in an auto accident than in a terrorist skyjacking, and though my concern for a terrorist attack on an airplane is great, it does not deter me from flying. Likewise, my fear of bears does not keep me out of bear country.

At airports, I do all I can to comply with any security measures they care to put me through—opening my bags, letting strangers in uniform go through my most personal belongings, taking off my shoes to put them through a security detector, and biting my tongue to avoid cracking any jokes around sometimes uncouth-looking security officers.

Likewise, I take every precaution in the backcountry to avoid an unpleasant encounter with bears. I abide by all the trail and camping regulations and suggestions to make my hike and camp safer. And lately I've added two items to my backpacking gear that give me a much greater feeling of safety in bear country, statistics be damned.

I have my first bear-resistant food container to carry into my favorite haunts in the Rocky Mountains. I also have my first canister of bear pepper spray and a belt holster to carry it at the ready, for a quick draw. Schneider tells me he carries his can of bear pepper spray all the time as well.

Since we backpackers and hikers constitute the majority of victims of bear attacks and hence are a greater threat to bears, we ought to do all we can to create less endangerment to bears. We are the ones intruding more upon their territory. So I propose we do three things:

> I always carry two carabiners. I tie them to an end of a long piece of parachute cord. I sling the 'biners over a limb high enough to hang my bear-resistant food bag. One carabiner does not have enough weight—two are just right. The carabiners also serve a variety of other purposes. Very handy.
>
> —*Dave Bates, national director*
> *of Camping and Conservation,*
> *Boy Scouts of America*

1. Hike with a bear pepper spray canister and know how to use it.
2. Carry your food and garbage in bear-resistant food containers.
3. Learn the bear safety rules and obey them.

You may not feel such strict precautions are necessary. That is up to you. But although you may be unafraid for yourself and your hiking companions, you might want to consider the harm you may bring to bears if one of you becomes a bear attack victim.

I've included a few bear encounter stories in this chapter. And I have enlarged the chapter to five times my original intentions, for I now believe that the unenlightened backpacker is the most serious threat to that last magnificent animal symbol of our diminishing wilderness.

RECENT BEAR ATTACKS

Consider the most recent bear attacks reported in newspapers in the four years from 2000 to 2003.

Though not a backpacker, the youngest to die was a five-month-old infant in New York's Catskills. The bear snatched her from her stroller right in front of her mother. The oldest also was not a backpacker, but a ninety-three-year-old woman in New Mexico. The bear broke into her home and killed her. The elderly Adelia Trujillo lived a short distance from me. Another bear ripped open a window and got into my next-door neighbors' home at 2:30 one morning.

All of these bears have been destroyed. Bears had become so accustomed to finding food in the homes around here—food left out to feed dogs, horses, sheep, llamas, hummingbirds, and such, and fruit from the apricot and plum trees in backyards, as well as food visible from house windows—that they had no fear of people and had become accustomed to finding food near them. Some bears became so sophisticated they waited until a home was dark, then broke in and opened the refrigerator door!

It isn't usually the one who enables bears to feed near human habitation who gets hurt. It is the next one in line—the innocent five-month-old Esther Schwimmer and ninety-three-year-old Adelia Trujillo—who get taken down by them. Neither of them was preparing or handling food at the time of the attacks.

Unprovoked Bear Attacks in the Backcountry During 2000 to 2003

Here is a list of fifteen of the bear attacks on backcountry users out of the twenty-three black bear attacks on twenty-seven humans in the four years from 2000 to 2003. The full list of newspaper clippings can be found on the website www.maineguides.org.

These fifteen attacks resulted in six deaths, about two per year. The numbers do not reflect attacks to others in more urban areas who were not engaged in some sort of backcountry activity.

There were no doubt more bear attacks to backcountry users than these. These are only the ones widely reported in newspapers that occurred in the lower forty-eight states and Canada. The list does not purport to be scientific.

May 2000. Hiker Glenda Bradley was attacked, killed, and parts of her body eaten by a black bear in Great Smoky Mountains National Park.

June 2000. Jason Sansom suffered puncture wounds to both arms after an unprovoked attack by a black bear on the shore trail of Two Medicine Lake in Glacier National Park.

July 4, 2000. Biathlete Mary-Beth Miller was attacked and killed by a black bear while out training near a military base in Val Cartier in Quebec, Canada.

September 2000. A black bear attacked both father and son bowhunters near Glenwood Springs, Colorado. The bear was scared off by shots from third hunter.

June 3, 2001. Eighteen-year-old hiker Kyle Harry was mauled and killed by a bear in his camp in Yellow Knife, Northwest Territories, Canada.

June 2002. While two campers were preparing to leave their camp in the morning, a black bear came into camp, ignored their food bag, and attacked twenty-five-year-old Sylvia Haert, pinning her to the ground while clawing her back. Her boyfriend screamed at the bear, startling it enough for Sylvia to break free and leap off a cliff into a lake in Algonquin Park, Ontario, Canada.

September 28, 2002. Jason Koller was sitting waiting for elk when bear cubs crossed in front of him, followed by the 200-pound mother bear, which saw him and attacked. He let his father know on his radio what was happening. The father ran to him, screaming at the bear, which then came toward him. He managed to let an arrow fly that took the bear down and stopped the attack.

September 16, 2002. Miles Becker was studying woodcocks with a team of biologists in Four Brooks Wildlife Management Area near Milaca, Minnesota, when he was attacked by a black bear shortly after noon. He survived the attack with broken bones and lacerations of his face, head, and leg.

September 2002. A hunter was attacked and killed by a black bear in Gaspé, Quebec, Canada.

September 2002. A black bear attacked and killed an oil worker in British Columbia, Canada.

April 17, 2003. A black bear stalked, attacked, and killed a logger surveying cut sites in Ontario, Canada.

July 3, 2003. A black bear mauled a hiker as he arrived in a campground in Angeles National Forest north of Glendora, California, while he was stashing his food. The bear knocked down the hiker and took his backpack with the food.

July 10, 2003. While fourteen National Outdoors Leadership School (NOLS) students were camped on the Green River in Utah, a bear grabbed eighteen-year-old Nick Greeve by the head and neck and tried to pull him from his sleeping bag.

July 15, 2003. Two hikers were mauled by a black bear while camped in Colorado's Rocky Mountain National Park. They "did everything they could to store food properly. There was no food in the tents. The bear was going for the campers," said park spokeswoman Kyle Patterson.

August 12, 2003. A five-foot-three, 105-pound, eighteen-year-old woman was hiking in Wawayanda Park in New Jersey when she came upon a black bear. She stopped and slowly backed away, but the bear charged and attacked. She managed to elbow it in the eye, stunning it enough for her to escape with only claw welts on her stomach.

DEADLY NIGHT OF THE GRIZZLIES

For more than half a century, while our national parks were in their infancy and still in their most primitive wilderness conditions, hikers, backpackers, hunters, and fishermen were hardly ever bothered by bears, despite their very sloppy backcountry camping practices compared with how bearwise we camp today.

That all changed in the summer of 1967. To this day, no one has adequately explained what went wrong. Whatever the cause, however, grizzlies began a series of maulings of campers in Glacier National Park. Things have gotten steadily worse over the years.

In fairness, though, quite recently, as the NPS education and bear management plans kicked in at parks like Glacier and Yellowstone, they have had a much lower number of bear incidents now than they had in the past, and far fewer deaths than are occurring many other places outside the national parks.

Before that fateful 1967 season, grizzlies had snooped at camps. But they had never before been so bold as to enter camp when anyone was present. And they would leave when campers made loud noises, such as banging pans or shouting.

In the early morning hours of August 13, 1967, however, bears attacked campers at two campgrounds some twenty trail miles apart, on opposite sides of Livingstone Mountain Range's 9,000-foot peaks.

Sixteen-year-old Paul Dunn was attacked while in his sleeping bag. Then a nineteen-year-old girl, Michelle Koons, was attacked in her sleeping bag. The bear crunched sharp teeth into Michelle's shoulder and chest and dragged her in her sleeping bag into the woods, where he finished killing and eating her.

Across the mountains at Granite Chalet campground at roughly the same time, there were other grizzly attacks. Eighteen-year-old Roy Ducat was awakened in his sleeping bag by a grizzly crunching its teeth into his shoulder and arm, tearing it out of its socket before Ducat could fight his way free.

He screamed to other campers: "I tried playing dead. But it didn't do any good. Help her! The bear's got that girl."

He meant college student Julie Helgeson, another nineteen-year-old. A griz had grabbed her while she was in her sleeping bag and was dragging her, screaming, into the woods. She was unable to free herself while the bear savagely mauled her to death and continued eating her.

About a month later, just outside Glacier National Park, a hunter, Bert Bell, was attacked by a griz. Within another month, still another hunter, Robert Gilmore, was attacked by another grizzly on the park boundary near the North Fork of the Flathead River.

The NPS offered a variety of theories as to what had caused all this grizzly aggressiveness so coincidentally—everything from "too many people feeding the bears" to "lightning activity" to "errant grizzlies" to "girls with menstrual cycles." And critics have blamed park rangers for not taking more aggressive management measures against the bears before that fateful night.

STATISTICS, AND BEAR STATISTICS

I contacted all national park and forest supervisors where there had historically been bear encounters with humans and found that the new bear attacks are not taking place on their turf, and fewer grizzlies have been attacking hikers recently. Rather, it is predatory black bears.

According to my bear conscience, Bill Schneider: "Black bears are more dangerous than grizzlies only because there are so many more of them and their range is many times larger than that of grizzly bears. More black bears in more places mean more encounters. The other reason is that people are more nonchalant around black bears and don't take the proper precautions."

I've been aware of black bears in the East and in New Mexico for several decades, and I cannot recall any deaths from their attacks until recently.

PREDACEOUS BLACK BEARS ARE MORE DANGEROUS THAN GRIZZLIES

The latest bear attacks have been mostly to people doing the "right thing" in bear country. None of these attack victims were feeding or molesting bears, nor getting too close in order to photograph them. The attacking bears have been labeled "predaceous" by bear experts like Stephen Herrero.

A typical predaceous black bear attack caused the first fatality to a hiker from a bear in the history of Great Smoky Mountains National Park. The NPS bear management program had reduced the number of bear incidents in the park from 359 in 1997 to less than half that, 147, in 2000. Yet this was the year that experienced hiker Glenda Bradley was attacked unprovoked and killed by a black bear.

Two months after Bradley was attacked, biathlete Mary-Beth Miller was killed by a black bear outside Quebec City, also a first for that part of Canada. A month later, two backpackers were mauled by a black bear in Glacier National Park. Both survived with injuries on thighs and hips. Twelve hours later, another man was mauled by a grizzly a few miles from there in the Canadian Rockies. This was the first bear attack in that area of the Rockies in twenty-two years.

The increasing risk of black bear attacks is in many ways worse than the old risk of attack by grizzlies for two simple reasons. First, predaceous black bears stalk hikers to kill and feed upon them, whereas grizzlies attack hikers mostly out of self-defense or because they have found food around them. So precautions against grizzlies are simpler and more assured than precautions against predaceous black bears.

Another reason black bear attacks are becoming more of a problem is because they are attacking in wider, more spread-out geographic areas. Grizzly problems occurred primarily in two national parks, where it was far easier to implement a bear management program, as the two areas were administered under the same central agency, the National Park Service. But black bears are attacking in widely disparate land management governances. Some are local or state lands, some private, and some in various Canadian jurisdictions, making development of any unified management program difficult and slow.

NOW THE NEW CONTROVERSY: PLAY DEAD OR FIGHT BACK?

On August 2, 2004, at about 4:30 P.M., Roberto Cataldo of Medena, Italy, was hiking in Alaska's Denali National Park. He was taking photos of caribou when he heard something behind him, turned, and saw a bear with two cubs about forty to fifty feet away. He stood his ground and waved his arms as the NPS advises, but the bears continued coming at him. When they were about twelve feet away, he dropped to the ground into a fetal position, still holding his ice ax in his right hand.

The mother bear pounced upon his left shoulder and neck. Roberto raised himself the best he could and swung his ice ax at the bear, plunging it into the animal's left side. The bear became agitated and fled with her cubs.

In the Denali press release, representative Kris Fister said: "It is never recommended that a person fight back when a brown bear [Alaskans' term for the grizzly] attacks. . . . Park managers do not recommend fighting back or striking a bear unless the attack is prolonged."

Now if you were Roberto, would you have waited to fight back until the bear's attack was "prolonged"? Would you wait until you figured out just how long "prolonged" might be?

I'm fairly certain I would have taken the same action as that taken by Roberto and not waited for the attack to become "prolonged."

Perhaps Roberto read the park brochure distributed at the visitors center, which says: "If the bear makes contact fight back vigorously! . . . Kick, punch, or hit the bear's face, eyes and nose."

The brochure titled *Bear Safety* in Alaska's national parklands goes on to clarify as follows: "IF IT IS A BROWN BEAR, PLAY DEAD. . . . IF IT IS A BLACK BEAR, DO NOT PLAY DEAD; fight back vigorously! NEVER PLAY DEAD WITH A BLACK BEAR! . . . FIGHT ANY BEAR THAT ATTEMPTS TO ENTER YOUR TENT!!"

If you cannot tell whether it is a brown/grizzly or black bear, you might follow these brochure instructions: "If the attack is prolonged and the brown bear begins to feed on you, fight back vigorously!"

This brochure does not tell you how to distinguish between the two species, but another brochure distributed by the NPS says, "Color or size can **not** be used for identification as both species vary greatly." Then the brochure goes on to inform you that you can tell it's a brown/grizzly if you notice the extra length of its claws, the concavity of its face, and the hump on its back.

If you're being attacked, however, these features may not be quite so readily discernible. How sharp do you think your discernment would be if you were being attacked by a bear?

I also noticed in the description of the first major attacks by grizzlies in Glacier National Park, on that bloody night in August 1967, that all four attack victims did not fight back. Two ended up dead, and two were severely mauled. So, really? Play dead or fight back? Grizzly or black bear?

I am being a bit snide, of course. For a reason. Roberto was criticized by the press for not following NPS guidelines. He hurt the grizzly while defending himself. Easy to criticize him from the safety of a newsroom, not so easy when you are being clawed and bitten by a bear while lying in a fetal position beneath the beast.

How much of Roberto's story is true? Some rangers are skeptical. But whether true or not, the story illustrates the difficulty of complying with NPS guidelines for defense against bear attack. And even if or when you ought to put up a defense at all.

The confusion arises, even among rangers who have extensive experience with bears, because of the skimpiness of the scientific data. Stephen Herrero is the expert in this area, and he writes in his book *Bear Attacks:* "Because of the difficulty in quantifying these situations, I have not used statistics to test for significance. My recommendation for playing dead under such circumstances is therefore based mainly on my impressions from examining incidents and my understanding of bear behavior."

So then, once a bear begins an attack, it really does become murky as to what you can or should do to protect yourself from harm. The bottom line is that any defense against a bear attack is a matter of probabilities and not certainties.

The question then is, Should it be a matter of reducing the intensity of the attack or of surviving it?

When I wrote this chapter, my bear counselor, Bill Schneider, told me that "this sort of dates your book, because I'd bet heavily that this advice changes soon to reflect the new 'read the behavior, not the species' thinking."

I chose not to change what I had written, for the "experts" keep changing their minds, and I seriously question how much I can depend upon the "latest" expertise on such life-threatening issues.

As Thomas S. Kuhn, the science history author who coined the term "paradigm shift," points out, a paradigm doesn't shift until those scientists who hold the view die off and a new generation of scientists grows up.

So even if Bill Schneider does believe that in a year or two the NPS advice to play dead if attacked by a bear may change, there will still be a host of books and literature promoting that view. Note, too, that in the current NPS bear literature, that advice is heavily emphasized, though it is not consistent with advice given in some Forest Service areas. In the Cibola National Forest, for example, the bear warning signs say, "If attacked by a bear, fight back with all you've got." If the NPS changes its warnings, so much the better.

My advice: IF ATTACKED BY A BEAR, FIGHT BACK WITH ALL YOU'VE GOT. PERIOD.

The best defense is avoidance of the attack in the first place. As Herrero says in his book, "Your best defense in bear country is your brain—your knowledge and understanding of bears."

The simplest solution that protects hiker as well as bears is to carry bear pepper spray deterrent and know how to use it. Never mind whether you are or are not afraid of bears. The bear in the story above is being searched down and likely will be shot if found with Roberto's ice ax in its back. And the cubs probably will be killed as well. Bear pepper spray likely would have stopped her from coming any closer and saved this sow's life and the hiker from injury.

So even if you are macho-unafraid of bears and know very well all you should know about hiking and camping safely in bear country, how about concern for the bears that might wind up being offed because machismo deemed it wimpy to carry bear pepper spray deterrent?

HOW TO SURVIVE A BEAR ATTACK

There is a certain amount of confusion among Park and Forest Service rangers about what to do if you are the unfortunate victim of a bear attack. The old version was to play dead and protect your neck and the back of your head while allowing the bear to maul you.

More recently, they changed that suggestion to playing dead if attacked by a grizzly and fighting back if it is a black bear attack.

You may still get either suggestion from rangers in the same park.

There is now a new view advocated by bear experts Stephen Herrero and Tom Smith, after several years of study of human-bear encounters, that still was not in official bear safety literature in the national parks or forests as recently as 2004. This defense is bear-behavior based, and it makes no difference whether an attack is from either grizzly or black bear: Should a bear attack for defensive reasons—a sow defending her cubs, a bear defending food, or a bear you have startled—then play dead. If, on the other hand, the bear is aggressive or predatory, then defend yourself for your life.

Without the scientific data to support it, James Gary Shelton, who runs bear-awareness classes for rangers, outfitters, hunters, and backcountry workers of all types argued for this defensive tactic as far back as 1994 in his *Bear Encounter Survival Book*. Here is what he had to say about how to survive a bear attack:

> I believe there are stronger and better survival strategies which are based on my knowledge of bear aggressive behavior, and also on the following three important facts that I have learned during the past five years [1989–1994] of developing my bear safety program.
> 1. The frequency of different attack categories for both black and grizzly bears has been changing since the mid-1960s.
> 2. Many bear encounters and bear attacks do not clearly fall into a category where Herrero's basic strategy will work. [Back in 1994, Herrero recommended playing dead when attacked by a grizzly, fighting back if by a black bear.]
> 3. Those types of encounters and attacks where playing dead with grizzlies and fighting back with black bears does not work, have been increasing over the last few years.

Shelton advised that instead of trying to figure out whether you are being attacked by a black bear or a grizzly, you try a much simpler distinction: Is the bear attacking defensively or offensively?

How can you tell?
- If you are attacked while in your tent, then fight back.
- If the bear stalks you and then attacks, fight back.
- If you have not surprised the bear with cubs and it charges you, fight back.
- If you have not come upon a bear at the carcass of a kill, fight back.

These are all indications of a predaceous bear. On the other hand, if the bear is defending cubs, is feeding upon a dead animal, or has been startled by you coming upon it by surprise, the best defense is to play dead. Lie down on your stomach, feet apart, and protect your neck and the back of head with your hands.

RULES TO FOLLOW IN BEAR COUNTRY

Reading a book is not enough, any more than reading the driver's manual was all you needed to learn to drive. You need to study enough to know how to handle yourself in bear country. But it is necessary to practice these measures as well.

> I wouldn't go hiking in Alaska without at least two forms of bear deterrent, one of which must be bear pepper spray.
>
> —*Terry D. DeBruyn, Ph.D., Alaska regional wildlife biologist, National Park Service*

Practice with your bear pepper spray deterrent in the way the manufacturer suggests. Master your food storage system before you leave home. Be sure everyone in your hiking group understands these techniques.

Rehearse how you will hike, how you will set up camp. Measure off the key distances that you need to know, and see what they look like: 100 paces, twenty-five to thirty feet, fifty to twenty feet, ten feet. Everyone in your group should understand what these distances look like before you get out onto the trail.

Before backpacking anywhere, find out which bears inhabit the area and the perceived risk you run among them. According to Bill Schneider, grizzly bear populations of North America have been spreading out from their normal habitats over the past few decades. So when local lore has it that "no grizzly has been sighted in this area for more than forty years," it could be that this has changed recently.

Land managers usually have up-to-date information about bear activity, as well as trail and camping closures. They close trails or camping temporarily when risk is highest, such as when excessive garbage has accumulated, where there is a dead animal's carcass on which bears are feeding too close to a trail, or if a recent mauling has occurred.

Pay Attention While Hiking

Be aware of your surroundings. Observe rules about areas that have been closed or warnings that have been posted. Far too many hikers have been taken out of the woods in body bags after failing to pay attention to closure signs.

Bill Schneider's little pocket-size book *Bear Aware* is a good item to carry in your pack for quick reference. He explodes many myths about bears—both those that exaggerate the danger and those that trivialize it.

But *please,* don't pull it out to study after a bear is on your back chewing your neck. That may make a great cartoon—but it's not something to laugh about if you're beneath a bear!

Hike in a Group

To a certain extent, a group provides some protection. Most bear maulings occur to hikers alone on trails. Rarely has a group of hikers experienced any difficulty. Some rangers recommend that you hike in parties of four or more.

Stay together on the trails. If you are a family hiking together, don't let the children run on ahead of the rest of you. If in a larger group, persuade stronger hikers to slow down to the pace of the group. The best way is to have the slowest member of the group lead.

Stay on the Trails

Bears expect people to be on trails during the middle of the day and usually avoid going near them at those times. The opposite is true off trails as well as on seldom-used trails. Bears do not expect people bushwhacking. Hence, in bear country, it is wise to diminish the possibilities of running into one by sticking to the well-traveled trails. Leave the bush to the bears.

Hike in the Middle of the Day

Bears ordinarily prowl in the late evening, at night, and in the early morning. Leave the dim and dark hours to the bears. The 1967 bear attacks occurred in Glacier shortly after midnight.

Best to stay off the trails until after the sun has risen at least into midmorning. And stop hiking sometime in midafternoon. Schneider suggests 11 A.M. to 3 P.M. in mid-August as the safest hours to hike in a place like Glacier National Park. But even this is only a general guideline. Bears can be active at any time of day, depending upon weather conditions. It is hazardous hiking in bear country. You need to be bear aware all the time.

Make Noise

Ordinarily, it is rude and impolite to other hikers to carry on loud conversations as you hike. And it is one reason I stay well away from well-traveled trails. In bear country, however, reverse the courtesy—make plenty of noise so as to let the bears, with their highly sensitive hearing, know you are on the trail. The bear bell is standard equipment in Glacier for its deterrence to bears. And frankly, it is a lot more soothing to the nerves than a lot of loud voices. But in Alaska's national parks, bells are said not to work very well and are not recommended.

If you are in open country with a wide view ahead, no need to make noise. These are places, too, where noise travels farther and you would best consider the annoyance to other hikers. So be considerate. Use common sense.

While in camp, using marine air horns, banging pots and pans, and shouting can produce loud enough noises to scare away most bears. In Great Sand Dunes National Park, I recently saw a ranger set off firecrackers to scare bears away from the campground. Obviously, firecrackers are not allowed in most national parks. The air horns are highly recommended by some NPS rangers in Alaska as a deterrent. But only those with a low-pitched sound.

Keep Your Distance

Bears, particularly cubs, may look cute and cuddly. But in the wild, they may be cute, but they sure aren't cuddly. Cubs' mothers are usually nearby and ruthlessly protective. A mother bear will maim or kill anyone she even thinks may hurt her cubs. Keep your distance!

That goes for photographing bears as well. Many people are mauled merely trying to get a better angle for their bear photos. Bears will likely take your crowding closer as an act of aggression and respond accordingly. Stephen Herrero reports in his book that some two-thirds of bear attacks are on people who crowd in too close to a bear—photographing, feeding, harassing, or (can you believe?) "petting" it.

Throw Sticks or Stones at Black Bears

Black bears can often be chased away by tossing sticks or stones at them, just to scare them. But grizzlies are more likely to get annoyed and become more aggressive.

Do Not Use a Gun

Besides being against the law in most national parks, unless you are a skilled marksman under pressure, you are going to annoy the bear into an even more vicious attack than if you did not use a gun.

Use Bear Pepper Spray Deterrent

If properly used, bear pepper spray is the best deterrent. Better than bells. Better than playing dead or fighting back or climbing a tree. But used the wrong way, it can attract bears.

It's important to learn how to use it before you start your hike. Read the directions and test-spray it before you get into your hiking territory. Aim it downwind to keep it from drifting back onto you. Test it well away from bear country, else the lingering scent could actually attract bears. *Do not spray it on yourself, on your gear, or in your campsite.* The spray's odor could attract bears to your camp.

When hiking or in camp, always carry the spray where you can pull it out into action immediately. If you sight a bear, get your bear pepper spray deterrent out into your hand ready for action.

Wait for the bear to be within twenty-five to thirty feet before spraying a warning blast toward it. If the bear approaches closer, give it another couple of blasts when it is within fifteen to twenty feet.

If the bear continues approaching, when it is within ten feet, blast the canister directly at its face, especially its eyes. Keep spraying until the bear leaves or the canister is emptied.

If none of this works and the bear makes contact with you, fight for your life with all you can. The bear is acting aggressively.

Keep Dogs and Other Pets Out of Bear Country

Pets are not permitted on backcountry trails of national parks, but there are plenty of public lands in bear country that allow pets. If you feel you must take your dog, then be absolutely sure you can control it. Bears are not frightened of dogs. In fact, they are annoyed by them to the point of attack.

Trail Runners Beware!

Don't run. Not in bear country. Not at all! Speed on the trail is simply an invitation to disaster. Runners rarely make enough noise as they run, nor do they usually run during the heat of the day. If you are determined to run regardless, then carry a loud bell with you, though even this is discouraged by bear experts.

The runner covers distances more rapidly than hikers and tends to surprise all manner of wildlife because of this. Bears hate being surprised! Also, when running, you're watching where you'll plant your next foot. And that is not very far ahead of you or to the side, and therefore you are not being bear aware.

Bear Pepper Spray Deterrents

The main ingredient in bear pepper spray deterrent is an extract of red pepper oil, oleoresin of capsicum (OC), which is sprayed in a high-pressure cloud. The canister has a sophisticated dispersal system that creates an atomized blast, producing a pepper cloud that is slow to dissipate. It does not kill or harm the bear. The spray temporarily affects the upper respiratory system of the bear, triggering involuntary eye closure and intense burning.

The Federal Government Inter-Agency Grizzly Bear Committee reviewed various types of bear encounters and determined that, in most cases, bear pepper spray worked extremely well. In some encounters, the bear pepper spray did not work as well but nonetheless diminished the severity of the mauling and shortened the attack. In lab studies at the University of Montana Border Grizzly Project (BGP), the bear pepper spray deterrents stopped and turned away every bear tested—six grizzlies and almost sixty black bears—during almost 500 tests.

Bear pepper spray deterrents must be registered with the Environmental Protection Agency (EPA) as pesticides. The accompanying chart shows the specifications of each of the bear sprays approved for use by the EPA. Counter Assault meets all of the guidelines of the wildlife specialists. None of the other bear pepper spray deterrents meet all of the specifications. Some professional guides and backcountry workers do use the other sprays, however, and attest to their effectiveness.

Bear pepper spray deterrents are weapons and ought to be handled as such. Before going out on the trail, it is essential that you learn how to use the spray. One bear expert, Gary Shelton, recommends buying three canisters of spray: one you practice with to test different wind conditions, and the other two you carry on your belt at the ready in bear country. Each canister contains roughly ten seconds of spray, or ten one-second bursts. This is enough to deter a bear, but not if you waste it in sprays that miss the bear because of wind direction or because the bear is too far away.

Stay Away from Carcasses

Should you happen upon the carcass of a dead animal, move along as quickly as you can get past it. Report it to a ranger as soon as possible. Bears find dead animals a feast and jealously guard them from other animals, including human beings.

Hang Your Pack

Bears know your pack contains food. So even if you take a short side trip from the trail, make a practice of hanging your pack from a branch of a tree a good ten feet above the ground and four feet from the tree trunk so as not to attract bears.

In camp, always hang the pack a good 100 paces from your tent, ideally ten feet or more above the ground and four feet or so from the trunk of any tree. (See the illustration of hanging your pack on page 164.)

Obey Park and Forest Regulations

In most places, hiking on public lands means regulations. Find out what they are and obey them. They are put together for your protection. If you obtain a hiking permit,

This chart represents all current EPA Registered Bear Pepper Spray Products*

Ingredients/attributes	Guidelines (established by bear biologists and wildlife specialists)	COUNTER ASSAULT (Counter Assault) (manufacturer)	GUARD ALASKA (McNeil River Enterprises) (independent fillers)	BEAR GUARD (manufactured by Defense Technologies) *Subregistrants and distributors Pepper Power (UDAP)	Bear Peppermance (MSI)	FRONTIERSMAN (Security Equipment Co.) (manufacturer)
EPA registered / #	Must be EPA registered	Yes / 55541-2	Yes / 71545-1	Yes / 71920-1-72007-1		Yes / 72265-1
EPA establishment #	(Indicates state of manufacture)	Montana	Contract fillers, locations vary	Arizona		Missouri
Minimum net weight	7.9 ounces 225 grams	9.1 oz. 230 grams	9.0 oz 255 grams	7.9 oz. 225 grams	9.0 oz. 260 grams	9.2 oz. 260 grams
Derived from (OC) oleoresin capsicum	Yes	Yes	Yes	Yes	Yes	Yes
Capsaicin & other	1%–2%	1.73%	1.3%	2.0%	2.0%	1.4%
Megaphone shaped cloud	Yes	Yes	Yes	Yes	Yes	Yes
Minimum range	25 ft.	30 ft.	15–20 ft. (does NOT meet guidelines)	30 ft.	30 ft.	18-25 ft. (does NOT meet guidelines)
Time of continuous spray	6 seconds	7 seconds	9 seconds	4 seconds (does NOT meet guidelines)	5.4 seconds (does NOT meet guidelines)	5 seconds (does NOT meet guidelines)
Meets guidelines		YES, Counter Assault meets all guidelines	NO	NO	NO	NO

*Subregistrants/distributors purchase a registered product and relabel the can with their own labels. The EPA registration number, formula, contents, and specifications are the same as their respective registered product.

The chart specifications were developed in the early 1980s by bear biologists and wildlife specialists in the development stage of COUNTER ASSAULT BEAR DETERRENT.

This information is from the EPA label of each product.

For additional information, see these websites:

Environmental Protection Agency (EPA): www.epa.gov/region8/toxics_pesticides/pests/beardeter.html

Interagency Grizzly Bear Committee: www.fs.fed.us/r1/wildlife/igbc/background.htm

Bear Expert Killed by Grizzly

On February 20, 2001, Timothy Treadwell appeared on CBS's *Late Show with David Letterman,* laughing and joking about his life as a defender of the grizzly. In promoting his book *Living with Wild Bears in Alaska,* Treadwell showed close-up videos of himself with fearsome grizzlies, even creeping on all fours among a grizzly sow and her cuddly cubs.

Treadwell contended that grizzlies are really "harmless, party animals" that enjoy affectionate nuzzling and actually spend little time being aggressive. He said the key was to not frighten them, but talk to them in a soft singsong voice.

Shortly after his television interview, Treadwell chartered a pilot, Willy Hall, to come pick him up at the end of his season's work in his thirteenth summer camped among Alaska's most dangerous grizzly population.

When Hall arrived at the designated spot, he found a 1,000-pound grizzly sitting atop the shredded remains of Treadwell's body, having a feast. The odds were against Treadwell's getting mauled, even in Katmai National Park, home to 3,000 of the largest grizzlies in North America. He and his girlfriend were the first deaths by grizzlies in the park's eighty-five-year history.

With the thousands of visitors to that park, this isn't bad odds. But Treadwell could have improved his odds had he followed the safer-camping instructions of park rangers and friends concerned about his safety and the message he was sending to the public. Park superintendent Deb Ligget said: "At best he's misguided. At worst he's dangerous. If Timothy models unsafe behavior, that ultimately puts bears and other visitors at risk."

Bear expert Bill Schneider says point-blank that Treadwell was reckless in teaching people, particularly schoolchildren, that it is perfectly safe to consort with grizzly bears.

you will be given a copy of the regulations that apply. If not, check the bulletin board.

And since Forest Service has not been as diligent in managing bears, observe the NPS rules when hiking in adjacent national forests or BLM lands.

I once was hiking with Rick Graetz and his friends in the Madison Mountains, near Yellowstone National Park, where we believed we were out of grizzly territory. But we ran across a posting near a mountain pond where we intended to camp that advised that grizzlies had been spotted recently in the area. We knew the NPS guidelines and set up our camp accordingly, even though there were no Forest Service rules for that area.

Today, Bill Schneider says, grizzlies range throughout not only the Madison Range, but Big Sky and Spanish Peaks as well. All of which points up the fact that even outside the parks, it is foolish not to follow NPS bear safety guidelines.

CAMPING IN BEAR COUNTRY

Most national parks assign you backcountry campsites sight unseen until you hike in to the campground. Nonetheless, an artful discussion with backcountry rangers will help you obtain the safest site available when they issue your permit. In some national parks, such as Yosemite, Kings Canyon-Sequoia, and Denali, though the campgrounds are designated, sites are not, and you have freedom to choose on a first-come basis. Likewise in most national forests. A good many national forests and BLM lands permit camping at large, though their regulations will require you to camp a certain distance from water or trails.

How to Make Camp

This decision may be the most important of your camp safety measures.

Do not camp at a site where there are food scraps, litter, or grease of any sort from previous campers. This is an almost certain invitation for a bear to come for dinner.

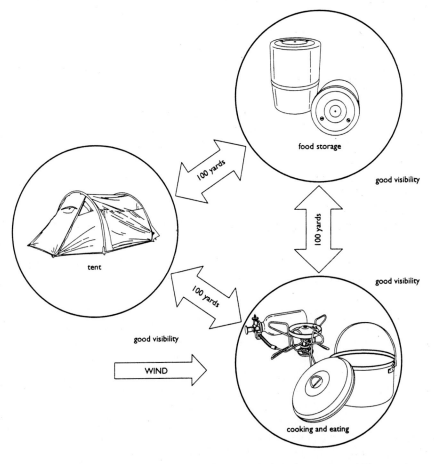

The bear-resistant triangle: when camping in bear country, situate your tent 100 paces from where you cook and eat; and store food 100 paces from where you sleep and 100 yards from where you cook and eat. Bear-resistant food containers are the safest way to store food on the trail. Many national parks provide them either free or for a small rental fee.

FROM *MOUNTAINEERING: FREEDOM OF THE HILLS.* COPYRIGHT © 2005 MOUNTAINEERS BOOKS.

It is unfortunate that people who leave garbage are not the ones who usually get hurt by bears. It is a subsequent user of the site that gets attacked, for the original culprit is long gone by the time bears discover the leavings and return for more.

It is a good reason to arrive at your campsite early, so you'll have plenty of time before nightfall to make your inspection to be sure that you have the safest campsite possible.

Finally, do not sleep out under the stars. It may seem unlikely that a tent could provide any protection from bears, since tent walls are so thin. But the tent does create the impression of something much bigger than a sleeping bag.

If you see fresh sign of bears anywhere—paw marks on the ground, clawed tree trunks, bear scat—or worse yet, you see a bear, do not camp there. Even if you have a reserved site and a permit for it, do not camp there. Camp instead in an undesignated area, and be sure to report your findings to the ranger when you return from your hike.

With that exception, do not camp in an undesignated area. There is too great a danger that you could be choosing a perfect habitat for bears. Besides, it is illegal and could get you in trouble with park authorities.

Cooking and Eating at Your Campsite

Bears love fish. So do not camp near a fishing area, especially stream inlets to lakes. If you cook fish, clean them twice as far away from camp as you store your food, at least 200 paces from your tent area.

Cook your meals and eat them a good 100 paces from your tent. Change your clothes after you have eaten, and leave the clothes you ate in stored, along with your food, in a bear-resistant place. You do not want the slightest trace of food odors near your tent in bear country.

Storing Food in Camp

Bears are attracted to food odors, as well as scents of cosmetics, toiletries, toothpaste, and sunscreen, as flies to honey, and bears have a much keener sense of smell than flies.

There are old and new ways to carry and store food in bear country. I'll tell you about both, because some parks still recommend the old way while many prefer the new. The aim of both is to keep food scents sealed so as not to attract bears.

The new method is far superior to the old and is working in parks in Alaska, as well as those where bears have figured out how to outfox the old method.

The New Method

Yosemite Park has dealt with bear problems on a megascale—not in deaths, but in far more bear nuisances than other parks. Bears have become so wise to park visitors that they have figured out where the food is in ice chests, coolers, and cars. They regularly break into locked cars, even into trunks.

Yosemite bears do not need to have the scent of food, for they can identify packages and even chewing-gum wrappers. Thus park management has had to clamp down rather hard with penalties for leaving food in cars. Violators can get citations or even have their property confiscated.

Bears at Yosemite have also figured out how to get food down from the best bear-resistant hanging devices. Thus the new method of food storage for the trail: the bear-resistant food container. It is quick, simple, and easy to use, made of polymer with smooth sides and rounded edges so bears have nothing to grip. It seals tight with a stainless-steel lock that is easy for humans to open with a coin but impossible for bears to open. A container holds six days of food for one person.

These containers are required for food storage at camps above timberline in Yosemite and strongly urged to be used elsewhere. Most Alaskan national parks provide bear-resistant food containers gratis for backcountry use.

Despite being bear-resistant, these food containers still need to be stored 100 paces from your tent. For food odors may still be present on the exterior of the containers.

The Old Method
Designated campsites in many national parks have bear poles on which to hang your food safely out of reach of bears. If you are hiking in a national forest or on BLM land, check with the rangers beforehand to find out what to expect for storing your food in their backcountry campsites.

If your campsite does not have a device for hanging food, then you will have to improvise one. Find a limb of a tree that is sturdy enough, and hang your food bag from it a full ten feet above the ground and four feet away from the trunk. Or find a tree leaning against another that provides such a food-hanging mechanism.

Before hanging your food, prepare it to store in the food bag so as to cut off all food odors. First of all, put food and garbage in odor-resistant containers, such as zipper-lock bags. If the food is particularly smelly, then store it in two zipper-lock bags, one inside the other.

Also store other items with odors, such as toothpaste, hair spray, lotions, sunscreen, and makeup, first in zipper-lock bags, then in tightly sealed trash bags, before packing them in a large stuff sack to hang. Better still, leave as many of these items as possible at home. Store water bottles this way in the stuff sack as well. They have odors, especially if you have carried any mixed drink in them.

The stuff sack you use to hang your food ought to be waterproof and large enough to contain all of your food and cosmetic items, as well as any cooking utensils.

You will also need a good 100 feet or so of nylon cord. It should be of clothesline thickness. Parachute cord will do the trick as well if you are hanging a small amount of food.

Bill Schneider recommends concocting a small pulley system to make the hoisting easier. This is particularly useful when hanging food for a long trip or larger group. Makes sense and can be obtained very reasonably at most hardware stores.

Plan to hang your food well before dark. It is tricky after dark. The usual way is to tie a rock or branch to the end of a rope, then toss it over the limb. Tie your food bag to one end of the rope, then haul it up, and tie down the loose end to secure the load.

A better way, and one that some national parks require, is the balanced-load system. You will have to prepare for this in advance of your trip. You'll need to carry an extra stuff sack. When you arrive at the campsite, fill it with a few small rocks before tossing it over the hanging limb. Then, when you begin hoisting the food storage bag, you can

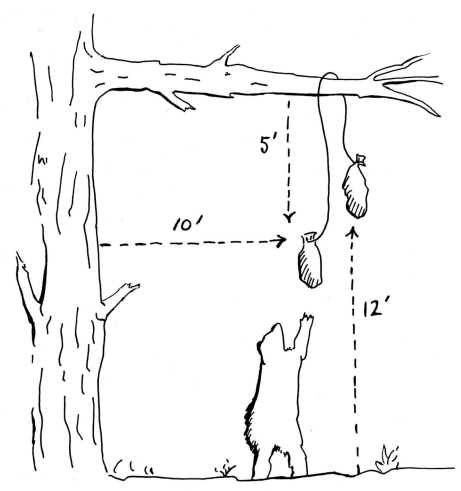

Hang all food, garbage, clothing with food odors, and cosmetics well out of reach of bears. Counterbalance the food bag with a bag full of rocks at other end of rope to hold the food bag well above the reach of bears, at least twelve feet from the ground.

fill the ditty bag with more rocks until its weight equals that of your food bag. When the food is hoisted high enough, your rock-filled ditty bag will hold it in place, and it is all right if it is close to or even on the ground, for it presumably has no food odor.

When bringing the food bag down, untie the food bag, making sure there are no knots left in the rope, then gently haul it back over the branch. Do not jerk it, or you could get it tangled around a branch and have to leave it.

Gear to Take into Your Tent
Do not take your pack into the tent. It is impossible to keep food odors off it. Take into your tent only sleeping bags, clothes, flashlight, camera, binoculars, and bear pepper spray deterrent.

For Maximum Safety in Bear Country

- Be on the alert at all times, especially when coming around bends in the trail or going through thickly forested or bushy areas.
- Make noise as you hike.
- Hike in larger groups.
- Carry bear pepper spray deterrent where it can be quickly pulled out and used in event of a surprise encounter with a bear.
- Eliminate all scents and odors of food, drink, and toiletries by packing smelly items of any sort in odorproof, bear-resistant containers.
- Cook and eat at least 100 paces from where you camp.
- Store all foods, utensils, cooking gear, sunscreen, toiletries, even clothes you wore when you ate in odorproof containers at least 100 paces from your camp. Use the bear-resistant containers that have been developed for use by backpackers at Yosemite National Park, instead of the old way of hanging bags of food up out of reach of bears.
- Do not leave your pack unattended anywhere for even a few minutes.
- Sleep inside a tent, not out under the stars.
- Do not have sex in bear country.
- Do not go into bear country during menstrual periods.
- If you see a bear, do not run or try to climb a tree.
- In the presence of a bear, stop. Stand still. Loom as large and tall as you can. Back away from the bear slowly.
- If approached by a bear, use your bear pepper spray deterrent, but not before the bear is within thirty feet of you.
- Hike in midday from about 11 A.M. to 3 P.M. Avoid hiking in early morning, late afternoon, evening, and at night.
- Stay on the more heavily used trails in bear country.
- If attacked by a bear that is not defending itself or its cubs and you do not have bear pepper spray deterrent, do not play dead. Fight the bear off with whatever you can get your hands on. Scream and yell.
- If attacked by a bear that is defending itself or its cubs, play dead. If it continues the attack without leaving, then fight back.

The most essential piece of equipment you must carry in bear country is bear pepper spray deterrent. It is easy to use and highly effective in deterring a bear from approaching you if it gets too near.

But bear pepper spray deterrent is a last resort—and even at that, it is not a guarantee of survival. Do all you can to avoid a bear encounter. Once a bear begins to attack you, there is no sure way of survival.

Avoid Sex and Menstrual Periods

Avoid having sex in camp. And it is wise for a woman having her menstrual period to avoid bear country. There is no proof that either of these attract bears, but there is a strong suspicion, though there are conflicting views. But why take the chance? For details, see www.nps/yell/nature/animals/bear/infopaper/info7.

19

Cougar Alert

One beautiful April morning, Barbara Schoener drove her Intrepid to the Auburn Lake Trails subdivision in California. She drove past the gates, past daffodil-trimmed lawns where children were playing, a man was washing his car, and two others were mowing lawns.

She parked at the trailhead near gate number three, slipped her car keys into the pocket of her purple shorts, pulled on a white visor, and warmed up. Then at about 8 A.M., Barbara started off on her jog. Her route would go seventeen miles to Brown's Bridge and back on the Western States Trail. She was training for an ultramarathon like the Cool Canyon Run she and her husband, Pete, had run together a few weeks earlier.

About an hour into her run, she rounded the long, U-shaped curve that gives a glimpse of the American River far below. Barbara had not noticed she was being followed, quietly, in a slow, studied, creeping way, by something hidden behind the bushes just out of sight. Seemingly as though there was no movement at all, the cougar slipped slowly closer, its color blending conveniently into the background of earth and rocks beneath the trees.

At the appropriate moment, the cougar leaped upon Barbara from behind and sunk its teeth deep into her neck, straddling her back with its four paws digging into her flesh from all sides. It hit with such force that it carried her off the trail, down the steep ravine at the side of the trail.

Having either killed or severely crippled her, the cougar loosened its grip on Barbara's neck and sank its teeth into her skull to drag her further down the ravine away from the trail. Then it chewed a hole in her back, crunching through ribs to feed upon the woman's organs.

She never had a chance to fight back. Anything she could have done to save her life needed to have been before she left her car—become far more sensitive to what lurks in the trailside foliage, run with at least one other companion, and carry a stick or other deterrent.

This is a disturbing image. But cougars must kill often and expertly in order to eat the ten pounds of flesh a day they need to live.

Today there is a memorial, Barbara's Bench, on the trail near where her body was found. One of the men who located her badly mauled remains, veteran ultramarathon runner Kurt Fox, is quoted by James Raia Communications (www.byjamesraia.com) as saying: "I pass women on the trails by themselves—a lot. When I see them out there all I can think to myself is, 'If you would have seen what I saw, you would take more concern.'"

Barbara Schoener was attacked in 1994. It was the first death from a cougar attack in California in 100 years. In the 10 years following, there were five more cougar attack fatalities in California—virtually all of them hikers, trail runners, and bikers.

Though the risk is still not great, it is ominous. But compare it to driving: Even with the improbable risk of getting hit by someone running a stop sign or red light, we don't stop driving. We simply become aware of the risk, take extra precautions when we encounter those situations,

Believe it or not, I wouldn't go out on the trail without my recorder—the musical instrument, not the writer's tool. It reminds me to sit down and relax now and then.

—*Jo Deurbrouck, author of* Stalked by a Mountain Lion: Fact, Fear and the Uncertain Future of the Puma in America *and, with Dean Miller,* Cat Attacks: True Stories and Hard Lessons from Cougar Country, *as well as magazine and newspaper articles about the outdoors*

and remain alert. Likewise, with cougars, we ought to know what the risks are, how to look out for them, and what precautions to take. And what to do if someone "runs the red light."

INCREASED COUGAR ATTACKS IN THE PAST TWO DECADES

The cougar is known by various names: mountain lion, puma, panther, or occasionally just lion. Its normal diet is ten pounds of raw meat a day, which it gains from killing deer, small game such as porcupines and raccoons, and even smaller game such as squirrels, mice, and chipmunks. Unlike wolves or coyotes, which hunt in packs, the cougar hunts alone. It stalks its prey and pounces upon it from ambush.

Numbers are not easy to come by; there are various ways of counting cougar attacks, and it is not easy to compare the studies of reliable researchers. Antihunting groups tend to bend the numbers to their point of view, tending to minimize them. And there are differences in the time periods that are studied by different researchers, the most thorough of whom is Northern Arizona University's biologist, Paul Beier.

Even the most conservative of the counts indicates that there have been an increasing number of cougar attacks on humans since the 1970s, when data became more accessible and reliable. The data show a 600 percent increase in cougar attacks on humans in the 1990s over the number in the 1970s, and the number is still increasing into the twenty-first century.

In the 1990s, there were four times more attacks on humans than there were in the eighty years from 1890 to 1970, and 50 percent more than there were in the two decades before that. On average now, there are fourteen attacks per year, mostly on hikers and trail runners. These attacks are savage, leaving victims badly scarred and often crippled.

Deaths from cougars, too, have shot up alarmingly in the past ten to fifteen years. And here researchers are pretty much in agreement. Up to 1970, there were no more than four cougar attack deaths over a ninety-year period. There is now an average of about one such death per year since Barbara Schoener was killed in 1994.

Close Encounters with Cougars

Cougar attacks on humans are extremely rare. In North America, around twenty fatalities and a hundred nonfatal attacks have been reported during the past hundred years. But more cougar attacks have been reported in the western United States and Canada over the past twenty years than in the previous eighty. In Washington, according to the Department of Fish and Wildlife, one fatal cougar attack was recorded in 1924. Since then, twelve nonfatal attacks have been recorded, eleven of them since 1992.

In the earlier figures, it was primarily younger children who were killed in western parts of North America in cougar attacks. But lately the victims have been adults, and the attacks have been moving east to places like Colorado, Oklahoma, Arkansas, and Ontario, Canada. And most of these places report that it was the first such death by cougar ever.

The concern for us is that most attacks are on hikers or trail runners. Though compared with other types of risks cougar attacks are still low on the totem pole, they are more significant because of the alarming rate at which they are increasing and how little is known about how to avoid them or protect yourself if attacked.

There are three reasons for this rapid increase. First, the numbers of cougars has increased because of changes in management. There was a bounty on them up until the 1950s. Since then, the bounty has been discontinued, and a number of laws have been enacted by various states limiting the hunting of cougars. Second, residential building has encroached upon their habitat, putting humans in greater contact with them. And third, there have been rapid increases in the number of hikers and trail runners in the past couple of decades, putting more of us at risk.

Because of urban expansion, the cougar has found dogs and even young children as fair game for a meal. The place where attacks are most prevalent is British Columbia's Vancouver Island. Seventeen of the fifty-four attacks in the 1990s occurred in or near its towns and villages.

HOW TO IDENTIFY A COUGAR

The cougars in North America are usually tawny to light cinnamon colored, with black tips on both tail and ears. They are much larger than lynx or bobcats.

Males average eight feet from nose to tip of tail and a weight of 150 pounds. Females average seven feet tip to tip and a weight of a little under 100 pounds. Their tails average about a third of their total length.

Their habitat ranges from desert, brush, rain forests, and woodlands all the way up to subalpine levels of mountains. They are most plentiful where deer are abundant.

Cougars are most active at night, particularly at dawn and dusk, but they do hunt in daylight hours as well. In addition to their diet of wild animals, they have a propensity toward livestock and a variety of domestic animals such as dogs and other pets. As I write this, there is a section of Colorado where several dogs have been attacked by cougars in the past three months—seven in one town alone. In a recent year, park and fish and game managers in Kalispell, Montana, received 2,800 complaints of cougar or bear problems.

Cougars, for the most part, kill their own prey, taking it by ambush. Once it has spotted a likely animal, a cougar will stalk it, hiding in whatever cover is available, then suddenly attack, usually from behind.

They kill with a powerful bite, breaking the neck just below the base of the skull. They then drag the carcass to a sheltered spot to feed upon it. Once their appetite is sated, they bury the carcass beneath leaves, dirt, snow, whatever is available, and return from time to time over several days to feed. After each feeding, they drag the carcass to a new location and bury it again.

Cougars live an average of about twelve years. Their only enemies are larger animals—bears, larger lions, and wolves. They also die from other causes—diseases, accidents, and being killed by human beings.

Newborns weigh about a pound and are about a foot long. They have dark spots. At about six weeks old, their mother takes them to her kill to feed, and they begin learning how to hunt. They don't lose their spots until they are about six months old, when they weigh about thirty pounds. They remain with their mother, improving their hunting skills, until they are about two years old. Immature cats are responsible for many attacks on humans.

HOW TO AVOID COUGAR ATTACKS

While cougar attacks are rare, so are deaths from drunk drivers crashing into you. The best protection is an awareness of the risks and how to recognize them if they occur. Because most attacks occur to runners and hikers, here are some precautions that reduce those risks:

- Know the territory. Is it cougar habitat? Have there been prior encounters in the territory? Check with land managers or fish and wildlife agencies in the area. State fish and wildlife managers in cougar country all provide literature on their prevalence and what precautions to take. If no information is available, you can assess the territory the best you can by one major consideration—deer. They are the cougar's primary prey. Another consideration is that trails closer to developed areas are most vulnerable, for a number of reasons spelled out elsewhere in the chapter. Cougars are less likely to reside in more open areas such as deserts and grasslands, though they might be found along rivers running through them.
- Observe warning signs or notices of cougar activity in the area posted by land management agencies.
- Be keenly aware of what is around you. Cougars are enormously seclusive and are rarely seen, even when they are close by. So it is essential that you be particularly aware of the trees and bushes through which you hike or run. This advice is just as useful for cougars as it is for bears.
- Hike with others—a companion or group.
- Keep small children close to you, especially when traveling through woodlands and brush where you cannot see very far ahead or behind.
- Know what to do if you do encounter a cougar.
- Carry a weapon or deterrent device within quick access. (Remember that firearms are illegal on most public lands.) And be aware that most attack victims get little to no warning of being attacked.

Cougar Encounters

Cougars are seclusive. They move about quietly, calmly, and in hiding. The likelihood of seeing one in the wild is remote. The likelihood of them seeing you is far greater. They generally want to avoid contact with humans, however.

They are most abundant where there are plenty of deer to hunt. These conditions exist more and more in residential mountain subdivisions and on the fringes of urban areas. The number of encounters in these areas has increased dramatically in recent years, as residential communities have expanded further into the countryside and more people are hiking, biking, and running on trails close to these communities.

Cougar attacks do not occur in remote backcountry, where you might most expect them. From the perspective of cougar attacks, perhaps the safest place you can hike is in remote wilderness. The only attacks in national parks I could find documented were on the more frequently trafficked trails. Following is a breakdown of the fifty-three attacks in the 1990s reported on by Jo Deurbrouck and Dean Miller in their book *Cat Attacks*. The locations of fifteen of the attacks are unknown because wildlife agencies do not always provide information about where the attacks occurred.

Within sight of human dwellings	7
Developed campsites or campgrounds	6
Trails or roads	24
Remote backcountry	1
Unknown	15
Total	53

- Do not hike at night or in the early morning or early evening. Cougars are nocturnal, and most likely to be encountered at these times.
- Do not hike with a dog. If you do hike with a dog, be sure it is under your control even under stressful situations. A dog is easy prey to cougars. Dogs do not provide any protection whatsoever against this threat.
- Do not leave food or garbage unattended in camp, which can attract animals. Even attracting animals such as deer or raccoons can, in turn, attract cougars.
- Make noise as you move about, especially at dawn and dusk.
- Stay away from dead animals. They may well be prey of cougars or bears.
- Talk to your children and other members of your hiking group beforehand about the dangers of cougar attacks.

WHAT TO DO IN AN ENCOUNTER

There are no reliable studies of what to do if you encounter a cougar. Based upon the experiences of some who have encountered them, however, there seem to be some patterns of behavior that may be helpful. Here are some suggestions:

- Quickly assess the risk as follows: If the cougar is fifty yards away or more and changes positions, directing its attention toward other things as well as you and your group, it may only be curious. The risk is slight, but it is greater to unattended children. Back away slowly, while keeping the cougar in your peripheral view. Take out your deterrent or pick up rocks or branches or something to use as a weapon in case the risk increases. If the cougar is closer than fifty yards and is staring intensely and hiding, it possibly is preparing for attack. If the staring becomes even more intense, accompanied by crouching and creeping, it indicates that the risk is getting very serious. Be prepared for it to attack!

- Never approach a cougar. Give it a way to escape. Most seem to want to avoid human contact. Stay calm if you do encounter one. Talk calmly, yet loud and authoritatively.
- Stop. If possible, back away slowly. Do not run. Running seems to stimulate a cougar's instinct to chase and attack.
- Stand upright. Do not crouch or bend down if at all possible.
- Face the cougar, and keep eye contact with it. Do not turn your back to it.
- Do all you can to appear larger. Raise your arms and wave them slowly. Open your jacket and hold it open.
- If you have children, pick them up. Try to do this with the least amount of bending down possible. Keep them from panicking and running.
- If the cougar approaches you, throw stones or sticks at it without crouching down or turning your back to it.
- If, God forbid, you are attacked, fight back with all you have. Some people who have been attacked have managed to survive by fighting back with stones, sticks, jackets, tools, knives, bear pepper spray deterrent, even bare hands. Remain standing if at all possible. If you are knocked down, try to get back up.
- Defend your children with all you have. But do not defend your pet. Some people have successfully defended their children from attack. It is extremely dangerous but has, of course, been worth it to those who managed to do so.

COUGAR DETERRENTS

Much of the cougar literature recommends carrying deterrents, which is an excellent precautionary measure. There are a number of possibilities here, with varying degrees of effectiveness, none of which have actually gone through any important study. Because cougar attacks are sudden and unexpected, usually from the victim's back, the effectiveness of the deterrents, no matter how good, is very limited. Still, it is better to be prepared than to ignore the threat.

Weapons and deterrent devices may include walking sticks, knives, bear pepper spray deterrent, and firearms. Firearms are forbidden on most public lands, however, except with a hunting license. And their use would seem to be rather limited in a sudden attack from the rear. Whatever you choose to carry, be sure you know how to use it in a defensive situation. Be comfortable and confident of its use before setting out on the trail.

Though unproven, it would appear that pepper spray designed specifically for bears, such as Counter Assault Bear

I always carry a two-ounce featherweight zippered shell that is wind-resistant and water-repellent. It has saved me great discomfort over the years.

—Gudy Gaskill, "mother" and builder of the 500-mile Colorado Trail

Pepper Spray, would be the most useful and effective of all the deterrents. First of all, it is easy to use quickly. And though it will likely drive away the animal, it will not inflict permanent damage and hence will give you a lot more moral confidence than would something that may well kill the animal.

Note, too, that people have successfully fought off cougar attacks with rocks and sticks, and even in rare cases their bare hands.

One other factor to keep in mind, though not very comforting to the victim: Should you or any member of your party be a victim of a deadly assault by a cougar, that animal will be tracked down and shot. So you may help save the life of a cougar too.

Section Five

THE HIKING PARTY

Sky so blue it makes you wonder
  If it's heaven shining through;
Earth so smiling 'way out yonder,
  Sun so bright it dazzles you;
Birds a-singing, flowers a-flinging
  All their fragrance on the breeze;
Dancing shadows, green, still meadows—
  Don't you mope, you've still got these.

  —*from "Comfort," by Robert Service*

20

The Fine Art of Picking
Your Hiking Companions

Because you've started reading a chapter with this title, I presume you are much in the same sort of boat I was in for many years: loving the trails but not finding others who love them as much—or at least not in the same way—as you.

Like me, you may already have tried a few dozen different companions, and though they are all good people whom you love doing other things with, the trail is just not where your compatibilities meld very neatly.

As we become more immersed in our backpacking, the more we find out about ourselves, devoid of societal constrictions. While we are out there in stillness, away from TV, computers, cell phones, radio, family, and friends, we begin to truly see our innermost foibles, our compatibilities, our harmonies as well as our discordances. We discover that we deeply like some attributes about ourselves, as we also become aware of some of those ungracious sides of ourselves. But in the backcountry, we learn to accept ourselves, more for what we truly are than for any of the falsities of persona that we put on in our everyday lives back home.

Yes, long before we became backpackers, we knew we had two inner selves—the one being our social persona built by our nurturing, and our other truer, deeper, God-given nature. And the more we get away from the limiting influences of our everyday life, the more we get in tune with this more fundamental side of who we are.

Our upbringing, no matter how well intentioned our parents, was largely shaped by the word *don't*.

"Don't play with fire; you could get burned!" "Don't play in the street; you could get hit by a car!" "Don't be impolite; that's your grandmother who loves you!" "Don't pick that up off the floor and eat it; it's dirty and could have germs!" "Don't hit your little sister. It's not nice!"

"Don't do this . . ." "Don't do that . . ." On and on . . .

And later in life, the *don'ts* get couched in more and more sophisticated, genteel-sounding language.

"You wouldn't want people to think you were an idiot, would you!" (Not as a question, but as an epithet.) "*Yuck!* Who dresses like that!" "*¡Caramba!* Not another one of those!"

It is such a relief to be free of other people's ideas of who we are—to be able to see thoughts for what they are and where they come from, knowing underneath it all is a more authentic "me."

This is the psychological freedom of the outdoors. We cherish it. And because of this side of our backcountry experience, the more we get out there, the more we want to have around us others who jibe with our more authentic self. Whom we choose as backpacking companions becomes most important.

If you are married and have family, you likely already have a good many companions whom you might say are "built in" to your social structure and make perfectly wonderful trail companions—*most of the time.* There may be other times, though, when, like me, you want more trail time than your family is inclined or able to give you.

If it hasn't already done so, likely over the years your backpacking will boil down your trail-enduring matchups to a handful of stalwarts.

Mine include a fair number with whom I enjoy backpacking, but who have quite limited amounts of time to go with me. For example, my daughter Kate, who is joining me shortly for a week's hiking in Colorado's Weminuche Wilderness, will be with me on our first backpacking together in a number of years. She has a different lifestyle and a lot on her platter to allow for much hiking. She is a great trail companion, though. I truly enjoy her company. We enjoy the same pace of trailside living and have mutual passion for the feelings we get in the outdoors.

There are others among my immediate family with whom, for one reason or another, I don't find the time to get together. A number of friends fall into this category as well. Yet my need to be on trails erupts too frequently for these occasional get-togethers. I find myself gathering my gear and checking maps far more often than I have companions available for my hikes. Thus I go solo much of the time, which I enjoy as much as, if not more than, going with my best hiking companions.

MY FAVORITE TRAIL COMPANION

I have one reliable trail partner, though: my nephew Kenn Petsch, who defies my solo bent. He often seems to find the time for backpacking jaunts when the whim hits me. Fortunately, we both love the same sort of backcountry agenda. We both have heightened passions for Grand Canyon as well. Luckily, the canyon lies halfway between us. He lives in San Diego and I in northern New Mexico, each of which is a nine-hour drive from South Rim trailheads. And we both have flexibility in our work schedules—he owns his own business, and I live the life of an author.

One time, for example, Kenn called for-some reason unrelated to either the canyon or hiking but missed me. Then when I returned his call, he wasn't there. I left word with his wife, Cheryl, that I would not be home for the

Molly Kemsley and William Kemsley III starting down the North Kaibab Trail in Grand Canyon.

On my hikes, I carry the wisdom of individuals who have helped me remember that we are who we are because of those we have come to know along the way: my father, Dennis Ward; my USFS friend, Pete Wingle, who introduced me to the "Forest Service family"; Dos Chappel of Volunteers for Outdoor Colorado, who gave me an understanding of how to "give back" to the land; outdoorsman Jean Campestre, who died at my feet in an avalanche; and longtime trail advocates Ira Spring and Louise Marshall.

—*Bruce Ward, executive director, Continental Divide Trail Alliance*

next few days, but that if Kenn wanted to reach me sooner, he could call me later that night at my hotel in Grand Canyon Village. Just earlier that day, I had made an impulsive decision to take a quick trip to the canyon.

I arrived at Maswick Lodge just after midnight that night. Kenn had called and left a message saying he would try again later. Then at 3 A.M., I awakened from a dream. I thought I had heard loud knocking at my door. But then when fully awake, I heard a voice calling my name.

"Uncle Bill!"

Kenn had decided that I was not going on a hike in to our favorite spot by myself. When he heard where I was going, he hopped into his truck and drove straight across to the canyon, arriving at 3 A.M. to knock on my door.

That was several months ago. On our most recent hike, we intended to spend a few days hiking a four-day loop, but the first night we got a very late start and made it only a third of the way to our destination. We were forced to make camp prematurely, though it was still in our permitted camping area and also another of our favorite campsites. So no hardship.

That night, I came down with some sort of viral ailment. I was nauseous through the night, and it sapped all the energy from me. In the morning, I was unable to raise my head, never mind get out of my sleeping bag. I was achy, had no appetite, and felt generally too punky to hike. Except for occasionally coming to, I slept for thirty-six hours straight.

I felt guilty, as if I were a disappointing bore to him. But Kenn quite lovingly said, "Uncle Bill, could you have picked a better place to be sick?"

He was right, of course. We were sleeping under the sky, with priceless views all around in every direction.

He was a wonderfully understanding trail buddy who found plenty of interesting activities in which to engage himself while I pooped out. The next day, I was energized enough to get up and about. We aborted the next two days of our trek, hiked back out the way we had come in. Who else would have put up with me?

Then, to end the story, once we were back on the rim, Kenn came down with the same debilitating viral attack. He was pooped, depleted of energy, and had to sleep the whole day through as well!

ANOTHER BACKCOUNTRY BUDDY

Another favorite hiking companion, Jim Kern, is someone I only hike or canoe with for a few days once every few years. But we probably have spent as much time with each other in the backcountry as we have at all other times.

When we do get out on treks, I must say they always turn out to be the most unusual backcountry excursions. For example, Jim called one day and said, "Why don't we both read the same book so that we can discuss it on our next hike."

I love chatting with Jim on hikes—at rest stops, over lunch, and in camp in the evening. I always learn so much hearing him talk about bird species and wildlife. He is a patient listener to what I have to say as well. Could it get any better?

This time, though, he caught me off guard, suggesting we each read *Understanding Poetry,* by W. H. Auden. It sounded a bit heavy, but why not?

One reason that Jim is such a good backcountry companion is that we both camp alike. Our pace is similar. Our needs for conversation are similar. Our camping styles are too. We share a love of John Burroughs as well as our natural curiosity, a common-sense interest in whatever is going on around us.

We each go about our interests of the moment, never intruding on or excluding the other. It is difficult to describe this characteristic, which we seem to have acquired gradually over a lifetime spent outdoors.

Both of us grew up in the Boy Scouts, for one thing. Then, my experience has a good dash of tricks learned from my father, whose boyhood was spent on a homestead in northwest Canada and who cherished his time spent in the woods. As I was growing up, he often took our family on Sunday drives in the country. And on these drives, he often pulled off the road and took us for walks in the woods whenever we came to places Dad found interesting.

I am not quite sure what it was that Dad found interesting about any of these places. But we'd go for our walk, actually a hike, either along an old two-rut wagon road or just making our way through the bush without a trail.

Dad had this beguiling curiosity that would rise at just about any time.

"I wonder where this road goes?" Or he'd say, "I wonder what's around that bend in the path up there?" There would always be genuine curiosity in the tone of his voice.

I can't say that we ever marveled especially over what we found "up there," "over there," or "around the next bend," though Dad sometimes gave names to these places reflecting his love, such as "secret sanctuary," "sacred hiking grove," "cathedral in the pines."

No doubt I acquired Dad's sense of curiosity. I never know what I am looking for, nor whether or not I have ever found "it." But with this sense of wonder ever fresh, the search continues to compel me to take another peek around the next curve in the trail, needing to see what is just over the next hill. I am never disappointed and usually somehow exhilarated by my finding, whatever that might be. Yes, often it is a magnificent scene, although my joy has been raised to peak pitch as well from just another resting spot along the trail or setting up a plain camp in the woods.

Jim Kern's curiosity takes a more biological turn, turning him into a bird and wildlife expert. He seems able to tell the species of bird simply by hearing its song.

We'll be trudging along a trail, and he will hesitate, his nose up and ears cocked.

"Hear that?" he'll say, peering over the tops of shrubs in the direction of a break of balsam firs. "That's a blackpoll warbler. They usually aren't in this area."

It is these sorts of facts that intrigue me. I love hearing it from someone like Jim but have little patience to find them out on my own.

I always take popcorn— wouldn't leave home without it.

—*Christine Woodside, editor of AMC's* **Appalachia** *magazine and AT end-to-ender*

One time because of Jim, I read one of John Burroughs's essays on Slide Mountain in which he described identifying the Baird's thrush, a rare bird that he said was found only on Slide Mountain.

I enjoyed climbing Slide Mountain from various routes, and that summer while climbing it, I had my eyes peeled to find the Baird's thrush, which Burroughs said was abundant on top. And I was overjoyed at finding one!

Then when I got home, my delight descended to despair as I discovered that though I had seen a thrush all right, it could have been one of several subspecies. Yes, it could have been a Baird's thrush. But it may also have been a Swainson's, or an olive-backed, or even just a plain gray-cheeked thrush. So how to tell the difference? Well, the Baird's is smaller, like six and a quarter to seven and a half inches, while the others range from seven and a quarter to eight inches. Okay, so how about the ring around the eye and the gray cheek? Yes, they are less distinct on the Baird's. So, all right then, I looked up again what John o'–the-Mountains said about it.

He admitted flat out that he couldn't tell the difference from just seeing it, though its song is different from other thrushes, "as if the bird was blowing in a delicate, slender, golden tube, so fine and yet so flute-like and resonant," as John Burroughs described it *(In the Catskills)*.

End of my patience. I prefer to get my bird information from Jim o'–the-Mountains.

Jim Kern read the draft of this chapter on a flight to Washington's Olympic Peninsula for a week of birding. He dropped me a note with his only comment about the chapter: "Baird's may have been a name in use in Burroughs's time but it is not now. Not with regard to a thrush. There used to be a Bicknell's thrush, but it has been lumped with the gray-cheeked thrush. And there used to be an olive-backed thrush, but it has been lumped with the Swainson's thrush. The American Ornithological Union decides these things. There are the 'lumpers' and the 'splitters.' With regard to the thrush, the lumpers are ascendant!"

This was Jim's gentle way of correcting me. And I could simply have changed the name from Baird's to Bicknell's thrush in the manuscript and been done with it. Dumb mistake, for I see this was exactly what Burroughs had called the thrush, now that I looked it up for the third time! But I decided to keep it as I wrote it so that I could give this chapter a bit of the flavor of why I love hiking with Jim.

My confusion came from my lack of patience in reading Burroughs. Here is more of what he said: "In its appearance to the eye among the trees, one would not distinguish it from the gray-cheeked thrush of Baird, or the olive-backed thrush."

Without Jim, I wouldn't have the patience to "split" Baird from Bicknell and their thrushes. To confound me even more, there is a footnote in Burrough's book that says, "Bicknell's thrush turns out to be the more southern form of the gray-cheeked thrush, and is found on the higher mountains of New York and New England."

On one of our hikes in the Catskills, bushwhacking across a couple of ridges, Jim showed me, merely by doing it, a trick I'd never seen before. We were high on the side of a mountain, next to a spring bubbling from beneath rocks.

We decided to camp there, though there wasn't a flat stretch of ground anywhere. Jim laid out his sleeping bag horizontally on the side of the mountain, uphill from a large tree so that he would not roll downhill during the night. What a simple and useful idea. I did likewise.

COMPANIONS WHO HAVE DIFFERENT HIKING STYLES

Though Jim is one of my all-time favorite hiking companions, there are limits that we both acknowledge. Jim would just as soon not hike in deserts, carrying large containers of water. And I would rather not hike in some of the swamps Jim loves, where wildlife is abundant. So when I head to Death Valley or Jim to Corkscrew Swamp, we go with other hiking companions.

I'm convinced that most people, if not all, have this innate simpatico with nature that Jim and Kenn and I enjoy. It is just not as developed in some people. Whenever and wherever it is that I stop at a scenic overlook someplace along a highway, for example, numerous other people are already parked there. Clearly they are not backpackers, nor are they even hikers. Nonetheless, I have to believe they are enjoying the view as much as I am. I am also convinced that when we touch this chord in other people, we are doing for the environment the very best possible for its ultimate salvation.

I've hiked with a wide enough variety of people that I can fairly well tell in advance if I am going to enjoy hiking with someone. Recently my friend Linus Meyer and I took a couple-day hike on a very busy trail. We did very well together in both directions. But there came a point in my socializing with other hikers on the trail when Linus had enough. He excused himself to get along the trail ahead of me and waited for me at the end of the trail.

You too must have a fair idea whose company you are going to enjoy most on the trail. How well you like to be with people in everyday life can be a fair gauge as to how you will get along with them on the trail. Of course, in the backcountry, our personality quirks tend to come out more prominently because we are in such close contact with each other for protracted periods of time, engaged in the most personal types of activities. If there are peeves that arise in ordinary daily conversation with another person, they become exaggerated on the trail after just a few hours.

We generally hike with family or our closest friends. When I started hitting my stride in backpacking, there were very few people I knew who had any interest in the backcountry—so few that I had to introduce people to the sport in order to have hiking companions. Some of these worked out well. Others were sickening disasters, for me as well as them. And the majority of these matchups were only so-so, not warranting a repeat journey.

GOING WITHOUT TRAIL COMPANIONS

This brings me around to the reason that so many of us have chosen to defy the odds and go out on our own. But as a warning, it is folly to go on the trail overnight by yourself unless you have a considerable amount of outdoors experience.

My dad was the first to take me hiking and backpacking. Toward the end of his life, I took him on annual hiking and camping trips into the southwestern deserts. He loved being on the trails with me. One night as we laid out camp under the brilliant stars in Death Valley, he confessed that he would never backpack by himself, and more particularly, he would never camp out under the stars alone. You know when this is right for you or not. Follow your heart in this. But understand the risks you are taking—at all times.

Now I have to tell you one last story about my dad. When I was a kid, he gave me my first gun, a .22-caliber pump-action rifle. The only time I was allowed to use it was when he took me squirrel hunting. Almost always it was in late fall, when the leaves had already fallen from the oaks in our part of the woods. We would walk through the woods for an hour or so, then Dad would find a large oak tree with a huge leafy nest up in its branches. He would have us both sit quietly on the ground beneath the nest, our backs leaning against trees, and wait for squirrels to show up at the nest.

Dad told me to watch. Then he would fall asleep. Now as strange as this sounds, I truly enjoyed these "squirrel hunts" with Dad, though I cannot ever remember us shooting any squirrels.

As he lay dying and I gave him my last hug, telling him, "Dad, it won't be long before I'll be over there with you," he said, "Yeah, I know. And I'll take you squirrel hunting when you get there."

Those were his last words to me. Any wonder that I love the woods so much?

And this brings me to one further point about companionship. Many people want to avoid at all costs getting to know their inner selves.

It is easy to speculate why. But then, it's always easier to analyze another person than it is to analyze yourself.

Instead, let me leap past this and talk a moment about a still deeper part of our selves that we can begin to know in the backcountry—provided we have that inclination. That is the mystical self that many metaphysical writers spell with a capital S, that Self that the poet sings about, as Wordsworth did in "Ode: Intimations of Immortality":

> *O joy! that in our embers*
> *Is something that doth live,*
> *That nature yet remembers*
> *What was so fugitive!*

Though no doubt the backcountry can aid in our quest to know this cap-S Self, it is far more likely that the backcountry enables us to become acquainted with that part of our nature we've come to keep hidden over the years, being the less socially redeemable though nonetheless more authentic part of who we are.

21

Family Hiking and Backpacking

You are lucky if you were a hiker before you got married. It is easier to get your family into hiking as you acquire the family—first just you and your spouse, then the two of you and your first infant, and on until the child becomes a toddler, then another infant as your family grows. Family hiking just naturally evolves.

It is far easier and safer to develop your techniques as your family evolves than it is to hatch them for immediate use with a full-blown family that's never hiked before. Nonetheless, if this is your starting point, it can still be enormously gratifying.

START CHILDREN ON EASY DAY HIKES

If you are not already hiking with your children, you'd be wise to start them on short, easy day hikes. Make it enjoyable for them, or you will lose them as hiking partners as they get older and are allowed a choice.

The best way I found was to pack a picnic lunch and take a short walk somewhere in the woods. A local park is fine. It does not have to be backcountry. Honestly, consider the child's pleasure factor. After walking a reasonable distance, which for toddlers might be no more than a half mile or so, stop and have a leisurely picnic lunch.

Try to find out what it is that your youngsters like about the woods. Try to listen to them, rather than asking them loaded questions such as "Isn't that a great view?" or "Don't you love that waterfall?"

And don't be disappointed if they don't like anything at all about it. Of my six children, four loved backpacking, one "liked" it, and one never, ever took to it at all. He hiked and backpacked with us repeatedly all the years of his childhood. And he enjoyed the other children's company. But as an adult, he hasn't spent a single day on any hiking trail! The other five have all continued their hiking interest to some extent.

BE PREPARED FOR THE WEATHER

Start your family hiking regimen on short walks in the most favorable weather. But always carry extra clothes and raingear in expectation of the worst changes in weather for that time of year. Nothing will more discourage your family from hiking than to run into a sudden summer shower without raingear and extra warm clothes, with the children ending the hike blue-lipped and shivering—if more serious harm does not occur.

The easy-does-it strategy discussed in chapter 1 is doubly important for breaking the family into this activity. Let the first few hikes be not more than a mile. Build up

Warning: Don't Let Children Run Ahead

There are four reasons for this precaution:
1. Missing a key turn on the trail, the child could easily get lost.
2. The child could surprise a poisonous snake. In the Northeast, there are countless copperheads that, though not aggressive, do not give any warning before striking. At one Nature Conservancy preserve in a bedroom community just outside New York City, for example, it is rare to hike on its trails and not come across at least one copperhead.
3. Bears. There have been an increasing number of predaceous black bear attacks and deaths in the past few years. One young child was attacked and killed in the Catskill Mountains near New York City. Another was attacked near a town in central New Jersey.
4. Cougars. Though attacks are rare, young children are especially vulnerable.

gradually to three to four miles on later hikes. A great benefit in doing this with your family is finding out what the comfort factors are for each of them. They will vary a great deal among your children and spouse. One of my children, Kate, was hardly ever cold, regardless of how little she wore. Another, Andrew, needed extra clothes whenever the slightest breeze blew up. By all means, do not fight these needs; cater to them. They will benefit you in the long run.

Woodland hikes are excellent for youngsters for the variety of terrain, including ponds and streams such as these in New Hampshire's White Mountains.

Foul weather can also be fun if you bring along the right weatherproof clothing and a tarp that can be slung up quickly for protection while you eat lunch.

WHERE TO TAKE CHILDREN ON THEIR FIRST HIKES

There are simple walks you can begin with for which you need hardly anything other than your desire to take them. These are mostly the walks and nature trails in various national, state, county, and city parks. In New York City, for example, I can think of no more interesting walk to take than a Sunday stroll in either Manhattan's Central Park or Brooklyn's Prospect Park. Every major city has similar parks. And if you don't enjoy this sort of walk, I can't imagine why you would even be considering hiking or backpacking!

Take it easy and be patient when getting your family into hiking—or you could lose the opportunity of having your children as hiking companions. More serious still, you could get into dangerous situations that could be avoided with greater caution and preparedness.

Turning children into backpackers requires patience and resolve. First of all, you have to throttle way down, in both the distances you intend to travel and the pace at which you hike. In raising our children on the trails, I discovered that I had been missing a lot of extraordinary pleasures by hiking too rapidly and too far. With the children, as the saying goes, I was able to "smell the flowers."

Hiking at the children's pace enabled me to see that I'd been passing by things my children saw that in fact were fascinating. They asked questions I never would have dreamed of asking, things that pointed me to sides of nature I'd never noticed before. Zany people-type questions like "Who put this trail here?" and "Who was the first one to walk on it?" And more intriguing nature questions like "Why does this tree's leaves turn red and that one over there's leaves turn yellow?" and more practical ones like "Will we get any blueberries on this hike?"

> Besides the essential water, I always take one of my beloved children, Alyda Rose, age six, or Elliott, eight. We each must always find one piece of trail trash to carry out with us.
>
> —*Janet Wyper, manager of community relations, L.L.Bean*

Family hiking is very popular in the Lake District of Wales, United Kingdom. JIM BARKER

They turned the backcountry into a far more enchanting place. So give them a break. Follow their interests without forcing yours on them. Take it very easy introducing the children to backcountry trails.

The proof that our family took the proper amount of time and consideration introducing the children to the trails came when my oldest son, William, was five. We asked him what he wanted for his birthday. He said he wanted to go for a hike and have a birthday party "out there."

Bear Safety for Children

Be especially watchful of young children, particularly infants, in black bear country. Two incidents involving infants occurred just recently in woodlands close to New York City.

A five-month-old baby girl was snatched from her stroller and killed near the family cabin in a resort area of the Catskill Mountains of New York. And a two-year-old toddler was mauled on the back porch of a suburban home in New Jersey.

I don't know if they would have been protected in either of these situations, but I never let my children out of my sight in black bear country. Black bears habituate just about every woodland in the lower forty-eight and Canada. They have become considerably more accustomed to people, seem to have lost their fear, and have become much more aggressive in recent years.

Be especially concerned about letting your older children hike on ahead of you on the trails where you are unable to see them.

At one point on a backpacking trip when my children were toddlers, we were clearly following in the fresh footprints and steaming scats of a bear on the low-lying Long Trail alongside Long Lake in New York's Adirondack Mountains. Luckily our youngsters were all close beside us.

Let the Slowest Child Take the Lead

Your hikes will grow in enjoyment if you consistently allow your slowest hiker to take the lead. That one will probably be the youngest in your party. It gives the youngster pride to get there first and not be the last to be dragged along to the next rest stop.

We of course were accommodating. We took him, his sisters and brother, and a couple of his friends on a short hike in a nearby woods, stopped after a short distance, spread a blanket on the grass, had a picnic lunch, and cooked up a trail-mix birthday cake decorated with five candles. As I write about this years later, it brings tears of joy to my eyes, for it was a very special event for all of us.

GIVE CHILDREN ADDED INCENTIVES

At age three, we began to introduce each child to the "M&M technique." When the kids would tire on longer trails, I'd point out some spot on the trail up ahead, such as a bend or the top of a hill or a tall ponderosa pine, and tell them they'd get an M&M stop once we reached it. We were good on our promises, stopping when we did get to that spot. And the children would each get a single M&M. After resting a moment or two, we were then again hiking. This worked miracles for at least two hiking seasons. But then, you might say, it lost its flavor. We needed more grown-up sorts of lures.

One lure that worked very well for virtually all of my six youngsters in their early years on the trails was discovered on hikes we did on portions of the Appalachian Trail. There are sections of the AT near enough to White Plains, New York, where we lived at the time, that run in four- to five-mile stretches between roads. We would hike in from one end of a section from one road, stop about halfway to the next road, have lunch, and then hike back out to the car. On our next hike, we'd come in from the other road, stop at the midpoint to which we had hiked the previous time, have lunch, and hike back out that direction to the car.

This prompted a fascinating game for them. They would bring a toy, such as a doll or car, leave it hidden at the midpoint, and see if they could find it when we hiked in from the other direction. It gave an incentive to them that was even better than the M&Ms.

Other hikers have their own enticements that work for their kids. Some play games

Tropical beaches are great places for hikes, as on this trail on St. John's, U.S. Virgin Islands.

Backpacking Toys for Ages Three to Eight

Here is a list of simple items to help your younger children enjoy the leaves, stones, frogs, mosses, and pebbles they find and pass evenings in camp:

- crayons
- notebook
- small flashlight
- magnifying glass
- small beach sand bucket
- large spoon
- plastic trowel
- favorite book
- special items your child likes that are portable enough to bring along

The more enjoyable camp can be for your children, the more they will want to go with you on these treks.

---

with the children on hikes. You might want to check out a few other good sources of ideas for making the trails more interesting for children. The American Hiking website, www.americanhiking.org, has useful information under "Family Hiking" and "Hank's Handout." Also take note of the "Top Ten Family Friendly Trails." The book *Backpacking the Kelty Way,* by Nena Kelty and Steve Boga, is loaded with excellent tips on games and activities to make family hikes and backpacking treks fascinating to children of all ages. *Hiking with Kids,* by Robin Tawney, is a pocket-size book that provides advice for adults ready to take that first step onto the trail with kids.

GET CHILDREN INTO BACKPACKING SLOWLY

We got into the backpacking phase of our family backcountry experience slowly too. We started car camping along with our day hiking. Our infants rode in kiddie carriers on our backs at first. One of my daughters, Kate, from her very first hike on her mother's back, would lift her nose to take in the backcountry scents with a beautiful contented smile the moment we headed out into the woods. She happens to be the one in the family who attracts the most bug bites. But they have never deterred her love of the backcountry, even at times when her little eyes would be swollen shut from blackfly bites.

Today, many years later, Kate is likely to call me as she did last summer to see if I'd like to go on a backpacking trip with her. We joined up at the airport—just her and me—and headed out for a great hike along the Continental Divide in Colorado's San Juan Mountains. What a precious reward for our careful coddling of Kate's hiking comforts in her infant, toddler, and teen years!

As our infants turned toddler and learned to walk, we alternated some walking with some carrying, enabling them to get their trail legs as they grew. By three years old, we expected them to walk the whole distance. The distances we traveled, though, were always scaled

When hiking with my daughter, I always bring a candy bar that I break in half. She gets half when I see that she's dragging a little and needs a goal to get to the top of a hill or just hike another mile. And she gets the other half when we're done. For the rest of her life, this kid's going to associate hiking with chocolate!

—*Pete Olsen, director of membership for American Hiking Society*

back to a level appropriate for the age of our youngest.

HIKING WITH AN INFANT

When taking a very young infant on the trail, it is best if Mother carries it in a convenient baby carrier in front that enables baby to face in toward Mom. Some mothers may want to carry a small day pack as well, with a handy supply of necessities for baby.

Children brought into it gradually can become real backpackers, as they are in this family in the Cascade Mountains of Washington.
MARILYN S. DOAN

I recommend that fathers do not carry very small infants only weeks old on the trail. Mothers are far more sensitive to the child's safety and needs, and Dad can carry an extra share of the infant's paraphernalia. We had a near-tragic event on a Grand Canyon trek carrying our eight-month-old, Maggie, in a carrier. To relieve her mother on an afternoon side hike, I carried Maggie. And I almost lost her by bending over too low for something, not being nearly as sensitive to her safety as her mother. I don't think it is just me when I say that fathers do not seem to be as sensitive to the fragile needs of the very young. Culture or genes? Makes no difference when the safety and care of the infant are at stake.

Depending upon the child's growth, a backpack-type carrier that has the child facing your back is far more versatile. Most come with a mechanism for standing up on their own when not being carried. Be careful, though. Some are too tippy for safely standing up in camp.

I recommend the Kelty K.I.D.S. carrier. It is more expensive than most but has a number of other features as well— an overhead shade, a kickstand, easily adjustable shoulder straps and waistband, and supply-carrying capability. It weighs a bit more than five pounds. Sound like an ad? True. But Kelty doesn't even know I am writing about it here.

A larger, stand-up baby carrier can also handle a number of other items carried in its cargo portion.

Plan Rest Days in Your Backpacking Treks

Allow for frequent days of rest on hiking vacations. On backpacking trips, allow at least one rest day after two days of hiking. And on day-hiking vacations, plan to stay at one stop every three days to give the kids a chance to play.

Don't consider hiking play for them, unless the hikes are very short walks to very interesting places. "Interesting," that is, from your child's point of view.

Cautions When Carrying Baby

Observe the following cautions when carrying an infant:

- Do not bend over from the waist. Bend at the knees to prevent losing baby from carrier.
- Be extra careful going under low tree branches. Duck very low when passing under them.
- Take care when sitting down so that you do not sit on your child's feet.
- Expect baby to fall asleep while you hike, so cushion the child's face with a towel or sweater.
- Cushion a towel or blanket between carrier and baby for baby's comfort.
- Use compartments on carrier for necessities while hiking.
- Check baby often for rashes or irritations from rubbing against carrier.
- Do not take any chances of falling anywhere. You have a precious cargo.

Do's and Don'ts of Backpacking with Infants

These are rather commonsense thoughts, but they are useful to bring to mind when you set out to backpack with infants.

- Premeasure the infant's meals, making separate packages for each meal. Label them. It will save much time and energy on the trail.
- Repackage foods in plastic containers, for glass bottles or jars break too easily.
- Take some extra containers of baby's favorite food. You never can tell when it will be useful.
- Work up to an overnight by taking several daylong hikes. Try the suggestions given for backpacking while on your long day hikes.
- Use disposable diapers. Be sure to pack the used ones out with you. Take along extraheavy trash bags to haul out the waste.
- Bring plenty of warm clothes for the baby. More is far better than less. (See "Baby's Clothing Checklist.")
- Bring a toy, especially baby's favorite.
- Don't worry about dirt. It's impossible to keep your baby clean of dirt in the backcountry.
- Include long-sleeved shirts and long pants—even in heat of summer. Nights can get chilly.
- Take your first overnight close by home on a trail with an easy escape route.
- Try to keep as close to your baby's home routine as possible while on the trail— same foods, same feeding times, same clothes, same sleeping blankets. If you adhere as much as possible to what your infant is used to at home, both you and the infant will enjoy the trip a good deal more.

Trail Safety for Children Checklist

Here are some precautions that will make you feel more comfortable with your children in the backcountry.

- See "Bear Safety for Children" sidebar.
- Dress your children in colorful clothing that you can see from a distance, to be sure they will not get lost.
- Hang a whistle around each child's neck so that if they get separated from you, they can blow the whistle until you find them. As in shopping malls, advise your children that if they should get lost, they should stay put and calm the moment they realize they're lost. Wandering around looking for Mom and Dad will certainly make things worse.
- Teach them that even on day hikes, they are not to turn over rocks or pieces of wood without checking to be sure they are not hiding a venomous snake, scorpion, or spider.
- Teach them not to put their hands in places they cannot see, such as into holes or over rocks, logs, or ledges, so as to avoid encountering snakes, scorpions, or any other kind of hazard.
- Teach them to identify poison ivy and poison oak and avoid them.
- When on trails with steep drop-offs, such as in Grand Canyon or high mountains, rope toddlers with a hank of climbing rope and carabiners to tether them from a fall. Be sure to get expert instruction on safe ways to attach rope to your youngsters.
- Keep children from bridges without sufficiently protective guard-rails over fast-running streams to avoid their accidentally tumbling in.

It is a good idea to rope up young children when taking them on precipitous routes, such as those in Grand Canyon.

Baby's Checklist

The baby's mother will no doubt have a more thorough list. This one is merely to jog the memory. It is essential that all baby's necessities be with you when you arrive at your backcountry camp. Add any particular needs for your infant to this list so that you don't forget them.

- ☐ disposable diapers
- ☐ blanket
- ☐ premoistened towelettes
- ☐ plastic bottles
- ☐ formula
- ☐ baby food repackaged in plastic containers
- ☐ juices in plastic containers
- ☐ baby spoon
- ☐ diaper-rash cream
- ☐ powder
- ☐ washcloths
- ☐ bibs
- ☐ infant sunscreen
- ☐ garbage bags, large and small, to carry out diapers and trash
- ☐ ammonia-soaked sponge to control odors in diaper disposal bag

Baby's Clothing Checklist

Again, this is just a starter list. Mother should add any special items for your infant to it. Better to carry too many than not enough clothes for the infant.

- ☐ sweater
- ☐ hats
- ☐ mittens (even in summer weather)
- ☐ socks
- ☐ booties
- ☐ jumpsuit
- ☐ hooded sweatshirt
- ☐ footed sleeper
- ☐ rain suit (does not have to be breathable, *but must not cover baby's mouth and nose!*)

22
Women-Only Groups on the Trail

Though I have backpacked or hiked with dozens of top-notch women hikers, and admired their skills and endurance, I have paid little attention to any differences between the sexes of hikers.

I can name a few hardy women who put my backcountry skills to shame, such as Gudy Gaskill, founder of the Colorado Trail, and Laura Waterman, first editor of *Backpacker* magazine. And I've known others with whom I'd hate to compete on the trail, including Melanie Miles, a guide for Grand Canyon Field Institute (GCFI); "Butch" Henley, who has hiked and biked across America from coast to coast, and incidentally squired the hiking community's support to bring America's trails from sickness to health as executive director of the American Hiking Society; Carole Latimer, founder of Call of the Wild wilderness treks; and my sister-in-law, Kathleen Kemsley, who has spent her career as a park ranger and fire dispatcher in the Arizona and Alaska backcountry.

Then there are the nameless numbers I have met on the trail, such as the two I bumped into on the still-dark January morning tromping up through the snow to the rim of Grand Canyon after their seven-mile, 5,000-foot ascent from Phantom Ranch as I was just starting down; or the German Fräulein storming up the perilously steep trail in the Swiss Alps as my wife and I struggled down. This does not include the women rock climbers with whom I spent many an adventure on steep-walled cliffs, such as Marguerite Bauman, Lilli Meissinger, Krist Raubenheimer, and Mary Sylvander.

Still, it would be foolish for me, a male, to attempt to represent myself as any kind of authority on women in the backcountry. But I do claim to be an authority on finding authorities. I know how to ferret out the women authorities and get their views. This, I can assure you, may be the single most valuable part of this chapter.

THE AUTHORITIES: VIVE LA DIFFÉRENCE!
I've sought out women who have pioneered the way for a relatively new backpacking phenomenon—women-only backpacking groups. I've spent countless hours interviewing them, reading their literature, and recording their suggestions. The advantage that I gained from this approach is that you'll hear not just one woman's seasoned guidelines for backpacking, but the points of view of several. They all have distinct personalities and preferences, as you would expect from the individualists that they are.

Which of these authorities is best? Well, I'll do my best to describe their characteristics later in the chapter, and you can choose which style has the greatest appeal to your way of doing things. You can't possibly go wrong with any one of them. That's the beauty of it.

But first let me tell you how I became acquainted with the phenomenon.

THE INCREASING NUMBER OF WOMEN-ONLY BACKPACKER GROUPS

One day recently, my nephew Kenn and I hiked down the heavy-use corridor of Grand Canyon toward Phantom Ranch, where he was going to treat me to a steak dinner for my birthday. When we stopped to rest at the Tipoff into the Inner Gorge, Kenn asked, "Uncle Bill, what's going on here? There must be some sort of convention going on up there in Grand Canyon Village."

"Convention?"

"Yeah. I've never seen so many women with packs, but without men, in a lifetime of hiking."

I began to take notice. The women were mostly in their thirties and forties. They were well equipped with the latest, most expensive hiking gear and clothing.

Later that day, down at Phantom Ranch, I asked a woman park ranger what was going on.

"Nothing special," she said. "There are lots of women backpackers. They've been coming for many years now."

Judging from her age, she couldn't have meant more years than you can count on the fingers of one hand. It didn't satisfy my curiosity. I asked James Blankenship, a somewhat older male ranger, back up top at the backcountry office.

He said, "Yes, I've noticed an increase in all-women hiker groups too."

He thought it had been going on since about 1998. Heidi Seller, a ranger also in the backcountry office, said she thought they were divorcées who'd become used to backpacking with their spouses and did not want to give it up once they separated.

Made sense. But I couldn't see how that could account for such a sudden increase in numbers.

Heidi's view was somewhat biased, however. "Maybe I have this idea because one of my early heros was Anne Labastille," she said. "Her book, *Woodswoman* [still in print], was a real inspiration to me. Anne said she started backpacking alone because she and her husband went their separate ways after their failed marriage."

A Hiking Woman to Emulate

Hulda Crooks was sixty-six when she started hiking.

It is difficult to know what prompted Hulda to want to climb the 14,485-foot Mount Whitney, the highest mountain in the lower forty-eight United States. It is an eleven-mile backpack from the trailhead to the summit and an equal distance back out.

That first climb was but a tasty treat. Hulda was captured by the enjoyment of the ascent and climbed Mount Whitney almost annually until she was ninety-three, some twenty-three times over those twenty-seven years.

She was not known to be a particularly strong woman at the time she began her hiking stint, though she was determined.

Indeed, Anne Labastille was the first woman I knew who'd taken to the woods alone, and she was the first woman state-licensed Adirondack guide permitted to lead groups into the wilderness.

I ran a photo of Anne and her dog, Pitzi, on the cover of a 1977 issue of *Backpacker* magazine featuring the story of her solo hike of the 132-mile Northville-Lake Placid Trail in New York's Adirondack Mountains. Back then, such an adventure was cover-story material. Women just did not go out on the trails without men. And back then, it wasn't that common to see women on the trails *with* men, either.

One pioneer solo woman backpacker is Anne Labastille, who became an Adirondack guide. She is the author of Woodswoman, *a series of four books on her treks, as well as the Sierra Club book* Women and Wilderness.
ANNE LABASTILLE

When women began testing their mettle on trails here and there during the early days of the modern women's movement, they sometimes made headlines. A couple of young women were killed by grizzly bears in 1967 in Glacier, and others were maimed at Yellowstone National Park. Then there was a female version of *Deliverance* on the Appalachian Trail, with the women being raped and murdered at their campsites.

Like Kenn, I grew more and more curious as to what was going on. Had the trails become less dangerous? Women more courageous?

Before this hike, Kenn and I usually took to Grand Canyon's more primitive trails, where we rarely saw any other hikers. This was our first time in years to hike in the heavy-use corridor. We wondered if this was why we hadn't noticed a greater number of women before. Maybe they were sticking to these safer routes?

That did not prove entirely true, though. Blankenship said he had been giving women-only groups camping permits for primitive trails in Grand Canyon and at Shenandoah, Glacier, and Grand Teton National Parks, where he had put in stints at their backcountry offices.

There are still other views of the phenomenon. Backcountry ranger Steve Bridgehouse, who has been around a number of years—not just in the backcountry office, but as a fanatic hiker of Grand Canyon trails in his off-time—explains it thus: "I think it's part of a broader category of hikers who are taking a mid-age milestone fling. Mid-age women, like mid-age Italians, mid-age Irish, mid-age accountants, mid-age executives, mid-age-you-name-it, all are part of this 'once before I die' or 'once the kids are off to college' type of thing."

Mike Buchheit, director of the Grand Canyon Field Institute (GCFI), which runs a variety of guided group backpacking treks in the canyon, agrees with Steve—somewhat: "Yes, it is a milestone phenomenon. But with women it is more than that. Sort of a self-confidence-building experience as well."

According to Melanie Miles, a backpacking guide who spends more than four months a year leading Grand Canyon Field Institute group trips on various trails: "Our

All-women backpacking group at Indian Point on Tonto Plateau in Grand Canyon. Grand Canyon Field Institute trip leader, Marji "Slim" Woodruff has her hand on the sign. MARJI WOODRUFF

all-women backpacking treks bring out more of the feminine aspect of the backcountry experience. These trips are less competitive than mixed-sex groups. When a woman feels like she is having difficulty keeping up and thinks she's becoming a drag on the group, there is an entirely different sort of response from women hikers. In an all-women's group, the other hikers offer help and encouragement, whereas in a mixed group, there is a lot less of that. And of course, this builds confidence in the hiker who has the difficulty."

Once women have taken their initial training backpacking trip, she says, "About three out of five soon get out onto the trails again. Many come back on our more advanced backpacking treks."

There are other aspects of all-women backpacking trips that help build self-confidence and independence. When a mixed couple backpacks together, subtle things occur unthinkingly between them. The man, without thinking, usually takes charge of chores like putting up the tent, lighting the stove, refueling it, and route planning.

"It isn't that the man is at fault," Melanie says. "The woman is also involved. She usually tacitly agrees to this division of trail chores. But on an all-women hike, she has to do these things for herself. It gives her a new perspective on her independence."

It isn't that the woman needs to take charge of these tasks on her next hike with her male partner. But she has the freedom to do so at appropriate times and knows that she can do it with reasonable competence.

Another traditional backpacking group leader for the Grand Canyon Field Institute, Marjorie "Slim" Woodruff, says there's a noticeable difference between men and women on backpacking treks. She leads both mixed-sex groups and women-only groups.

A couple months ago, Slim ended up taking an all-male group on a backpacking trek—quite by accident. It started out as a mixed-sex group, but the only woman who had signed up backed out at the last minute because her partner broke his wrist just before the trip began. It gave Slim a firsthand observation of the differences between her all-male and all-female groups.

"The men came in pairs—fathers-sons, two best friends—and talked about sports and politics. They had very serious conversations. The women didn't stay in their groups or pairs. They talked about their families, their jobs, and their personal problems. They also critiqued the men in their lives. They got sillier by the day, and

I wouldn't go into the backcountry without two large, black garbage bags, which become my solar-heated bathtub out on the trail. No kidding, it's the best, and on a sunny day, the water gets really hot.

—*Carole Latimer, owner and trip operator of Call of the Wild since 1978.*

The Carole Latimer Backcountry Bath

Here are author and trail guide Carole Latimer's instructions for devising a solar-heated bath from heavy-duty black plastic garbage bags. "It's hysterically funny to see a bunch of people sitting in a meadow in water-filled garbage bags," she says. "But the hot water is heavenly. It facilitates group dynamics—and it makes for the most fantastic photo opportunities on the trip."

- Start with two garbage bags (one for the wash, one for the rinse), thirty- to forty-five-gallon size each. The bags must be black, not brown, and not have a silver lining.
- Prepare the bath by spreading a ground cloth or other puncture-proof material in direct sun, keeping in mind that a nearby tree, for example, could throw the bathtub into shade, resulting in no hot water.
- Be sure to set up your personal spa 300 feet away from all water sources for environmental reasons.
- Place the garbage bags on the ground cloth several inches apart, making certain they're on a completely level surface. Otherwise the water-filled bags can travel off the cloth and may be punctured.
- Bring water to the bags from a nearby lake, creek, or pond. Don't attempt to fill the bags and bring them to the bath site; that doesn't work. Don't overfill the bags, or the water won't get hot; around five or six gallons each is plenty. A little hot water is better than a lot of tepid water.
- Try to get rid of as much air as possible, to avoid insulating the cool water.
- Tie the bags with easy-to-untie slip knots.
- Leave the bags in the midday sun for about four hours. While you're out hiking, the sun will warm the bathwater.
- To take a bath, open the wash bag and hold its edges up while sitting cross-legged inside. Pull the open edges of the bag up to neck level. Hold the bag around your shoulders like a shawl and soak. Get a friend to shower over your head as you shampoo and luxuriate.
- When you move over to the rinse bag, toss your dirty clothes into the soapy water bag. Let them soak for a few minutes while you rinse off. Then they can follow you into the rinse cycle while you're grooming your clean hair and body.

at one point I was laughing so hard I had to stand up to keep from choking. One of the men on the all-men trip told me he had been on a mixed-group hike before and found the ladies much livelier."

Slim said another difference was in their bathing. "The women set great store by taking as much of a bath as they could in the cold water and washing their hair. The men took little spit baths and didn't really seem to think about it much."

GCFI's Denise Traver also makes some comparisons: "Interestingly enough, on the women's hikes I lead, there is little talk of men. Food tops the list of discussions.

"One of my goals with trips is that whoever and whatever the women were at home, out there they are on equal footing. I truly believe it helps the groups meld together. It really doesn't matter if they are married, divorced, had children, or whatever. It doesn't matter if they are doctors, lawyers, or housewives.

"One of my greatest joys is watching women of all ages turn back into ten-year-old girls and tomboys, playing in waterfalls, splashing around without a care in the world. I lead mixed groups. And once I was specifically asked to lead an all-male group that didn't want to just talk sports and other guy things. It was one of the most fun trips I've ever led. All these men in their fifties and sixties turned into little boys. It was a blast!"

WOMEN'S CONCERNS
Trip leaders told me of several concerns women have expressed on their first backpacking trips. Most of these, of course, are the same concerns that many men have when they are first starting out. But this chapter is about women and for women.

How Well Will I Do?
The leaders of women-only backpacking trips, as well as those novices who have been on them, tell me that women will feel more at ease under the tutelage of women trip leaders than they would with male leaders. And this holds true whether or not your husband or boyfriend wants to introduce you to the sport.

The Bathroom Thing
According to Betty Leavengood, "Women who are first-time backpackers worry more about going to the bathroom than anything else."

I can tell you up front that I have few words for you about this, except that you cannot go on a backpacking trip without a few calls of nature someplace or other along the trail.

One thought I do have, though, is that if you choose to get your introduction to backpacking on a GCFI trip, you will have the opportunity to use modern outhouses that are spaced conveniently a few hours apart along the route you take on your first hike.

On my wife's first few overnight backpack treks, she had difficulty using the bushes, so she brought along a swatch of our bathroom wallpaper, which she used for a little mnemonic device. It worked for her those first few times. Now she has no difficulty.

Fear of Snakes, Spiders, and Scorpions
This is an overblown fear that a lot of us have when we first go out on the trail, no less for men than for women. The advice I give on these subjects elsewhere in the book applies to women as well as men. A women-only trip will likely provide a far more supportive environment for you in coping with these fears.

Fear of Bears
What this book has to say about bears applies as much to women as it does to men, but there are two points I want to emphasize here. Menstruation is suspected to make a woman more susceptible to bear attack. Some rangers and bear experts argue that this is not as dangerous as others think. Still, I strongly advise my daughters and spouse to play it safe, an ounce of caution being worth a pound of cure. Why play with fire? The first two bear tragedies in Glacier National Park were nineteen-year-old women who were either having their period or about to. Was this the cause of the bears killing them

in their sleeping bags that tragic night? Possibly not. But then, it is up to you as to what you want to believe about it.

Second, there is some indication that having sex may also attract bears. This is a caution not just to women, but to men as well. Again, why add to the possibility of an unpleasant, if not tragic, experience?

Fear of People
GCFI guide Melanie Miles puts it quite simply: "I fear people more than any other creature in the outdoors." I do too. Remember, *Deliverance* can occur to women as well as men. An excellent source that more fully addresses these concerns is Judith Niemi's fine book, *Basic Essentials: Women in the Outdoors.*

ALL-WOMEN'S GROUP OUTFITTERS
Betty Leavengood, author of *Grand Canyon Women,* which is worth its price just for her introduction, in which she describes some of her own adventurous hikes, has this to say about women-only treks: "Women have fun together, away from men. They are more relaxed, talk about any subject under the sun (including men, of course). With men around, especially husbands or significant others, women revert to the role of caretaker. On an all-women trip, you never hear, 'Bring me a cup of coffee, dear.' Women are more self-conscious when men are around. They worry about how they look. They just act differently." With that, Betty highly recommends the Grand Canyon Field Institute.

Grand Canyon Field Institute
After witnessing firsthand the Grand Canyon Field Institute (GCFI) organizing one of its trips, and interviewing director, guides, and women students, I too am impressed. GCFI is an educational program of the Grand Canyon Association, a nonprofit partner of Grand Canyon National Park. Its trips are inexpensive and cover some extraordinary backcountry trails. Visit the website www.grandcanyon.org/fieldinstitute.

Denise Traver, who spent a few seasons as a backcountry ranger at a remote inner canyon campground in Grand Canyon, first organized the GCFI's all-women hikes. "After observing people at Cottonwood Campground," she says, "I noticed most women start out hiking with guys. Men hike differently than women. Men are out to conquer things . . . but women want to stop and see the flowers and stop at the creek to wiggle their toes. If you are talking to a man, he will say, 'How long did it take you?' and not 'What did you see?'"

It was because of these observations that Denise proposed the idea of all-women groups to John Frazier, the founding director of the GCFI. He bought the idea and put Denise to work organizing them.

Denise developed a style of leading that has been adapted by many other group leaders. She leads by following the slowest hiker in the group, telling those who are faster where to stop and wait for the group to catch up. This allows everyone in the group to go at her own pace. Those so disposed can race for the fast prize. And those who would rather can take in whatever pauses they like along the way.

From the first women-only hike in 1995 through 2004, Denise led all-women groups for the GCFI. She said women are just as good backpackers as men, even if they are not as fast as their husbands. "Women are the mules of the human race," Denise says. "We are slow, steady, and have the endurance if we are allowed to go at our own pace."

Karen Berger, an Appalachian Trail end-to-ender and author of several books on backpacking, takes this view a step further. She says in *Hiking and Backpacking:*

> Women are often more successful backpackers than their male counter-parts. . . . Certainly, women can hike as far and climb as high as men. In addition, backpacking rewards endurance rather than strength, and emotional flexibility rather than goal orientation, and it punishes those who would push too far and too fast for too long. Clichés about tortoises and hares apply. Not that men can't be flexible and women can't be strong, but there do seem to be marked (if somewhat stereotypical) differences in the attitudes of men and women in the backcountry. These differences seem to work in favor of women, particularly over the long haul.

But the GCFI is not the only outfit offering all-women beginners' backpacking trips.

The First All-Women Trip Outfitter

One of the earliest to get into the field—or should I say, "onto the trails"—was Call of the Wild (www.callwild.com), started in California in 1978 by Carole Latimer. I have heard nothing but top praise for these trips that Carole serves her clients, many of whom have been repeat customers for years. And incidentally, she is author of a terrific backcountry cookbook, *Wilderness Cuisine,* worth having a peek at before your next trip.

Of the women who take her beginners' backpacking treks with all-women groups, Carole says: "Most are in the thirty-five to fifty-five-year range. Their children are grown, and they are looking for new challenges," as well as relief from the stress of their jobs.

What about the theory that they are mostly divorced women?

"Sixty-five percent are married," Carole says. "Some of the women are doing it so they can go backpacking with their husbands with greater confidence."

Though she didn't have it specifically in mind when Denise suggested the idea of all-women backpacking groups, she notes that women do gain confidence, self-esteem, and spiritual renewal. She claims, as does Kate Borgelt of Outward Bound, that the women often have life-changing experiences on their initial backpacking trips.

Outward Bound's First Women-Only Wilderness Trips

Outward Bound (OB) offered its first women-only wilderness course in Minnesota back in 1966. Like its Minnesota courses for men, the OB MG-1 Course was more canoeing than backpacking. And as with male OB courses, the women were trained in rock climbing, wilderness camping, and survival skills, toward the end of their adventure spending three nights camped out solo in utterly wild country without tent, sleeping bag, food, or insect repellent.

Today more than 40 percent of OB course students are women. OB offers a variety of self-confidence-building trips for a variety of clienteles, not the least of which are women-only backpacking trips in a variety of places. For more information, visit www.outwardbound.com.

The purpose of the OB courses is not to transform students into more avid outdoors people. It is to build character, to demonstrate that they can do things they didn't think they were able to do. Barbara LaFontaine, a thirty-four-year-old *Sports Illustrated* reporter who accompanied that 1966 first women-only OB trip, wrote: "None of us, I suspect, who was not an outdoors woman before all this has become an outdoors woman because of it,

> **I'm not real big on equipment. I use an external-frame Kelty pack, my sleeping bag is a fiberfill North Face, the tent has external poles, and my stove is a canister-fuel Coleman.**
>
> *—Betty Leavengood, author of* **Grand Canyon Women** *and* **Tucson Hiking Guide**

but that was never the point; in fact, whichever girl liked it the least has probably come off best, having learned more than any of us what she is capable of. And that is the point."

According to marketing manager Kate Borgelt: "Outward Bound has been offering women-only wilderness experiences since 1966. True, these are more canoeing than backpacking. However, and that is a big 'however,' the Outward Bound wilderness course does include a Quiet Walk through swampland and heavy brush, alternately hiking briskly and running and wading through mucky waist-deep river waters, each time getting swifter and deeper. And the backpacking is called 'portaging'—sixty-five-pound canoes and packs with all their other gear over these marshy trails from one lake to another."

Other Outfitters

There are several other women-only group trip outfitters. One of the most pioneering groups, Woodswomen of Minneapolis, has since been disbanded, and its activities taken over by a successor organization, Adventures in Good Company (www.goodadventure.com).

Woodswomen founder Judith Niemi continues to offer a variety of outdoors programs, including writing programs in wild places and trips for cancer survivors, with her new company, Women in the Wilderness (www.womeninthewilderness.com and www.judithniemi.com).

There are others as well. And many are no doubt good. Trouble is, there are also those that aren't so good. My preference would be one of the above. But then, you see, note my gender.

THE NUMBER OF ALL-WOMEN GROUPS TODAY

It is difficult to nail down the number of those who backpack in all-women groups or even come to reasonable estimates. No one keeps track of these numbers. The best I could gather was merely impressions of various national park backcountry rangers, equipment makers, and group leaders.

In my visits to sporting-goods stores that carry backpacking equipment, I have noticed lately a lot more clothing and equipment for women. Some leading manufacturers are producing women's sleeping bags, backpacks, and boots. There are good reasons for this, for these pieces of equipment do fit women differently than they fit men. My daughter Kate is re-outfitting for a two-week trek around Mont Blanc in the Alps.

She is enthusiastic about the better fit of her new sleeping bag and pack for her very womanly body.

According to the Albuquerque REI store manager, Mitch Herbert: "A good percentage of our customers are women, though it is hard to say how many. But for the first time, in 2004 we noticed we sold more products to women than to men."

National Sporting Goods Association research confirms these estimates, with the proviso that while the number of women backpackers has increased, their percentage of the total number of backpackers has actually pulled back slightly.

All of which tells us little to nothing about the number of women-only groups of backpackers on the trails today. It is still Kenn's and my impression that the "Call of the Wild Girls"—as Gail Sheehy dubs them in her popular book on the stages of life, *Passages*—are far more prevalent than numbers indicate.

I like to think of the image I have of two women from San Francisco I met at the Bright Angel Campground at the bottom of the canyon last fall, who slept out under the stars. When we talked about that, they told me that while they were avid day hikers, they had never camped out on the trail before. They had planned to hike to Phantom Ranch and had already bought their airline tickets, but then they couldn't get reservations to sleep at the ranch. So this was their alternative.

WOMEN BACKPACKING AUTHORITIES

Would it help to know who these women pioneers are and what qualified them to give advice? Well, consider them and make up your own mind.

Susan "Butch" Henley, executive director of the American Hiking Society.
REESE LUKEI JR.

Susan "Butch" Henley

Butch has been an avid hiker since Girl Scout days. She end-to-ended the Appalachian Trail in 1978, then two years later hiked across the nation on the thirteen-month HikaNation event of the American Hiking Society (AHS). That route became the foundation of the American Discovery Trail.

Butch is most proud, though, of her hiking up and down the halls of Congress lobbying for trails. In five years on the board of AHS, then ten years as executive director, she spearheaded efforts to get funding for all the national trails and a tenfold increase in federal funding for trail maintenance—up from $9 million in 1986 to $90 million in 1996, the year she retired.

She recently was pulled out of retirement to serve as the executive director of the American Discovery Trail Society. She was honored for her tireless service to trails with the Lifetime Achievement Award from the Partnership for the National Trails System in 2003.

Kathleen "Kit" Kemsley

Kit is on this list not simply because of her name. Call it nepotism. But I call it guts. Kit is a woman to be admired. She tells how she got started in her lifelong career in the backcountry in her book, *Places of Power,* now out of print. But Kit knows how to put her hands on a copy here and there. Check with her at kitknm@hotmail.com to see if she can find one for you.

Kit's love of the backcountry began in Yosemite's craggy valley, where she spent summers at the family cabin in Fish Camp. Her taste for the backcountry was honed working as a waitress during her college years for Yosemite Park and Curry Company, the concessionaire that ran the hotels and other guest facilities there. She hasn't stopped working in the backcountry, having put in twelve years at Grand Canyon and Denali National Parks and another dozen years for Fish and Wildlife, Forest Service, and BLM units, the last few years of which have been in fire control dispatching.

Carole Latimer

Carole started her all-women backpacking trips back in 1978 under the trade name Call of the Wild. Hers is the longest-running organization outfitting these kinds of trips. As of this writing, she has taken twenty-two annual treks up Mount Whitney, as well as to such exotic backpacking spots as Mexico's Copper Canyon, Peru, and Alaska.

Carole grew up in northern California, backpacking with her family since as far back as she can remember. She's the author of a backcountry cookbook with 150 gourmet recipes, *Wilderness Cuisine,* which is now in its second edition and has been completely revised for today's tastes. These are all trail-tested recipes that have won favor with hundreds of her backcountry clients. See her 12,000-Foot Oriental Stir-Fry in chapter 28, or visit www.callwild.com.

Betty Leavengood

The author of *Grand Canyon Women,* Betty is less of an outfitter than an avid backpacker who has introduced numerous people to backcountry trails, mainly in the southwestern deserts and Grand Canyon. Betty's book gives some accounts of her own treks that will impress the most seasoned backpacker. She recently has been hiking in Switzerland and climbing to 15,000 feet on Africa's Mount Kilimanjaro, but her second-favorite hiking area is the mountains surrounding Tucson, Arizona. Her *Tucson Hiking Guide* is now in its third edition.

Melanie Miles

Melanie is a special backcountry woman. She is a women-only backpacking group guide for Grand Canyon Field Institute and occasionally for Call of the Wild. She is an offspring of the Woodswomen organization, where she guided for seven years. She sets a personal standard for guiding both mixed-sex and all-women groups in Grand Canyon. When she is not guiding backpacking trips, she is running rafting trips down the Colorado River through Grand Canyon. She is a Brit who fell in love with Grand Canyon at first sight and stayed on ever since. She joined the GCFI staff as a guide in 1998.

Judith Niemi

Judith is the first of the more recent pioneers of all-women backpacking trips. In Minneapolis in 1977, she founded the prototype of all-women outdoors organizations,

Woodswomen, which offered backpacking treks in addition to canoeing, climbing, and biking trips. Judith's aim was to get women outdoors, stirring up interest in these activities as well as in the naturalness of women-only groups. She set a standard, in one way or another, that has been adopted by most other organizations since then.

Woodswomen trained guides under the same strict standards of all good leadership training programs. Many of these guides have carried these tenets with them to other organizations, outfitting similar trips for women. Woodswomen ceased operations in 1999, but its most experienced guides started a successor organization offering the same types of trips in the same tradition called Adventures in Good Company, and Judith has a new company that offers outdoors programs called Women in the Wilderness.

Judith is also the author of an excellent book, *Basic Essentials: Women in the Outdoors.* Packed with useful information for wilderness travelers, it focuses especially upon the special difference between men's and women's attitudes toward and affinities for the backcountry.

Laura Waterman

Laura was the first editor of *Backpacker* magazine. When she married Guy Waterman, she left the magazine to homestead in the Vermont woods a mile's hike from the nearest dirt road. She and Guy built their tiny cabin so that it fit around his grand piano. The reason I mention their homestead is because of the purpose in it: Both loved backpacking and technical mountaineering so much that they rid their lives of clutter so as to live simply. They had no electricity, no plumbing to freeze when they were away. They grew, canned, and preserved their own vegetables but had no farm animals so that they could stay free to leave for a climb at any time of year. For the next twenty-seven years, they hiked and climbed year-round when they weren't writing books.

Laura Waterman gets crowned and toasted with grape juice at Isolation Shelter in New Hampshire's White Mountains for achieving her first round of 4,000-footers on a chilly February 4 by her husband, Guy (right), and me (left).

Laura's hiking, backpacking, and climbing statistics are impressive: climbing all forty-eight of the New Hampshire 4,000-foot peaks six times, three in winter; climbing Mount Lafayette, their favorite mountain, 123 times, 20 in winter; and setting some impressive ice-climbing records. Laura was the first woman to climb Cannon Cliff in winter, with her ascent of Black Dyke in 1975, and the first woman to lead Mount Washington's Huntington Ravine ice climb of Pinnacle Gully. Rather than for these accomplishments, though, Laura would like to be known for the alpine conservation work she and Guy did in the White Mountains. Their friends have set up the Guy Waterman Stewardship Fund to provide financial resources for continuation of this work.

With Guy, Laura wrote the first book on the new backcountry ethics, called *Backwoods Ethics,* which won the National Outdoor Book

Get Started with a Hiking Club

Many women get started by day hiking with a local hiking club and move on into some easy weekend backpacking. Most cities have a hiking club, which can give you a list of its organized hikes. It is best to start slowly, going on a beginners' day hike first to find out your comfortable hiking pace.

You may find a hiking club by checking with your newspaper or library. The American Hiking Society (AHS) has national affiliated clubs in many areas of the country. AHS does not sponsor trips itself, but it maintains a database of clubs that do.

American Hiking Society
1422 Fenwick Lane
Silver Spring, MD 20910
www.americanhiking.org

Another way is to contact one of the national outdoors organizations, such as the Sierra Club, to see if it has chapters in your area.

Sierra Club
85 Second St., Second Floor
San Francisco, CA 94105
www.sierraclub.org

American Volkssport Association is a national environmental organization that also has local chapters that sponsor hikes and other outings.

American Volkssport Association
1001 Pat Booker Rd., Suite 101
Universal City, TX 78148
www.ava.org

Local chapters sponsor frequent walking events, oriented more to country roads than to trails. But this is an excellent place to get started.

Award. They also authored *Wilderness Ethics* and climbing histories in their books *Forest and Crags* and *Yankee Rock and Ice.* Her memoir of her marriage and life on the homestead, *Losing the Garden: The Story of a Marriage,* is a touching story that in its first three pages will hold you until the end.

Marjorie "Slim" Woodruff

Slim is another group backpacking leader who's been around. I first met her in Buena Vista, Colorado, in the 1970s, when she was guiding trips in the Rockies. It would be pretty difficult not to have met Slim over the past several years, for she has been a guide and trip leader for several different outfitters, camps, and education programs, including the Sierra Club, Rocky Mountain Expeditions, and Grand Canyon Field Institute, leading hiking, backpacking, and cross-country ski trips. Not exactly what you would expect from a Ph.D. But then, Slim has this love affair with rocks, trees, peaks, and canyons.

23

Seniors Take to the Trails

On a beautiful April evening, we were gabbing with other hikers in a dining room full of them, all waiting for dinner to be served. We all had hiked the seven and a half miles down the South Kaibab Trail to Phantom Ranch at the bottom of Grand Canyon. We chatted about where we were from and why we decided to hike down the mile of elevation to have dinner there.

When the meal was over, the servers cleared the table, lowered the lights, and brought dessert, a large chocolate sheet cake lit with a forest of candles, while singing happy birthday to me. My nephew had treated me to a steak dinner and a cabin at Phantom Ranch for my seventy-fifth birthday. He had secretly arranged to have the cake and birthday celebration at one of my favorite hiking places.

This is nothing unusual at Phantom Ranch, for they frequently host birthday guests. But not many seventy-five-year-olds.

Next morning at breakfast, we chatted with some of the guests, one of whom was Hal Braun from Bozeman, Montana. "What a great idea to celebrate your birthday down here!" he said. "I wish I'd thought of that. I could have celebrated mine last month."

Hal had turned eighty in March. Again, nothing remarkable about this. Many people in their seventies and eighties continue hiking on even more demanding routes than this. But Hal was on his first big hike and wanted it to be special. Hal is a retired cardiologist, and though he is very sensitive to the stresses on his heart, "It wasn't my heart that bothered me," he said. "It was that last mile down to the bridge! That got me right here in the legs. The ranger said I am walking with the 'Kaibab Shuffle.'"

"That is a killer!" I said. "Just when you can see the bridge, it looks such a short distance away, yet it seems to take forever!"

Otherwise, eighty-year-olds are perfectly capable of enduring this sort of hiking.

When I was in my mid-teens, my father got heavily involved in politics and gave up his interest in hiking. He was sedentary for most of his life thereafter. When he was sixty-eight, however, my brothers and I took him on an eight-day backpacking trip through a slickrock canyon in Utah. He survived it quite well. The trick was to watch his endurance limits. And to make sure we covered short enough distances each day, with a built-in rest day, so that we all had a good time.

There have been a rash of large-circulation magazines running articles about elders participating in adventure sports, such as one in the September 2003 issue of *Time* magazine entitled "Aging Rockers," referring to active mountain climbers fifty and over. The article mentions that a third of the members of the American Alpine Club are

Soloing the 2,000-Mile Appalachian Trail at Sixty-Six

Emma Gatewood had raised eleven children, was divorced, and was sixty-six years old when she read a magazine article about the 2,000-mile Appalachian Trail. Why not beat the boredom and try hiking it?

She decided to give it go. She started on Mount Katahdin at its northern end in Maine. Coming down the mountain, she took a wrong turn, wandered about for a few days, broke her glasses, and ended in defeat. But the next year, she was better prepared. She started out from the southern end of the Appalachian Trail and hiked on through to Maine's Katahdin, the first woman to solo its entire length.

That tasted so good to her that she hiked it twice more over the next ten years. Hiking was so much fun, she spent much of her time out on various long trails. At seventy-one, Grandma Gatewood, as she had become known, also hiked a number of other long trails, including the 2,000-mile Oregon Trail from Independence, Missouri, to Oregon City, Oregon.

now over fifty. It tells of Lou Whittaker still guiding climbs up Mount Rainier at seventy-four, Royal Robbins still climbing the Yosemite cliffs at sixty-eight, and fifty-one-year-old Dick Bass summiting Mount Everest.

Today there is a much larger group of people who have stayed fit and who have the resources as well as the time to devote to such outdoors recreation activities.

In April 1997, I accompanied a group of American Hiking Society members ten miles down into a remote canyon bordering Arizona and Utah. They carried picks and shovels as well as their packs with a week's supply of food and gear. They were on a mission to "do something worthwhile." They spent the following week repairing a section of backcountry trail in a side canyon of the vast Kanab Canyon.

The leader of the trek was twenty-nine-year-old Richard Sheets and another team member was thirty-two-year-old Jon Erickson, but all the rest of the "workers" were over sixty. Well, Toni Martinez was only a few weeks over sixty. But Len Bjork was sixty-three, Joseph Burton sixty-four, Ray Hakata sixty-seven, and Joe Shute sixty-eight.

This was Joseph Burton's first AHS Volunteer Vacation. He took to it so enthusiastically that in the next seven years he went back out on eighty more trail-building treks with the AHS Volunteer Vacations. What a way to spend retirement years!

One recent fall, my wife and I hiked in one of our favorite spots, Zermatt, Switzerland. This is sort of a luxury

My Thermarest sleeping pad is essential for any trip I take.

—Brian Kemsley, retired heavy equipment mechanic, Denali National Park

---

Conservationist Dale Ball

by Ashleigh Morris, editor-in-chief of Santa Fean *magazine*

Thirty-one miles of single track wind through the foothills of the Sangre de Cristo Mountains thanks to the efforts of this former banker, who, at 75, spearheaded the creation of the hiking system that bears his name.

Today, the Dale Ball Trails stretch from Hyde Park Road to Camino Cruz Blanca across a network of easements that Ball managed to secure. His mission: to create low-elevation trails that would offer year-round use.

"I had a dream that Santa Fe would become a hiking center," says Ball, now 80. Call it mission accomplished.

Also to Ball's credit: coming out of retirement in 1992 to found the Santa Fe Conservation Trust, then serving as its executive director for nine years, during which he helped save 28,000 acres from development. Plus, he was a force behind the Santa Fe Rail Trail, the 15-mile recreational corridor that runs from Santa Fe to Lamy.

Ball's take on his trail-blazing feats: "What else is an old man with a lot of energy to do?"

---

hiking trip we treat ourselves to once every three years. We stay at a particularly nice hotel, where we have a five-course gourmet dinner every evening with the other guests of the hotel, most of whom are there for the hiking. This year, we were amazed at how many of the other guests were in their seventies, spending their days hiking some vigorous mountain routes.

I recently helped host a National Trails Day event at Cloudcroft, New Mexico, with leaders Barbara and Tom Springer, who unabashedly admit they are both in their seventies. They and their Rails-to-Trails Conservancy members have spent the past ten years restoring by hand enormous steel railroad trestles to turn a twenty-seven-mile spur of abandoned railroad into hiking trails.

Like anything else in life, if undertaken with proper attention to stress, the body is capable of enduring most anything. Age need not necessarily be a constraint.

There is a measure by which you can gauge the safety of your stress level. It is a simple test you can take at any time, anywhere, given in the sidebar "How to Establish Your Target Heart Rate." Look it up. Follow its suggestions. Pay attention to the results of the test. Do not press beyond those limits. If you pass this test, any type of physical activity will more than likely be safe for you.

But before you even take this test, and before you follow any of the suggestions in this chapter, if you are up in age and have not been getting regular aerobic exercise of some sort, then by all means check with your physician first to get professional counsel on what degree of stress your body can safely endure.

All I am saying is that age itself does not have to be a limitation to your getting into hiking and backpacking, if you keep common sense foremost. The simple phrase "easy does it" will stand you in good stead.

I live in a town where there is a club of retirees who meet for lunch every Monday at one of the local restaurants. They call themselves the Old Geezers Club. The only requirement for membership is that the retiree be at least seventy. The oldest member automatically becomes president. This title is currently passing, since our friend, eighty-nine-year-old president Wayne Kraxberger, has just said his last "so long."

Their chief activity is hiking and cross-country skiing. The Monday meeting is primarily to plan the next excursion, though when you hear their chipper chatter, you would seriously question that this was the purpose of the gatherings.

Back east in New York's Catskills, where I spent so many of my years hiking and backpacking, there is a similar club, the Over-the-Hill Boys, though perhaps it is even

How to Establish Your Target Heart Rate

Health professionals know what the proper pacing should be for you during exercise for whatever physical condition you are in. If you have been active in some regular aerobic activity for some length of time, then this test will give you a clue as to what limits you ought to observe when you start strenuous hiking or backpacking. If you have not been active, then even before you take this test, you should consult your physician to get expert advice on what limits you need to respect.

The following are standard limits set by the American Heart Association. The simple test is to measure your pulse rate as you increase your physical stress. If you have not been regularly active in aerobic sports, keep your pulse rate while under stress at a maximum figure you have calculated for your age.

Beginners should keep their pulse rate at half the maximum allowable rate for their age, which is simply 220 minus your physical age divided by two. So, for example, a person sixty-five years old should keep the pulse rate to $(220-65)/2 = 78$. This is the maximum pulse rate for an out-of-shape sixty-five-year-old on the first brisk walks.

As you take more and more brisk walks, it is all right to allow the pulse rate to fluctuate between 50 and 75 percent of the maximum pulse rate for your age. That is to say, you should keep your pulse rate to a range of half to three-quarters of the 220 minus your age.

Here is a table for quick reference to target heart rate zones for ages fifty and over:

Age	Maximum heart rate	Target heart rate zone
50	170 beats per minute	85–127 beats per minute
55	165 beats per minute	83–123 beats per minute
60	160 beats per minute	80–120 beats per minute
65	155 beats per minute	78–116 beats per minute
70	150 beats per minute	75–113 beats per minute
75	145 beats per minute	73–109 beats per minute
80	140 beats per minute	70–105 beats per minute
85	135 beats per minute	68–101 beats per minute
90	130 beats per minute	65–98 beats per minute

An even simpler method to keep your heart rate within a safe zone is to carry on an ordinary conversation as you hike. If you are able to do this, you are walking at a safe pace.

How Long Can You Keep Hiking?

How long you can keep hiking depends upon your career, for one thing. An example was set by Ulrich Inderbinden, a Swiss mountain guide who was still leading climbers up the Matterhorn and surrounding peaks until he was ninety-seven. High-adventure sports freaks might want to challenge Ulrich's 370-plus climbs of the 14,692-foot Matterhorn, a technical rock climb from the Hornli Hutte at the 10,700-foot level. Ulrich climbed the peak steadily, year after year, for seventy-five years, so many times that he actually lost count.

Ulrich said, however, that one of the best periods of his life didn't come until he was eighty-two and took up competitive skiing. He won every meet in which he competed, primarily because there were no others competing in his age group.

Once he climbed the 13,658-foot Breithorn on skis. On the ski back down, he fell, broke a leg, and had to toboggan down upon his skis to the base.

He finally gave up climbing, hiking, and skiing altogether the night of June 14, 2004, when he died in his sleep at 103.

a bit more gung ho. The "Over" in the name refers to the mountains but also has the generational connotation of its members' ages. This club's overt purpose is to climb all thirty-five of the Catskill's 3,500-foot peaks—over and over and over again. It has just about a hike a week, and a good number of members are always on them. And as you no doubt have guessed, after they've climbed them all, the next exercise is to climb all of them once more in winter.

24

Taking Your Pet

There is not much neutrality in opinions about pets on the trail. Either you love them or you hate them. When we talk about pets on the trail, we are generally speaking of dogs, though I have seen some interesting cat fanciers on the trails. One in particular stands out in memory, though I saw the chap but once, and that was many years ago on the Appalachian Trail in New Jersey. On top of his backpack, he had a cardboard box with a hole cut out in the front of it, through which I could see a cat's smiling face. He told me that cats are not long-distance hikers like dogs, so they have to be carried.

Though I've had my own dogs on the trail, I am more inclined toward the unfriendly view. Every time I see someone coming with a dog, I expect it to be unruly and out of the owner's control. Perhaps the reason is my experience with my own dog, Blue. He was obedient to me at home, and I expected the same on the trail. For the most part, this was true, except at a time when I needed his obedience most.

We were hiking up Divisidero Trail in northern New Mexico, and Blue went charging around a corner of the trail, barking fiercely. He spooked a horse, which almost tossed its rider over the side of the mountain. That was the last time I took him on a hike. I did not want to have a more serious incident occur.

THE CASE AGAINST DOGS ON THE TRAIL

The dog problem became serious a number of years ago—so serious that they have been banned from most backcountry trails in national parks, except for specially trained dogs to guide the blind or impaired. Three rangers were attacked by a dog in Rocky Mountain National Park when they tried to get the owner to leash it. Several children have been bitten by dogs in the national parks. Some people have been known to take attack dogs along on trails to "protect themselves." And park visitors have set their dogs loose to chase down mountain sheep. One park official in the East stated his opinion quite candidly about people who bring their pets on the trails: "It is selfish on the part of the dog owner, inconsiderate of other people, and unfair to the animal itself."

Those who object to dogs on the trails give the following arguments:

- Dogs harass wildlife. Many dogs do chase squirrels, rabbits, and large game, especially deer. There is a fine for dog owners in many states if their dogs are found chasing deer. Some forest rangers argue that even well-disciplined dogs scare off wildlife with their mere presence.
- Dogs harass other hikers. It is true that there are many dog owners who are proud of their dogs' aggressive protectiveness. These dogs can be frightening, if not

How to carry a cat the distance of the Appalachian Trail. Look closely to the ears sticking out of the top of the pack on the man on the right.

dangerous, to other hikers on the trails. Young children can feel especially threatened by encounters with large barking dogs.

- Dogs are noisy. The peace we seek in the backcountry is shattered by dogs whose owners cannot control their barking, especially at night.
- Dogs are intrusive. Our serenity can easily be disquieted by the sudden appearance of a dog sniffing and nosing around us uninvited and out of the owner's control.
- Dogs steal food. It is not safe to leave our lunch or other food unattended when there is an uncontrolled dog around. And a child holding a sandwich or snack can be intimidated by an uncontrolled dog that suddenly appears in camp.

Backcountry Ethics for Dog Haters

- Be friendly toward the dog and its owner. A dog's aggressive behavior is often touched off by subtle displays of emotion in people.
- Be considerate of other people's enjoyment in the backcountry, so long it as does not impinge on your own.
- If you have children, keep them well away from other people's dogs. And let them know that there could be danger if they do not keep away.
- Be reasonably prudent about keeping your food stashed away out of sight of people's dogs.
- Try not to complain unreasonably to rangers.

  Consideration and tolerance can go a long way toward reducing unpleasant confrontations and make for everyone's greater enjoyment of the outdoors.

- Dogs foul trails and campsites. An uncontrolled dog may urinate on corners of tents and in other places campers try to keep clean.
- Dogs harass horses. Where horse riders frequently use trails, land managers report an excessive number of complaints that dogs have scared horses and endangered riders.

> **My trail favorites are my border collie, Petunia, and as big a book as I think I'll be able to read while I am out there.**
>
> —*Mary Margaret Sloan, president, American Hiking Society*

- Dogs fight other dogs. Anyone who has been near a dogfight knows how upsetting it is to try to pull apart two dogs that have gone at each other, snarling, growling, biting, and barking.
- Dogs can be hurt by wild animals on the trails. Park officials report that numbers of dogs have been killed or injured by bears, mountain lions, snakes, scorpions, and spiders.

THE CASE FOR BRINGING ALONG YOUR DOG

On the other hand, I have friends who have hiked extensively with their dogs and have never given another hiker a single unpleasant experience. Laura and Guy Waterman climbed all 4,000-foot New Hampshire peaks with their dog, not once but four times, and got only warm greetings from other hikers.

A dog is a person's greatest companion. Especially if hiking alone. Anne Labastille, the famous ecologist, hiked extensively in the Adirondacks alone with but her dog, Pitzi, for company. Seventy-year-old A. C. Van der Kas bemoans: "My only companion on the trails is my dog, who loves hiking. Why should I be denied my companion and my dog his joy of hiking?"

And dog owners argue that many children on the trails are just as uncontrolled as some people's dogs. They are noisy, intrusive, and harassing, yet we would never think of stopping children from hiking.

Laura and Guy Waterman argue: "It is not right to condemn the whole species because of the faults of a few—or more likely the irresponsibility of their too-casual owners. A well-behaved, responsible pet does none of those things that disturb other hikers."

If you do plan to take your dog on the trail, be absolutely certain that you are able to keep it under control at all times—including when it runs into unexpected situations. And check the regulations beforehand so that you do not violate pet regulations in the area in which you intend to hike.

What better company on a hike?

Backcountry Ethics for Dog Owners

- Never let your dog chase wildlife.
- Keep your dog close to you when you approach other hikers. If they are nervous around your dog, grab it by the collar and hold it close, even if you know it is perfectly safe to other people.
- Keep your dog even under tighter control when there are small children around, even if you know it will be friendly toward them. The children don't know this.
- Keep your dog quiet. Other people do not want to hear barking, growling, or whining. If you can't keep it quiet, don't take it on the trails or to campgrounds.
- Train your dog to stay away from all food, especially other people's food.
- Do not let your dog drink at springs from which people draw their water. Have your dog drink downstream from all people.
- Do not allow your dog to foul the trail or campsite. Use common sense, and take the dog well off the trail and away from camp for it to eliminate. Should the dog foul a trail or camp, be sure to get the feces off into the woods where it will not be tracked back under other people's feet.
- When meeting another dog and its owner on the trail, grasp yours by its collar and ask the other owner to do the same.
- Should you come upon a horse on the trail, take your dog by the collar and hold it until the horse passes.
- Use common sense and be courteous to others.

There are many people and rangers who do not want dogs on trails or in camps anywhere. Do not give them ammunition to justify further restrictions.

A book on the subject that you might find useful is *Hiking with Dogs: Becoming a Wilderness-Wise Dog Owner*, by Linda B. Mullally. The author includes recommendations on raising a hiking dog, bonding, training, trail etiquette, and preventing wildlife conflicts, with a special section on dog-friendly public lands.

25
Going Alone

We spend most of our lives almost completely secluded from nature. As you read this, you are likely in a room furnished only with things made by humans—chairs, carpets, clothing, curtains, curios—and lamps powered by electricity generated by a people-made power plant. And you are reading a book written by a human, edited, printed, and distributed by human beings. Whatever there is of the natural world in your surroundings right now is most likely caged or potted, or at best a free-roaming cat or dog.

Thus, when we go out onto trails, we enter a foreign world. Presumably, this gives us greater appreciation for nature. At least, that is the way I see it. It is the prime reason why I go alone, for being alone intensifies that deeper immersion into the breezes, the forest scents, the ghostly sounds, and the shifting moods of the wilds.

Now, no doubt this chapter belongs in the section about the dangers of backpacking, for in every bit of advice that books and rangers give about the risks of backpacking, going alone ranks near the top of the list.

So-o-o-o-o-o-o-o-o, Bill, why are you now telling us to go alone? A question for which I have only a lame non sequitur: It's well worth the risk. *For me.*

This sense of finding my true home on a solo hike in the backcountry, especially the canyon country of the Southwest, prompts me to reread again and again Colin Fletcher's classic backcountry book on solo hiking, *The Man Who Walked through Time.* His book about his two-month hike end to end through the Grand Canyon is far more than a description of his hike. He masterfully tells the inner side of his journey, from the initial idea, through the planning stages, on to each step of the long, long hike.

Listen to the words Colin Fletcher wrote as he swung around an outcrop to the lip of a terrace between Fossil Bay and Apache Point several days into his solo trek, as quoted in Bruce Babbit's *Grand Canyon: An Anthology:* "I was meeting the silence—the silence I thought I had grown accustomed to—as something solid, face to face. And just for a moment I felt once more the same understanding and acceptance of the vast, inevitable sweep of geologic time."

Colin Fletcher's canyon solo has been a lasting inspiration to me. Not that I have ever considered attempting such a feat myself. It's just such a high standard of solo immersion into the cosmic order of things that it borders on the spiritual.

OUTWARD BOUND'S CLASSIC SOLO EXPERIENCE
Outward Bound has wilderness solo experiences built into its adventure-education expeditions, which now serve roughly 60,000 students each year. Students are given an

Since I entertain clients so often in the backcountry, I have developed a personal taste for eating just as well when I am off fishing by myself. I take along a light grill on which I broil trout I catch. Or when luck is not with me, I broil an elk steak I've brought along from my freezer "just in case." Salt and one of those little packs of soy sauce for a marinade tips it into gourmet class!

—*Taylor Streit, "legendary guide"
in Freshwater Fishing Hall of Fame
and author of* Instinctive Fly Fishing:
A Guide's Guide to Better Fishing
and Guide to Fly Fishing in New Mexico,
www.streitflyfishing.com.

option of participating in a final exercise of a solo expedition, camping alone in the wilderness for as many as three days.

The student makes a wilderness camp with sleeping bag, tarps, appropriate clothing, water, and journal, leaving behind watch and books so as to remain in the present moment without getting immersed in others' writing or worrying about the time. A student taking the wilderness solo is assigned to a designated spot with specific boundaries, is not allowed to leave the area, and for safety reasons is continually checked by instructors.

This is a voluntary part of the Outward Bound program. Its main purpose is not backcountry survival, but rather more monastic, an exercise in reflection and self-awareness. According to Kate Borgelt, Outward Bound's marketing manager: "Solo has become one of Outward Bound's most valuable tools as well as one of its most defining elements. It's a period for rest and reflection for our students. They take a mental and physical break from the rigors of the expedition and time to consider the impact the expedition's experiences will have on their lives back home. For many, being alone in the wilderness contrasts so dramatically with their daily lives. And of course, the wilderness experience is always healing for them." What do instructors tell students about reflection on their solos? "When students are ready," Kate says, "they come together as a group and talk about possible feelings of apprehension they might have on the solo. They commonly come up with questions such as, What will I be afraid of? What is it I appreciate most about my life? What is there about myself I'd like to change? What is my vision of my biggest, wisest, most admirable Self? What holds me back from bringing these visions to reality in my life? How does the Outward Bound course enable me to change? We encourage them to journal about these questions. Most students do take the solo. And virtually all of them claim it changes their lives."

SOLOS AS THERAPY

My son-in-law, Doug Shafer, had that same sort of solo experience in the Maine woods during his years as summer counselor at Camp Deerwood in New Hampshire. In order to achieve the highest level of merit, he was given three matches, a knife, and a fishing line to spend three days solo in the woods. "It certainly was a rite of passage," he says.

My solo jaunts all have been considerably less ambitious, but in many other ways, they emulate Fletcher's canyon-walk inner experience.

Soloing for the Sheer Joy of the Backcountry

Group backpacking leader Denise Traver likes to solo for the sheer joy of the backcountry: "It opens my eyes to the unbelievable beauty that surrounds me. It is addictive."

She got into backpacking with a good friend who was highly experienced in desert hiking. He made sure they each had the right equipment and sufficiently checked it out before they ever set foot on their first hike. After many backpacking trips in the desert, he moved away from the area. Denise was so addicted that she continued backpacking, but now it was solo hiking.

"I took my first backpack trip on my own, a six-day trip in the Superstition Mountains near Phoenix, and I haven't looked back since," she says. "All my personal backpacks are solo. I need my downtime when I am not leading groups on backpacking trips. I will go out for two weeks by myself and never talk or sing to myself. If I am lucky, I won't see a single soul on the entire trip. Leading trips feeds my extrovert side, and taking my own personal hikes feeds my introvert side."

I got into soloing only because I had a lot of difficulty finding hiking partners, never mind ones who were compatible with my hiking style. Looking back on it, my solos were at first blushingly modest—just an afternoon walk alone in the park.

The urge came on me late one night after a long study session during my college years. The nearest park was along Riverside Drive on the Hudson River. In those days, there was an amusement park on the Jersey side of the Hudson, its dancing lights flickering deep into the darkest part of the night. It was quiet on the Columbia University side of the Hudson, and the contrast created a wonderful soothing respite from the textbooks.

Oftentimes I've considered the woods as something akin to therapy. One technique I used was an anxiety-reducing palliative from Norman Vincent Peale. He suggested taking a walk alone on the beach or into the woods, sitting down well away from people, and bringing your worries to mind, one by one. Then he advised writing down the first worry that comes to mind with your finger into the sand or dirt, in a single word. Say it was "rent," for a worry about how I was going to pay the rent on Monday.

Then, as the next worry arose in my mind, I'd write the word for that worry in the sand on top of the first word. Say I've had a quarrel with my girlfriend, Jackie. I would write "Jackie" on top of "rent." Then I'd scroll down in my mind through all my other worries, one at a time, writing each worry in the sand, one upon the other.

I tried this at times over the years. Though it never magically gave me the rent money or settled matters with Jackie, it did put my worries into perspective, just as talking them out with a therapist would do. And at a much better fee!

Without even writing down the worries, though, I have found walks alone in the woods have a tremendous healing effect.

My tent is a two-person A-frame Gerry, which I have been using long after everyone turned to domes. OK, maybe they have the "most efficient square footage" for round or square people, but people are linear, especially me.

—*Eric Seaborg, executive director, American Discovery Trail Society*

In time, I extended these walks to quick overnight hikes for similar reasons—to get away for a rest from my daily difficulties. At times when I felt overwhelmed by so many problems, I'd make sure things were in order at home, then toss my pack into the car and head for the nearest trailhead.

I recall rather nostalgically some nights I camped trailside in the Hudson Highlands, atop some knoll overlooking the Hudson River with the lights of New York City aglow in the distance.

It is difficult for worries to keep their clutch upon me when I'm lying out on my sleeping bag beneath a starry sky with a view like that before me. Then, next morning, after an early breakfast, I would be ready for the short drive back home to face my routine again.

As I write this, I can't think of a better way of getting into soloing. It is a lot safer to get into it gradually than to take your first solo on a longer backpacking trek, where the risks are a lot higher. After all, a walk in the park is pretty safe. And a walk on the beach about the same. Extending that into a short overnight near home is not much of a step further up the risk ladder. So consider the more gradual approach.

TAKE EXTRA PRECAUTIONS WHEN SOLOING

Today there are many extra precautions I take when I backpack alone, since I am off on much more extended treks. Now then, let this part of the chapter warn of the dangers. And then let's talk about the extra precautions that can reduce the risks, though they cannot by any means eliminate them. For it is true that hiking alone at least doubles the ordinary dangers of the backcountry.

When you are alone on the trail, you invite trouble. Should you experience the slightest difficulty and need help, you are uppa-da-creek! A sprained ankle could disable you enough that you are marooned for days, especially if you are in an area seldom if ever visited by other human beings.

If you encounter any of the dangers discussed earlier—hypothermia, heatstroke, snakebite, lightning, bear attack, or anything else we have not thought of—your chances of survival plummet. I know this. My wife knows this. My children know this. Yet we all accept that the solitude of the outdoors is a vital part of my life. They know, too, that I take whatever precautions possible to reduce those risks.

Mostly I hike alone. I use my Gregory Denali Pro pack for longer backpacking hikes, though on short overnights I carry a North Face Stamina pack.

—*Steve Bridgehouse, Grand Canyon backcountry ranger, 1997–2004*

Whenever I go alone, I leave my wife a detailed USGS map with my itinerary clearly indicated on it. I also leave phone numbers of the police and rangers' offices nearest to where I'll be hiking. I mark the place on the map where I will park my car. And I write down, so that there is no failure of communication, exactly when I expect to be back to my car. In the event that I do run into difficulty, she will know where to have a search begin.

I also take extra precautions in everything I do on the trail. I am bear alert, stay aware of changes in the weather, stay out of slot canyons, and take all the other precautions that are mentioned throughout this book.

I take care where I camp, how I set up my campsite, where I cook and eat and store my food. I am even careful of the way I walk on the trail, stepping over logs and stones onto firm ground to avoid any slip that could result in a turned ankle.

TYPES OF SOLO HIKES

Last February, I took a three-day solo into Grand Canyon, starting out through several inches of snow on the South Rim, hiking down into warm weather in the Sonoran desert climate at the bottom. Here my risks of soloing were minimal. Park rangers refer to these trails as the "heavy-use corridor," as if they were hallways in some gigantic building. Though the risks were low both because this was one of the safest times of year to hike in the canyon and because of the huge number of hikers on the trails, my hike gave me a limited amount of solitude.

William Kemsley Jr. at a solo backpacking camp in Big Bend National Park.

Some of my other solo jaunts are considerably riskier but provide more solitude. Once or twice a summer, I attempt a climb up one of Colorado's prize mountains. This is an entirely different sort of backpacking. It requires more planning, greater concern about weather and timing, and a more disciplined camp routine. Because many of these peaks are less frequently climbed, the risks are higher, there being fewer hikers who could help should I run into difficulties.

Regardless of the difference between the two types of hikes, the benefits of going alone, at least to some extent, are available to me on both. I am able to get periods of time away from the throng, even in Grand Canyon's heavy-use corridor. And in either place, of course, I have the advantage of setting my own hiking pace. It is all a matter of degree.

MY SOLO TRIP WHILE WRITING THIS CHAPTER

One of the pleasures I am getting from writing this book is that I am able to write most of it in the outdoors. I carry a notebook and pen in my pack and a laptop in my car. For this chapter in particular, I wanted to be alone for several days running, both with backpack and camped by my car.

There is a side of my backpacking trips that makes the backcountry speak to me in a different voice, in the stories of those who passed there long ago. This particular trip

Extra Precautions for Hiking Alone

- Provide the following information to your family or friend who will take responsibility for beginning a search should you get into difficulty on the trail: a detailed USGS map with your itinerary clearly marked, including the location where you will park your car; an indication of when you expect to return to your car; and the emergency phone number of the ranger's or sheriff's office closest to your car.
- Do not deviate from your planned itinerary without advising someone.
- Take extra precautions on the trail, watching where you step so as not to turn an ankle, and avoiding slot canyons during storms or threatening weather.
- Keep on the lookout for bears and any other potential hazards in the area.
- Make noise as you hike in bear country.
- Camp safely in bear country, preparing meals and eating 100 feet or more from your tent. Bearproof the camp in all the ways described in chapter 18.
- Camp safely out of flash-flood areas.
- Carry an adequate first-aid kit.
- Familiarize yourself with all the cautions in this book about bears, floods, lightning, snakebite, hypothermia, heat exhaustion, and more.
- Play it as safe as you possibly can, for even if help arrives, it may be too late.
- Some would take a cell phone or GPS for what search-and-rescue people are calling the "911 syndrome." This is a serious business today. Some states are considering and passing legislation that requires you to have either a cell phone or GPS along with you; if you don't and have to be rescued, you can be heavily fined. A good host of rock and mountain climbers resist with this slogan: "Don't come to rescue me if I get in trouble." My own view is quite simply that having either a cell phone or GPS is certainly not solo hiking.

was inspired by a fascinating book I had just finished reading about the history of the U.S. Southwest. *Cities of Gold* author Douglas Preston told of an area a day's drive from my home that is still a wilderness and is replete with colorful imaginings of the history of the first encounter of Europeans with the North American Indians.

Preston was so intrigued with this period of history that he retraced on horseback the Spanish explorer Francisco Vásquez de Coronado's 1540 route on his discovery of the great landscapes of the Southwest, including Grand Canyon. Coronado's encounter with Native Americans changed the face of North America ever after.

Something that Preston noted was that although much of the land he was tracing was less than 100 miles from downtown Phoenix, it was as desolate and impenetrable as it was in Coronado's day! Hard to believe. I had to see this.

As I say, I enjoy writing in camps deep in the woods, so I took this weeklong journey to see this area for myself.

My first day was driving, a few hours on the interstates, then down narrower and narrower state highways to the town of Globe, Arizona. I'll give you enough details of this trip that you, too, can take the route.

I first stopped in for the night to visit with my brother and sister-in-law in Truth or Consequences. Getting a late start from their place, I was up in the Continental Divide on Highway 152, where I eat my lunch back in the woods at a horse trailhead just off an S-curve. I decided to spend the afternoon there with my laptop in the craggy desert beneath towering pines, writing for a while. Then I drove across and north of Silver City to the edge of the Gila Wilderness to make camp for the

> **A whittling knife is my best company on a solo hike, when I sit by my campfire whittling.**
>
> *—Kenn Petsch, my nephew and veteran desert hiker*

night. Probably car-mile distance for the day was less than 100 miles. I am in no hurry. This is my job, you know! And I must take the time to write.

Leisurely breakfast with lots of coffee in the morning. I simply love coffee, and I make it with beans that I grind fresh at home just before I take the trip. I also treat myself on a car trip like this with fresh cream in my coffee. And before I pack up for the road, I write a few lines that come to mind on my laptop. I have a laptop cord that plugs into my cigarette lighter while I drive along to recharge the battery.

This day, I travel a little more than 200 miles before making camp. I drive through Globe, Arizona, where I gas up about early dinnertime, so I pick up some fast food and head on out of town on the road toward Payson. But before I get to Theodore Roosevelt Dam, I cut north on a dirt road variously marked as 288, 88, and some other numbers along the way. Not possible to get lost, though, as it is the only road, and the few that cross it in the next 100 miles or so dead-end in but a few miles.

This is my destination. The road goes across the mountains and drops down into a near ghost town called Young that has an extraordinary history. It is where one of the most bloody range battles of the Old West took place. And until just a few decades ago, if you were a stranger entering this valley, you would be hanged on the spot without a trial.

If you love this sort of history-mongering, I recommend Preston's book. He is a gifted writer and an inveterate outdoorsman, with a passion for history. He gained a grant from the Smithsonian Institution to take his trip, which his book is all about.

Just one note about the area I am now traveling through. It is Coronado's route, with hundreds of soldiers, colonists, slaves, and cattle. It is also the historic route of the Basque sheepherders, who have been driving their cattle from the south across this range up through the Pleasant Valley, past the town site of Young, and up the Mogollon Rim. They are still doing it today, north during the spring and back south in the fall. When you drive through here, you have to wonder how they manage to get through. It is a tangle of desert foliage twisted among the craggy canyons, miraculously traversed by this narrow, sharply winding dirt road so rugged it is barely passable in a two-wheel-drive vehicle.

Though I have been alone since I left my brother's place, I am now truly alone. No cars pass me all afternoon long, and once I'm past Globe, there are no signs of human habitation except the lonely dirt road.

I stop at another primitive horse trail that crosses the road and decide to make camp a short distance in from the road. It is late May as I make this trip, so the days are conveniently long. After dinner, I read what I have written and tidy up some of it, letting ideas gel for the rest of the chapter.

The morning dawns beautifully crisp and dry, for this is the Southwest. And I am at a fair altitude of about 7,000 feet in the Sierra Ancha Mountains. Again, my leisurely breakfast, then an hour's walk up the trail where there are some fine viewpoints.

I make my way slowly through Young, which is merely a name on the map, for it has nothing there, no gas, no store, no post office, only a few rather weather-beaten houses and barns, many with For Sale signs.

The route past town rolls across meadowlands, where I stop for a spell to eat lunch and do some more writing. The road then crosses Haigler Creek. I mean, this is the West, and you "ford" the creek—that is, drive across it in trust without a bridge. Then the route winds treacherously up the Mogollon Rim, which stretches across all of Arizona and part of New Mexico, rising precipitously some 1,000 feet in most places.

At the top of the rim, I come to my first paved road, which somehow is almost deserted. I take a Forest Service road into the Sitgreaves National Forest. The high desert is now beneath first juniper and piñons, then towering ponderosa pines. Camping at large is allowed in this area, so long as it is fifty feet from the dirt road and not near water of any sort, which is something of a joke in this area, for it is dry as a bone.

I drive several miles into the pines, looking for a perfect place to make camp. For I intend to stay here the rest of the week. About ten miles into the forest, I find a pristine spot that appears as though no one has ever been there before me. I drive off the road the required distance and make my camp on a sweet, soft bed of ponderosa pine needles. It is more magnificent than I can describe.

I make my base camp here for the rest of the week. I hike each day in a different direction, and one day I find an even more perfect spot on the rim of a small side canyon where I can camp and get a first-light view of the sun rising in the morning.

So this is the other way I love to get off by myself. Now on this trip, I did not let my wife know where I would be each night. But I did give her my probable route and timing. There wasn't much that could go wrong, even though this is bear territory.

Section Six
WHERE TO GO

Grand Canyon becomes enchanting in winter. Colorado Trail founder Gudy Gaskill imbibes the serenity of a December snowfall.

Yes, they're wanting me, they're haunting me, the awful lonely places;
   They're whining and they're whimpering as if each had a soul;
They're calling from the wilderness, the vast and God-like spaces,
   The stark and sullen solitudes that sentinel the Pole.

They miss my little camp-fires, ever brightly, bravely gleaming
   In the womb of desolation, where was never man before;
As comrade-less I sought them, lion-hearted, loving, dreaming,
   And they hailed me as a comrade, and they loved me evermore.

And now they're all a-crying, and it's no use me denying;
   The spell of them is on me and I'm helpless as a child;
My heart is aching, aching, but I hear them, sleeping, waking;
   It's the Lure of Little Voices, it's the mandate of the Wild.

                              —from "Lure of Little Voices," by Robert Service

26

Deciding Where to Backpack

Assuming that you have tried hiking and take to it rather enthusiastically, you are ready for your first overnight on the trail. Again, I cannot urge you more strongly to start slowly. Try camping at a trailhead near your car and day-hiking from there.

This can be serious hiking. Most hikers who climb Colorado's 14,000-foot peaks camp at a trailhead to get an early start day-climbing one of these impressive peaks. If they have to—and for some of these peaks they must—hikers will backpack farther into the backcountry to climb them. For these hikers, it's the hikes that count, not the backpacking.

The same is true, of course, of climbing the peaks in Washington, Oregon, California, and many of the northeastern peaks. Many of my early backpacking trips were in the Catskills, where I usually set up camp at a roadside campground Friday night, backpacked across the peaks to camp on the other side of the mountains Saturday night, and headed back to my car Sunday.

For your first backpacking trips, take short overnights close to home. Find a trail close by that enables you to get out in the backcountry but not be so far from your car that you can't handle emergencies if they arise. As you spend more time camping out, you will learn to more confidently cope with those that do arise.

Some of the more common anxieties on first overnights are caused by the strange forest sounds which can be rather disconcerting. I will never forget one of my early solo backpacking journeys on the Appalachian Trail. I was camped in a state wildlife refuge in Pennsylvania, where there was an abundance of wildlife sounds that were unfamiliar to me. I spent much of that night lying awake with flashlight in hand, sure that my sleeping bag was going to become a roost for some porcupine or wild partridge.

RESPECT THE *WILD* IN WILDERNESS

Take backpacking seriously. There is a lot more risk to it than appears at first blush. Too many people today get into backpacking with little to no concern for the risks. Hence there are a lot of backcountry accidents that could easily have been avoided with better preparation. Michael Ghiglieri and Thomas Myers, the authors of *Over the Edge: Death in Grand Canyon,* don't think of them as accidents, but rather "rare outcomes that one would expect to happen given a set of specific conditions or decisions (such as not wearing a life jacket while boating on the Colorado River)."

As you become more familiar with what it is like to carry a load, set up camp, and cook your meals in the backcountry, it will be easier to make your decisions about where you want to go. But do consider the risks discussed in this book.

My research has alerted me to new risks that have developed in the past few years, as well as old ones I had no idea were so serious and new ways of coping with some of the most severe dangers.

I've hiked hundreds of days in Grand Canyon, for example, yet I never realized the serious danger of flash floods. It wasn't until I made an innocent inquiry of the park historian, Mike Anderson, about a flood that occurred some years ago that I discovered that a man who had spent thousands of days hiking the Grand Canyon had died in a sudden flash flood in an area in which I have hiked and never realized the possibility of such an occurrence. The story is told in chapter 30.

> **I never go out on the trail, even on day hikes, without an umbrella, which I've carried for fifteen years and never taken out of my fanny pack.**
>
> —*Gudy Gaskill, "mother" and builder of the 500-mile Colorado Trail*

Likewise, what I now know about bear attacks is more daunting than ever. I have always known of the risk. And I have never been quite comfortable with it. But I have discovered that in recent years, there have been a growing number of attacks by black bears. And I've always believed they were rather harmless. Then, too, the guidelines about how to cope with a bear attack have been changed—not once, but twice—since I had last read the literature.

On the trail on sunny days of summer, the entire world seems so cozy that risks of backcountry travel seem remote. It is difficult to imagine anything could possibly go wrong. But they can, and they do. And it is plain foolish to be deceived by balmy summer sunshine.

Find out, as best you can, what kind of risks you are likely to confront in the area you plan to hike. Forewarned is forearmed.

HOW TO GET INFORMATION ABOUT TRAILS IN AN AREA

The best source of information about trails is the website of the American Hiking Society, www.americanhiking.org. Its "Trail Finder," powered by trails.com, lists a variety of 30,000 trails. The AHS site also links to its online partners, such as hiking equipment retailers, trail tool information, and National Geographic maps.

Here I am hiking in one of my favorite ranges, the Swiss Alps, in the shadow of the Matterhorn.

Another way to find out where to hike is from local hiking clubs. The best source of information on hiking clubs is also the AHS website. If you are planning hikes with your family, check out the "Top Ten Family Friendly Trails" on the AHS site.

Another good Internet source of trail information is a site conveniently named trails.com. It has considerable detail about the 30,000 trails, including guidebook descriptions and maps. Or you can inquire at your state, county, or federal government recreation department office. There is also a wealth of areawide guidebooks with names like *Sixty Hikes within Sixty Miles of* _____ (insert your city's name in the blank).

Once you determine which part of the country you want to take your hike in, find a trail guide for that area. There are many good ones to choose among. REI carries a stock of 1,000 different hiking-guide titles. Eastern Mountain Sports (EMS) stores have a similar line of trail guides. And the Internet sites can be enormously helpful. Likely you will be able to narrow down from these sources just where you want to go.

On some trails, aids are provided to help the hiker over the most difficult parts. This ladder is on the seventy-four-kilometer West Coast Trail in the Pacific Rim National Park in Vancouver, British Columbia, Canada.
TIMOTHY MANNS

PLAN LONGER TRIPS WELL IN ADVANCE

Find out ahead of time the rules and practices for the area you intend to backpack. They vary from one place to another. Some, like Grand Canyon, require advance reservation for any backcountry backpacking campsite. These campsites are so popular that you are not likely to get a reservation without requesting it at least three months ahead of time. The park gets some 30,000 requests annually for permits for these campsites, but only 13,000 are issued.

Also find out what the weather conditions will be like at your chosen time of year, what the backcountry camping may be like, and what precautions you ought to take against potential hazards.

The answers to these questions will give you clues to the type of gear you need. Will you be hiking in forests, as on the Appalachian Trail or Washington's Cascade Mountains, where you'll need extra protection against wet weather and good bug repellent? Will it be desert backpacking, requiring you to carry an extra amount of water? Or mountainous terrain above tree line, where nights will be particularly cool?

In the desert in springtime, you may want to tent simply to keep away from insects that tend to come out at dusk. I am dry camping in Forest Service land in desert of New Mexico's Chama Valley.

One Fourth of July weekend, we were heading to the Weminuche Wilderness in Colorado and noted that we had to prepare for unusually cold weather. While temperatures here in New Mexico are in the high eighties, nights there at the higher elevations above tree line where we would be backpacking were dropping well below freezing.

Will you be hiking in and out of streams, as in slickrock canyons, and need to consider boots that can get soaking wet and take special care protecting your feet from blisters? Should you expect to be hiking across snowfields, where crampons and ice ax would be useful? I'm not talking technical climbing now, but simple backpacking in various types of terrain. Many western mountain ranges regularly have snowfields that trails cross in summer but do not have the hazards of glaciers.

27

Overnighting at Inns and Huts

Even if you can't wait to go backpacking in Gates of the Arctic National Park, you may want to start your more serious backcountry adventure by hiking during the day and staying in an inn at night, where you also take dinner and breakfast. A variety of inns, lodges, cabins, and huts offer such accommodations for hikers. This can be both an adventurous and a wonderfully sociable way to go. In places like Vermont and Grand Manan Island in Canada, you can hike a backcountry trail during the day, and then enjoy the evening ambience of a country inn with other people who are also hiking these trails.

HIGH-MOUNTAIN HUTS AND LODGES

Inns and their cousins in a variety of forms—chalets, huts, lodges, cabins, and on down to hostels—vary in accommodations offered, some with cooked meals, while others are places to which you bring your own food and prepare your own meals on their cookstoves and bring along your sleeping bag to use in bunks.

A bit more rustic are places where you get simple meals and a bed. Then there are the more primitive accommodations in huts to which you hike, but prepare your own meals on their cookstoves and bring along your sleeping bag to use on bunks.

Any of these variations of overnight accommodations is a splendid way to see what it is like in the backcountry at night without having to go full-tilt camping out. I defy anyone, for instance, to spend the night in the Appalachian Mountain Club (AMC) hut on the shoulder of Mount Monroe in the Presidential Range, and hear the pensive song of a white-throated sparrow across the pond in the evening, without catching the backcountry bug. The AMC operates a string of nine huts each an easy day's hike from another in the White Mountains of New Hampshire. You get your own bunk and all your meals at these huts, including a bag lunch for the trail.

In New York, the Adirondack Mountain Club (ADK) operates several huts conveniently situated for day hikes in the higher peaks. Like the AMC's, the ADK huts provide meals as well as bunks.

In Colorado, a series of seventeen Tenth Mountain Division ski huts, most of which are situated above 11,000 feet in elevation in the Rocky Mountains, are available for use by hikers. They have a romantic history, having been built to train ski troops during World War II.

In the Southeast, the historic LeConte Lodge, situated atop a mountain in the Great Smoky Mountains National Park, plays host to overnight hikers. It was built by the advocacy group that successfully lobbied for designation of the Smoky Mountains as a national park.

Appalachian Mountain Club huts, as this one on Mount Madison, are nestled near the summits of peaks in the Presidential Range of New Hampshire. PAUL MOZELL, COURTESY OF THE AMC

The Sperry and Granite Park Chalets are lodges with overnight accommodations in Glacier National Park to which you must hike. There are others in California, Washington, Alaska, and Canada.

HELICOPTER HUT HIKING

Yes, the twenty-first century has impinged upon even the backcountry huts. In the Bugaboo Mountains of British Columbia, you can helicopter in to a backcountry inn.

Food and supplies are carried in by the hut men and women to the high mountain huts in the White Mountains of New Hampshire. Trash is carried out via same method.

Heli-hiking has become popular in some remote areas, such as the Bugaboo Range in British Columbia, Canada, where you helicopter in to a remote spot and hike back out. Here Betty Leavengood gets aboard to try it out. BETTY LEAVENGOOD

From there, you can hike upon glacial moraine beneath the towering rock spires that pierce the sky thousands of feet from their roots in the glaciers around you. Or helicopter from your roadside inn to a trail high above for a day's hike. Visit www.cmhski.com to learn more about this unique experience.

I'm sure there are many other places where you can helicopter in to hiking huts. One I know about is in an Indian nation to which there are no roads. The normal way in to its principle village, Supai, is via a ten-mile mule trail, which most people hike. But because of the invalidism of some of its older residents, the Havasupai people have issued a permit for helicopter service to Supai. They also have built a rustic resort hotel at which you may stay. From there, you have a variety of hiking options, including a good, strenuous, exceedingly beautiful hike down to the Colorado River past three blue-green waterfalls that spill into enticing pools of mineralized water, in which you can take a swim en route. See www.havasupaitribe.com.

EUROPEAN MOUNTAIN HUTS AND INNS

Trekking long distances while stopping nightly in inns and huts is very popular in Europe. Some I've stayed in at 12,000 to 15,000 feet in altitude in the Italian Alps regularly accommodate more than 200 hikers and climbers on a typical summer night. But throughout Europe, there also are mountain huts at lower elevations in mountains and hills, as well as small inns in country villages, that hikers use with great frequency during the hiking season.

One of the most popular hikes for Europeans is the Tour du Mont Blanc, which takes about eleven days' hiking through France, Italy, and Switzerland around the massive Mont Blanc, stopping each night at inns or mountain huts. Another popular route is along the crests of Switzerland's Bernese Alps.

When I hiked this route, the huts and inns along the way varied in how rustic the facilities were, though all were in fine repair and exceptionally clean, much more so than any of the hostels I have found in the United States. Speaking of hostels, those in Britain are rather luxurious and are situated in some of best scenic locations in the areas.

The nice thing about this sort of hiking is that you carry only a daypack. You can ship heavier items you don't need daily along to a drop-off destination farther along your route and pick them up later.

Day-hiking from inn to inn is a more gentle way of breaking into overnighting, and you may even decide this is a better way to go. Huts and inns are very popular among the few who know about them, so it is best to get in touch with their managers well in advance of your planned trip.

FINDING HUTS AND INN-TO-INN HIKING

You can do a search online to find other huts and inns that accommodate hikers. There are many more than you might suspect. My area, for example, has a series of four yurts that a cross-country ski enthusiast built in a national forest on the New Mexico-Colorado border. They are available for hikers as well as skiers. Rent is reasonable if you are a family with children.

For the AMC huts, check www.outdoors.org/lodging/huts. For Sierra Club lodges, see www.sierraclub.org/outings/lodges/. Try www.adk.org/huts for Adirondack hut information. For information on Colorado's Tenth Mountain Ski Huts, go to www.huts.org. For Alpine Club of Canada, visit www.alpineclubofcanada.ca/facility.

Wall Tent Bed-and-Breakfast

There are even more genteel, though nonetheless rustic and nostalgic, places to spend the night while hiking during the day. How about a wall tent with bed, linens, woodstove, and kerosene lantern at MaryJanesFarm in Idaho farmland? Lend a hand with the farm and garden chores, go for a hike on the scenic backroads and trails in the surrounding hills, or relax in the peace of your private outdoor sitting area.

Mary Jane Butters, the Mary Jane of MaryJanesFarm, is an interesting backcountry personality worth getting to know. She was the first woman station guard at Moose Creek Station, the most remote Forest Service ranger station in the lower forty-eight. She spent two eight-month seasons living in the backcountry, renovating an old historic log cabin, growing a wilderness garden, tending stock and the station and grounds—all sort of a prelude to her bed-and-breakfast farm. Good evening chats can be a bonus for a visit if you can connect with her. For more information, visit www.maryjanesfarm.com.

A wall tent with wooden platform floor and cots is the most primitive accommodation at MaryJanesFarm in Idaho.

WWW.MARYJANESFARM.COM

Spending the evening in backcountry huts enables children to be occupied with enjoyable activities. Nine-year-old Kate Kemsley found fun building a house of cards, even when Miss Pussy came to investigate.

For others, search for "huts." It helps to use the qualifying word "hike." Or try "inn to inn" in your search, again with the qualifying word "hike." You will find possibilities in dozens of states and many countries of the world. For instance, how about hiking a route from hut to hut in Lapland, described as "an eight-day hike around the Kebnekaise massif in Swedish Lapland, all but two days above tree line"?

AMC huts are now supplied with heavy equipment and building supplies by helicopter.

TOUR OPERATORS

Tour operators can put together a swanky inn-to-inn hiking trip for you, with everything provided according to your tastes, such as moving your gear from one inn to another, serving candlelight gourmet meals, and turning down your bedcover, with a mint on your pillow. All you need is foot power to get along the trail of your choosing.

Don't knock it until you've tried it. Though I love camping deep in the wilderness, getting away from all semblances of human appurtenances, I have to confess that I have thoroughly enjoyed many nights in huts, lodges, cabins, and refuges. More than anything, it is being in the backcountry that counts.

Here are a few tour operator websites you may want to check out: www.randonee-tours.com specializes in hikes in British Columbia and Alaska; www.inntoinn.com focuses on Vermont inns; www.gorp-travel.com will arrange hikes in Montana's

Glacier National Park; www.callwild.com deals exclusively in all-women trips to won-derfully exotic wilderness places; www.gfic.org offers both backpacking and inn-based hikes with an educational bent at very reasonable prices; www.coloradotrail.org pro-vides an excellent short summer-season wilderness education program in tents at its cabin high in the San Juan Mountains of Colorado; and both REI (www.rei.com) and EMS (www.ems.com) offer group tours.

SOME OF MY FAVORITES

It is said we take a hike three times: once as we plan and prepare for it, once when we walk it, and yet again when we tell our friends about it. One of the special joys of stay-ing at inns is the fellowship with other hikers in the evening, talking about the hike you took during the day and the one you plan for tomorrow.

Let me share two of our favorite inns at which we've enjoyed that sort of fellowship. One is a couple hours from New York City, on the southern rim of the Catskill Moun-tains. The Mohonk Mountain House (www.mohonk.com) has eighty-five miles of trails for hiking, biking, horseback riding, and cross-country skiing on about 11,000 acres of craggy mountain terrain, where we hike all day, then dine in luxury, chatting with other hikers.

But let me wax a bit more about our all-time favorite hiking spot. I began writing this chapter on the balcony of our spacious room, with late-afternoon sun rays tinting pink the surrounding snow-covered peaks. We have just returned from an eight-hour hike. Shortly we will have dinner with new companions we've met here in Zermatt.

Yes, I enjoy backpacking deep in the backcountry, and in a couple weeks I will be back in the United States in another favorite hiking place on a four-day backpack. But I confess that I also love these Swiss amenities. For a modest rate, which includes breakfast and a five-course gourmet dinner, we are staying in the very special three-star Butterfly Hotel (www.hotelbutterflyzermatt.com), from which we can walk out the door onto trails to snow-covered peaks in every direction.

Yesterday my wife, Joy, was not feeling well, so I made a solo ascent of a 4,000-meter glacier-covered peak that, though an easy mountaineering climb, nevertheless is a technical climb that takes its toll of climbers' lives. A gravestone in the church cemetery commemorates the recent death of twenty-seven-year-old Donald Stephen Williams of New York City.

I mention this climb in contrast to the many other levels of hiking available on the 250 miles of trails here in Zermatt, where everyone walks. We walk because no cars are allowed in town. The only vehicles are bicycles, horse-drawn carriages, electric-powered taxis, and small delivery trucks.

Today Joy and I hiked along a trail that meanders gently through Alpine meadows and forests of hemlocks, pine, and larch, the pungent aroma of sun on pine needles fill-ing the air. After an hour or so, around a bend in the trail, we saw a red Swiss flag with its large white cross flying above a quaint, colorful chalet with geraniums in the win-dows. The flag was a sign that the inn is open for business, inviting us to stop for a café au lait and a nibble of sweet roll. Probably the best part of that stop was the wait for service with the wide panoramic view of mountains in every direction and the Matter-horn dominating the middle. What a way to wait. Please, don't hurry.

My wife and I have a snack at the Hornli Hutte, 1,000 meters below the summit of the Matterhorn.

After another couple hours hiking through Alpine forests and meadows, it was time for lunch. And surprise. We stumbled upon another country chalet with Swiss flag flying. Yes, we took a table on the porch beneath a red-and-white umbrella and still, that everlasting Alpine view, Matterhorn center stage.

Does it matter what they serve for lunch in such a setting? We both chose *rosti mit oeufs,* a special way the Swiss have of serving hash-brown potatoes topped with fried eggs. Joy ordered a beer. I had *mineral wasser mit gaz.* Notice the delightful mixture of French and German? That's Switzerland's four languages for you—French, German, Italian, English.

We ate our food leisurely. Half its taste was in the autumn sunshine. To linger longer, we shared a piece of apple pie with a café au lait. I am a coffee freak and proclaim Swiss café au lait even better than that I've been served in Paris!

Then the hike back down, more direct, a bit steeper, through mostly thick pine and larch forests, coming out into town on narrow paths among private homes.

We had time for a sauna at the hotel before dressing for dinner, where we shared our hiking stories with other guests. Lucy and Eddy Bartaby, our new friends from England, had hiked back to town from the Furi cable-car stop. We'd taken the same hike a few days earlier. John and Helen from southern France had hiked a strenuous trail on the other side of the valley, with lunch of *spaghetti arrabiatta* and a Swiss red wine at a mountain hut much farther up the mountain than any of the rest of us had hiked.

A young couple from the United Kingdom had taken a picnic lunch to a high alpine meadow while doing the most strenuous hike of all. They were in fine hiking shape, for this was the last day of their eleven-day high-mountain hike from hut to hut across the Alps from Chamonix, France, to Zermatt, Switzerland.

28

Enjoying the High Mountains

Mountain hiking is one thing at lower elevations and quite another at higher altitudes, though there are some similar characteristics. All mountains have fickle weather. Some, like the Rocky Mountains, usually whip up ugly afternoon lightning storms in midsummer. The trick in these peaks is to climb them early and be off shortly after noon. Each range has its own weather personality, and the more arctic the summits, the wiser it is to take into account the personality quirks.

No matter whether you backpack in high- or low-elevation mountains, though, you should carry clothes for quick changes in the weather—wind, rain, much cooler temperatures toward the summits, and unseasonal sleet or snow.

Typically, when hiking in the mountains, we take trails that wander along the bases of the higher peaks and make camp somewhere in forests, positioning ourselves to climb the peaks on day hikes. This type of backpacking is much the same regardless of the height of the peaks.

One of my favorite less crowded areas that provides days and days of wandering among high peaks is the High Uintas on the Utah-Wyoming border. A trail wends gently below the summits at about 10,000 feet in elevation, offering an enviable variety of primitive campsites each affording climbs of numerous nameless 11,000- to 12,000-foot peaks. Another network of such trails that I love is on the westward side of the Wind River Mountains out of Pinedale, Wyoming. And still another favorite is in the Bitterroot Mountains of Montana, on a gentle trail leading out from Hamilton following the Blodgett Creek, with rugged rocky peaks along both sides. On a hot day, I've stopped from time to time to take dips in the creek's chilly pools. There are so many possibilities that you need never tire of them, each seemingly better than the one before.

I no doubt give far more attention in this chapter to the perils than to the pleasures of high-mountain backpacking. But you don't need a book to be persuaded of the marvels of the mountains. It is important to know about the potential perils, however, so that you may enjoy the mountains all the more.

Face it, you learned to drive an automobile safely so as to avoid potential road hazards. Backpacking is no different. It has its hazards that can be avoided by observing simple, safe trail procedures. Unless you know about them, how will you learn to stop on red?

The best place to start learning about dealing with mountains and their hazards is the classic *Mountaineering: The Freedom of the Hills,* edited by Steven M. Cox and Kris Fulsaas. This book has gone through several revised updates. Be sure you get the most recent one.

WHERE TO PITCH A HIGH-MOUNTAIN CAMP

Unless you stop at a developed campsite, picking a spot to camp in the high peaks is much the same as elsewhere. You want the same characteristics—a level spot situated on ground high enough to permit rain to run off away from your tent, located 100 paces from the edge of any pond or stream, and where you can arrange for a latrine in privacy near camp.

One caution, however: No matter how tempting, never camp on ridges or mountaintops. They have such an attraction, you want to linger longer with those beautiful views. Spend as much time as you like lolling there. By all means, though, do not make camp on them. It is extremely dangerous. A sudden storm can arise out of the blue. And an exposed area on a mountain or ridge is a lightning rod in a storm.

Second, peaks and ridges attract unpredictable winds that come up from seemingly nowhere. They can be so fierce they literally blow you off your site. Jet streams have hit 193 miles per hour in Colorado's Fourteeners, where they commonly knock hikers off their feet.

Finally, as you may suspect, these exposed ridges and tops are the coldest places in the mountains.

The ideal camp is down in the woods, somewhere on a mountainside between the valley floor and the summit. Trees provide protection from both the wind and sudden lightning storms. A location halfway up the mountainside is the warmest place to camp, inasmuch as the warmer air rises from the valley floor as the evening cools.

If it is bug season, try to locate your camp someplace that catches a light breeze to move insects away from camp.

HIKING ABOVE TIMBERLINE

Since most of us backpack most of the time at lower elevations, in wooded mountains, when we hit peaks above tree line in the West it is something of a surprise, if not a shock.

My hand warmer that heats up when I shake it is really handy in these cold mountains, where you can get snow in August. Sometimes I pop it into my sleeping bag before I climb in. You'd be surprised how long it keeps it warm and cozy.

—Cindy Schacher, Nez Perce National Forest archeologist, Selway-Bitterroot Wilderness.

There are few peaks above the limits of trees in the East. And those that rise above it don't top tree limit by much. New York's highest peak, Mount Marcy, barely rises more than 100 or so feet above the tree line. New Hampshire and Maine have a few where the weather does emulate the fickleness and brutal weather of the western peaks.

Mountain treachery is due in part to how benign they look on a lovely sunny summer morning, yet suddenly can present such dangerously severe weather that it takes lives every year.

Colorado's peaks have no summer weather above 13,000 feet. This applies to peaks of even lesser elevation north of

A Tragic Death from Altitude Sickness

The saddest mountain story I have ever heard is that of the death of Nanda Devi Unsoeld, the daughter of mountain climber Willi Unsoeld, one of the first Americans to climb Mount Everest.

When his daughter was born, Unsoeld wanted to name her Nanda Devi after the magnificently beautiful Himalayan mountain by that name, which he dreamed of conquering one day, perhaps even with his infant daughter.

When Nanda Devi was twenty-two years old, her father's dream was about to be fulfilled. She had become an accomplished mountaineer and joined him on his dream-of-a-lifetime climb of her namesake Himalayan peak.

Before the summit attempt, they were marooned four days in Camp IV at 24,000 feet, waiting out a storm after the first party made the ascent. It had taken fifty-six days to get this far. Nanda Devi had complained along the way of high-altitude-sickness symptoms. But since she still was able to carry heavy loads, all presumed she was simply stressed from the climb.

Then the morning of September 7, 1976, Nanda Devi was stricken suddenly with the acute symptoms of cerebral edema. She said, "I'm going to die."

Within fifteen minutes, Willi Unsoeld's dream turned into a nightmare, as his beloved daughter died.

there. And you can anticipate winter weather at any month of the year. This means you could unexpectedly confront a peak covered by ice from a sudden storm on a mid-July afternoon. And consider that Washington's Mount Rainier is barely as high as fifty-four of Colorado's highest, yet is a mountaineering event all the way to its summit from 8,000 feet.

Despite the dangers, the higher peaks present some of the most spectacular beauty seen anywhere. And hiking in them is one of the greatest pleasures in life. One area just east of Pinedale, Wyoming, in the Bridger Wilderness is such gentle mountain terrain that it is difficult to imagine anything other than sublime serenity at any time. It is a fisherman's paradise, each of the high mountain ponds having been stocked years ago by Finis Mitchell with a different species of trout—rainbow in some, brown in another, cutthroat, speckled, and on down the line of freshwater trout—which you can see swimming about as you hike by.

Yet it is called a wilderness for a reason. It does have wild weather changes that can become a challenge to the most experienced. Hike there, by all means. Know what you can expect, go prepared for unexpected emergencies, and enjoy. Dressing properly, timing your hikes, and using good judgment are your greatest safety measures for high-mountain hiking adventures.

ADJUSTING TO HIGHER ALTITUDE

After flying from sea level, say from New York or Chicago, to backpack in Colorado at altitudes of 10,000 to 14,000 feet, you or someone in your party may experience altitude sickness. Plan to spend an easy day or two adjusting to the elevations before

Types of Altitude Sickness

There are several degrees of altitude sickness, each more severe than the other.

Acute Mountain Sickness (AMS)

This is common at 7,000 to 8,000 feet. Its symptoms are headache, nausea and sometimes vomiting, and shortness of breath. These usually improve after a day or so. Treatment involves fluids, aspirin, and limiting activity. Descent is usually not necessary.

High-Altitude Pulmonary Edema (HAPE)

This is rare below 10,000 feet. Symptoms are weakness, shortness of breath, and increasing cough beginning twelve to forty-eight hours after too rapid an ascent. To treat HAPE, descent is advisable. Oxygen may help.

Cerebral Edema (CE)

This usually occurs above 12,000 feet. Symptoms are severe headache, hallucinations, weakness, and a staggering gait. Coma develops twenty-four to sixty hours after too rapid an ascent or too strenuous work. To treat CE, descent is mandatory. No other choice. There is a chance of permanent damage if victim survives.

beginning any strenuous backpacking. There are over-the-counter herbs available that may assist you with altitude adjustment, but don't rely on them. The best way to deal with the altitude is acclimatization.

Himalayan guides recommend acclimating at 1,000 feet per day above 10,000 feet. They advise sleeping 1,000 feet higher each day. During the day, you can climb another 1,000 to 2,000 feet above that, returning at night to sleep at the lower elevation. Not a bad suggestion. Worth trying.

Should someone in your party begin to experience symptoms of altitude sickness, the only remedy is to get down to a lower elevation as soon as possible. Do not continue on in hopes it will pass. Take it seriously.

Altitude sickness is a mystery illness that comes in a variety of forms. It is unpredictable. You can be in top physical condition, yet it can bring you down. You can have climbed to high altitudes many times before, with no problem, yet it can bring you down on your next climb. It can nail you at elevations as low as 8,000 feet. It is no respecter of age. It can cut down a youngster just as quickly as an oldster. But few who climb in mountains of 8,000 feet or higher know much about it, or what to do if they are stricken.

Altitude sickness kills the young, the fit, and the audacious, because they are the ones who go into the high mountains. The best and only way to prevent altitude sickness is to take the time to adjust to the altitude before the climb. No medication, no treatment—not even oxygen—can substitute for getting back down to the richer oxygen supply at lower altitudes.

CROSSING SUMMER SNOWFIELDS

Another aspect of high peaks to be wary of is year-round snowfields. Glaciers look so benign when approached on foot—seemingly just another walk through the park.

Mostly where trails traverse them, they are not more than that. But the rub is that they present more different hazards than we become accustomed to at lower elevations.

In crossing glaciers or snowfields where no well-marked trail is evident, you'd best have crampons and ice ax, and practical knowledge of how to use them. For one, the snow conditions change from the heat of the sun during the day. What can be safe in early morning can turn hazardous in midafternoon—or vice versa. A snow bridge across a glacier that was safe to cross in the morning can collapse in the afternoon after the sun softens the snow. Or a snow slope facing the sun in the morning is soft, allowing you to kick in steps to climb it, but it falls in shadow in afternoon and freezes hard, making the snow toboggan slick on your return.

Do *not* try to learn the necessary skills to cross a snowfield or glacier from a book. Learn them from competent professionals who put you through actual practice drills on glaciers. I mention this now, for last summer I witnessed a number of well-equipped leaders of roped-up climbers who clearly did not know how to use these safety tools. The leaders were, in fact, endangering the climbers in their parties more than if they were not roped together.

These groups of roped-up climbers in the Swiss Alps were climbing a glacier with leaders using ski poles and not even carrying an ice ax. Should one of the party tumble into a crevasse, the leader would be unable to stop the fall, which probably would drag some of the other climbers in as well. Or if one of the climbers lost footing and fell down the thirty-five-degree slope, it likely would have pulled others down too, with no way to arrest the fall. The graveyard in the town down below has markers attesting to the risks of this mountain.

If you go in for mountaineering, then get training from one of the top mountaineering

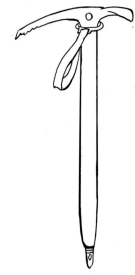

Having an ice ax and knowing how to use it is essential for hiking on snow in the high mountains. The ax handle should be of such a length that the adze end fits comfortably in your hand when the tip is on the floor and your elbow is slightly bent. It is impossible to use an ice ax for your safety without having instruction and actual practice.

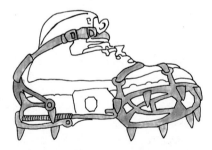

For any extended crossing of snow and ice in the mountains, full-length crampons make the going easier and safer. Be sure they fit on your boots snugly before you set out on a trek. Avoid front-pointed crampons, which are for ice climbing and mountaineering. If not used properly, they can cause you injury.

Two major dangers of hiking in the high mountains are avalanches and cornices. Avalanches can begin under various conditions on steep snow slopes (left). Avoid steep slopes if possible, and certainly do not zigzag your way up them, since each zig may precipitate an avalanche. Cornices may be even more deceptive. You must test for them when walking across any innocent looking covering of snow on a mountaintop (right). Probe with an ice ax (not a ski or trekking pole) to see if the layer of snow is hollow underneath you.
FROM THE WINTER 1973 ISSUE OF *BACKPACKER* MAGAZINE

schools that are practiced in ice and snow climbing, as well as rock climbing. Your life depends upon it, as do the lives of others in your party.

There are three basic types of dangers to avoid on snowfields.

Cornices

You can be walking on a most innocent-looking wide and rounded mountain snowfield and have it suddenly break off from the edge of the mountain, taking you with it. For what you had taken to be solid snowpack turned out to be an overhanging cornice, jutting out from the mountain, hollow below. And your weight on it was sufficient to break it free, carrying you to your death on the rocks hundreds of feet or more below. An ice ax is a tool to test for cornices. I'm not telling you how to do this. I'm just saying that unless you do have an ice ax and know how to use it, you may quite innocently approach a fatal mountain accident.

This is hardly an exaggeration. Recently, my friend Steve Bridgehouse and I were backpacking in the San Juan range in Colorado. We intended to climb Mount Wetterhorn, which is more than a novice climb but usually does not require technical gear.

According to volume 2 of *Dawson's Guide to Colorado's Fourteeners,* by climbing expert Louis Dawson II, "You should have climbed other fourteeners, have some knowledge of safe movement on steep, loose rock, and know how to judge the safety of a snow slope." Otherwise the climb will "have harder route finding and might bring you closer to hazards like cliffs, loose rock, or steep summer snow."

When Steve and I got to the beginning of the summit ridge, we found it covered with snow, which appeared to be corniced. We had no ice ax or crampons. So we passed. And climbed a different peak instead.

We didn't have to be The Gambler to see the wisdom of walking away.

Crevasses

Most crevasses are obvious wide gaps in the glacier, and you naturally try to skirt your way wide around them to avoid falling in. The dangerous ones, though, are the ones you don't see and that break open under your body's weight when crossing them. An ice ax provides a couple of aids in glacier work to avoid this accident. You use it to probe for the soft spots that indicate danger. And it serves as an anchor for a roped party should someone fall in. The leader or another in the roped party thrusts the ice ax deep into the glacier as an emergency anchor and spins an end of the climber's rope around the top of it to properly belay the falling climber.

Again, I cannot urge you more passionately to learn from master guides such as those in the mountaineering courses at places like Mount Rainier. What you can learn from this book is that crossing snowfields or glaciers without equipment and expertise invites disaster.

Sliding Falls down Snowfields

Crossing a snowfield on a footpath is not the same as hiking on a similarly narrow path on rock or dirt. You cannot as easily regain even the slightest misstep as you can on dirt or rock. It can easily turn into a nonstop slide down the snow slope into whatever rocks and ice are at the bottom. Every year, climbers and skiers die from sliding falls on snowfields. Crampons will help you avoid this, and the ice ax is a tool for self-arresting a fall.

The ice ax self-arrest, as Dawson says in his guide, "is a skilled acrobatic maneuver. You must practice until it becomes instinct. If you're new to the game, a snow climbing course is your best bet for learning. If you are an expert, you should still practice periodically."

None of what I have said about snowfields is meant to teach any techniques. Rather, it is meant to warn that what often looks quite lovely and innocent can become deadly.

DANGERS OF THE MOUNTAIN FALLING ON YOU

I've mentioned the types of hazards that can occur from your falling or health conditions. Another category of danger in the mountains is when the mountain falls on you, in one of three ways.

Falling Rocks

One of the dangers of hiking behind another group of hikers is the possibility of falling rocks. A careless hiker can dislodge a rock and send it plummeting down on you. This can occur on low mountains as well as high ones. It is very important to both be on the lookout for people climbing above you at any time and be cautious about knocking

Beware of Sunburn at High Altitudes

At higher altitudes, the sun burns the skin far quicker than at sea level. It is more like noonday sun at a tropical beach. Use high-SPF sunblock on your bare skin, especially your nose, cheeks, and ears.

High Mountain Oriental Stir-Fry

This Call of the Wild trail recipe from Carole Latimer's book *Wilderness Cuisine* is irresistible. I had to include it. This is a "must-have" book if you like good trail foods. If makes four servings.

Carole writes: "This is the meal I usually serve to my group the night before we climb Mt. Whitney at the end of a 13-mile day. Serve with instant miso soup and Minute Rice; hot chocolate and fortune cookies for dessert."

Here's the recipe:

A selection of freeze-dried or dehydrated veggies to equal about 5 oz. Such as:

bell peppers	green beans
mushrooms	corn
peas	small onion, diced

1 TB fresh grated ginger
2 garlic cloves, minced
2 TB safflower oil
2 TB sesame oil
Optional: 1 small can of Oriental veggies: bamboo shoots or water chestnuts
    or bean sprouts
½ cup cashews
24 snow peas
8-oz package of vacuum-packaged tofu, cut in squares
soy sauce

At Home: Put all freeze-dried or dehydrated vegetables together in a boilable plastic bag. Pack cans and vacuum packed tofu. Pack produce in brown paper bags. Bring a small nalgene bottle of soy sauce. Mix oils and carry in a nalgene bottle. Package cashews in plastic bag.

In Camp: 1. Re-hydrate vegetables. 2. Saute onion, garlic and ginger in oil. Add dehydrated vegetables and canned vegetables and cook for about 5 minutes. Add cashews and snow peas. 3. When snow peas are almost cooked, add tofu and gently stir in and heat through. Sprinkle with soy sauce and serve.

---

even small rocks over the edge that can hit hikers below you. This is particularly critical in places like Grand Canyon as well.

In the higher mountains, rocks also can become dislodged when no one is there to knock them loose. This can happen on steep slopes where rocks are embedded in snow or ice. If the snow or ice melts during the day, it can loosen the rocks enough that they cut loose and tumble down toward you. So extra caution is needed in crossing even fairly gentle snow slopes on warmer days.

There is a route up Mount Rainier that is no longer used as it was when I climbed that peak. It skirts along the bottom of Gibraltar Rock, a high cliff of rock with thousands of smaller rocks frozen into the ice and snow above the trail. Accordingly, climbers traveled this route in darkness to avoid having the rocks careen down at them when the sun warmed up enough to melt the snow and ice. Though we passed beneath Gibraltar Rock shortly after midnight, we still could hear missiles flying past us in the dark as if we were being shot at.

> **Lip balm and sunglasses are musts at our high altitude.**
>
> —*Gudy Gaskill, "mother" and builder of the 500-mile Colorado Trail*

Falling Ice

Like falling rocks, large icicles can break loose from overhanging cornices and steep rock faces. These fall frequently in nice, warm weather that follows cold and stormy days. Experienced climbers avoid these places or know how to pick their way gingerly through the least dangerous sections at the least dangerous times of day.

Usually you can detect these areas by the ice debris that has collected at the bottom. If in doubt, though, avoid the area.

Avalanches

Avalanches are probably the most underestimated danger of the mountains. They are more common in the winter months, it is true. But there are significant avalanche dangers in the summer months as well.

There are two main types of avalanches. The slab avalanche occurs when a plate of snow breaks loose and slides down, bringing with it a gathering of more snow, trees, rocks, and such. The powder avalanche is less frequent in summer, for it is triggered by a small amount of snow that accumulates into a big slide.

There is much to learn about avalanche safety. First, find out if there are avalanche dangers in the area where you will be hiking. Second, avoid crossing beneath precipitous snow slopes, especially in warmer summer afternoons.

29

Desert Hiking

If you grew up in the green-forested East, Northwest, or Midwest, then desert country is foreign territory for you, as it is for me, and needs to be approached entirely differently than where you have been accustomed to hiking.

Once I was lured to the Southwest, I came to prefer desert hiking. But some fellow New Yorkers I've introduced to this land have said it was a fascinating place to visit, though they wouldn't want to hike here.

Let me start with some of the desert's allure.

Probably my biggest attraction to the desert is its dryness. I needn't worry too much about rain, for it is less of a concern than it was back in Michigan where I grew up, or in New York where I spent so many years backpacking in the Catskills, Adirondacks, and Presidentials.

Still, we do get some wet days out here. I've been rained out of Grand Canyon on more than one occasion, and out of Death Valley, where precipitation averages less than one and three-quarters inches per year. Actually, I should say "flooded" out, for the rain came down so hard for so long that all but one road was closed going in or out of the valley. We no doubt had four or five years' rain all in about an hour that night. But rain is as infrequent in the desert as it is frequent in the East, Northwest, and Midwest.

Because of the infrequency of rain, desert dryness quickly returns once the rain stops. One night some years ago, four of us had just snugged down beneath a tarp in our camp, high on a side of a canyon wall in Grand Canyon, when a storm suddenly blew in. During the early part of the night, my sleeping bag got soaked through to my legs. The surprise was that after the rain stopped around midnight, my sleeping bag dried thoroughly by the time we got up in the morning.

Some will find the dryness unpleasant, for it tends to dry the skin and dehydrate the body. Any lengthy trek in the desert requires some sort of oil for the skin and plenty of drinking water. There are long stretches when you need to carry all your water, for water sources are few and far between. Also, I find desert water highly unappetizing because of its mineral content.

Carrying a gallon of water is eight deadweight pounds in the pack. And actually, a gallon is not even enough for one hot summer day. Even after you have chugged as much as you can for breakfast before you leave camp, you need to carry at least two gallons for each night you will sleep out. That is the truly tough part of desert hiking.

One more advantage of desert backpacking I'll admit is truly a confession of intimate details. And perhaps I ought not mention it. But what the hell!

Who can resist climbing and cavorting on the sand dunes in places like Death Valley or Great Sand Dunes National Monument in Colorado?

The scents of the accumulation of dust upon the body, even after several days on the trail, is far more pleasant than the odors that build up after a few days on the trail in humid forests. When I first shower after a week or longer backpack in the desert, the scent of the dust being washed from my hair and body gives me a jolt of nostalgia for trails I just hiked. It's the same pleasant aroma when I sort out and put away my sleeping bag, tent, and clothes from the hike, while back east I always needed to give all my gear and clothing a good airing and washing to remove the repugnant odors.

FINDING WATER IN THE DESERT

If you hike in a more heavily used area such as Grand Canyon, the rangers have an excellent read on where water is and isn't. They collect reports from hikers and rangers who hike in even the most remote areas of the canyon.

When hiking in less traveled areas, it could well be fatal to rely solely on topo map indications of water sources. On one eighteen-day trek in a remote desert area, we discovered that the water source indicated on the map was there all right, but covered by the rotting remains of dead animals and deep piles of dung. Ugh!

We spent the better part of two days excavating a new source of water uphill from where the seep emerged from the ground. Then we had to fill our containers by a drizzle of water seeping drop by drop from the new hole.

One source of water in emergencies is the pocket holes in the rock where water remains from rains and winter snowmelt for considerable periods of time. The problem with this water is that it almost always looks unappetizingly scummy. Yet

> Since I hike mostly in the desert, carrying an adequate amount of water is my first consideration. My second is salt tablets to replace what I lose to the heat and avoid muscle cramps.
>
> —*Sherry Fletcher, school superintendent, Truth or Consequences, New Mexico*

Descumming Stagnant Desert Water

Start this process early, as it requires considerable time for the entire operation.

Slit a large plastic trash bag open along one side and bottom. Spread it over a depression in an otherwise flat rock surface. If you are near a sandy area, dig a hole in the sand and spread the plastic bag over the hole.

Pour as much muddy river water or scummy water from a water pocket as you need into the plastic sheeting over the hole. Skim off surface scum. Let the water sit overnight in this plastic basin, allowing all free residue in the water to settle to the bottom.

In the morning, gently scoop out water from the top to either boil or treat with your water-purifying devices. If you boil the water, let it settle and cool. Then pour it back and forth from one container to another to reoxygenate it.

To clean muddy or scummy water, spread a plastic trash bag over a dug-out hole, and fill with water. Allow to settle overnight, then skim off surface debris and gently scoop out clear water. Purify this by boiling or other method.

if you are as desperate as it is possible to become in the desert, you will eventually drink that water. The sidebar "Descumming Stagnant Desert Water" tells you how to clean it up into more palatable form.

Another source of water that you would not ordinarily want to consume is the muddy water of a river, creek, or stream. This too will become more potable when you get thirsty enough. But be sure to purify it. These sources of water are the most likely carriers of disease.

DANGERS OF DESERT HIKING

Like me, you probably heard of the desert's prickly, poisonous perils long before you ever got near one. And to a great extent, all we heard was true. But I did not let it stop me from allowing the desert to become user-friendly.

One of the most impressive aspects of the desert when I first encountered it was that it seemed full of land mines of unfriendly things. It seemed that all plants had prickers at least, some with the seeming uncanny ability to jump onto me, while others brandished razor-sharp sword points. Many desert rocks, too, had brutal cutting edges.

And I was certain that I'd meet snakes, scorpions, and spiders beneath every bush and in every crack in the rocks. It took a while for me to realize that though the desert certainly has its share of prickly, poisonous perils, most desert flora and fauna were quite friendly and benign. But it took time for me to discern friend from foe among desert plants, rocks, and creatures.

What I've found, though, is that a little knowledge, some familiarity, and a lot of caution enabled me to become even more comfortably at home in the Southwest's deserts and canyons than I am in the thicker forests of the Northeast where I spent so many of my backpacking years.

Most of the plants, animals, and rocks are not poisonous. They just require some watchfulness and familiarity to avoid their cuts and stings.

Snakes

One of the most deadly snakes in the world, the coral snake, resides in the southern Arizona deserts. You are hardly likely to see one, never mind be bitten by it. They are small, reclusive, secretive, and timid. The coral snake is so rarely seen that scientists know little about its habits. Its mouth is so tiny that Natt Dodge says in *Poisonous Dwellers of the Desert,* "It would be difficult for it to bite an adult human."

What makes the coral snake so dangerous is that its poison is transmitted through the nerves much like the venom of a cobra. It bites with its short teeth and must chew the victim in order to inject its venom.

There are several varieties of nonpoisonous desert snakes that have the same coloring—red, cream, and black bands circling the body. What distinguishes the coral snake is its black head.

Yet the desert may be the most notorious place of residence for a variety of other poisonous snakes you may come across. Almost all are in the rattlesnake family. Of the thirty species of rattlers in the United States, half of them live in the southwestern deserts. But not all desert rattlers are equally poisonous. The bites of all but one variety of desert rattler are about equally toxic. If bitten by one of these species, the poison that gets into your blood is rarely lethal and moves through the body rather slowly. The treatment for these snakebites is pretty much the same regardless of rattler variety. See chapter 17 for information on how to treat snakebites.

To avoid snakebites, walk cautiously, aware of where you are stepping. Do not reach into cracks, over ledges, under rocks, or anyplace that you can't first see into. Since snakes are cold-blooded, they can't stand the intense heat of day. They come out more at night and in the early morning or evening. So do not walk around in the dark without a flashlight to see where you step. One of the precious few times I have seen a rattler in the backcountry was early morning in Chaco Canyon when I got out of my tent to take my morning relief.

Scorpions

"Some authorities consider the scorpions to be potentially the most menacing of desert animals," says Natt Dodge. "Not all scorpions are deadly. Danger from the deadly species is greatest to children under four years of age. . . . Older children may die from

The scorpion can inflict very painful bites, and some can be serious enough for medical treatment. They can be deadly to the elderly, infirm, and to small children. But there is little likelihood that a scorpion can inject enough venom to kill a healthy adult.

the effect of several stings; and adults, especially those in poor health, may suffer serious injury."

There are more than twenty species of scorpions in the deserts of the Southwest, but the deadly species occurs only in southern Arizona and at the bottom of the Grand Canyon. This scorpion is straw colored, about two inches long, and all of its features—legs, pincers, tail, and body—are slender and long.

All scorpions have a stinger at the end of the tail. They sting and do not bite. The sting of the nonlethal scorpions is painful, causing local swelling and discoloration of the skin. The sting of the deadly variety affects the body generally all over, with intense pain at the sting site, but no inflammation or swelling.

There is an antivenin for scorpion bites, and most hospitals in Arizona have a supply. The treatment is complicated, but medical treatment ought to be sought immediately after being bitten. It is advisable to find out more information on how to treat scorpion bites before entering areas where they are likely to be found.

Scorpions come out at night and are rarely seen during daytime hours. They remain in hiding during the day, usually in places like beneath the bark of old tree branches or in piles of firewood.

To guard against scorpions in the backcountry, use a flashlight when moving about at night to be sure you do not step on one inadvertently. Shake out your sleeping bag thoroughly before using it. And shake out boots before putting them on. Inspect your clothing before getting dressed.

Spiders

Tarantulas are the ugliest spiders in the desert, with the worst reputation. They really don't deserve the reputation, though, since they are quite harmless.

They live in web-lined holes in the ground. They are active in spring, summer, and fall, males commonly noticed traveling across country.

Tarantulas can inflict a painful bite if molested. But any ill effects of the bite are more likely due to infection than to its toxins.

The two spiders whose bites are most painful and can cause serious illness are the black widow and the brown recluse. The bites of both can cause severe sickness and discomfort but are only rarely known to be lethal.

The black widow is black, with long, thin legs, and has a characteristic red hourglass mark on its abdomen. The brown recluse is small, only about a quarter inch long. It is brown with long legs. Its distinctive mark is a violin-shaped spot on the upper side of its head.

The black widow bite causes some pain and swelling at the site, spreading throughout the body, mostly in the victim's hands and feet, which become cramped. It also causes muscles in the abdomen to tighten, with nausea and vomiting, difficulty in breathing, dizziness, ringing in the ears, and headache. Blood pressure is raised, eyes dilated, and reflexes overactive. Despite these symptoms, most cases generally clear up on their own. There are very few deaths from black widow bites.

Tarantulas, though big and scary, are not very venomous. Their venom is painful and feels like red-hot chili peppers, but it's not too serious. There are no known human deaths from their bite.

Very few people are bitten by the brown recluse in the backcountry. In fact, far more are bitten at home. At the time of the bite, there is little stinging but some pain. Some people are even unaware they have been bitten until two to eight hours later. The bite may cause fever, chills, weakness, vomiting, joint pains, and skin eruption within a day or two after the bite. The most serious aspect of the brown recluse bite is the deterioration of the skin tissue spreading from the bitten area. The bite has been known to be fatal to young children.

Medical treatment needs to be sought as soon as possible for either spider bite. Though not much can be done as first aid for either bite, cold compresses do reduce the pain and sting. And if bitten, you should absolutely not use alcohol or narcotics.

Natt Dodge quotes medical professionals to the effect that "internal use of alcohol is dangerous, and a person bitten when intoxicated would have much less chance of recovery."

Centipedes

One centipede species residing in the desert is poisonous. It is six to eight inches long, with jaws of sufficient strength to inflict a painful bite. The bite causes swelling, inflammation, and fever, but there are no recorded deaths. Since the bite tends to clear up on its own, though it is painful and inconvenient, no specific treatment has been developed for it. Prompt treatment by a physician can reduce the duration and intensity of the pain, however.

Gila Monsters

Gila monsters are occasionally seen ambling slowly across open stretches of desert, mostly in springtime. These are docile animals that exert every effort to escape any encounter with other animals, particularly humans. When prodded, however, either intentionally or inadvertently, the Gila monster can attack, with mouth open, hissing and sputtering.

Though otherwise slow, when attacking, the Gila monster is particularly adept at swinging its head and snapping at anything it perceives to be harmful. Should it

The Gila monster is a large, slow-moving animal that resides in desert country. Its slowness is deceptive because it can bite quickly, and when it does it hangs on tenaciously, chewing its venom into the victim. The bite is painful and can cause nausea, but there are no reliable reports of human fatalities caused by it.

manage to sink its teeth into a victim, it will grind in its poisonous venom. If the victim is able to break away quickly from the bite, the venom will have little effect. Victims unable to break away from the bite experience symptoms similar to rattlesnake poisoning, though the Gila's venom is more neurotoxic, spreading quickly through the body via the nerves. The victim's breathing and heartbeat are quickened, and muscles around them are slowly paralyzed. If you are bitten by a Gila monster, avoid stimulants and get medical treatment as soon as possible.

Bears

Yes, there are bears that eat cactus!

I've been hiking all my life, about half of it in desert, yet it was just while I was writing this book that I discovered that there are bears that frequent deserts.

Okay, it is only a few places, they have shown up very recently, and they have never had an incident with humans—yet. That *yet* is important. For Glacier National Park never had an incident with bears in fifty-seven years until 1967. Then one night, bears went nuts and mauled four different people, killing two of them.

The first bear since Big Bend became a national park came across a wide desert in the 1980s and crossed the river from Mexico. By 1988, twenty-seven park visitors reported seeing bears. Since then, the Park Service took action, employing a number of measures to avoid human-bear encounters. It has worked out safely so far without incident, and the number of sightings is steadily increasing. Though these bears are comfortable in the Big Bend National Park deserts, they tend to frequent the forests on the mountains in the park.

There have been bears in the high mesa deserts of Apache-Sitgreaves National Forest in Arizona as well. Likewise, there are numerous bears in the Lincoln National Forest in southern New Mexico that make their way into the high mesa desert country.

Good bear management policies have so far avoided any incidents. There may be other public lands upon which bears are roaming. These are the only areas that have come to my attention. And I have not done any sort of survey to find out where bears may roam.

So although I don't want to frighten you off from desert hiking because of bears, it is as good an idea to know how to backpack in bear country as it is to know how to drive on snow and ice. It can be done quite safely, if you know what you are doing. See chapter 18 for how and what to do in bear country. Because there are bears in some desert areas, you should find out ahead of time from the land managers if bears frequent the area you intend to hike.

THE HAZARDS OF EXTREME DESERT HEAT

Deserts have some dramatic weather that can become far more lethal than snakes, scorpions, spiders, Gila monsters, or bears. According to Grand Canyon National Park physician Tom Myers, in his paper "The Unforgiven: Heat and the Desert Crucible," delivered to a group of backpacking leaders at a training workshop: "Brutal and unforgiving summer heat is potentially the most dangerous hazard to backcountry travelers in the desert southwest. In Grand Canyon, heat accounts for roughly seventy-five percent of the 250 annual emergency evacuations from the Inner Gorge. . . . more common in young, healthy people, i.e. athletes."

One obvious suggestion is to avoid backpacking during the hottest months of summer—June through August—when midday temperatures become suffocating.

Should you happen to come into severe desert heat, you might try confining your hiking to early morning, late afternoon, or even nighttime if you have good moonlight. One caution, though: Early morning, evening, and nights are the times when you are most likely to surprise a rattler on the trail. So remember the Revolutionary War rattlesnake motto, "Don't Tread on Me," and use a good flashlight.

There are obvious precautions you should take wherever you spend much time in midday sun. Use plenty of sunscreen, and above all, wear a hat with a wide brim all around. It is simply insane to wear only a baseball cap and let the sun crisp your ears and neck.

The other dangers of too much heat for too long are heat dehydration, heat exhaustion, heatstroke, and hypothermia. Why risk them and ruin a perfectly good hike, never mind imperiling your life? Drink lots and lots of water, and eat salty foods each time you drink to avoid hyponatremia, which is caused by drinking all the water you need without replenishing the salt your system is losing through perspiration and urination.

Wear clothes that cover the skin, including arms, legs, and neck. Take breaks often. Try to find shade to get out of the sun. This is not easy in the desert, especially at midday. If necessary, pitch a tarp and hunker down beneath it for a half hour or so when the sun is most intense.

DESERT NIGHTS

Don't be fooled about the heat of the desert when it comes to the clothes you take along. The temperatures characteristically drop forty to fifty degrees at night. So from daytime highs of 100-plus, it is not at all unusual for temperatures to drop into the sixties at night, possibly to the fifties. Bring clothes to dress accordingly.

Nights in the desert can be particularly enchanting. There is a stillness that settles in, with the sounds of a few insects. But the desert has more stillness than sound at night. And the cooler temperatures are a relief from the overwhelming heat of day.

DESERT WINDS

One of the most unpleasant things I find about the desert is the wind. When winds blow up, and they often do, they penetrate everything you have with an ultrafine powdery dust. In these conditions, you will definitely have a use for your neckerchief, bringing it up over your nose and mouth in order to breathe without filling your lungs with desert dust.

Desert camping under the stars in Pariah Canyon, Utah.

It is also very difficult to pitch camp and cook when winds blow as hard and persistently as they often do in the desert. Be prepared. Try to camp on the lee side of large rock outcroppings or trees. And try out your stove's windshield in a stout breeze before you take it on a desert hike.

BUGS

Bugs are a nuisance. You don't get bug pests at all times of year in the desert. Nothing like the mosquito hatches in late May in the Michigan forests. But you do get one pesky little critter that is an even nastier pest: the no-see-um. These bugs earn their name honestly and are an intense problem. They come in swarms, usually sometime in early June or even late May.

Their bite is nasty. They love the edge of your hairline, as well as your eyelashes and eyebrows. Your tent net is not perfect protection from these pests. The only solution I know is to find out when they are likely to be out in the area to which you are headed, and pick a different time for your hike.

BEST SEASONS FOR DESERT BACKPACKING

It is a pleasure to hike in desert country in September or October. But where is there a place to hike that *isn't* great at this time of year?

Because of this, you will run into far more hikers in the backcountry. So it's tougher to be completely alone—if that's what you like. Nonetheless, once you fall in love with the desert, you will find more and more places where no one ever goes.

Next best time of year for me is April and early May. This is the time when desert flowers are first coming into bloom and the insects are not yet out. Days are balmy, nights divine! During my father's final years, he and I went to the southwestern deserts every year to celebrate his birthday on May 11. What a time that was for us! We four-wheeled on backcountry jeep tracks, set up camp, and hiked during early-morning hours. Some of the finest times I have ever spent in the backcountry were with Dad in his twilight years.

Winter isn't a bad time of year either, although most of the high-desert areas are a bit too cold for me. If you want winter desert hiking, take a look at the state and country parks located near Yuma, Arizona. Here is some very rugged desert, but it's warm enough to make you forget the snows back home.

30
Canyon Hiking

There are canyons and then there are canyons. The grandest of course is Grand Canyon, which is one of my all-time favorite places to hike. But besides this magnificent gorge, there are hundreds of other canyons that provide excellent backpacking as well.

Grand Canyon drops down a full mile in altitude from the South Rim and another 1,000 feet if you start down from the North Rim. In hiking down into it, you traverse five of the seven life zones in North America, more than any other place on the continent. It is like hiking from cool subalpine weather on the slopes of the Canadian Rockies down to the intense desert heat of Baja Mexico's Sonoran Desert. For Grand Canyon backpacking, you need clothing for all those life zones.

This is desert hiking at its trickiest. The tricky part is that you start hiking down in pleasant morning subalpine weather at the rim and end up shocked senseless to find it so damnably difficult to hike back up from the Lower Sonoran Desert with the heat blasting you at midday.

You become further fooled by its being the reverse of mountain climbing—easiest hiking down, hardest hiking back out. These delusions are mostly what account for the canyon each year taking an average of four hikers' lives and requiring 250 Inner Gorge emergency rescues, mostly to young, male athletic types.

Despite numerous signs along the rim at every trailhead warning visitors not to try to hike to the river and back in one day, a madness takes possession of some to whom signs merely create more of a challenge.

DEADLY CANYON HIKING

In the ten-year period from 1991 to 2001, there were 112 deaths in the Grand Canyon area due to everything from heatstroke, falls, lightning, and exhaustion to hiker negligence, airplane crashes, suicides, and a few murders. But virtually all 38 deaths below the canyon rim were hikers, most of which could have been averted by greater caution.

In 1997 alone, the NPS conducted 482 searches and rescues for 377 sick or injured people down in the canyon. Eighteen of those people died.

Several hikers died on or close to the easiest-looking footpaths in the entire canyon, called the heavy-use corridor. This most popular combination of trails begins innocently enough from a cluster of buildings on the South Rim by the Bright Angel Lodge. Yet as placidly seductive as this corridor appears, it took nineteen hikers' lives in the 1990s, many of whom were in exceptional athletic condition.

It is a combination of things that makes canyon hiking so lethal—heat, sudden storms creating unexpectedly inclement weather, a hiker's lack of stamina or poor health. But more often than not, it's a hiker's inability, or unwillingness, to judge difficulties early enough to avert them.

Canyoneering is the opposite of mountaineering. A canyon's degree of difficulty comes long after the hiker has been lured into its seductiveness, unlike mountaineering, where the difficulties increase as one plods upward toward the summit. In mountaineering, you can turn back if the weather suddenly turns or the going gets too difficult, and the return is a lot easier when hiking downhill.

It is quite the opposite in canyon hiking. Descending Grand Canyon is a piece of cake, especially on a balmy summer morning, even if you are entirely out of shape. You begin from the rim at a higher altitude, usually in cool morning temperatures, which increase into torrid heat as your hike progresses. Both the midday sun and Sonoran Desert conditions intensify the heat as you hike deeper into the canyon. Add to this the toll the body's dehydration takes in these intense hot and dry conditions. Most of us are just not accustomed to the way our energy is drained. Then there are the rapid changes of weather that often occur during the busiest tourist season of the year, with lightning storms and unexpected flash flooding.

Add up all these factors, and it is easy to understand why Grand Canyon can be a seductive death trap to unsuspecting hikers.

Hiker Deaths on Grand Canyon's Easiest Trail

Hikers become lulled into overconfidence by the ease at the start of the heavy-use corridor hike. Sixteen hikers died between 1991 and 2000 on what is known as Grand Canyon's easiest trail. Many of these hikers were highly experienced. None made it back out alive. Most of these deaths likely could have been avoided. The details given here are from *Over the Edge: Death in Grand Canyon,* by Michael Ghiglieri and Thomas Myers.

April 21, 1991. Vernon Bollinger died of exhaustion hiking the Bright Angel Trail.

September 3, 1991. George Fairchild died of heatstroke four miles into his return ascent in attempting an overnight rim-to-river-to-rim hike.

April 17, 1992. Jose Ordierez hiked merely the six and a half miles from rim to Tonto Plateau and died from heat exhaustion on his way back up.

August 21, 1992. Walter Jaskowiak and Miriam Epstein died in a flash flood at Horn Creek, a short distance west of Bright Angel Trail.

September 11, 1992. Robert Kier collapsed of exhaustion hiking down the North Kaibab section of the heavy-use corridor.

March 24, 1994. Gary Clausen collapsed of exhaustion while hiking.

May 5, 1994. Beverley Collins slipped and fell 100 feet into the rocks below the Bright Angel Trail.

June 10, 1995. Miloslav Hanacek hiked down six miles—only two-thirds of the distance to the river—to Plateau Point and collapsed on his return hike up Bright Angel Trail.

June 14, 1996. David Kruse was attempting the twenty-one-mile rim-to-river-to-rim hike and died of exhaustion partway up the last section of trail.

July 23, 1996. Phillip Grim died of heatstroke alongside Colorado River near Bright Angel Creek.

October 16, 1996. Wesley Johnson was hiking from river to rim after a boating trip when he collapsed from exhaustion.

September 11, 1997. Patty and John Moran and John McCue were drowned in a sudden flash flood coming down Phantom Creek canyon just off the North Kaibab Trail.

October 11, 1997. John James was attempting the twenty-one-mile rim-to-river-to-rim hike when he collapsed near Phantom Ranch of exhaustion.

May 8, 1998. Sheryl Flack took a short walk from a mule trip and slipped over the edge of the rim off Plateau Point.

April 28, 1999. Thomas Pacewicz hiked out after a river trip and collapsed of exhaustion above the three-mile rest house on the Bright Angel Trail.

February 6, 2000. Orda Smedley, attempting the six-and-a-half-mile hike to Plateau Point and back, dropped dead one and a half miles from the rim on the return hike.

FLASH FLOODS

Flash flooding is one of the more serious dangers to experienced hikers. They are the Southwest's equivalent of tornadoes. They come up fast, without warning, and carry incredible destructive powers. They are fascinating furies of sound, wind, water, and wreckage. Flash floods are almost always underestimated, even by highly seasoned canyon hikers.

These floods occur most often in remote canyons where few people ever go. Not even local residents know about the floods, except from what they leave in their wake, in the massive rock carvings and tumult of rocks, trees, and debris.

Their genesis is in rain falling on barren, rocky terrain of the Colorado Plateau in southern Utah and northern Arizona. With nothing to hold the waters back, the flood begins in a frenzied race toward openings in the rocky plateau floor, gathering momentum, mass, and debris as it rushes like a freight train down dry streambeds and arroyos, engulfing everything in its path. By the time it gets to the bottom of a drainage, it has become a debris-choked tidal wave of mud, house-size boulders, and trees. All this can begin from a local storm over a small area several miles away, while the sky may be perfectly clear where you are.

Flash floods are the greatest problem in side-canyon explorations during the July-through-September stormy season. There have been eleven deaths from flash floods in Grand Canyon. They were all hikers, some of whom were highly experienced canyoneers.

A storm can occur 100 miles upstream from you, so far away that you would have no inkling of its becoming a threat. Then, all of a sudden, without any warning whatsoever, a wall of water crashes through the narrow canyon walls and takes everything with it—boulders, trees, your camp, and you if you are in its path.

To avoid flood danger, camp well away from the water at the bottom of narrow canyons and high enough to be out of the floodplain, which could be fifteen to twenty feet high. And stay alert. The summer I began writing this chapter, six campers were drowned in southern California's Old Waterman Canyon when such a flash flood came without warning.

Yes, you do face flash-flood danger in the narrow side canyons of Grand Canyon. And even the wider heavy-use corridor trails have experienced flash floods that have

The Tragic Death of One of Grand Canyon's Most Seasoned Hikers

Tom Myers, Grand Canyon NPS physician for more than a decade, describes in "Casinos of Stone: Monsoon Gambling and Playing the Slot Canyons" a flash-flood tragedy over which he personally grieves, inasmuch as one of its victims was his good friend George Mancuso:

> It was mid-June and very hot when we approached the confluence of the Colorado and Little Colorado rivers. Across the Little Colorado, lean and tanned, George walked swiftly with a seasoned hiker's confidence.
>
> Calling me over, he introduced me to his new hiking companion, Linda, who was soft-spoken, in her early fifties. It was her first canyon hike. George, on the other hand, was a bona fide canyon hiker and professional photographer. He had plodded at least 6,000 miles in the canyon over roughly 25 years. This was his favorite spot in the canyon. A perfect place for us to meet.
>
> George was his usual bundle of nervous energy. Like always, his enthusiasm rivaled the setting, his passion as deep as the canyon itself. . . .
>
> When I left them they were heading up the Little Colorado to explore some side canyons for photographs.

There were several afternoon thundershowers, which George knew to be dangerous in side canyons, so he and Linda camped well above the Little Colorado at the base of the Salt Creek Trail. On August 7, Linda wrote in her journal that they were going to Emerald Pool in Big Canyon, a narrow tributary to the Little Colorado, where she was looking forward to washing her hair in clean water.

About ten days after Tom bade them good-bye, George and Linda were reported missing. Since George was such an experienced hiker, a search party was not dispatched until August 18, a few days later. When the search party arrived at George and Linda's camp near the base of the Salt Creek Trail, they discovered it had been abandoned for some time.

It took four days for the search party to find Linda's body, which was wrapped around the base of a tamarisk tree near Emerald Pool in Big Canyon. But the searchers could not find George. His body was eventually found by a passing boatman, who noticed ravens hovering around it near the confluence of the Colorado and Little Colorado Rivers, George's favorite place in Grand Canyon.

George Mancuso. MICHAEL QUINN

taken lives. In the 1990s, four hikers lost their lives to flash floods close to these trails—two at Horn Creek and two at Phantom Creek, where thousands of people take day hikes from Phantom Ranch to Ribbon Falls.

How to Avoid the Danger of Flash Floods

The most important thing for safety is to be aware that there is extreme danger of flash flooding in narrow slot canyons. In Grand Canyon, Bright Angel Trail is in a slot canyon that has had its share of flash flooding. Others of its obvious slot canyons are Phantom, Deer Creek, Horn Creek, Havasu, and Little Colorado.

Avoid hiking in slot canyons during July to September when it is raining, appears to be raining anywhere else, or even looks like it might rain. Avoid hiking into these canyons when the skies look at all threatening in any direction, as this is a clue that a sudden storm can develop almost anywhere, at any time.

If the sky is clear, hike into these canyons only in the morning hours, giving yourself enough time to get back out before noon. All of the deaths from flash floods occurred in the afternoon or early evening.

LIGHTNING

The frequent thunderstorms during July to September that often bring lightning are almost as great a danger for hikers as heat prostration. Grand Canyon experiences more than 25,000 lightning strikes per year.

In addition to the precautions you should take to avoid danger of lightning in the mountains (see chapter 16), there are special cautions that should be taken in canyons. The one that is most difficult to observe is to stay well back from the rim at the top of the canyon. And be sure to stay well away from the metal handrails installed at most viewpoints.

Lightning Precautions

First of all, avoid hiking during thunderstorms. If you are already on the trail and a storm comes up, take these precautions:
- Avoid handling metal objects. Put down your pack and get well away from it. Do not get into your tent, and get away from any other metal gear you have. Take your sleeping pad or sleeping bag with you to sit upon as a cushion to give you a little protection and insulation from the ground.
- Stay well away from rivers and streams.
- Take shelter in a building if possible, or hunker down in a cluster of small trees that is surrounded by larger trees. It is the height that attracts the lightning bolts. Do not get underneath a ledge or seek refuge in a cave.
- Stay away from tall trees or rock outcroppings, and do not take refuge beneath one, as the height attracts lightning.
- Seek lower ground. Drop down into an arroyo, where you can get below the higher terrain around you.
- Avoid wide-open spaciousness like the Tonto Plateau or the Esplanade, where you would be the tallest object.
- Stay off ridges and away from the edge of cliffs.

- If caught in the open with no place to hide, crouch upon the balls of your feet and cup your hands over your ears. Do not put your hands on the ground.

Should you feel your hair standing on end or your skin prickling, an electric charge is building up near you, an indication that lightning may strike you soon. Keep calm, but get into the best possible situation that can offer some protection.

SLICKROCK CANYONS

Slickrock hiking is unique to the four-corners region of the United States, mostly in southern Utah, where there is an extensive network of weirdly eroded stone canyons. These canyons usually require a different type of hiking. They are steep-walled, narrow passageways, usually with a stream running through them. They, too, can become insufferably hot in summer months. Maybe even worse than Grand Canyon.

The big difference between these canyons and Grand Canyon is that you hike *through* them, rather than down into them. Start at one side canyon with easy access, and hike a route along the riverbed to an easy-exit side canyon someplace farther along. These make particularly enjoyable hiking in spring or fall. Wintertime is fine—except, of course, it's cold with short days and nights far too long. You'll want other hikers with you to stay up in the evenings to chat with you into the darkness, for who can sleep thirteen to fourteen hours?

Exploring these canyon mazes on foot is about the only way possible. You follow the washes at the canyon floor. It is especially enjoyable if there is water running through the wash, and many of these canyons are so gifted, despite the semiarid nature of slickrock country. Some canyons are worth hiking for forty miles or more with very limited access and egress. Many of them have ninth-century Anasazi Indian ruins as an additional attraction.

The flora and fauna of these canyons provide a special treat if you become aware of them. Trail guidebooks for an area can provide advance ideas of what to look for. For example, some canyons have a night-blooming species of primrose that grows up to eight feet tall; you just may catch an evening display of these blossoms. You will definitely be treated to communities of ferns and desert orchids during spring to fall seasons. One tree that blooms early in the year has always captivated my attention: The redbud scatters a carpeting of its magnificent magenta petals everywhere.

Most of these canyons have springs at various points along their routes. They are marked on USGS maps. Still, it is a good idea to check with rangers beforehand to be sure they are running at the time you plan your hike. Some of these canyons are in national parks or monuments, such as Canyonlands, Arches, or Grand Gulch, but most are scattered about in national forests or BLM lands. It takes some sleuth work to dig out all the information

> The main thing in canyon hiking is keeping cool, carrying a water bottle with spray nozzle to keep everything damp, a wet bandanna or hat, and a wet shirt in a Ziploc plastic bag. Worth their weight in gold! Recent tests found that a wet hat or bandanna reduced the outside temperature by twenty degrees, and that keeps heart rates and stress levels within normal range.
>
> —*Michael Quinn, Grand Canyon National Park archivist*

you may need for a good backpacking trip in slickrock country. But you will hardly be disappointed, no matter what your choice. I have been hiking in this part of the nation so many times over so many years, and I am always astounded at how much more I have left to see.

Water is a critical problem in southwestern canyons. Because its sources are extremely limited, your means of water purification is a top item for your don't-forget list. Should you not have along a purification filter or such, you can always boil the water. It may very well be the safest method of purification anyway. Simply bringing the water to a boil—even at higher elevations—is sufficient to kill any harmful bacteria. Want to be sure? Boil it five minutes.

My problem with desert water is not in purifying it, but its taste. Virtually every canyon country water source produces highly mineralized water with some combination of unpalatable residues. It tastes so bad that it discourages me from drinking sufficient water to prevent dehydration.

You have to face not only the same types of dangers in slickrock canyons as in other desert hiking, but a couple of additional ones as well. Some have quicksand. But the most dangerous risk of all is flash floods. Be aware that this is a serious danger. Find out all you can about them and how to avoid their risks.

Section Seven
WHEN TO GO

And the Northern Lights in the crystal nights came forth with a mystic gleam.
They danced and they danced the devil-dance over the naked snow;
And soft they rolled like a tide upshoaled with a ceaseless ebb and flow.
They rippled green with a wondrous sheen, they fluttered out like a fan;
They spread with a blaze of rose-pink rays never yet seen of man.
They writhed like a brood of angry snakes, hissing and sulphur pale;
Then swift they changed to a dragon vast, lashing a cloven tail.
It seemed to us, as we gazed aloft with an everlasting stare,
The sky was a pit of bale and dread, and a monster revelled there.

—from "The Ballad of the Northern Lights," by Robert Service

31

Extending Your Hiking Season into Fall

Unless you live in the South, you most likely have been taking your backpacking jaunts during summer. And if you love getting out on the trail, you hate hanging up your gear at the end of the season. That is the best time of year, though, to begin extending your hiking into the cooler months. There is something highly invigorating about hiking later in the year. And there is an added joy in sleeping out in cooler temperatures that soon becomes addicting.

My advice here again is to take it easy, one step at a time. The best time to start cooler-weather backpacking is early in the fall. Begin with short hikes, getting used to the cooler weather, and gradually turn them into overnight backpacking trips. Build up to more difficult weather conditions slowly.

Fall is better than early spring for other reasons as well. In early spring, you are more likely to run into patches of last winter's snow, where you will have to posthole through, sometimes sinking up to your hips in wet slush. Not fun. And the farther you go, the worse it gets.

Another problem of early-spring hiking is that the trails are muddy, and hikers cause far more trail erosion than at times when trails are drier. If you do go in early spring, use common sense, and stick to lower elevations.

In fall, you're still in pretty good shape from your summer hikes. And then, the bugs are gone. Less to worry about snakes and bears. The only difficulty is cooler weather.

HYPOTHERMIA: A HIDDEN RISK OF COOLER WEATHER

Those words slipped so easily off the tips of my fingers in writing this. It is no coincidence that "the only difficulty is cooler weather" followed so closely after less to "worry about snakes and bears," for cooler weather is far more hazardous than both snakes and bears. The very *idea* that cooler weather is a relief from hot summer temperatures slips so easily into mind that it deceives us into believing we are actually past any imminent danger. That is a danger in itself.

This way of thinking about cooler weather carries with it the common misconception that hypothermia is mainly caused by freezing temperatures. That is a dangerous misconception, for hypothermia takes most victims' lives in weather in the high thirties and forties, sometimes even in fifty-degree temperatures. See chapter 16 for how to identify and prevent hypothermia.

The Centers for Disease Control and Prevention begins one of its reports on hypothermia with such cases as these:

Ten Causes of Hiker Deaths

This chart, based on information at www.cdc.gov, shows that in a typical year, 600 hikers die of hypothermia, while snakes, bears, and all other wild animals together take just a little over 100 lives. Though not all of these victims were hiking, most of the hypothermia victims were.

Cause of death	Average number of deaths per year
Hypothermia	600
Storms	128
Falls from cliffs	83
Wild animal attacks	68
Lightning	64
Snakes	45
Avalanches	44
Bee, wasp, or hornet stings	43
Spiders	6

"In the fall of 2003, a man aged 44 years was found dead outdoors in Vermont. . . . Local investigators reported that he looked as though he just 'laid down and went to sleep.' Overnight temperature had dropped to 32° F. . . .

"In the fall of 2003, Alaska state troopers reported that a hiker aged 35 years was found dead alongside the highway. . . . The overnight temperature was 44° F, but conditions were wet and windy."

This report, available at www.cdc.gov/mmwr/preview.mmwrhtm/mm5308&2, emphasizes these cases to point out that temperatures had not dropped below freezing.

It is also true, though, that both of the deceased had a high alcohol content in their blood, which contributed to their deaths in two ways. It made them *feel* warm, though their body temperatures plummeted lethally. And it gave them a false sense of security that they were all right. As the investigators said, it seemed as if one of the victims just "laid down and went to sleep."

When hiking in cooler weather, you must be highly sensitive to shifts in your body temperature, especially when the wind suddenly kicks up, clouds cover the sun, you stop for a rest, or you walk into a tree-shaded area out of the warm sun.

The hiker's tendency in summer is to shrug off these seemingly subtle shifts in weather because of the nuisance of stopping to put on or take off another shirt or sweater. During summer hiking, when you work up a sweat climbing a hill, you don't stop to take off a shirt or sweater to cool the body. Perspiration wets your undershirt. Then when you reach the top of the hill, you stop sweating and your body

> When the trails have snow and ice, but not enough for snowshoes, I like my Yaktrax, which are "chains" for my shoes that grab slick surfaces much better than shoe tread can.
>
> —*Barbara Springer, New Mexico Rails-to-Trails Association*

I extend my backpacking into winter in the Catskill Mountains of New York.

cools rapidly because your clothes are wet. In summer, this feels good, so you do not put on anything to prevent the cooling. You want to cool down. But in cooler weather, this can quickly lead to disaster.

Heat is conducted from the body 240 times faster when it is wet than when kept dry. Preventing perspiration from dampening your clothes is the first safety precaution to observe in cool-weather hiking to avoid the onset of hypothermia.

It is a nuisance to stop when climbing a hill to take off a sweater. It is worth the trouble, though, when you realize that hypothermia is the most common killer of hikers. And this particular killer is the one over which you have the greatest control.

On cool days, stop often for clothing adjustments. Keep lightweight shirts and sweaters near the top of your pack to put on and take off as the mood of the weather demands. Layers of thin clothes are far better and more adaptable to the weather than thicker parkas and sweaters. Your raingear can also serve as an excellent retainer of bodily heat. Use this gear for warmth as well as for rain and snow.

Another consideration for keeping dry when camping in cooler weather: If the temperature drops to freezing, your tent walls will capture your bodily evaporation in the form of frost. Be careful when awaking in the morning not to knock the frost off onto your sleeping bag and clothes, where it would melt and dampen them.

GREATER WATER, SODIUM, AND CALORIC NEEDS

As you hike in colder weather, your body gives off moisture through evaporation without your noticing it. It is critical that you drink enough water to replenish this evaporation. Much as in desert hiking, you should drink more water than you think you need. If you stick to the eight-glasses-of-water-a-day adage, I doubt that you could go wrong. But then, I suspect a lot depends upon how strenuously you hike and how cold the temperatures. A certain warning sign is darker yellow urine. If you notice that your urine has turned a darker shade of yellow than normal, it is a clue you ought to be drinking more water.

The colder the weather and the more effort you put into your hike, the more water you need to drink. Use common sense.

When you drink, also eat a salty snack. Though the danger of hyponatremia is not as great in cooler weather, it is still a concern. And you need to replace the sodium that is dissipated from the body in evaporation. Salt replacement will also help you avoid muscle cramps when sleeping out in cool weather. I had to prove this to a hiking buddy, Dr. Lou Perez, on a winter backpacking trip. He had never heard of salt depletion causing muscle cramps on winter hikes. So one of us took some extra salt at bedtime, while the other did not. Guess who got the muscle cramps?

Hiking in cooler weather also requires more energy than hiking on a warm day. Not only is the body burning energy for the hike, but it is also burning energy just to stay warm. You need to eat more calories to provide sufficient fuel.

SUDDEN CHANGES IN WEATHER

Another hazard of fall hiking is the probability of encountering a sudden deterioration in the weather, especially unexpected rain or snowstorms. The risk is greater the higher you go in altitude. The Rocky Mountains and Sierras are notorious for sudden unexpected snowstorms in early September, even in midsummer. The danger looms heavy in the mountains of both the Northwest and Northeast as well. New Hampshire's Mount Washington also is infamous for its fickle weather, which has taken hikers' lives.

I once ran an article in *Backpacker* magazine about an experienced California backpacker who got stranded in an early snowstorm in Yosemite. He was marooned for nineteen days in the mountains before being rescued. I ran another article about a hiker in New York's Adirondack Mountains who got similarly trapped by a sudden turn in the weather but didn't survive.

HOW TO AVOID AN UNEXPECTED SNOWSTORM EMERGENCY

More often than not, people get into snowstorm emergencies in wilderness because they are not prepared for adverse weather. Here's what you can do to minimize the risks:

- Plan your hike before you leave. Consult trail guidebooks and maps. Draw up an itinerary and follow it the best you can.

Craig Evans puts on his down booties in a Catskill Mountain camp. Feet, hands, and head get coldest first. Note that Craig is wearing his mittens and wool hat as well.

- Prepare for Murphy's Law: If things can go wrong, they will. Be prepared for the worst weather that could occur at that time of year.
- Pack adequate clothing, food, and sleeping accommodations for the worst weather you could possibly encounter.
- Always carry map and compass, knife, flashlight and extra batteries, matches, and first-aid kit.
- Leave a copy of your itinerary and map, including the location of your car, with a friend or family member, giving the time and day you expect to be back out.
- Leave the same information with a Park or Forest Service ranger.
- Do not hike alone.
- Know your limits. If you become tired, stop. Avoid places that are beyond the level of your skills.
- Be modest. Do not hesitate to turn back if that is the sensible thing to do. Reaching your destination may be the most foolish part of your plans if weather indicates otherwise.

Camp can be cozy during chilly weather. Laura Waterman enjoys evening soup at Northwest Basin lean-to in Baxter State Park, Maine.

- Stick to your itinerary—if possible. Stay on trails. Do not cut cross-country, for two major reasons: You may more easily get lost, especially in a sudden blanket of fog or snow, and it makes it far more difficult to find you should a search become necessary. I understand that more mountain deaths have occurred in Colorado's high peaks from very experienced climbers getting lost in sudden blankets of fog.
- Let rangers know when you get back. Drop in, call them, or send an email letting them know you got out safely.

HOW TO SURVIVE A SUDDEN SNOWSTORM

If your best plans go awry and you get caught in a sudden snowstorm, there is a prescribed way of dealing with the situation that will avoid adding to the risks:

- Keep calm. Panic only compounds your difficulties and solves nothing.
- Get protection from the weather as soon as possible. If necessary, improvise the best shelter you can from whatever is handy. Best, of course, is to pitch your tent and get into it.

- Get as warm as you can as quickly as you can. Add clothing; put on raingear to reduce heat loss.
- Get into your sleeping bag with all your clothes on. Pay special attention to your head, neck, feet, and hands. If you can, use your stove or build a fire.
- If possible, lie close to another person to conserve the body heat of both.
- Keep warm. Sit or lie on an insulated surface. Wiggle your toes and fingers. Prewarm inhaled air by breathing through a wool sock, hat, or sweater.
- Drink hot liquids and nibble on high-carb foods to replenish your energy.
- Remain still and quiet to conserve energy.
- Stay put until the weather improves. Travel in storms consumes far too much energy and increases the possibility of getting lost.
- When you do walk, do not move about aimlessly. Plan your route on a map and use your compass.
- Find a vantage point from which to orient yourself. Remaining calm can be your greatest help at this point.
- Avoid getting your clothes or sleeping bag wet and avoid perspiring. If necessary, take off a shirt or sweater. The body loses heat much faster when wet than in dry clothing.

Backpacking on skis allows me to work my way through Rocky Mountain National Park in winter.

Tips for More Comfortable Cool-Weather Camping

Here are a couple of tips that will help you enjoy these trips with less annoyances:
- Keep your water bottle wrapped in warm clothes. I often carry my water bottle inside my shirt to keep it from freezing. Or wrap it in some of your extra clothing, being sure the top is tightly fastened.
- Heat water to fill your bottle before you go to bed, and take your water bottle with you into your sleeping bag. It makes a delightful bed warmer.
- Use a larger-size winter sleeping bag and take your boots into the sack with you so that they do not freeze during the night.

Guy and I believe in early starts, especially when days are short. We'd rather be be-dayed than benighted!

—*Laura Waterman, first editor of* **Backpacker** *magazine, author of* **Backcountry Ethics** *and many more*

- Be alert to the possibilities of frostbite or hypothermia, take precautions, and be on guard for their symptoms.
- Should you get lost, find shelter and stay put.
- Signal for help if at all possible. Know the means of signaling and do not hesitate to use them.
- Ration your food as though you will be there many days.

Backpacking in fall and winter is a serious undertaking. Great fun, but potentially deadly for the unprepared. Many hikers set out on beautiful warm fall mornings only to find themselves, because of an unexpected afternoon freezing rain or snow, returning in a grisly feat of endurance with all sorts of resolves about "Next time I'll . . ." Before you get too far along in your season stretching, it is an excellent idea to become acquainted with some survival books. The best one I know is Greg Davenport's *Wilderness Survival.*

32
Getting Started Winter Backpacking

Those of us who have a good deal of summer backpacking experience in varying kinds of terrain and weather are easily lulled into overconfidence in tackling the trail in mid-winter. But this is a completely different activity. The only similarity is the pack and the overnight stays on the trail. Otherwise, you need a whole new set of techniques.

If approached with caution, winter backpacking can provide immense enjoyment. Getting out in the woods and mountains with far fewer people around, no bugs, and nature in its cloak of crystalline snow with clear, freezing air is exhilarating beyond measure.

Those who leap right into it without some gentle buildup to its wiles, however, can end in a huge unpleasant fiasco, compelling them to vow to never ever do it again, if they manage to escape frostbite and hypothermia.

Winter backpacking is a serious business. Its main difficulty, of course, is contending with freezing temperatures, ice, and snow.

A small mistake in the summertime can be a mere inconvenience, whereas the same mistake in winter can cost you your life. Moreover, slight changes in weather are far more dangerous in winter than in summer.

GET INTO IT GRADUALLY
I grew up in the Midwest and went to college in New York, where I lived during my career. Both places offer nippy winters. Once I got into it, though, I got so accustomed to winter backpacking that winters never got cold enough or lasted long enough. Still, I got into winter backpacking slowly.

If you are going to keep on backpacking because you love it, you will find a way to acclimate to the winter and want more of it. So take it from me, don't jump into your first try on a full-fledged zero-degree backpacking trek in a foot of newfallen snow. That is guaranteed to turn you off to the joys of the winter trails.

Get started winter backpacking much the way I advised getting into backpacking itself, by taking day hikes until you can't stand not being out on the trail later at night and waking up out there at first light of day.

Once you have done a fair amount of winter day hiking, then you are ready for your first cold-weather overnight on the trail. I suggest you do it much like I did: Ease into it.

It happened inadvertently. In my early days of rock climbing, I camped with a group of other climbers at New York's Shawangunk cliffs, under the stars near a magnificent clear creek.

Wildlife is rather scarce in the mountains in winter. But you may luck out and find ptarmigan.

That first year, as with so much else in my life, enthusiasm carried me to the cliffs every weekend that spring, summer, and fall. Then one night I reached for my water bottle and discovered the water was frozen. My first lesson of winter camping: Water freezes in my canteen. Sounds so simple as I write about it. But out in the woods, snuggled deep in my sleeping bag against the cold that had dropped enough to freeze the water in my canteen, I was not ready to crawl out of my bag and go to the creek for more water.

I learned that day how to keep my water from freezing and have used the technique ever since. The water bottle is filled, tightly closed, and tucked down inside my sleeping bag. In fact, when the weather is really cold, it is nice to fill the bottle with hot water before slipping it into the sleeping bag. This can be dangerous, though, if the top is not screwed on tightly. In cold weather, you need to keep everything dry. So lesson two the same day: Close the canteen tightly before putting it in the sleeping bag.

A few weeks later that fall, I awoke in the morning to a snow-covered sleeping bag. Another lesson, easily learned, in how to deal with the first snowfall. Since we were not deep in the woods, but only about a half mile from our cars, I could pick up my dampening sleeping bag and trek on out to the car, where I could start the engine and turn on the heater. I knew that next time I slept out in late fall, I needed to sleep under a tarp or in a tent.

Rock climbing becomes more of a challenge when the cliffs start getting cold and are crusted with snow and crispy frost. That did not stop us from climbing for the season, though, which meant we camped out. So I learned how to make camp when even deeper snow covered the ground. Okay, you will do it differently. But the principles will be the same. We needed an insulating layer between our sleeping bags and the snow. So we uncoiled our climbing ropes and snaked them back and forth to provide an insulating cushion, upon which we laid our ground cloths and then our sleeping bags.

Staking out the tarp was difficult, too, in frozen ground. It took a bit of hammering to drive in the stakes. So I learned some other tricks, such as pitching it near fallen logs or large rocks to which I could tie the corners of the tarp. Little problems to deal with each week as the weather got colder and the snow deeper.

Then, when the snow covered the cliffs and climbing ledges, we gave up climbing for the season. Since I liked the camping part so much, though, I began my first serious season of winter backpacking. And what a great way to stay in shape for my summer backpacking! Now I needed snowshoes.

Sixteen Unique Winter Backpacking Problems

There are a number difficulties that are likely to come up sooner or later in winter backpacking:

1. Having water freeze in the canteen.
2. Becoming dehydrated due to failure to drink enough water.
3. Getting clothes wet from perspiring on the inside or snow melting on the outside of parka, pants, socks, hat, or mittens.
4. Overestimating the distances that can be covered and falling short of the intended campsite.
5. Overestimating the amount of daylight on winter days.
6. Having difficulty in finding a camping spot in deep snow.
7. Having difficulty tamping out a level camping spot in deep snow.
8. Having far greater difficulty putting up tent with freezing bare hands or mittens. (At *Backpacker,* we once gave an otherwise excellent winter tent a ho-hum rating because it did not have knurled sliders on its tent poles, making it all but impossible to assemble with mittens.)
9. Staking the tent out with pegs that don't hold in the kind of snow found at that particular time and in those weather conditions.
10. Spilling the cookpot at least once on things that ought not get wet in winter.
11. Learning that it takes enormously long to melt snow, and that it burns up far more fuel than anticipated.
12. Having clouds of steam fill the tent from cooking inside, with the vapor dampening the sleeping bag and clothing.
13. Finding that boots have frozen during the night and are both difficult to get on and, once on, painfully cold on the feet.
14. Having tent walls frost up during the night, so that the slightest movements cause particles of frost to fall on sleeping bag and clothing, melting and getting them wet.
15. Encountering sudden weather changes that require changing clothes layers, but not doing so in time to prevent your body temperature from dropping severely.
16. Having your bare skin bind fast to cold metal parts in below-zero temperatures.

For Christmas, I got a decent tent for snow camping. I don't want to tell you how much it weighed! It was sold as a "lightweight" backpacking tent. But to give you a hint, it was made of treated cotton, and though it was not as heavy as car-camping tents, it weighed about as much as all the gear I now carry on an overnight hike in summer.

THE BEST WAYS TO GET STARTED

The best way to get into deep-winter backpacking is to take a course with one of the professional tour outfitters. Or go with someone who is highly experienced who will take the time to teach you the techniques.

Next best, follow these five steps:

1. First get a good, solid base of summer, spring, and fall backpacking, meaning that you have gone on a half dozen or more backpacking trips during these three seasons, especially in the spring and fall. Be completely at home with the equipment you will be taking on the trail. Do not take any new equipment that you have not tried out before.
2. Study one of the manuals on winter backpacking to get a thorough understanding of what to expect. Read more than one book, for each author emphasizes different aspects of the activity. Ask experienced friends for advice. See if there is a club in your area that either teaches or takes beginners on winter backpacking jaunts.
3. Work into overnighting gradually. Start with winter day hikes in various kinds of weather and snow conditions. After a few hikes in the dead of winter, take along your fully loaded winter backpack as if you were going to stay out overnight. This will give you a lot better idea of what travel is going to be like.
4. Take your first overnight to a spot that is no more than a quarter to a half mile from your car, so that you can get back out quickly if the weather takes a nasty turn dur-

Winterizing Tips

It can be much more difficult to do the simplest tasks in winter. Things you ordinarily do in seconds will take much longer. A combination of things contribute to this—bulky clothing, more of it, mittens or gloves on your hands, and a host of other unfamiliar things to deal with in winter that you don't have to deal with in summer. And you have far less daylight in which to do them. Here are some tips to make winter camping easier:

- Put long tabs on zippers so you can handle them without taking off your mittens.
- Secure your mittens to a long cord that runs through the sleeves of your parka.
- Take foods that are quick and easy to prepare.
- Take a parka with large, roomy pockets and a pack that is especially roomy.
- Use a larger stuff sack for your sleeping bag.

To prepare for your cold-weather hikes, it is useful to tie tabs onto all of the zippers and openers of your clothes, pack, and gear for easy opening with mittens or gloves. It is also a huge advantage should you be stricken by the early stages of hypothermia and lose the sensitivity of feeling in your fingers.

ing the night. Camp well below tree line on your trial run. Take this trip early in the winter when the snow cover is still rather light. Get used to camping in cold weather before you undertake deep snow and cold at the same time.

5. Make camp early. In midwinter in the northern tier of states, start making camp no later than 3 in the afternoon, as it will be dark by 4:30. You do not want to make camp after dark, for it's too difficult and dangerous.

HOW TO STAY WARM ON THE TRAIL

Because we spend most of our time indoors in winter, we have little respect for the cold. If we do not give it our full attention and respect, the cold literally can kill us. One adage worth memorizing immediately is this: *It is far easier to keep warm than it is to warm up once you get cold.*

Be sensitive to the temperature as you hike. When you feel yourself heating up at all, stop, take off an outergarment, then continue the hike. If you are still too warm, take off another layer. And likewise, when you feel you are chilling down the least bit, stop and put on another layer of clothing. This is bothersome. Especially when you are hiking through woods and come out into the sunshine for a stretch and then go back into the woods again. Each time, you will probably have to stop to adjust your clothing layers.

Nevertheless, this is critical. I failed to do this one time—even after many years of backpacking experience—and had to be nursed through a bout of hypothermia I suffered as a result. If you are by yourself, you are at far greater jeopardy if hypothermia sneaks up on you. Layering can save your life!

Snack often on sweets with lots of carbs to keep up both your energy and your body temperature. Drink lots of water to keep from dehydrating. You will not notice evaporation from your body so much in winter. Nonetheless, it is occurring, perhaps even more rapidly than in summer. Should your urine become a darker yellow, this is a definite clue to drink more water.

And, each time you drink, eat a salty snack to replace the salt your body lost from evaporation. You risk hyponatremia at worst, and muscle cramps at best, if you don't replace the sodium lost.

WINTER GEAR
Winter Pack

You will need a far roomier pack for winter backpacking than you use in summer, for you will be carrying a lot more clothing and other items. It needs to have exterior fittings to lash on crampons, ice ax, skis, and snowshoes as needed.

When snowshoeing, I prefer an external-frame pack. But for skiing, it's best to have an internal-frame pack so that you can carry the load lower to give you better balance on your skis.

Another consideration with your winter pack is what to do with it when you stop even for a short rest on the trail. Do you lay your pack down in the snow and thus risk getting it and the things in it wet? I attach a small strap to the top crossbar of the pack, which I fasten around a tree to keep the pack up off the snow.

Once you start hiking in snowy conditions, a problem that presents itself is where to set your pack down when you stop to have lunch, make camp, whatever. If you are in woodlands, you can hang it conveniently from a tree limb or, preferably, strap it to a tree trunk. Carry a loose strap that you can circle around the trunk and draw tight. Friction will hold it firmly out of the snow.

Sleeping Bag

You will need a sleeping bag rated for colder temperatures. Consider buying a longer winter sleeping bag than you ordinarily need. The longer bag enables you to accommodate your boots, water bottle, and anything else you need to keep from freezing.

I have a lightweight summer bag that I can fit inside my winter sleeping bag. This, along with a sleeping-bag liner, gives me a system that gets me through any kind of weather, from warm to cool to cold to extreme cold.

Boots

You may need a different pair of boots than you use in summer to accommodate extra socks. If the boots are too tight, they will give you cold feet, possibly even frostbitten toes. I use a pair of U.S. Army boots designed for the Korean War. They are made of insulated rubber and take me down to twenty below with no problem. In fact, my feet sweat in above-zero temperatures when wearing only one pair of socks with these boots.

If you are taking crampons, be sure they fit on your boots properly before starting out on your hike. Likewise for snowshoes. Don't get out on the trail to find out you may have an improper fit or wrong-length straps. Try everything out before you leave home.

If you are skiing, you will need ski boots. It is best to also carry along some other kind of boots to put on in the tent at camp. I use a pair of down booties in camp.

At night, you do not want your boots to freeze up. The best way to avoid this is to take them into your sleeping-bag with you. I put them into my sleeping-bag stuff sack, turned inside out.

Clothing

Layering clothing is key to maintaining body warmth. A typical outfit includes two wool shirts or sweaters, wool or silk long johns both top and bottom, a waterproof nylon shell with hood, wind or rain pants, wool mittens, outer mitten shells, a wool ski hat or balaclava, and two pairs of socks. Everything ought to be loose fitting and comfortable. You also need gaiters to keep snow from getting into the tops of your boots and wetting your socks and pant legs.

As soon as you stop for a rest at any time during the day, slip on a parka, shirt, or sweater. Take it off when you start hiking again. When you get to camp, immediately put on more clothing. Keep putting on layers to stay warm. Even if you do not feel the need for additional clothing, when you stop it's better safe than sorry. Put it on and keep it on to stay warm. Remember that it is a lot easier to stay warm than it is to get warm once the body has cooled down.

Because of the extra weight carried on winter treks, it is a good idea to take clothes that can serve dual purposes. Instead of two pairs of pants, wear one pair and carry wind pants, which can be used separately or together with the pair you have on. Instead of one heavy shirt, carry two medium-weight wool shirts. Carry a lightweight wool sweater and a windshell instead of one heavy sweater.

You'll be warmer in several layers of clothing than in one layer of thick, bulky garments. Layers give you far more flexibility in adding and taking off clothes to control

Dave Sumner amazed me with the amount of gear he carried on our winter treks—not only food and winter gear for both skiing and backpacking, but a 4x5 Linhof folding camera, a 35-millimeter Nikon, extra lenses, sturdy tripod, film holders, film, and changing bag. And he never even asked me to share any of his extra load.

your body temperature. They also serve as insulators that trap the air between, keeping the body warmth from escaping.

Wool garments are preferable to cotton. And some of the fleece synthetics work as well as wool and in some instances are even lighter weight. Be on guard, though, about claims of water repellence and resistance in these materials. They aren't always as claimed. Check them out at home before committing to a long-distance trek.

I take a top and bottom set of synthetic sweats, but also wool pants, sweater, and shirt. I love that lightweight soft angora wool. And I love silk long johns. For outerwear, I take lightweight nylon wind pants and parka, as well as a rain parka in milder winter weather or a down parka for below-zero temperatures.

How to Get the Most Warmth from Your Gear

You can improve the warmth of your camp by these simple techniques:

- Zipper up your tent except for small vents to provide fresh air. Tents increase the outside temperatures by five to ten degrees and cut the windchill factor. *Important: Leave vents wide open when operating a stove inside the tent!*
- Pitch your tent on the leeward side of a cluster of trees and shrubs for shelter from the wind.
- Place two or more hikers' sleeping bags close together to increase your bodies' heat retention.
- Make camp on the side of a hill rather than at the bottom of a valley or the top of the hill. The warmer daytime air rises from the valley floor upward during the night, and wind usually draws it away from the tops of exposed hills. This can provide as much as fifteen degrees more warmth on the sides of hills.
- Cover your feet with stuff sacks inside your sleeping bag, and sleep in layers of clothes inside the sleeping bag.

- Use a sleeping-bag liner or overbag to increase the warmth of your winter bag.
- Use foam sleeping pads rather than air mattresses. They provide more insulation from the cold ground.

STAYING WARM IN CAMP

The easiest way to stay warm is to move about. The more active you are, the warmer you will be. In camp in the evening, though, it is not so easy to keep active. And evenings begin about 4 P.M. in midwinter, but daylight does not come until close to 7 A.M. So you have a lot of dead time to kill on winter nights in camp, as temperatures drop quickly once the sun goes down.

Put on layers of additional clothing the moment you start making camp. When the tent is up, if it is very cold, slip into your sleeping bag, then prepare dinner. Nighttime in your tent is why you take your headlamp along, with fresh extra batteries. You need it to keep both hands free to do the cooking. Eat snacks and read if you need to kill time camping more than one night.

It is a good idea on cold nights to consume lots of carbohydrates to provide quick energy to heat the body. Hot Jell-O is a perfect quick-energy drink. Eat candy, dried fruits, gorp. A good idea that Paul Petzold promoted at NOLS is to suck on a hard candy as you crawl into your sleeping bag to go to sleep.

WINTER BACKPACKING MEALS

This is no time to be on a weight-loss diet. Save that until you return home. You need all the carbs you can get from your food. Eat often at rest stops during the day. Keep breakfast and dinner simple and easy to prepare. I have hiked with friends who even take time on the trail to heat up hot soup for lunch, though I've always found this to be too time-consuming in midday. You'll have lots of time for preparation of dinner. But you need to be prepared to melt snow, which can take forever, or other such time-consuming tasks that you hadn't planned on. Just consider that everything that takes minutes in the summertime takes an inordinately longer amount of time in winter.

I included some simple, easy-to-make recipes for winter backpacking in chapter 9. They are high-energy, quick-energy meals. You particularly might want to try the Green Mountain Stew and, for a degenerate dessert, Grand Canyon Java. They are energy-abundant and easy to prepare on the trail. Then, too, I am partial to three of the make-at-home recipes in that chapter: Mountain Bars, Gorp Breakfast Bars, and especially Mount Rainier Logan Bread, which I love to eat at lunch in winter covered with strawberry jam. See if that doesn't keep your legs going in the toughest weather!

All of these require pretrip preparation, however. And call me lazy, but I

> It is always very cold in winter when we stop in late afternoon to set up camp. This is the only time I ever put on a hat. Then I light up my stove to heat water while I set up my tent. When it's up, I drink hot Jell-O to give me enough warm energy to do other camp chores. One thing I learned in Girl Scout leadership was "If your feet are cold, put on your hat."
>
> —*Susan "Butch" Henley,*
> *membership director,*
> *American Discovery Trail Society*

keep the food very simple. This is where freeze-dried meals are particularly useful. They are lightweight and prepared simply by bringing water to a boil. This latter characteristic is also an attribute of several supermarket offerings. Take the instant soups, for example. Can anything beat Lipton's instant broccoli, creamed chicken, or mushroom soup? And don't forget Knorr's soups. Perhaps you don't eat these at home, but I'll tell you, camped 11,000 feet up in a snow-covered meadow in the shadows of Mounts Sheridan and Sherman in Colorado's Mosquito Range, they are rather tasty.

Or the ramens. I like the Curried Mushroom Top Ramen recipe in chapter 9. You can find a wide variety of packaged ramens on supermarket shelves, and even more delicious versions in health food stores. The key words are *lightweight* and *simple to prepare.*

No doubt I am lazy when it comes to trail cooking, but if my trail companions are big on cooking, I am a very appreciative partner!

Sitting in a tent in the mountains on long, cold winter evenings is a great time for me to eat and eat and eat—slowly, mind you—but a bit of this and a bit of that. And talk. Dave Sumner and I solved all the world's problems on our long midwinter nights camped high in Rocky Mountain National Park or in our favorite campsite near Frigid Air Pass in the Maroon Bells Wilderness. Though it is true nobody wanted to hear our solutions, how we loved to talk them all out!

Cooking is probably the most delicate part of your winter backpacking treks. You need a cookstove that you have become well acquainted with on summer and fall hikes before you take it out winter camping. All tasks should be well practiced before you do them when winter backpacking.

You are going to have to cook some of your meals in your tent. There are high risks here. First and foremost, you must keep the tent well ventilated, for the stove gives off deadly carbon monoxide gas, which is odorless and can easily creep up in a deadly assault upon you without your realizing what is happening. Ventilate by keeping the doors open while your stove is running, regardless of the weather outside.

Also, your stove needs to be set upon something fireproof and impervious to heat. I ordinarily use my snowshoes for this. Or skis, if it is that type of trip. But you need another piece of relatively fireproof material to place on top of the skis or snowshoes

---

Using Plastic Produce Bags for Warmth

I learned a trick about plastics from Jack Stevens of Stevens Tent Company fame. Putting plastics next to the skin can reduce the body's natural evaporation and thus retain some of the heat that is ordinarily lost. Jack incorporated much of this in his body vapor capture system of equipment design.

One trick that I derived from Stevens's plastic system is to employ those ultrathin plastic bags used in grocery departments for bagging fruits and vegetables. Try putting one of these bags on each foot before you put on your wool socks. See the difference. Do the same with your feet or hands inside your sleeping bag at night. But be aware that the plastic captures the moisture emitted by the body, and hence it will wet any clothing that you have on between the plastic and your bare body.

so as not to affect their surfaces. A six-to-eight-inch-square piece of eighth-inch wood or Formica works well for this.

The next concern is that when boiling water or soup, the steam billows out and condenses on the tent walls. The more ventilation you have, the less condensation on the tent walls, and the less probability of having moisture collect on your sleeping bag.

And the trickiest of all is to avoid knocking into the stove or pots of water and spilling things on your sleeping bag, tent floor, or clothes. This is an enormously delicate situation, especially if there are two or more of you in your tent. Everyone has to be reminded many times to be extra careful around the stove and food.

Need I warn that firing up the stove in your tent is extremely dangerous? I've always done it in the open area of the vestibule formed by my tent fly. If you can manage it, fire up your stove outside the tent before bringing it in.

> **Guy and I carried a heavy Optimus stove on our winter backpacking trips, which probably weighed four pounds without fuel, to be sure of its reliability for melting snow.**
>
> —*Laura Waterman, first editor of* **Backpacker** *magazine, author of* **Backcountry Ethics** *and many more*

DRINKING ON WINTER TREKS

Cold weather is especially dehydrating. It is therefore particularly important to drink far more than you think necessary to quench your thirst. A nice touch to my winter hikes is hot, sweet tea.

I also fill the canteen with hot, sweet tea before leaving camp in the morning so that I have hot tea along the trail. Of course, it gradually cools, but then I have iced tea. Not a bad drink at rest stops.

At night, I fill the canteen with hot water and take it into my sleeping bag with me. It warms the bag much like those bed warmers used in olden times.

Water freezing in your canteen is a tricky business. It is one of the first things you have to get used to in winter hiking. A memorable night on one of my first winter overnights, in the Hudson Highlands a few miles above New York City, was when a friend and I chose to try out our winter techniques and snowshoed in to a lean-to set atop the crest of one of the hills, with a beautiful view of surrounding forestlands.

We lay in our sleeping bags chatting after dinner, sipping a cup of hot chocolate. While drinking it, I had set the pot with the remaining hot water on the lean-to floor beside my sleeping bag. When we decided to have another cup, I picked up the pot. It couldn't have been more than ten to fifteen minutes after I had poured our first cup, but the boiling water by that time had already frozen solid in the pot!

Because you need to drink your water, you must keep it from freezing. Carry the canteen upside down in your pack so that if it does freeze, the ice forms on the bottom of the canteen and not at the top, where it could seal off easy access to the water.

Some packs designed for winter hiking come with insulated pockets to protect the water from freezing. It has been my experience that the fellows who carried their water bottles in them in subzero weather still had the tops of their water bottles freeze up. Your own experience will tell you which works best for you.

Some conditions require you to take both snowshoes and skis.

SKIS OR SNOWSHOES?

You'll need to either take skis or snowshoes. Even if there is no snow when you start out, there likely could be before you return. But which you take is an individual choice. You need somewhat different backpacking gear for each. The key is to learn to snowshoe or ski long before you attempt to take on a full-fledged deep-winter backpacking jaunt. Carrying the pack with all the extra weight of winter gear is quite a different thing from simply skiing or snowshoeing.

If your choice is snowshoeing, first master using them in deep snow that buries them with each step. The tough part of snowshoeing with a pack is lifting the snowshoes high enough to clear the snow for your next step, and carrying the extra snow on the snowshoe while taking each step.

I have done a good deal of both skiing and snowshoeing. It is said that a hard day's snowshoeing with a pack consumes 6,000 calories, and I don't doubt it. The weariest I have ever been on any hike was on a climb I did with Ron Zisman, bushwhacking up the Catskills' Westkill Mountain from its north side. We didn't arrive at the summit until dark, and on the way down, we daren't sit for a rest for fear we would not have enough energy to get back up! Such a joy when we got down to be met near our car by Karl Schwarzenegger, who invited us to dinner in the homey ambience of his cozy Sunshine Valley House.

MOUNTAINEERING AND USE OF THE ICE AX

Do not assume that if you become good at winter backpacking, you are a mountaineer. Mountaineering is an entirely different activity. It does involve winter camping, but much more technical knowledge is required as well—most particularly, the use of an ice ax and crampons. There are excellent schools of mountaineering, and you ought to take a course in technique before taking this next step, regardless of how simple it seems. Not only is your life at risk, but so are the lives of those who go with you and those who may have to try to rescue you should things go awry. And things do go awry, mostly because of a lack of technical knowledge on the part of the climbers, including poor judgment.

Along these lines, much oversimplification also has been given to backpacking and the risks it entails. One popular hiking and backpacking handbook on the market, for example, says about ice axes, "Self-arrest isn't difficult, but you do have to learn it, and in order to learn it you have to do it, not read about it." That author may be particularly gifted and dexterous. But the idea that ice ax self-arrest isn't difficult and can be learned by practicing it a few times is dangerous advice.

Here is what mountaineer Louis Dawson, the author of the most respected *Dawson's Guide to Colorado's Fourteeners,* has to say about ice ax technique in volume 1: "A successful self arrest is a skilled acrobatic maneuver. You must practice until it becomes instinct. If you're new to the game, a snow climbing course is your best bet for learning. If you're an expert, you should still practice periodically."

If this sounds too cautionary, it is because the current fad of extreme sports tends to scoff at commonsense concern for safety. There have been sufficient numbers of deaths from this foolishness to cause alarm.

I cannot recommend more highly reading *Mountaineering: The Freedom of the Hills.* This book has been the standard book for mountaineering—for novice as well as advanced climbers—for more than sixty years. The author and publisher is the Seattle Mountaineers, a solid old-time mountaineering club. It has gone through seven heavily revised editions, updated every few years to incorporate the latest technique developments and gear.

Though you may well never get into mountaineering, winter camping is the first step of mountaineering. And this book has a wealth of information from more than thirty highly experienced mountaineers on techniques and the dangers of winter backpacking and hiking. You should know far more than you need to know in order to avoid the catastrophic errors that can easily be avoided if you know about them. Just one example is avalanches, which occur in the most innocent and beautiful-looking snow conditions imaginable. An ounce of prevention is worth your life. No other winter backpacking book compares!

Whoops! Be prepared for a nasty tumble with a heavy load on a winter backcountry trek.

Afterword
Why I Love America's Trails

Nothing makes me feel more fortunate to be an American than our backcountry and its system of trails. Although one of my favorite places to hike is the Swiss Alps, even its magnificent hiking opportunities are nowhere near as varied and as plentiful as those provided by America's system of backcountry trails.

Don't we take this magnificent public-lands system of ours entirely too much for granted, as if it is our natural right to have and enjoy such priceless possessions?

In my view, the vast number of seemingly trivial everyday issues accomplished by the ranger ranks at all levels, including the most inconsequential, count as much as the work at the big-vision levels. It is the implementation of the visions carried out in these "trivial, everyday" decisions by our lands' custodians that make American public lands particularly enviable to the rest of the world.

Take, for instance, my camp here in Apache-Sitgreaves National Forest. While roaming the American Southwest from one public land to another with hardly a break between them, I see far more damage to these lands by people enjoying their recreation than I do from ranchers' overgrazing. There is a great deal of construction along the edges of public lands, little enclaves of tourist accommodations and suppliers, as well as deeper incursions of vacationers on power boats, ATVs, trail bikes, horses, rafts, canoes, kayaks, bicycles, and boots. Why, then, is there so much complaining from recreationists about ranchers' use of the lands?

Still, it seems that there are unlimited lands surrounding all of us users that have been preserved and protected by the guardians of the lands, our rangers. These lands have been used over and over again, yes, with heavy impact from sheep and cattle, mining, and logging. As deep as I have gone into wilderness areas, I have seen the signs of previous users: tumbled-down miners' shacks deep within the Snowmass-Maroon Bells Wilderness; stumps of large trees sawed off for lumber in numerous other western forests; huge, dead cadavers of hemlock trees in New York's Catskills, downed and stripped of their bark for tanning shoe leather decades ago; caves where asbestos and copper have been mined in Grand Canyon; sheepherders' camps at 12,000 feet in Colorado's San Juan Mountains; even the abandoned villages of Anasazi dwellers from ancient times in Chaco Canyon and Grand Gulch. These uses have had a far greater impact upon the land than today's recreationists.

That little editorial is a prelude to my own justification for using these lands for the past few days on my explorations of what the sixteenth-century Spanish explorer Coronado, in his search for the Seven Cities of Gold, called the *despoblado*, meaning "uninhabited land." Though the *despoblado* is only ninety air miles from downtown

280

Trekking through Switzerland's Bernese Alps.

Phoenix, it probably is more desolate and less populated today than it was in Coronado's day.

I am writing this in the depth of the Apache-Sitgreaves National Forest, at a campsite that is as pure as ever I can imagine. So far as I can tell, I am the first ever to have camped here upon a bed of pine needles beneath a towering forest of ponderosa pines, morning sun streaming through their thin-needled tops. The only debris I had to clear for my tent was a scattering of pinecones. I built no fire, moved no rocks, left no trash, in fact left no traces that I can see.

And this site was available for me at my own choosing along a ten-mile stretch of rough dirt Forest Service road. The land is not designated a wilderness, meaning that I can still access it by car. And what is barely noticeable to the undiscerning eye is the subtle way that the Forest Service rangers have managed this enormous chunk of land so as to both keep it accessible to the public for recreation and preserve its natural integrity as untrammeled backcountry. Along the state highway, there are developed campgrounds in which fully equipped RVs can hook up and campers have the convenience of flush toilets, showers, coin laundries, and pay phones.

Get off the paved highway a bit and you can enjoy more primitive campgrounds that cater only to tent campers, though they still have drinking water, flush toilets, and showers. A bit farther away from traffic, there are more rustic campgrounds with drinking water, outhouses, and more primitive tent sites spaced farther apart. Then, for a still greater degree of roughing it, there are really primitive campgrounds where signs notify, "Camp Only Within Fifty Feet of Signs," and the signs that say "Camp Here" are spaced out at good distances from each other. These primitive campgrounds have outhouses but no drinking water.

And if these are still too civilized for your taste, you can keep on driving, as I did, and camp virtually anywhere in the woods along hundreds of miles of backcountry roads as long as you are within 300 feet of the road. These primitive camping spots are wilder and wilder the farther you penetrate the forest.

I am camped about ten miles from the paved road. I could have driven considerably deeper into the maze of these primitive dusty roads. But this was far enough away that I have not seen another person all the time I have been here. A more idyllic camping experience I could not have had anywhere else!

Thank God and the rangers' passion for the land. For the managers of this forest to provide this sort of experience and still keep it so untrammeled has required a great many subtle decisions. You can still enjoy this sort of camping experience, not just in Apache-Sitgreaves, but in a myriad of other national forests throughout our great nation.

Bibliography

BOOKS

Aitchison, Stewart. *A Naturalist's Guide to Hiking the Grand Canyon: In Depth Information on Hiking 30 Grand Canyon Trails.* Englewood Cliffs, NJ: Prentice Hall, 1985.

Anderson, Michael F. *Along the Edge: A Guide to Grand Canyon's South Rim from Hermit's Rest to Desert View.* Grand Canyon, AZ: Grand Canyon Association, 2001.

———. *Living at the Edge: Explorers and Settlers of the Grand Canyon Region.* Grand Canyon, AZ: Grand Canyon Association, 1998.

Ashley, Clifford. *The Ashley Book of Knots.* New York: Doubleday, 1944.

Babbitt, Bruce, comp. *Grand Canyon: An Anthology,* Flagstaff, AZ: Northland, 1978.

Barnes, F. A. *Canyon Country Hiking and Natural History.* Salt Lake City, UT: Wasatch Publishers, 1977.

Berger, Karen. *Hiking and Backpacking: A Complete Guide.* New York: W. W. Norton, 1995.

Burroughs, John. *In the Catskills: Selections from the Writings of John Burroughs.* New York: Houghton Mifflin, 1910.

Davenport, Greg. *Advanced Outdoor Navigation: Basics and Beyond.* Guilford, CT: Falcon, Globe Pequot Press, 2005.

———. *Wilderness Survival.* Mechanicsburg, PA: Stackpole Books, 1998.

Dawson, Louis II. *Dawson's Guide to Colorado's Fourteeners,* vol. II. Colorado Springs, CO: Blue Clover Press, 1995.

Deurbrouck, Jo, and Dean Miller. *Cat Attacks: True Stories and Hard Lessons from Cougar Country.* Seattle: Sasquatch Books, 2001.

Dodge, Natt N. *Poisonous Dwellers of the Desert.* Globe, AZ: Southwest Parks and Monuments Association, 1976.

Fizharris, Tim. *National Park Photography: How You Can Take Great Pictures of the Best Views in America's Most Beautiful National Parks.* Heathrow, FL: AAA Publishing, 2002.

Fletcher, Colin. *The Man Who Walked through Time.* New York: Knopf, 1968.

Forgey, William. *Basic Essentials: Wilderness First Aid.* 2nd ed. Guilford, CT: Falcon, Globe Pequot Press, 1999.

———. *Wilderness Medicine: Beyond First Aid.* 5th ed. Guilford, CT: Falcon, Globe Pequot Press, 1999.

Ghiglieri, Michael P., and Thomas M. Myers. *Over the Edge: Death in Grand Canyon.* Flagstaff, AZ: Puma Press, 2001.

Grubbs, Bruce. *Desert Hiking Tips: Expert Advice on Desert Hiking and Driving.* Guilford, CT: Falcon Press, 1998.

Guten, Gary N. *Injuries and Outdoor Recreation.* Guilford, CT: Falcon, Globe Pequot Press, 2005.

Hart, John. *Walking Softly in the Wilderness: The Sierra Club Guide to Backpacking.* 4th ed. San Francisco: Sierra Club Books, 2005.

Herrero, Stephen. *Bear Attacks: Their Causes and Avoidance.* Rev. ed. Guilford, CT: Lyons Press, 2002.

Hodgson, Michael. *Basic Essentials: Weather Forecasting.* 2nd ed. Guilford, CT: Falcon, Globe Pequot Press, 1999.

Jacobson, Cliff. *Basic Essentials: Map and Compass.* 3rd ed. Guilford, CT: Falcon, Globe Pequot Press, 2007.

Jardine, Ray. *Beyond Backpacking: Ray Jardine's Guide to Light Weight Hiking.* Arizona City: Adventurelore Press, 1999.

Kelty, Nena, and Steve Boga. *Backpacking the Kelty Way.* New York: Berkola, 2000.

Labastille, Anne. *Woodswoman IIII: Book Four of the Woodswoman's Adventures.* New York: West of Wind Publications, 2003.

————. *Women and Wilderness.* San Francisco: Sierra Club Books, 1984.

Ladigan, Don. *Lighten Up!* Guilford, CT: Falcon Press, 2005.

Latimer, Carole. *Wilderness Cuisine.* Berkeley, CA: Wilderness Press, 1991.

Leavengood, Betty. *Grand Canyon Women.* 2nd ed. Grand Canyon, AZ: Grand Canyon Association, 2004.

Leopold, Aldo. *A Sand County Almanac.* 2nd ed. New York: Oxford University Press, 1968.

MacKaye, Benton. "The Appalachian Trail: A Guide to the Study of Nature." *The Scientific Monthly* 34, no. 4 (1932): 330–342.

McGivney, Annette. *Leave No Trace: A Guide to the New Wilderness.* Seattle: Mountaineers Books, 1998.

Mountaineers. *Mountaineering: The Freedom of the Hills,* 7th ed. Seattle: Mountaineers Books, 2003.

Mullaly, Linda B. *Hiking with Dogs: Becoming a Wilderness-Wise Dog Owner.* Guilford, CT: Falcon, Globe Pequot Press, 1999.

Myers, Tom. "Casinos of Stone: Monsoon Gambling and Playing the Slot Canyons." Unpublished paper, 2001. The intimate story of the flash-flood fatality of George Mancuso.

————. "The Unforgiven: Heat and the Desert Crucible." Paper delivered to the Grand Canyon Field Institute leader training workshop, February 28–29, 2004.

Nessmuk, George W. Sears. *Woodcraft and Camping.* New York: Dover Publications, 1963.

Niemi, Judith. *Basic Essentials: Women in the Outdoors.* 2nd ed. Guilford, CT: Falcon, Globe Pequot Press, 1999.

Olsen, Jack. *Night of the Grizzlies.* Moose, WY: Homestead Publishing, 1969.

Ongert, J. E. "Backcountry Water Treatment to Prevent Giardiasis." *American Journal of Public Health* 79, no. 12 (1989): 1633–37.

Petzold, Paul. *Wilderness Handbook.* New York: W. W. Norton, 1974.

Preston, Douglas J. *Cities of Gold: A Journey across the American Southwest.* Albuquerque: University of New Mexico Press, 1999.

Saijo, Albert. *The Backpacker.* San Francisco: 101 Productions, 1972.

Schneider, Bill. *Bear Aware: The Quick Reference Bear Country Survival Guide.* 2nd ed. Guilford, CT: Falcon, Globe Pequot Press, 2001.

————. *Where the Grizzly Walks: The Future of the Great Bear.* Guilford, CT: Falcon, Globe Pequot Press, 2003.

Shaw, Harley. *Soul Among Lions.* Boulder, CO: Johnson Books, 1989.

Shelton, James Gary. *Bear Encounter Survival Guide.* Hagensborg, BC: Pogany Productions, 1994.

Smolinski, Carol Simon, and Don Biddison. *Moose Creek Ranger District Historical Information Inventory and Review* Clarkston, WA: Northwest Historical Consultants, 1988.

Tawney, Robin. *Hiking with Kids.* Guilford, CT: Falcon, Globe Pequot Press, 2000.

Thybony, Scott. *Official Guide to Hiking the Grand Canyon.* Rev. ed. Grand Canyon, AZ: Grand Canyon Association, 2001.

Tilton, Buck. *Backcountry First Aid and Extended Care.* 4th ed. Guilford, CT: Falcon, Globe Pequot Press, 2002.

Tilton, Buck, and Frank, Hubbell. *Medicine for the Backcountry.* 3rd ed. Guilford, CT: Falcon, Globe Pequot Press, 1999.

Torres, Steven. *Lion Sense: Traveling and Living Safely in Mountain Lion Country.* Guilford, CT: Falcon, Globe Pequot Press, 2005.

Turner, James Morton. "From Woodcraft to Leave No Trace: Wilderness Consumerism, and Environmentalism in Twentieth Century America." *Environmental History* (July 2002), available at www.lib.duke.edu.

Waterman, Laura, and Guy Waterman. *Backwoods Ethics: A Guide to Low-Impact Hiking and Camping.* 2nd rev. ed. Woodstock, VT: Countryman Press, 1993. Still a classic in the field. Easy reading.

————. *Backwoods Ethics: Environmental Concerns for Hikers and Campers.* Boston: Stonewall Press, 1979. The original version of this classic book.

Whitney, Stephen R. *A Field Guide to the Grand Canyon.* 2nd ed. Seattle: Mountaineers Books, 1996.

WEBSITES

Abundant Wildlife Society of North America. "Mountain Lion Fact Sheet," by T. R. Mader, research director. www.aws.ven.com/mountain_lion_fact_sheet.html.

American Discovery Trail Society. www.adt.org.

American Hiking Society. www.americanhiking.org.

Appalachian Trail Conference. www.appalachiantrail.org.

Backpacker magazine. www.backpacker.com

BackpackingLite. www.backpackinglight.com.

Beier, Paul. "Cougar Attacks on Humans in the United States and Canada." www.users.frii.com/mytymyk/lions/beier.htm.

————. "List of Confirmed Cougar Attacks in the United States and Canada January 1, 2001–Now." www.cougarinfo.com/attacks3.htm.

Boy Scouts of America. www.bsa.org.

Chester, Tom. "Mountain Lion Attacks on People in the US and Canada." www.tchester.org/sgm/lists/lions_attacks.html.

Continental Trail. www.cdtrail.org.

Continental Divide Trail Society. www.cdtsociety.org.

Eastern Mountain Sports. www.ems.com.

GoLite gear company. www.golite.com.

L.L.Bean. www.llbean.com.

Pacific Crest Trail Association. www.pcta.org.

Pacific Crest Trail. www.pct.com.

Rails-to-Trails. www.railstrails.org.

REI. www.rei.com.

Waterman and Hill. "Attacks Are on the Rise." www.naturealmanac.com/cougars/attacks.html.

Index

About the Author

JOYCE JENSEN

William Kemsley Jr. may well be considered the father of modern hiking and backpacking. As founder of *Backpacker* magazine, for decades and still the most popular magazine for hikers and backpackers, and cofounder of the American Hiking Society, the voice of the American hiker, Kemsley has established his legacy as one of the most significant figures in the backpacking community. He is also a former board member of the National Parks and Conservation Association, Appalachian Mountain Club, and Big City Mountaineers and is a longtime member of the prestigious Explorers Club. He has authored numerous books on hiking and backpacking, including the best-selling *Buyer's Guide to Backpacking Equipment* and *Whole Hikers' Handbook*. Kemsley now lives in northern New Mexico, where he enjoys hiking and backpacking many times a year in the southwestern mountains, deserts, and canyons.